THE MUSLIM CONQUEST OF PERSIA

THE MUSLIM CONQUEST OF PERSIA

Lieutenant-General A.I. Akram

Edited by

A.B. al-Mehri

MAKTABAH
PUBLISHERS AND DISTRIBUTORS
Birmingham - England

Published by

Maktabah Booksellers and Publishers
PO BOX 13976
Birmingham
B11 9DQ
United Kingdom

Website: www.maktabah.net
Email: enquiry@maktabah.net

Wholesale Enquiries: wholesale@maktabah.net

Cover Design: H. Jundi
Front Cover Image: Sword of Uthman ibn Affan [ra] – Topkapi Museum, Istanbul

British Library Cataloguing-in-Publication Data
A Catalogue record for this book is available from the British Library

Maktabah Booksellers and Publishers

ISBN 978-0-9548665-3-2

CONTENTS PAGE

Editor's Preface ix

Foreword... xi

Chapter 1: In the Name of Allah 4

Chapter 2: The Change of Command 17

Chapter 3: The Victories and Defeat of Abu Ubayd 23

Chapter 4: The Battle of Buweib 40

Chapter 5: Umar and Sa'd 51

Chapter 6: Yazdjurd and Rustam 65

Chapter 7: The Eve of Qadisiyya 80

Chapter 8: The Day of Disorder 104

Chapter 9: The Day of Succour.. 115

Chapter 10: The Day of Hardship 128

Chapter 11: The Night of Qadisiyya.. 138

Chapter 12: On to Ctesiphon 151

Chapter 13: The Conquest of Ctesiphon....................................... 163

Chapter 14: The Battle of Jalaula 176

Chapter 15: The Consolidation of Iraq 196

Chapter 16: The Conquest of Ahwaz 207

Chapter 17: The Conquest of Tustar 220

Chapter 18: The Rest of Khuzistan 230

Chapter 19: The Persians March Again 239

Chapter 20: The Battle of Nihawand 250

Chapter 21: The Fall of Persia 273

Chapter 22: The Last of the Sasanis 284

APPENDIX A: BIBLIOGRAPHY 298

APPENDIX B: THE HIJRI AND CHRISTIAN YEARS 301

APPENDIX C: NOTES……………………………………... ……………..…..302

APPENDIX D: THE COMPANIONS.. 309

LIST OF MAPS

Map 1: The Early Campaigns 10

Map 2: The Movements of Abu Ubayd 28

Map 3: The Approach to Qadisiyya 61

Map 4: The Plain of Qadisiyya 79

Map 5: Qadisiyya Dispositions 101

Map 6: Qadisiyya 1st Day 111

Map 7: Qadisiyya 2nd Day 122

Map 8: Qadisiyya 3rd Day 132

Map 9: Qadisiyya 4th Day 144

Map 10: The Advance to Ctesiphon 157

Map 11: The Battle of Jalaula 1 180

Map 12: The Battle of Jalaula 2 186

Map 13: Khuzistan and Fars 213

Map 14: The March to Nihawand 247

Map 15: The Battlefield of Nihawand 251

Map 16: The Battle of Nihawand 1 252

Map 17: The Battle of Nihawand 2 255

Map 18: The Battle of Nihawand 3 260

Map 19: The Battle of Nihawand 4 262

Editors Preface

'It is He who sent His Messenger with guidance and the religion of truth to manifest it over all religion. And sufficient is Allah as Witness.'
[Surah al-Fath 48:28]

Following the publication of Khalid bin al-Waleed: Sword of Allah, there has been a huge revival in reader's interest for books dealing with early Islamic history. It was decided that we complete the task of publishing the [out of print] books by A.I. Akram on the first hundred years of Islamic military history. They are as follows:

- Khalid bin al-Waleed: Sword of Allah
- The Muslim Conquest of Persia
- The Muslim Conquest of Egypt and North Africa
- The Muslim Conquest of Spain
- Falcon of Quraysh
- Rise of Cordoba

Hence, present before you is second in the series of books written by A.I. Akram – The Muslim Conquest of Persia. **This version of the book has been edited** with the addition of footnotes, Anglicization of certain terms and the correction of minor spelling and grammatical errors. This edition also includes the original maps [digitized] drawn by the author from its original print.

Whenever civilizations have reached great heights, they have achieved inspiration from nothing but history. As the author notes, 'Muslim history is replete with great military achievements and glorious feats of arms....no battles that surpass, in brilliance and decisiveness, the battles of Islam; no commanders who surpass, in courage and skill, the gifted generals of Islam.'

If readers find any historic inaccuracies in the text, we ask that we are informed and we will endeavour to correct these for any future prints. Finally, I pray and beseech Allah [swt] to accept this effort from all those who helped with the publication of this book.

A.B. al-Mehri,
Ramadhan, 1430 AH [September, 2009]
Birmingham, United Kingdom

Foreword

It is not difficult for an author to persuade himself that his writings are a success, that his books are read, that people eagerly await more works from his pen. I have not needed much persuasion to believe that my book, *The Sword of Allah*, has found acceptance. The first, deluxe edition was sold out in good time; a second, paperback edition and an Urdu translation are shortly expected to be on the market; and the Supreme Council of Islamic Affairs in Cairo has rendered the book into Arabic. For all this, praise be to Allah!

The success of my first major foray into serious historical writing has encouraged me to continue with the programme of research in Muslim military history, which I had first conceived in 1964, a programme which involved a twenty-year effort culminating in what would be my last volume on the great battles of Muslim Spain. This is the second book, dealing with the Conquest of Persia, and upon it I have laboured with the same zeal and affection as on my first, and it has given me the same intellectual and emotional satisfaction.

I have used the same methodology of study and composition. I have based my research on Muslim historians who lived and wrote in the first four centuries of Islam, i.e. up to the 10th Century A.D., the only exceptions being the 13th Century geographer, Yaqut, and a modern Iraqi scholar, Muhammad Tariq Al Katib, whose researches in the geography of the Basra region have been of value to me. I have ignored later writers for the reason that they have based their writings on the chronicles of the early ones, and I prefer to get my facts first-hand from the early historians rather than second-hand from later ones. The library of early Arabic works of history which I had built up for my first book stood me in good stead for this one too, and my further requirements of historical works were met by a kind gift from Colonel S.H. Raza Rizvi, until recently our Military Attaché in Baghdad.

There is a certain amount of confusion in the accounts of the early chronicles. They have tended to record faithfully everything that came to their knowledge about events under study, and in the process have often given conflicting versions of the same event, leaving it to the reader to take his choice. I have not burdened the reader with these contradictions. Minor variations in historical versions have been ignored, the reader being presented with what appears to me the most logical and likely version, while major variations-and these are few-have been discussed separately in an appendix.

Everything that I have said in this book is historically factual. Every quoted statement in this volume is from an authentic source and the reference is given in a footnote. But although the acts of battle given in this volume are taken from history, their arrangement in readable narrative form is mine another garland of bright flowers which I have taken from better men, but threaded with my own thread.

In writing this book I have been conscious of the absence of a resplendent central figure like Khalid in *The Sword of Allah*. I have missed Khalid. In the present volume I have had to deal with many Muslim generals, some abler than others, and though none of these approaches the towering stature of the great Khalid, they were nevertheless fine soldiers, their military labours crowned with success and their mark indelibly printed on Muslim history. And although there has been no Khalid whose life and campaigns I could describe, I have stuck to the same literary style: a fast, free flowing narrative aimed at the intelligent reader - civilian or soldier, man or woman - rather than the professional soldier alone.

I started work on this book in early 1970, when I had finished with *The Sword of Allah*, and set about it in the same manner: studying historical writings, examining maps, making notes, preparing the first draft of the narrative. The draft was completed in about mid-1971, and I was to start my travels soon after, but my plans were interrupted by the tragic events which culminated in the dismemberment of Pakistan in December of that dreadful year. Two years were to pass, during which I continued to happily command my infantry division, before my travels could begin.

The first part of this book deals with Iraq, which was then a province of the Persian Empire: But I did not visit Iraq for a battlefield tour because I had already done so in 1968 when writing *The Sword of Allah*, and had acquainted myself with the region of Kufa, Najaf and Qadisiyya, where most of the early battles of this book were fought. I had also visited Ctesiphon, the ancient capital of the Sasanis, where the famous Arch still stands as a reminder of their departed glory. The only place I have not visited is Jalaula, for the reason that in the prevailing Iran-Iraq border situation, the place is "out of bounds."

The Euphrates and the Tigris have altered so much since the conquest of Islam, changing sometimes their main channels and sometimes their subsidiary ones, that very little remains of the towns and villages and topographical landmarks which featured in the battles. I have therefore depended for my construction of battles in Iraq upon the details given by early Muslim historians and geographers, particularly Tabari and Yaqut, aided by my visit to the ground in 1968 and by up-to-date maps of the battle areas. Because of the absence of many ground features which then existed, there may be inaccuracies in some of the battle maps which I have drawn, but these are not likely to be major ones.

My travels for this book were confined to Iran and began in mid-November, 1973. I flew to Tehran, the bustling, throbbing, glittering capital of Iran, and after finalising my tour plans, went on to Kirmanshah, a charming town which it is easy to fall in love with. I was struck by the clear, crisp autumn air and the clear, blue autumn sky, and found the inhabitants to be as beautiful as everywhere else in Iran but more so. This was the base for the first phase of my tour.

The next day I set off for the Hulwan Valley [known in Iran as Ajnand]. I saw Tazar and Marj-ul-Qila [now Khusrau-Abad and Karend, respectively], the valley where the Muslims assembled before marching on to fight the epic battle of Nihawand under Noman bin Muqarrin. I saw Hulwan, now called Pul-e-Zohab, captured by the dashing Qa'qa after the battle of Jalaula. And I went on to see Qasr Sheereen and examine the ruins of the fabulous Palace of Sheereen built by the Emperor Khusrau Parwez for his wife, Sheereen.

All that remains of the palace is a large structure of stone, a hall fifty feet square with walls nearly as high, above which the roofless round rim suggests the existence in olden days of a dome. The hall was obviously the main feature of the palace-an audience chamber or court full of colour and gaiety-where the royalty of Persia would entertain and be entertained. Khusrau Parwez was the last Persian emperor to score military victories against Byzantium, and Sheereen must have been a woman of rare beauty to earn such a glorious monument from her husband. No wonder she has become the main heroine figure in the romantic literature of Persia!

Continuing my journey in the path of the romance of Sheereen, I went to Bisotun, 30 kilometers from Kirmanshah, and looked with wonder at the massive mountain through which Farhad the engineer is supposed to have dug a tunnel to get to Sheereen. The story of this moving tragedy is narrated in Chapter 14. Farhad never made it.

The following day we made the long drive to Nihawand, the scene of the last great battle between the Muslims and the Persians, and here I drove back and forth and back and forth, examining the battle area. At first it was all very confusing but gradually, bit by bit, pieces of information which I collected and observations which I made, fitted like a jigsaw puzzle to make a fairly clear picture. I reconnoitred almost the entire battlefield and by the time I left in the evening, I had formed a good idea of how the battle was fought. There is room for doubt, of course, because geographical details given by the early historians do not fit exactly into the ground as we see it today, but I believe my reconstruction of this battle is as accurate as it possibly can be. Before leaving Nihawand, I stood at the poor, pathetic graves of Noman bin Muqarrin, the Muslim army commander, and Amr bin Madi Karib, knight and prince of the Yemen, and prayed to God to be kinder to their souls than men have been to their bones.

My work in Kirmanshah was over. So I flew to Ahwaz to follow in the province of Khuzistan the path of the Muslim conquerors who took the province in 18-20 Hijri. This is the richest province of Persia and I found the land here different from what I had seen in the Persian North-flat, desert, hot, oily; even the people were a little darker in complexion and could easily be mistaken for Pakistanis. But here too I found the same characteristic pride of Persia and the same characteristic charm of the Persians.

I travelled to Ram Hormuz-a quiet, sleepy town on the approach to which the Persian Hormuzan had suffered minor defeats at the hands of Juzz bin Muawia and Noman bin Muqarrin, but I was not able to locate the places which I sought. Many place-names have changed since the time of my history and there are no clues to connect the new names with the old. In any case, no great battle was fought here, nor is there a detailed description of the few actions which did take place.

I drove on to Shushtar, a very nice little town, which I have called Tustar in this book because that is how the early historians knew it. I marvelled at the engineering skill of the Sasanis, evidence of which is there for all to see and admire-the canals dug under the town through which the waters of the Karun flow to run mills just below the town; the dam on the Karun constructed to control the water of the river for irrigation; Valerian's Bridge, a stone bridge actually built by Roman prisoners; and the marvellous citadel known as Salasil on a hillock overlooking the town, where the Persian Hormuzan made his last stand against the Muslims and where he finally surrendered to Abu Musa al Ash'ari. The unusual way in which the fort was taken by the Muslims is described in the book.

As a tourist I also visited the Masjid-e-Jumeh, the great mosque started in the 9th Century but not completed till the 12th, and even saw a man saying his prayers there! And I was told of, but did not see, the shrine of a holy man known as 'the Pink Saint' and also as 'the Grass-eater', said to contain the bones of a man whose body turned green from an exclusive diet of grass. Why a green holy man was called the Pink Saint nobody could explain.

I then went on to Shush, called Sus in the book, the Elamite capital which is undoubtedly one of the oldest towns alive today. I visited the [alleged] tomb of Prophet Daniel who had been buried in the bed of the River Shahur before the river moved to a new [its present] bed. The Persians have built a monument over the Prophet's grave, with marble and silver and gold and mirrors, all used with a skill and delicacy of touch which are typical of Persian architecture. The reader will find the story of Daniel's grave in Chapter 18.

I could not see Junde Shapur, the last town taken by the Muslims in Khuzistan, because there is no Junde Shapur left. The ruins of the old town stand by the side of the village of Shahabad, not far from Dezful. Junde Shapur was the place to the townspeople of which a guarantee of safety on surrender had been given by a Muslim slave and the word of the slave had been honoured by the army commander.

I did a little more geographical investigation, as a result of which I discovered the location of some more places. My work in Khuzistan was now done, and I flew on to Isfahan, which is half the world!

Isfahan got me, as it gets most Visitors. I could not resist its charm, its allure, its grace and colour; the breath-taking beauty of its Safavi architecture which carried the famed blue tile work of Isfahan and the technique of dome construction to the zenith of perfection. Its unique imagery, its exquisite workmanship, its style and elegance stun the imagination and challenge the world to produce the like thereof. The people of Isfahan, known in earlier times as 'Sipahan' [military cantonment], are rightly proud of their city and do not fail to remind the visitor of the old saying: 'Isfahan is half the world...' In their understandable zeal, they leave out the second part of the saying: ". . . but for Lahore!"

I did not have much to do in Isfahan except to get the location and historical background of certain places which feature in the penultimate chapter of the book, but I stayed several days, savouring the special something that Isfahan has. Then I flew on to Shiraz. Shiraz is known in Iran as the: city of roses and nightingales, but when I visited it [beginning of December] there were few of the one and none of the other. It is also the city of Saadi and Hafiz and while the cold weather can take away the roses and the nightingales, it cannot take away the scent and music of the poetry of these masters. Shiraz seems to breathe poetry, and has perhaps the most beautiful gardens in Iran, and cypresses which could only grow in the city of Hafiz

Here again I carried out some historical and geographical investigation, with complete success, and returned to Tehran. In the last few days of my sojourn in Iran I drove around Rayy, now virtually part of Tehran, which had once been the capital of Parthia when Tehran, if it existed at all, could not have been more than a little village..

I also took the opportunity to visit the University of Tehran and meet a group of scholars, prominent amongst whom were Dr Mohammad Esmail Rezvani and Dr Abbas Zanyab Khoei. We had a long and lively discussion about various aspects of Iran's history, especially the era which this book is about, and I was deeply impressed by the scholarship, objectivity and depth of historical perception of these university professors. It was a pleasure to meet them and I thoroughly enjoyed the visit.

In the middle of December I returned to Pakistan. I returned with delightful memories of Iran ...the generous and spontaneous hospitality and affection of the people. . .the glitter and colour and gaiety of the cities ...the beauty of Iran which moved me so deeply that I have ended the book with a few paras on the subject ...the help which I received from the government and the army in Iran, thanks to the personal interest taken in my tour by General Gholam Ali Ovaisi, Commanding General of the Imperial Iranian Ground Forces. It was General Feredun Djam, the then Chief of the Supreme Commander's Staff, who in 1970 had extended to me an invitation to visit Iran for my book and promised to provide all the assistance that I needed; it was General Ovaisi who fulfilled that promise. I left Iran with a prayer for these two Generals, and for Colonel [now Brigadier] M. Daud Khan, our Military Attache in Tehran, whose cheerful cooperation. far-sighted planning and efficient staff work made my tour that much easier and that much more enjoyable.

My travels done, my battlefields seen, my maps drawn, I got down to preparing the final draft of the manuscript. I found that as a result of further research, I had to carry out some changes in my account of the early part of this Muslim conquest as presented in *The Sword of Allah*, and instead of repeating the part of that book which rightly formed the first phase of this conquest, I have given a brief summary of it in the first chapter of this volume. The work of rewriting was almost complete when, in the summer of 1974, I was posted to Ankara as

Pakistan's Permanent Military Deputy to CENTO. For some months my duties at Ankara kept me away from writing, and it was not until March, 1975, that I was able to send the final manuscript to press.

I owe a debt of gratitude to many friends for their encouragement and help. Of these I would like to make especial mention of two dear and distinguished regimental comrades: Lieutenant-General M. Attiqur Rahman and Major-General Ghulam Jilani Khan. My wife has assisted me by checking the manuscript and giving invaluable editorial help, and my younger son, Hans Masood, has done all the tedious work of drawing and copying the maps. The typing of the manuscript in all its many drafts has again been done by my faithful secretary, Naib-Subedar Abdul Sattar Shad.

So here it is, my second book: *The Muslim Conquest of Persia*. It is my second assault upon the ignorance which surrounds this field of Muslim history. According to an old Chinese proverb, it is better to light one small candle than to curse the darkness. This is my second candle. May it light the way for those who seek!

A. I. Akram
March, 1975
Ankara, Turkey.

A NOTE ON ARABIC NAMES

A brief explanation of the system of Arabic names would help the reader in understanding the filial relationship indicated by a name. It would also help him to understand why the same person is known by so many different names.

An Arab [and this custom is still prevalent in some Arab societies] was known by three names. One was his own personal name, say Talha. Another was the name of his father, say Abdullah, and in this case he was known as Ibn or Bin Abdullah, i.e. Son of Abdullah. The third was the name of his son, say Zayd, and in this case he was known as Abu Zayd, i.e. Father of Zayd. Thus he could be called Talha or Ibn Abdullah or Abu Zayd, the last being the most respectful way of addressing a person. In certain grammatical forms Abu is expressed as Abi, and both have been used in this book.

Since the father too would be known by the name of a son, the son would at times have a name like Talha bin Abi Uthman i.e. Talha, Son of the Father of Uthman [Uthman being a brother of Talha]. A man could even be known as Talha bin Abi Talha which, translated literally, means: Talha, Son of the Father of Talha. This may sound odd in English, but in Arabic it is normal, and in fact quite charming.

The same rule applied to women. A girl by the name of Asma would be known as Asma bint Abdullah, i.e. Daughter of Abdullah. And on becoming a mother she would be known as the mother of her son or daughter, e.g. Umm Zayd, i.e. Mother of Zayd.

In the pronunciation of Arabic names fine differences, as between S and Th or Z and Dh, have been ignored in this book, although to Arabs these differences are very real and the sound quite distinct. To simplify pronunciation, sounds commonly used in Pakistan - S and Z - have been used throughout the book.

THE MUSLIM CONQUEST OF PERSIA

Chapter 1: In the Name of Allah

In 550 B.C. Cyrus defeated the Medes, and at this battle the Persian Empire rose like a giant.

The dynasty took its name from Achaemenes [Hakhamanish], King of Anshan, but it was his grandson Cyrus who founded the Persian Empire - the first great empire of history and, in many ways, the greatest the world has ever known. The rise of this empire was: not a gradual affair but an explosion of elemental power, the reverberations of which were felt by the entire world. The mounted columns of Cyrus, led in person by the Great King, shattered every army which opposed their advance, and the entire civilized world from Greece and Macedonia in the west to Bactria and Makran in the east came into the Persian fold. Only Egypt remained outside the pale of Persian rule. Other, empires in history rose from humble beginnings and worked their way over generations up the ladder of power and glory, but the Achaemenian Empire was virtually born great, for within the lifetime of its founder it had established itself in power that would endure longer than any other empire of history.

In the two centuries that followed, the Persians ruled the world without a rival to challenge their authority, and the successors of Cyrus extended the imperial boundaries and annexed the Punjab and Sind also [though the Greeks revolted early in the 5th Century B.C. and forced the Persians to regard the Bosphorus as their western boundary]. Rulers like Darius, Xerxes, Ardsheer [Artaxerxes] further embellished the empire; but then came Darius 111 who was crowned in 336 B.C. and lacked the broad shoulders needed to carry the burden of imperial greatness. And he was unfortunate that in his day appeared Alexander the Great. Conversely, it was Alexander's good fortune that the Persia of his time was not ruled by one of the illustrious forbears of Darius, for then the world would never have heard of Alexander except as a Macedonian king whose ambitions were not compatible with his military prowess.

History has its own imperatives, and the youthful vigour of the Macedonian giant overwhelmed the mature but ill-directed strength of the Persians; and the Persian Empire collapsed. This was followed by the age of the imperial Greeks and the domain of Persia was ruled by the Seleucids with varying fortunes, until they were overthrown by the Parthians in the middle of the 2nd Century B.C.

Persia was again ruled by Asian rulers who, though not Persians, were nevertheless Iranian. The Parthian rule continued till 226 A.D.[1]

Ardsheer [Artaxerxes] son of Babak, of Fars, a vassal king under the Parthians, rose and challenged his overlord. In the battle of Hormuz, fought in 226 A.D., the Parthian king, Ardawan, was defeated and slain. Once again the Persian Empire rose like a colossus; once again the world trembled.

Ardsheer was no less ambitious and no less able than the founder of the Achaemenian dynasty. In the east he invaded India and levied tribute on the Punjab: in the north he overwhelmed Khurasan and Balkh; and he received the submission of the kings of Makran and Central Asia. In the west he trounced the Roman armies under the Emperor Severus Alexander and occupied Armenia. Ardsheer was not only a conqueror but also a statesman and empire builder and a man with considerable insight.

The Sasani Empire founded by Ardsheer went from strength to strength and remained in unending conflict with the Romans and the Turks and Huns. Ardsheer was followed by several brilliant monarchs who upheld the glory of the empire. There was Shapur I [known to the Arab Muslim historians as Sabur] who captured the Roman Emperor Valerian in battle and kept him as a prisoner until his death. There was Shapur 11 who ruled for seventy years-his entire life. [He was declared king while still in his mother's womb and thus is the only man in history to be crowned even before his birth.] He was known as Zul-Aktaf [the Shoulders Man]; and got this name because in his battles against the Arabs in the Persian Gulf he pulled out the shoulders of all able-bodied Arabs who fell into his hands. There was Behram Gor, the great hunter, who is reputed to have fought and slain a rogue elephant single-handed.[2] And there was Anushirwan the Just-the last of the glorious Persian monarchs.

Anushirwan reigned for forty-eight years and died in 579, nine years after the birth of Prophet Muhammad. He came to the throne after the empire had suffered a series of military setbacks, but re-established it at the peak of glory, where, by its distinguished heritage, the Persian Empire belonged. He shattered the Romans in several campaigns and wrested Syria and Alexandria from them. He vanquished the Turks and the Abyssinians, and placed the imperial frontiers beyond Balkh, Farghana, Samarqand and the Yemen. He even raided the island of Ceylon.

---

[1] The Parthians actually claimed descent from the Achaemenians but the claim is disputed by Persian scholars. Their being Iranian, however is universally acknowledged
[2] Ibn qutaiba : p.660.

But Anushirwan was more than a conquering hero. He was a superb statesman and reorganized the empire and the army and divided the political structure of his domain into four great satrapies, each of which was like a dominion ruled by a Satrap, or Viceroy, known as *Ispehbud*.

The north-eastern satrapy had its capital in Khrurasan and included the provinces of Khurasan, Sijistan [also known as Seestan], Kirman and Herat. Northwards its boundaries stretched to embrace Balkh, Bukhara and Samarqand, which had been conquered by Anushirwan from the Turks. The satrapy of the south-east covered Fars, Khuzistan and Baluchistan, with its capital at Persepolis. The satrapy of the south-west was all of Iraq. The satrapy of the north-west started from the centre of Persia-from Isfahan and Rayy [near modern Tehran] - and climbed north-west along the mountains to Azerbaijan and Armenia. All of Armenia, though in the past disputed and fought over by Romans and Persians for centuries, was now under Persia, but the hilly region, west of Armenia was in Roman hands. South of the hilly region, the plain east of and including, Mardin and Firaz, was Persian territory.[3]

And as if Anushirwan's political and military achievements were not enough to establish his claim to greatness, he was also possessed of a towering intellect. He read Plato and Aristotle in a Persian translation and established a university at Junde Sabur, where medicine, philosophy and other branches of literature were studied. He imported the game of chess from India.[4] One of his sayings runs: "Sovereignty depends upon the army; the army upon money; money upon taxation; taxation upon agriculture; agriculture upon justice; justice upon the honesty of public officials; the honesty of public officials upon the uprightness of the ministers; and ultimately all depends upon the king discovering his own self and exercising power over it, so that he controls it and is not controlled by it.[5]

Truly Persia saw glory and greatness in the golden age of Anushirwan the Just. With Ctesiphon as its capital, it was not only a formidable military power but also a centre of refinement and culture-a culture which still endures and the seductive charm of which even today captivates the visitor to Iran.

---

[3] Yaqubi: *Tareekh*: vol. I, p. 176: Dinawari: p. 67; Masudi: *Muruj*; vol. 1, p. 245; Abu Yusuf: p. 267.
[4] Masudi: *Muruj*; vol. 1, p. 267.
[5] Ibid: p. 270.

But after Anushirwan the empire declined and its western lands were recaptured by the Romans. Parwez, grandson of Anushirwan made a gallant attempt to regain the lost territories and succeeded in driving the Romans out of Syria, Asia Minor and Egypt, but was not able to maintain his hold over these lands. The Roman Emperor Heraclius, in a six-year campaign ending in 628, threw the Persians out of the disputed territories and pursued them to the gates of Ctesiphon Parwez, having lost the love and respect of his subjects, was dethroned by his own son Sheeruya [Ciroes], who first imprisoned, then blinded, then killed the aged monarch. The decline of Persia reached its climax in the time of Sheeruya, who, not content with the heinous crime of patricide, turned to worse cruelties. So that none may dispute his right to the throne or pose a challenge to his authority, he had all the male members of his family killed with the exception of his son, Ardsheer. The estimate of those of the house of Anushirwan who lost their lives to the maniacal fury of Sheeruya, adult and child, varies from 15 to 18. And Sheeruya reigned for only seven months before he too was dead.

With his death the confusion became worse. And there is confusion also in the accounts of the early historians about the order in which various emperors followed Sheeruya and the duration of their respective reigns. All that is certain and unanimously accepted is the position of Yazdjurd bin Shahryar bin Parwez, who escaped the assassins of Sheeruya and became the last Persian Emperor of the line of Sasan. This ill-starred young man was to see the final disintegration of the great empire of Persia.

Between Sheeruya and Yazdjurd there were about eight rulers in a period of six years, and these included two women-Buran and Azarmeedukht, both daughters of Chosroes Parwez. The first of these, Buran, proved a wise and virtuous monarch but lacked the strong hand needed to arrest the decline in imperial affairs. She was crowned during the lifetime of the Holy Prophet, who, when he heard of her coronation, made his famous remark: "A nation will never prosper that entrusts its affairs to a woman!"[6]

There were some strange incidents of crowning and killing during this unhappy decade. There was Shahr Baraz, a distinguished general who had spent a lifetime campaigning against the Romans and had lost several battles to Heraclius. Wishing to turn the chaos of the empire to his own advantage, he marched on the capital and captured it by guile, where after he killed the child-emperor, Ardsheer, and placed himself on the throne. But the public was

---

[6] Masudi: *Tanbeeh:* p. 90; Ibn Quteiba: p 666.

outraged and swore: "Never shall the likes of him reign over us."[7] Forty days later they killed him, and tying a rope to his feet, dragged him back and forth through the streets of Ctesiphon.

And there was Firoz who had no desire to be emperor and was led unwillingly to the throne. This man had an enormous head and when they forced the crown down it, he found it a most uncomfortable experience and protested: "What a tight crown!"[8] This unseemly remark left the courtiers aghast: and they killed him within the hour and placed another man on the throne. And so this absurd drama rolled on-around a throne on which had sat such glorious monarchs as Ardsheer bin Babak and Shapur and Anushirwan, the Just.

Yazdjurd[9], the last of the Sasanis, ascended the throne in 13 Hijri [634 A.D.], when the fortunes of Persia were at their lowest ebb.

What follows in the rest of this chapter is a condensation of Part III of *The Sword of Allah*, which describes in detail the invasion of Iraq by Khalid bin Al Waleed.

It was during the reign of the Empress Buran that Muthana bin Harisa turned his attention to Iraq. Muthana was a chief of the tribe of Bani Bakr which inhabited the north-eastern part of the Arabian Peninsula and the southern fringe of Iraq. Seeking adventure and spoils, and encouraged by the disarray which was apparent in the political affairs of the Persian Empire, Muthana took a band of his followers and began to raid into Iraq. At first he stuck to the periphery of the desert so that he could, withdraw quickly into the safety of the sandy wastes, but gradually his incursions became bolder and he struck as deep as Kaskar on the east bank of the Tigris.[10] His raids reached their climax during the year of the Apostasy, when Arabia was rocked by mortal combat between the Muslims and the Apostates - a combat which began with the death of Prophet Muhammad in June, 632, and ended with the crushing of the last revolt in March, 633. And Muthana varied his objectives, striking now in the east, now in the west. Most of his raids, however, were in the region of Uballa and he returned from these raids with spoils to dazzle the hungry Arab of the

---

[7] Yaqubi: *Tareekh*: vol 1. p. 173.
[8] Ibid.
[9] The Iranians refer to him as Yazdjird, but I have throughout the book called him Yazdjurd, which is the pronunciation used by the early historians, writing in Arabic.
[10] Kaskar stood where Waist was built by Hiajjaj bin Yusuf in 83 Hijri.

desert. The Persian garrisons were helpless against Muthana's ghostlike riders who vanished as rapidly as they struck.

Encouraged by his successes, Muthana approached Caliph Abu Bakr. This was in early February, 633 [late Zul Qada, 11 Hijri]. He painted a glowing picture- the vulnerable state of Iraq, the riches that waited to be plundered, the prolonged political crisis which bedeviled Persia, the inability of the Persian garrisons to fight mobile, fast-moving engagements. "Appoint me as, commander of my people," said Muthana, "and I shall raid the Persians. Thus I shall also protect our region from them."[11]

The Caliph agreed to his request and gave him a letter of authority appointing him commander over all the Muslims of the Bani Bakr. With this letter of authority Muthana returned to North-Eastern Arabia. Here he converted more tribesmen to Islam, gathered a small army of two thousand men and resumed his raids with even greater enthusiasm and violence.

Meanwhile, in the middle of February, 633, Abu Bakr wrote to Khalid: "Proceed to Iraq. Start operations in the region of Uballa. Fight the Persians and the people who inhabit their land, your objective is Hira."[12]

Khalid bin Al Waleed was at this time at Yamama, where two months before he had defeated the forces of the false prophet, Musailima, the Liar. Following the instructions of the Caliph, he mustered soldiers and in about the third week of March, 633 [beginning of Muharram, 12 Hijri] set off from Yamama. But before starting, he wrote to Hormuz, the Persian governor of the region of Uballa:

"Submit to Islam and be safe. Or, agree to the payment, of the Jizya and you and your people will be under our protection; else you will have only yourself to blame for the consequences, for I bring a people who desire death as ardently as you desire life."[13]

Hormuz was incensed by this threat from a nation which the Persians regarded with contempt, and marched with his army to Kazima, which lay on the direct

---

[11] Tabari: vol. 2. p. 552.
[12] Ibid: pp 553-4.
[13] Ibid: p. 554. The Jizya was a tax levied on non-Muslims. In return, they were exempt from military service and their protection was guaranteed by the Muslim state.

route from Yamama.[14] But Khalid did not go to Hazima, He marched to Nibbaj[15] where he picked up Muthana with his two thousand men, and then advanced towards

MAP 1: THE EARLY CAMPAIGNS

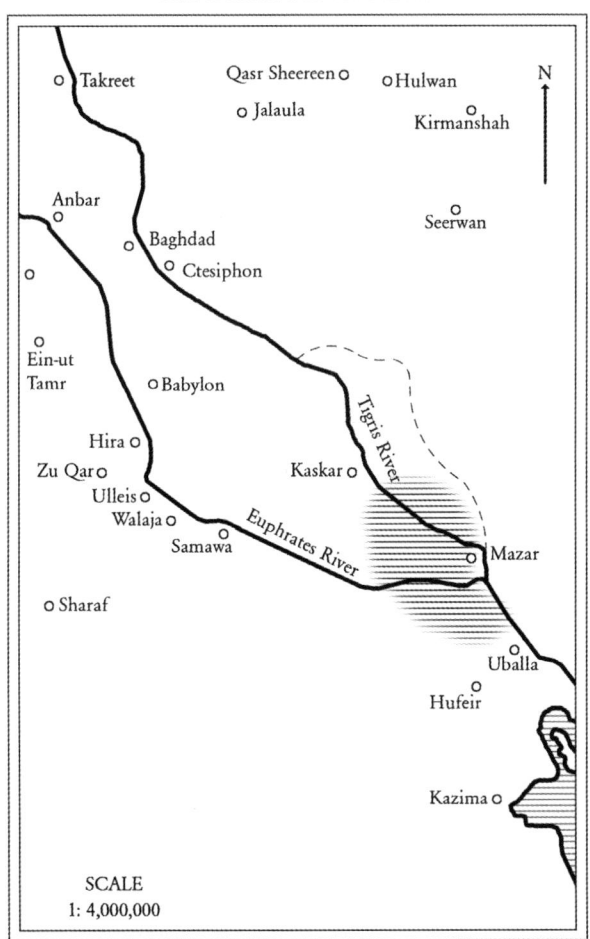

MAP 1: THE EARLY CAMPAIGNS

---

[14] Kazima was on the northern coast of the Bay of Kuwait, 5 miles from the present Basra-Kuwait road.
[15] The old Nibbaj is the present Nibqiyya, 25 miles east of Bureida.

Uballa on the Hufeir[16] route which bypassed Kazima. On the way he picked up another six thousand men and approached Hufeir with an army of eighteen thousand soldiers, many of whom were veterans of the Campaign of the Apostasy. [*See Map 1*]

Khalid knew the fine quality and numerical strength of the Persian army and the courage, skill and armament of the Persian soldier. He decided to exhaust his enemy with march and counter-march before fighting him. Hence the move to Hufeir which would directly threaten Uballa, the base of Hormuz.

Hormuz, seeing Hufeir threatened, marched thither from Kazima, but on arrival found that Khalid had changed his axis and was now marching to Kazima from where he could again bypass the Persians and make for Uballa. Again Hormuz reacted as Khalid wished, and by forced marches moved his heavily equipped troops to Kazima where Khalid awaited their arrival. At the end of the two-day march, as the Persians arrived at Kazima, Khalid formed up for battle, allowing the Persians no time to rest.

In the battle that followed, known as the Battle of Chains and fought in the first week of April, 633 [third week of Muharram, 12 Hijri] the Persians were roundly defeated and Hormuz was slain by Khalid in single combat. The remnants of the Persian army fled from Kazima.

Meanwhile the Persian court had sent another army under a general named Qarin to reinforce Hormuz, but Qarin had hardly crossed a certain river which joined the Tigris six miles above Uballa when he heard of the defeat of Hormuz. The survivors of the army of Hormuz also joined Qarin, and he prepared for battle near the south bank of the river.

Khalid, advancing from Kazima, arrived at the river and in the third week of April, 633 [beginning of Safar, 12 Hijri] was fought the Battle of the River. The Persian army was again shattered by the Muslims, and Qarin and the Persian generals commanding his wings, Qubaz and Anushjan, were killed in single combat by Muslim officers. The Persian survivors of this battle escaped by crossing the river in boats and retreated northwards. According to Tabari, thirty thousand Persians lost their lives in this battle.[17]

The twin disasters of Kazima and the River stunned the Persian court at

---

[16] The exact location of Hufeir is not certain, but I place it at the present day Rumeila, which is 21 miles from the old Basra.
[17] Tabari: vol. 2 p.558.

Ctesiphon, and for the first time the Persians realized the seriousness of the Muslim invasion. They correctly appreciated that Khalid would march westwards to Hira so that he would remain in Arab country and also be near the desert, where the Persians could not follow him in case he suffered a reverse. Another two armies were raised at Ctesiphon, and as soon as the first one was ready, it was placed under Andarzaghar who was ordered to proceed to Walaja and there await the arrival of the second army which was still in the process of being formed. The second army would be commanded by Bahman, one of the top military personalities of the realm, and at Walaja both armies would combine under Bahman's command and offer united resistance to the invaders.[18]

But the Persians had not allowed for the speed of Muslim movement. Khalid marched to Walaja and arrived there before the second Persian army could join the first, and faced Andarzaghar in battle. There, in early May, 633 [third week of Safar, 12 Hijri] the two forces came to grips in a fierce fight in which the Muslims again prevailed. Khalid carried out a brilliant Cannae-type manoeuvre- a double envelopment and annihilated the Persians and the Christian Arabs who comprised the army of Andarzaghar. The Persian general escaped the encirclement but lost his way in the desert where he died of thirst. Three Persian armies had now been cut to pieces by Khalid.

The fourth act in this bloody drama was enacted at Ulleis [4 miles west of Shinafia] where thousands of Christian Arabs had gathered to dispute Khalid's advance and were joined by the second army raised at Ctesiphon, which was now under the command of Jaban. Once again a large force faced Khalid, and once again he decided to do battle and destroy it. In the middle of May, 633 [end of Safar, 12 Hijri], on the bank of the River Khaseef, another titanic battle was fought between the invaders and the defenders of the empire.

This proved the fiercest and bloodiest battle of the lot. In spite of their superhuman efforts the Muslims could make no headway, and at last Khalid raised his hand; in supplication and prayed:-

"O Lord, if you give us victory, I shall see that no enemy is left alive until their river runs with their blood."[19]

Allah [swt] gave the Muslims victory, and Khalid set about keeping his pledge. Thousands of Persians and Arabs fleeing from the battlefield were captured

---

[18] Walaja was 5 miles south-south-west of present Shinafia.
[19] Tabari: vol. 2 p.561.

and herded to the river bank and beheaded. This slaughter went on for two days and two nights and as a result this river became known as the River of Blood. Jaban survived the annihilation of his army and lived to fight the Muslims again.

An idea of the courage and tenacity with which the Persians resisted Khalid can be gained from the words of Khalid himself: "At Mutah I broke nine swords in my hand, but I have never met an enemy like the Persians. And among the Persians I have never met an enemy like the army of Ulleis."[20]

Four great battles had now been won by Khalid as the relentless Muslim march continued towards Hira, the objective laid down by the Caliph. Seeing the fate of these armies, the Persian court decided not to undertake any further military manoeuvres to meet Khalid in the open. Meanwhile Khalid resumed the advance, sacked Amgheeshia, a large city near Ulleis, and arrived at Hira at the end of May, 633 [middle of Rabi-ul-Awwal, 12 Hijri]. The Persian general in command at Hira, one named Azazbeh, had sent mounted detachments forward to delay the advance, of the Muslims, but just before Khalid's arrival at Hira he crossed his Persian troops over the Euphrates and withdrew to Ctesiphon, leaving Hira[21] to be disputed by the local Arabs and the Muslims.

The Arabs had been known in Iraq since the time of Bukht Nassar [Nebuchadnezzar 7th and 6th Centuries B.C.] but did not then enjoy any power in the land. It was not until the early part of the Christian era, when a fresh migration occurred of Arab tribes from the Yemen to Iraq, that they began to command authority and influence. One of the great chiefs of these migrating Arabs, a man by the name of Malik bin Fahm, proclaimed himself king and began to rule over the western part of Iraq. Two generations after him the throne passed to Amr bin Adi, of the tribe of Lakhm, who started the Lakhmid Dynasty, which was also at times called "the House of Munzir." The kings of this dynasty ruled for many generations as vassals of the Persian Emperor.

The last of the House of Munzir was Noman bin Munzir who committed an act of disloyalty against Chosroes Parwez for which he was sentenced to death. The sentence was carried out in style-he was trampled to death by an elephant!

---

[20] Ibid: p. 569.
[21] The site of Hira is 12 miles south-east of Najaf and half a mile south of the present Abu Sukheir. Nothing remains of the ancient city except some traces of the White Palace which stood at the northern end of Hira.

This led to a revolt by the Arabs of Iraq which was soon crushed by the Emperor; and with this abortive revolt ended the house of Munzir.

Chosroes then appointed a new king, Iyas bin Qubeisa of the tribe of Tayy, to rule over Iraq, and for some years this man enjoyed a reasonable degree of autonomy. Then most of his authority was taken away and Persian generals and administrators took over the entire government of the land. Iyas remained a titular king, with his capital at Hira.

And now Iyas found himself facing the greatest soldier of the time, in command of the finest army of the time. After a day of nominal resistance in the four citadels of Hira, Iyas surrendered to the Muslims and was pleasantly surprised to find how generous were the terms offered by Khalid. All that the vanquished Arabs had to do was pay the Jizya, the rate of which was laid down; and they had to provide guides and spies for the Muslims.

After the fall of Hira. Khalid sent several columns across the Euphrates and the entire region up to the Tigris below Ctesiphon was subdued by the Muslims. Khalid also wrote to the Persian court:-

"In the name of Allah, the Beneficent, the Merciful. From Khalid bin Al Waleed to the kings of Persia.
"Praise be to Allah who has disrupted your system and thwarted your designs. And if He had not done so it would have been worse for you.
"Submit to our orders and we shall leave you and your land in peace; else you shall suffer subjugation at the hands of a people, who love death as you love life"[22] A month after Hira was taken, Khalid marched north and captured Anbar.[23] Then he turned south and captured Ein-ut-Tamr, where he first fought a battle with a Christian Arab army in the open and then took the fortified city.[24] While here, he received a call for help from Ayaz bin Ghanam, who had been sent by Caliph Abu Bakr to capture Daumat-ul-Jandal [the present Al Jauf in North-Western Arabia]. With part of his army Khalid

---

[22] Tabari: vol. 2, P. 572.
[23] Nothing remains of Anbar except some mounds 3 miles north-west up the present Falluja and about a mile from the Euphrates. One can still pick up pieces of old pottery on the mounds which cover an area half a mile square. According To Yaqut (vol. 1. p. 367) the Persians called this town Firoz Sabur.
[24] Ein-ut-Tamr, of which nothing remains but a spring, was located 10 miles west-north-west of the present Shisasa. Shisasa is also called Ein-at-Tamr these days but the original town was as stated above.

marched to Daumat-ul-Jandal, captured it and returned to Hira with Ayaz and his troops under command.

When Khalid marched to the aid of Ayaz, the Persians came to believe that he had left Iraq for good and determined to venture out again to deal with the Muslim invaders who remained in their land. They raised two fresh armies and placed one at Huseid and the other at Khanafis. [Both places were west of the Euphrates and north-east of Ein-ut-Tamr]. Meanwhile the Christian Arabs had also gathered in two large forces, one at Muzayyah [25 miles west of the present Heet] and the other at Zumeil [between Muzayyah and Ein-ut-Tamr]. The Persian plan was to concentrate all these forces into one mighty army and drive down to Hira where the Muslims would be crushed in one powerful, operation.

Khalid responded to the challenge with his characteristic speed and boldness. He first attacked Huseid and Khanafis, defeating each army in situ. The remnants of these armies marched to Mazayyah and joined the Arab army assembled there. Khalid followed and fell upon Muzayyah in a night attack in which almost the entire opposing force was annihilated. Then he moved rapidly to Zumeil and the Arabs at Zumeil also disappeared as if swallowed by an earthquake. These operations lasted about a month up to the middle of November, 633 [first week of Ramadhan. 12 Hijri]. And Ctesiphon withdrew once again into its shell.

A fortnight later Khalid marched to Firaz [near the present Abu Kamal on the Euphrates] which formed the frontier between Persia and Rome, and here, after a long wait, he fought and defeated a combined Persian and Roman army on January 21, 634 [the 15th of Zul Qada, 12 Hijri].

This was the last battle of Khalid in Iraq and marked the end of a brilliant campaign. He had fought and defeated ten Persian and Christian Arab armies in the field and captured three fortified cities. He had done this with boldness and offensive action and by using the elements of surprise and speed. Above all, it was the personality of Khalid which inspired the Muslims to perform prodigies of valour and endurance which few armies have performed in history.

Nothing would have pleased Khalid more than to attack and capture Ctesiphon, but this was not to be. In late May 634. he received a letter from Caliph Abu Bakr:

"In the name of Allah, the Beneficent, the Merciful. From the Slave of Allah, Ateeq, son of Abu Quhafa,[25] to Khalid, son of Al Waleed. Peace be upon you.

"I render praise unto Allah than whom there is no other God, and invoke blessings on His Prophet, Muhammad, on whom be the blessings of Allah and peace. March until you reach the gathering of the Muslims in Syria, who are in a state of great anxiety. I appoint you commander over the armies of the Muslims, and direct you to fight the Romans. You shall be commander over Abu Ubayda and those with him. Go with speed and high purpose, O Father of Suleiman,[26] and complete your task with the help of Allah, exalted be He. Be among those who strive for Allah. Divide your army into two and leave half with Muthana, who shall be commander in Iraq. Let not more go with you than stay with him. After victory you shall return to Iraq and resume command. Let not pride enter your mind, for it will deceive and mislead you. And let there be no delay. Lo, to Allah belongs all bounty, and He is the dispenser of rewards.[27]

---

[25] Although the Caliph is known to history as Abu Bakr, his actual name was Abdullah and he had also been given by the Holy prophet the appellation of Ateeq.
[26] This is how Khalid was usually addressed: Abu Suleiman.
[27] Tabari: vol. 2. pp 600. 605. Waqidi: *Futuh*: p. 14.

Chapter 2: The Change of Command

Early in June, 634, Khalid set off from Hira with 9,000 men on his march to Syria, to take command of the Muslim front against Rome. Muthana accompanied him along the caravan route up to Quraqir in Western Iraq, whence Khalid would strike out across the desert, in a perilous march, to keep his rendezvous with destiny.[28] At Quraqir, Muthana bade farewell to his beloved Commander-in-Chief. As they shook hands, Khalid said: "Return to your command; may Allah bless you, and raid as you please."[29] These two magnificent soldiers, who held each other in affection and professional esteem, did not know that they would never see each other again.

Muthana returned to Hira. He was now, the Muslim Commander-in-Chief in Iraq and responsible for the defence of South-Western Iraq against the Persian Empire. So far he had served as a subordinate general, albeit the fiercest and most dashing one, under a military genius who with 18,000 men had humbled the empire of the Chosroes and knocked the stuffing out of its armies in several bloody battles. But now he was on his own with 9,000-men a larger force than he had ever commanded, yet a very small one to carry out the task assigned to him. Calmly Muthana surveyed the strategic situation.

Khalid had occupied the region along the Euphrates from below Anbar to about Samawa. He had placed garrisons on the east side of the Euphrates which in turn had sent outposts in the land between the rivers, and he had raided up to the Tigris, which the Persians had grudgingly acknowledged as their military boundary with the Muslims. No Persian garrison remained west of the Tigris. But the southern part of Iraq, the area around Uballa, which Khalid had occupied in his very first move from Arabia, had been abandoned by the Muslims because in the later part of Khalid's campaign, with a shift in emphasis to the Euphrates, it had lost its strategical importance.

The Persians would no doubt take the offensive against the reduced Muslim army, and if Muthana remained on the defensive and awaited the Persian attack, his chances of holding on to Iraq would be slim indeed. Muthana decided that the best policy was, to maintain the psychological ascendancy which the

---

[28] The location of Quraqir is a not established beyond doubt. The point has been argued and explained in *The Sword on Allah*.
[29] Balazuri: p. 250.

Muslims had gained over the Persians and keep them on the defensive. He increased the violence of the raiding and his columns struck in the vicinity of Anbar and Ctesiphon and penetrated north of Ctesiphon and as far east as Kaskar on the Tigris. And Muthana awaited with confidence the next Persian move, which he knew would come. He was like a leopard worrying an ailing elephant, and wondering what the elephant would do when he got well again.

The next Persian move was not long in coming. The news of Khalid's departure for Syria spread rapidly in the empire and was received first with relief, then with jubilation, by all Persians. The most terrible invader of the empire was gone and only half the Muslim army remained on Persian soil under a general who had not been tested in high command. The Persians made the mistake of under estimating Muthana, but the mistake was forgivable. And the Persians decided to act fast, because the raids were hurting and the empire was screaming for vengeance.

There was nothing that they could do about the raids directly, for the Muslim raiders struck too rapidly and too unexpectedly to be forestalled or caught. The best course was to eliminate the base from which the raids originated and in doing so also destroy or expel the Muslim army from Persian territory. With this end in view, a new Persian army of ten thousand men was put together and placed under Hormuz, who was also given a war elephant. Hormuz was told to conquer Hira, and with this objective in mind, he set off from Ctesiphon.[30]

As Hormuz started his advance towards Hira, the Emperor Farrukhzad Khusrau wrote to Muthana: "I have sent you an army from the most degraded of the Persians, the swineherds and keepers of hens. I shall fight you only with these."

This letter is indicative of the arrogance and folly which frequently mark the political decline of empires. Farrukhzad was the last but one of the Sasani emperors and had been crowned a year before as successor to Firoz of the big head. While only two or three weeks before, when Khalid was still in Iraq, the best of the Persians were afraid to face the Muslims in the field, now the Emperor wrote of sending against them an army of swineherds and keepers of hens.

"Surely you yourself are one of these two," replied Muthana, who was the last man to be intimidated by such insulting threats. "Either you are an oppressor,

---

[30] There was another Hormuz, a high ranking general who had been defeated and slain by Khalid at Kazima. This one was obviously another man, probably of lower rank.

and that is evil for you and good for us; or you are a liar, and thus the most horrible in the sight of Allah. Praise be to Allah who has reduced you to the level of swineherds and keepers of hens."[31]

The contents of Muthana's letter were soon the property of all Ctesiphon, and the people in the capital wondered whether it was wise of their emperor to thus provoke a people whom the bravest of them had learned to treat with respect. But Muthana was already on the march when he received and answered the threat of Farrukhzad, for hardly had the Persian army left Ctesiphon when the Muslim outposts informed their commander of the move. The Muslim move was faster than that of the Persians, and they arrived at Babylon shortly before their enemy. A mile beyond Babylon, Muthana crossed a small river known as Sarat [now called Nahr-un-Neel] and deployed his army of about 8,000 men with the Hilla Branch of the Euphrates covering his left flank. Here, safe against outflanking manoeuvres, Muthana awaited his adversary.

The following day Hormuz appeared in sight and also arrayed his forces for battle, placing his one elephant in the centre of the front rank. This was some time in late June or early July, 634 [late Rabi-ul-Akhir or early Jamadi-ul-Awwal, 13 Hijri]. The two forces were fairly evenly matched, with the Persians a little superior in strength.

The details of the Battle of Babylon are not known, but it is described as a violent one with both sides giving as well as they took. After the combat had proceeded for some time, two Muslim stalwarts were able to blind the elephant with javelins, and the infuriated beast, not knowing where it was going and what it was doing, rushed madly about the battlefield, scattering the soldiers and breaking up lines of battle. Apparently it caused more confusion in the Persian ranks than in the Muslim, and as Muthana increased the pressure of his attack, the Persian front broke. The defeated army retreated hastily from the battlefield and made its way back to Ctesiphon. The withdrawal appears to have been an orderly one, even though Muthana followed the Persians up to their capital, harassing the retreat, before returning to reform his garrisons and outposts.

This was Muthana's first battle with the Persians since the departure of Khalid; and the Persians now knew, that the new Muslim Commander-in-Chief was a man to be reckoned with.

---

[31] Tabari: vol. 2. p. 606.

There were changes also in the higher political and military structure of Persia, the first of which related to an earlier event. Two years before, the Princess Azarmeedukht, the second of two royal sisters, daughters of Chosroes Parwez, ascended the throne. She was one of the most beautiful women of Persia.[32] Not many weeks had passed when the throne was coveted by one of the four satraps of Persia-Farrukh Hormuz, satrap of Khurasan. Seeking to gain with one stroke the satisfaction of supreme political power and the joys of love, he wrote to the new Empress : "I am today the hero of the nation and the pillar of the Persian Empire. Marry me!"

Azarmeedukht responded with distaste to what she regarded as pure insolence- a subject proposing marriage to his sovereign! She was, however, clever enough to conceal her feelings; and wrote to him: "It is not permissible for a queen to marry; but should you wish to satisfy your desire for me, come to me at night."[33] And she gave the night appointed for the romantic rendezvous.

Delighted at the exciting prospect which the invitation of the lovely Empress offered, Farrukh Hormuz journeyed to Ctesiphon. On the appointed night he came quietly to the palace, utterly unaware that he had a rendezvous not with love but with death. Azarmeedukht had given instructions to her captain of the guard to kill the impudent satrap as soon as he entered the palace.

The following morning the corpse of Farrukh Hormuz was found lying in the courtyard of the palace. The news of his death and the manner in which he was killed spread in the capital, and it was not long before it reached the ears of the son of the late satrap, who had been left by his father as governor of Khurasan and the commander of the front against the Turks and Huns. This man was a distinguished general, a veteran of many campaigns, and swore to wreak vengeance on the Empress for the murder of his father. He marched with an army to Ctesiphon.

At the capital a short battle was fought with loyal troops but their resistance was soon overcome and the rebel general captured Ctesiphon, and with it the Empress. On his orders the beauteous Azarmeedukht was blinded, and a few days later, killed. The general, supported by his troops, was now master of Persia.

In course of time another puppet was placed on the throne who found it safe not to challenge the authority of the general. And the general ruled Persia as the

---

[32] Tabari: vol. 1. p. 630.
[33] Ibid; Yaqubi: Tareekh; vol. 1. p. 173.

real power behind the throne and directed the course of its armies as supreme commander. It was he who conducted the campaigns against Khalid, and although the Persian armies were decimated in battle, his direction of the war was flawless.

This general was also a renowned astrologer and would seek to discover in the movement of the stars the course of future events. Because of his supposed insight into things unseen, and the chaotic conditions of the empire, one friend asked him confidentially, "What draws you to this? You can see how things are." The general replied: "The love of glory."[34] The general's name was Rustam.

An even bigger change which occurred related to the Persian throne and resulted from the Battle of Babylon. For the Muslims it was just another victory, but to the Persians it was more than another defeat. While they had acknowledged the superiority of Khalid's genius and bowed to the inevitability of his victories, it now appeared that even the successors of Khalid were cast in the same mould and would further humiliate the great empire. The Persians were a brave people, and reacted with anger to this defeat. A clamour went up in Ctesiphon against the Emperor Farrukhzad, who was blamed for provoking the Muslims unnecessarily with his uncouth insults. The clamour turned to violence; and the Emperor was killed.

Once again the throne of Persia was vacant and awaited the next occupant. This time, however, it seemed that there was none available, because after the massacre of the princes by Sheeruya, very few had been left who belonged to the ruling Sasani family; and these few had one by one ascended the throne and had one by one been killed by a fickle court and a fickle people. But a vigorous search was nevertheless conducted and it was not long before a prince of the royal blood was found living in obscurity in Istakhr [Persepolis].

Yazdjurd son of Shahryar son of Chosroes Parwez, a youth of 21, was brought to Ctesiphon and crowned. He was a fine young man who seemed to possess all the qualities of personality and character which the declining empire needed to arrest its decline. The Persians were filled with new hope. The young Emperor, in spite of his ignorance of political matters and court protocol, or perhaps because of it, threw himself with vigour into state affairs and the reorganisation of the military forces. Rustam remained Commander-in-Chief as before, for the Persians could not afford to lose the services of a man of such

---

[34] Tabari: Vol. 2, p. 635.

military talent and experience, but in his new relationship with the Emperor there was now a better balance between the army and the throne.[35]

The spirits of the Persians rose again. They looked upon Yazdjurd as a saviour who would throw the invaders out of the empire as many of his illustrious forbears had done. In any case, the martial quality of the Persian army and the Persian soldier was, and had always been high, for although the empire had declined politically, its military effectiveness had not declined.

The Persian Army, including its Arab auxiliaries, was the most formidable and most efficient military machine of the time. Led by experienced and dedicated veterans, it was a proud, sophisticated and well-tried force which gloried in its past achievements and its present might. The Persian soldier was the best equipped warrior of his day. He wore a coat of mail or a breastplate; on his head rested a helmet of either chain mail or beaten metal; his forearms were covered by metal sleeves and his legs were protected by greaves [like leg-guards covering the front part of the leg]. He carried a spear, lance or javelin, a sword and either an axe or an iron mace, the last-named being a favourite and much feared-Persian weapon. He also carried one or two bows with thirty arrows and two spare bowstrings hanging from his helmet.[36] Thus powerfully equipped and armed was the Persian soldier.

Muthana had always known that the resources of the Persian Empire were vast and only needed an organiser to be tapped and channelled against the Muslims. He had always had apprehensions that some day the military equation would turn unfavourable to him and his 9,000 troops. Now it appeared that his fears were coming true. The elephant which he had been worrying about seemed to be getting well again.

Muthana would need help. In the middle of August, 634 [middle of Jamadi-ul-Akhir, 13 Hijri] he set off for Madina to seek reinforcements.

---

[35] The year of accession of Yazdjurd and his age are in dispute, but from calculations carried out from past events and the reigns of the preceding monarchs, I find this version to be the most acceptable. There is much confusion on this point, and the early historians themselves are both confused and confusing.
[36] Tabri: vol. 1. p. 569; Dinawari: p. 73.

Chapter 3: The Victories and Defeat of Abu Ubayd

Muthana arrived at Madina to find the Caliph dying. He entered Abu Bakr's chamber and approached his death bed. The Caliph was alive enough and clear-headed enough to listen, judge and decide.

Muthana explained briefly the situation on the Iraq front: the adverse ratio of opposing strengths, the likelihood of a powerful offensive by the Persians and the difficulty of holding Iraq with his small army. He asked for reinforcements and urged the Caliph to allow the apostates to join his campaign.

Abu Bakr held strong views about the apostates, who had nearly wrecked the ship of Islam after the death of the Holy Prophet. Abu Bakr's greatest achievement had been his war against the apostates, and he was one of the very few men who could have carried the staggering burden which the apostasy had thrown on the Muslim state. After the destruction of the apostasy, Abu Bakr had ordered that no apostate would be allowed to take part in the holy war. The apostates had returned to the fold of Islam, of course, and the situation of the holy war had altered somewhat, but knowing that he was dying, Abu Bakr decided not to give any order on this point which his successor might not wish to implement. He sent for Umar, the caliph-designate, and a few minutes later Umar stood beside the departing Caliph.

"Listen, O Umar, to what I say to you," said the Caliph, "and act upon my words. I hope to die this very day, and when I am dead, let not the evening come upon you before you have exhorted the people to go with Muthana. And if I survive till nightfall, let not the morning come before you have exhorted the people to go with Muthana."[37]

Abu Bakr died early that night [634 A.H.] The same night he was buried; and the same night, after funeral prayer and before the prayer of the dawn, the new Caliph assembled the Muslims in the mosque and urged them to join Muthana in the campaign in Iraq. There was no response.

The following morning the Muslims of Madina assembled again, this time to take the oath of allegiance to Caliph Umar, and again Umar spoke about Iraq

---

[37] Tabari: vol. 2, p. 602.

and Muthana. Again there were no volunteers. The Arab feared the Persian - feared him with a deep, unreasoning fear which ran in the racial subconscious and was the result of centuries of Persian power and glory, during which the Persian had ruled other peoples with a heavy hand and treated the Arab of the desert with unconcealed contempt.[38] The Arab was willing enough to go to Syria to fight the Romans; but the Persians were another matter.

Umar was conscious of this. He also realised the vital importance of waging a successful war in Iraq, for no new Caliph could afford to surrender, immediately on taking the reigns of power in his hands, a rich dominion which his predecessor had conquered. Moreover, the torch of holy war had to be kept alive.

The following day Umar again assembled the Muslims and this time it was Muthana who started the proceedings. In a brief address, he spoke of the victories gained by the Muslims in Iraq and of the wealth which Iraq offered to those who had the courage to fight for it and hold it in their power. Then Umar spoke, and made a stirring appeal, in which he reminded the faithful of Allah's help to His servants and the promise of Allah that they would inherit the earth.

This time the response was better. The first man to stand and offer his services was one named Abu Ubayd bin Masud of the tribe of Saqeef. "Labbayk!" said the man. He was followed by others and after a little while a few hundred had come forward and volunteered to fight in Iraq, including many *immigrants* and *Ansars*-the seniormost of the companions of the Holy Prophet.[39]

Upon seeing the reluctance of the people to go and fight the Persians, Umar had made up his mind to reward the courage and keenness of the first volunteer by appointing him Commander-in-Chief in Iraq. He had hoped that one of the more senior and battle-tried members of the congregation would be the first, and although the first man to volunteer was a relatively younger man who was also not from among the early Companions, he determined to stick to his resolution. He announced that Abu Ubayd would command the army in Iraq and all others would serve under him, including Muthana.

---

[38] Ibid: P. 631.
[39] The Immigrants (Muhajireen) were those who migrated with the Holy Prophet to Madina; and the Ansars (Helpers) were the local residents of Madina who had invited the Prophet to live with then and had joined in the great movement of Islam. These were the earliest Companions and were always held in especial esteem by the Muslims who embraced the faith later.

A little later some of the older Muslims approached Umar and asked him to appoint one of the early Companions of the Prophet as commander since they had a higher standing in Islam. "Are you placing a man from the Saqeef in command over the Immigrants and Ansars?"[40] they asked. Umar replied that the Immigrants and Ansars held a high position only because they were the first to go forth to do battle with the infidel. This time they had shown no great keenness in answering his call to arms and so the first volunteer, even if he was not from among them, would be the commander.

Muthana left at once for Iraq to take up his station against the Persians while awaiting the arrival of reinforcements. Meanwhile a small force of 1,000 volunteers was gathered in Madina and placed under Abu Ubayd.

Abu Ubayd was an inexperienced soldier who, if left to his own devices, could lead the Muslims into serious trouble. He was a fearless and noble Muslim, but the conduct of war called for qualities of leadership which were not provided by just will and courage. Umar knew this, and appointed two older Muslims as Abu Ubayd's advisers, vis Sa'd bin Ubayd and Saleet bin Qeis, both veterans of Badr, the first battle of Islam. "Pay heed to the Companions of the Prophet, on whom be the blessings of Allah and peace," said Umar to Abu Ubayd. "Let them join you in matters of command. Do not act fast until the situation is clear, for war is war and goes best with a man of patience who knows when to seize an opportunity and when to wait. Haste in war leads to failure."[41]

In the meantime Rustam had laid his plans and launched his first move. His intention was to eject the Muslims from the Suwad, which was the name by which the most fruitful and populous part of Iraq was known. The Suwad was the land between the Euphrates and the Tigris from Basra to Ctesiphon and stretched further northwards to Mosul and Hulwan. It also included a wide strip of fertile land along the left bank of the Lower Tigris, which bulged in its southern part towards Ahwaz. Rustam determined to use direct military force as well as insurrectional methods against the Muslims. He wrote to the mayors of all the towns, urging them to fight in the cause of the Persian Empire, and also sent *agents provocateur* to incite the people to rise against the invaders. As for direct military measures, Rustam formed three small armies, two of which were placed under Narsa and Jaban. Narsa was sent to Kaskar [See Map 1] to re-establish Persian government in the eastern part of the Suwad and to act as a bait to draw the Muslims thither. Jaban was sent to the Euphrates to cross the

---

[40] Masudi: Muruj; vol. 2, p. 315.

[41] Tabari: vol. 2. pp. 631-2.

river in the region of Hira and manoeuvre directly against the Muslim base. These two forces, operating in separate areas, would either force the Muslims out of Iraq or cause dispersion in the Muslim army. They would engage in battle and weaken the Muslims, whereafter Rustam would send another force to further exhaust and bleed the Muslim army. Then, finally, Rustam would launch the fourth army - his big punch - under the formidable general, Bahman, to deliver the *coup de grace*. It was a finely timed and well thought out plan; and the Muslims, thanks to the inexperience of Abu Ubayd, reacted exactly as Rustam hoped, though with much more vigour and dash than Rustam wished.

Muthana returned to Hira to find the Persian moves under way and realised that a major offensive was in the offing. Having spent years as a raider, and having closely watched Khalid's strategy of fighting his battles close to the desert, he had no intention of getting involved in set-piece battles deep in Iraq against numerically superior forces. Some of the Muslim outposts had already pulled back from the Suwad, and now Muthana withdrew the remainder of his garrisons behind the Euphrates. In his next move, as Jaban approached the Euphrates, Muthana evacuated Hira and moved down to Khaffan in order to tempt Jaban to cross the Euphrates and draw him close to the desert.[42] The elephant seemed well again, and the leopard moved out of his path.

Abu Ubayd set off from Madina, and on his way to Iraq called upon all the Muslim tribes through whose areas he marched to furnish warriors for his army. The tribes responded fairly well and Abu Ubayd was able to recruit another 4,000 fighting men before he joined Muthana at Khaffan in early October, 634 [early Shaban, 13 Hijri].

Meanwhile Jaban had crossed the Euphrates and advanced towards the Muslims. He got to Namariq, near the site of Kufa, and stopped

Jaban had fought Khalid in the Battle of Ulleis in which most of his army of Persians and Christian Arabs had been annihilated in the River of Blood. Jaban himself had only just managed to escape and knew full well that to lose a battle to the Muslims meant virtual destruction of the army unless he kept his escape routes open. He consequently decided not to move beyond Namariq and here awaited the Muslims. He was a brave and skilful general who had earned for his troops a rare tribute from the great Khalid himself, as mentioned in Chapter 1.

---

[42] Khaffan was at or near the present Qawwam, which is 6 miles west of Shinafia.

After a week in Khaffan, Abu Ubayd moved forward with an army of 12,000 warriors, a good part of which was cavalry. He appointed Muthana as commander of the cavalry, and on arrival at Namariq both armies deployed and engaged in battle, of which no details are available. The Persians were defeated and retreated in disorder from the battlefield while Jaban was captured by a Muslim soldier. The soldier did not know the identity of his distinguished prisoner who talked him into releasing him on payment of ransom. Later, however, the Muslim discovered that his prisoner was none other than the Persian army commander, and wished to kill him, but Abu Ubayd, a fine, true Muslim, ordered Jaban freed for the reason that once a Muslim had given a promise of life and freedom to his prisoner, the prisoner could not be harmed.

This battle was fought, in the second week of October, 634. It was hardly over when Abu Ubayd decided to advance to Kaskar, 150 miles away, to fight the second Persian army which by its, very presence in that region, was disputing the Muslim hold over the Suwad. Muthana, as commander of the Muslim cavalry, was sent off at a fast pace while the rest of the army crossed the Euphrates and followed on camels. A fortnight later the Muslims fought and defeated Narsa in battle at a place named Saqatia, near Kaskar, and again the Persians retreated before the assault of the Muslims. Saqatia was sacked by the victors and a great deal of booty fell into their hands.

Abu Ubayd now ordered the return march. He was driving his men very hard, but the example of their tireless commander was enough to silence all complaints and the booty gained in battle made the sweat and blood worthwhile in the eyes of the men. Two weeks later, as the Muslims approached the Euphrates on their way to Hira, they found another Persian army awaiting them under a general, named Jalinus - the third army sent by Rustam against the Muslims. Abu Ubayd took no time to array his army for battle and at Baqsiasa, in the district of Barusma, the Muslims fought and defeated this third Persian army. Jalinus fled from the battlefield with rather more haste than was decent, but was able to extricate most of his troops.

MAP 2: THE MOVEMENTS OF ABU UBAYD

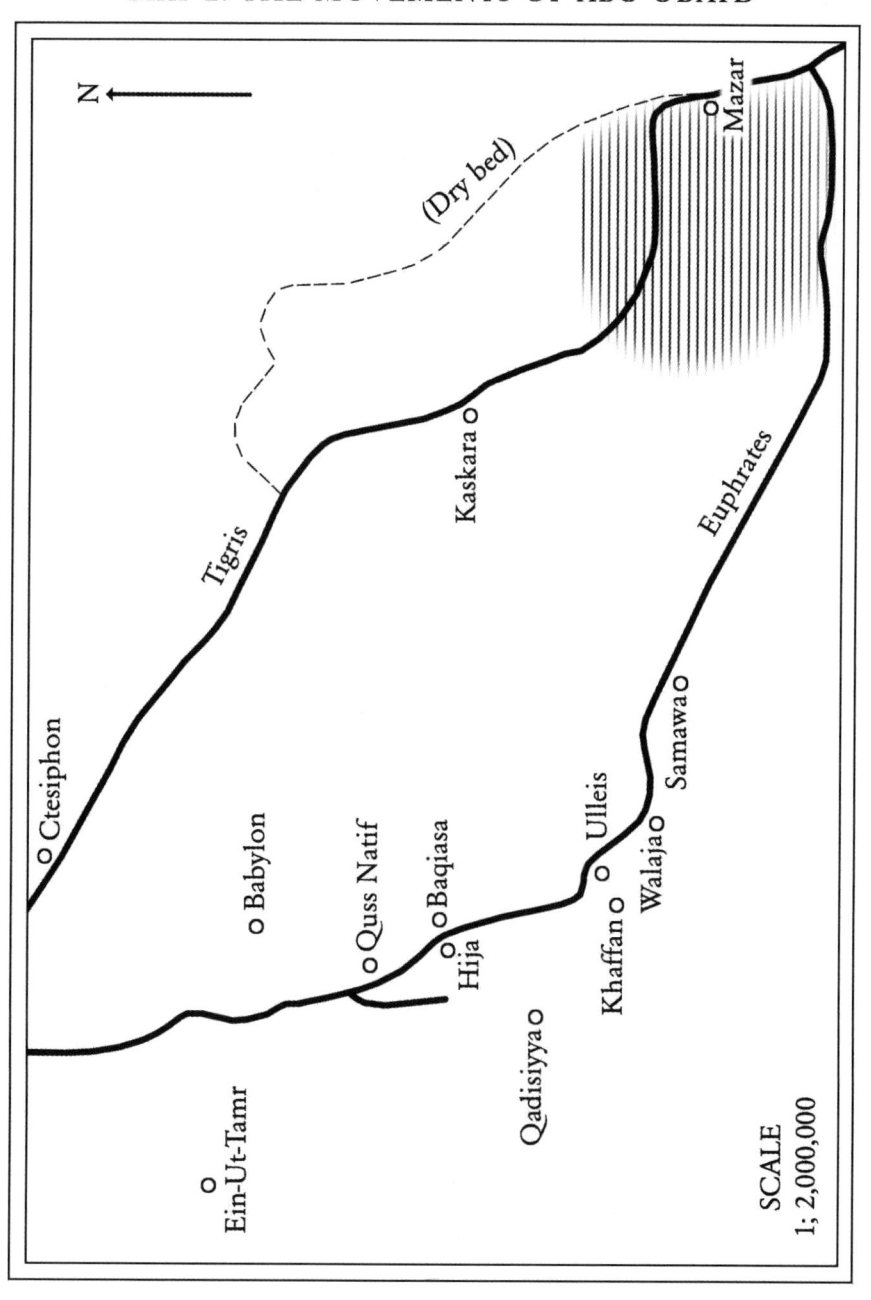

The day after this battle was fought, some local civil officials came to the Muslims and assured them of their loyalty, but this was received by the Muslims with less than total faith. One mayor brought some fine dishes of food to Abu Ubayd as a mark of respect to the Muslim commander and his officers. On being asked by Abu Ubayd if similar food would be given to all the soldiers, the mayor explained that it was just not possible to provide such a meal to everybody. Thereupon Abu Ubayd returned the fine fare with the remark: "If the army cannot have such food, we have no need for it. We shall only eat what all eat."[43] Abu Ubayd crossed the Euphrates and reoccupied Hira. He felt satisfied with the situation, not knowing that Rustam too felt satisfied.

By now even Umar was getting a bit alarmed at Abu Ubayd's wild marches across Iraq in search of glory and paradise. Thus, soon after his return to Hira, Abu Ubayd received a letter from the Caliph which read:

"You have entered the land of trickery and guile and dishonesty and oppression. You have marched against a people who love evil and know it well, and abjure goodness, of which they are ignorant. So be on your guard; and watch your tongue. Reveal not your secrets, for those who guard their secrets are secure against unpleasantness and loss."

Persia was a vast empire. Geographically it consisted of two great plains separated from one another by mountains. The western part of the empire comprised the plain of Iraq, which includes the valleys of the Euphrates and the Tigris and runs into the Syrian desert in the west and the Arabian desert in the south. As an eastern extension of this plain, lies the fertile land of Khuzistan, watered by the river Karun, which the Arabs knew as Dujeil. East of this plain stand the Zagros Mountains, rising near the Persian Gulf and running in a north-westerly direction to Azarbeijan, where they are joined by the Elburz Range in a high, tangled mass, and stretch further northwards to connect with the Caucasus Mountains. From Azarbeijan the Elburz Mountains run eastwards, skirting the southern shore of the Caspian Sea, to a little beyond Gorgan.

The second of the great plains was the arid Iranian Plateau, bounded in the west and north by the Zagros and Elburz Mountains and stretching eastwards to embrace Afghanistan and Baluchistan. North and north-east of the eastern end of the Elburz Range lay the steppes of Central Asia. The region with which we are most immediately concerned, however, is the western plain, which

---

[43] Tabari: vol. 2, p. 637.

meant mainly Iraq. Islam and Persia were now fighting for Iraq, specifically for the Suwad, the most productive part of Iraq over much of which Khalid had established Muslim rule. Iraq was one of the many lands which formed part of the Persian Empire, and it was undoubtedly the most prized possession of the Persians. It was a green jewel, on the rich soil of which many great nations and dynasties had risen, fought and perished since the time of the ancient Sumerians.

To the Arabs of the barren wastes of Arabia it was a land of milk and honey. Its two mighty rivers, the Euphrates and the Tigris, were the greatest known rivers of the time-west of the Indus and north of the Nile. But these rivers did not then flow as they flow now; nor were the cities of Iraq as the cities of today. Kufa and Basra did not exist; [they were founded in 17 Hijri]. Baghdad was a small though much-frequented market town on the west bank of the Tigris. The then glorious cities of Ctesiphon and Hira are now turned to dust.

Ctesiphon was a mighty metropolis and the capital and seat of glory of the Persian Empire. It sprawled on both sides of the Tigris and was known to the Muslims as "Madain" literally "the cities", for it consisted of several cities in one, of which more will be said in a later chapter. Hira was the capital of the Arab Lakhmid Dynasty. Situated on the west bank of the Euphrates, it was a glittering, throbbing city with many citadels. And there was Uballa, the main port of the Persian Empire which was visited by ships from India and China and other maritime countries of the East.[44]

The Euphrates and the Tigris have been known to change their course more than once since the time of Babylon. The maps in this book show the course which these rivers followed in the early days of Islam. The main change from today is in the course of the Tigris. In pre-Islamic times it had flowed in what is its present channel and is known as Dijlat-ul-Aura [the One-eyed Tigris], but then it had abandoned this channel and adopted a new course from Kut downwards, along the Dujeila [the Little Tigris] and the Akhzar, to enter a region of lakes and marshes comprising an area about a hundred miles square, just north-west of Uballa. The old bed of the river had then become a dry, sandy bed. The marshes extended much farther north than they do today, and the Tigris picked its way through these marshes to rejoin the bed of the One-eyed Tigris in the region of Mazar [the present Azeir] whence it flowed south

---

[44] Uballa stood where the part of modern Basra known as Ashar stands today.

and south-east into the Persian Gulf.[45] But the Tigris changed its course again in the 16th Century and returned to its old bed, the one marked on maps now as the Tigris. This is not, however, the largest branch of the Tigris, for the Gharraf, taking off from Kut and joining the Euphrates at Nasiriyya, is larger. The Dujeila, which in the early days of Islam was the main channel, is now a modest river-the third largest branch of the Tigris, after the Gharraf and the One-eyed Tigris.

The Euphrates followed a clear course down to the present Hindiyya whence it split into two main channels as it does today-both sizable rivers: the Hilla Branch and the main Euphrates. The main branch [the western one] again split up, flowing generally in one large and several subsidiary channels, which over the centuries have changed course several times, though not as drastically as the Tigris. The two main branches reunited at Samawa whence the Euphrates flowed towards the region of lakes and marshes already mentioned. While some of the water of the river lost itself in the marshes, one clear channel marked on today's maps as the Euphrates retained its distinct identity as it flowed eastwards to join the Tigris at Qurna. The marshes were drained by a large river which emptied into the Tigris a few miles above Basra, and from this junction all these waters flowed into the Persian Gulf as one mighty river, known today as the Shatt-ul-Arab.

This then was the state of Iraq, geographically, in the 7th Century. It was inhabited by Persians and Arabs and was the part of Persia nearest to the home of Islam.

The operations of the last few weeks had gone as Rustam had planned. The Muslims had reacted to his moves as Rustam had hoped and a certain amount of wearing down had been effected in the Muslim army, but Rustam had not expected that his three smaller armies would be beaten as badly as they were and was particularly angry with Jalinus who, considering that he had fought the Muslims soon after they had been engaged by Jaban and Narsa, should have done better than he did.

"Send him ahead," Rustam ordered Bahman, the commander of the main Persian army. "If he retreats again, cut off his head."[46]

---

[45] Ibn Rusta: pp. 94-5. At Mau (Azeir) today only a small river flows into the Tigris from the west-certainly too small to form the bed of the old Tigris. The old bed has probably silted up and ceased to be discernible.
[46] Tabari: vol. 2, p.639.

Bahman was charged with the mission of advancing towards Hira, bringing the Muslims to battle, destroying them in battle and driving the remnants out of Iraq. The strength of his army is not recorded but it included a group of war elephants; and to leave no doubt in the general's mind about the importance of his task, the Emperor gave him, to carry in battle, the great standard of Persia known as "Dirafsh-e-Kavian"- the most glorious and most venerated symbol of the empire.

The Persian society of the time was an imperial and aristocratic one, and as is inevitable in such societies, it had an elaborate system of ranks to indicate a man's social and official position at the court. The outward symbol of rank was the cap: as a man rose in rank, his cap became more costly. The highest rank below the Emperor carried a cap worth a hundred thousand dirhams, which was studded with diamonds and pearls and other precious stones. Of the Persian generals who had fought Khalid in the preceding year, Hormuz and Qarin wore hundred-thousand-dirham caps; and Andarzaghar and Azazbeh were one rank lower - fifty thousand dirhams. Of these only the last named had escaped alive from the clutches of Khalid. Bahman was a hundred-thousand-dirham man.

Bahman was also the top soldier of Persia. He was second to Rustam only because Rustam had seized political power and made himself the virtual ruler of the empire. An old veteran, he had fought with distinction under Anushirwan who had given him the name of Bahman as a title of honour. His actual name was Mardanshah. He was also known as Zul Hajib "the man with the eyebrows"-and was so called because he combed his eyebrows upwards. Today we would refer to him light-heartedly as General Eyebrows!

Eyebrows marched with his army towards Hira and camped on the east bank of the Euphrates at a place called Quss Natif, some distance north of Hira end a little below the site of Kufa. From Hira, Abu Ubayd moved up opposite the Persians and camped with 9,000 men on the west bank by a village called Marauha.

On the following day Bahman sent an emissary to the Muslim commander with the message: "Either you cross over to our side, and we shall let you, or we shall cross over to your side, and you must let us." When this message was delivered, the officers standing around Abu Ubayd said: "Do not cross, O Abu Ubayd. We forbid you to cross. Tell them to cross."

The obvious strategy for the Muslims was to let the Persians cross so that the great river would act as an obstacle in the way of Persian retreat while their own line of retreat would remain open in case of a reverse. But Abu Ubayd was no strategist; and he had become over-confident as a result of the clear but insignificant victories which he had won over the past few weeks. "There shall be none," Abu Ubayd asserted, "more willing to die than us. We shall cross to their side!"

The officers were horrified at the military blunder which their commander was about to commit - but Abu Ubayd's resolution was strengthened by the knowledge that in this battle he would drink the cup of martyrdom and enter Paradise. The night before his wife had dreamed that a man came down from heaven with a vessel from which first Abu Ubayd drank, then his brother Al Hakam and his son Jabr, and then a few others from his family. She had described the dream to Abu Ubayd, whereupon he had remarked: "This means martyrdom." For the true believer, this was the ultimate trial and the ultimate triumph.

Next Saleet bin Qeis, the man appointed by Umar as Abu Ubayd's deputy, said: "Never have the Arabs faced the Persians in battle since the beginning of the race, but the Persians have been vastly superior in strength and have met us with an abundance of equipment and material such as we never possessed. You are now in a place which gives us room for attack and a way of escape so that we can withdraw and counter attack."

"You are frightened." Abu Ubayd retorted, no longer amenable to reason.

Saleet was furious. "By Allah." he swore. "I am bolder than you. You have been advised and soon you will know." He said no more after this. Finally Muthana made an attempt to deter Abu Ubayd from the rash enterprise. "O Commander," he said, "do not cut your means of escape; and do not make yourself and those who are with you a target for the Persians." Muthana could claim to know more about the Persians than any other Muslim, but he too was silenced by Abu Ubayd, who said, "You too are frightened, O brother of Bakr."[47] The allusion was to Muthana's tribe.

As a result of the last exchange, Abu Ubayd removed Muthana from the command of the cavalry and appointed in his place his own cousin, Abu Mihjan. Abu Ubayd also announced that in case of his death the command

---

[47] Ibid: pp. 639-641.

would devolve upon his brother Al Hakam; in case of his death upon his son Jabr; and named several others who would follow in command. These officers were those who had drunk of the heavenly vessel in the dream of Abu Ubayd's wife. Muthana was left in command of his own tribal contingent - the Bani Bakr.

The decision of Abu Ubayd to cross the river was carried back by Bahman's emissary. The Persian could have hoped for nothing better. He pulled his army back some distance from the river bank and deployed it to await the Muslim crossing when it came.

Then a bridge was thrown across the river. It was a boat bridge and was constructed by neutral engineers - Christian Arabs working under Ibn Saluba, son of the mayor of Quss Natif who had submitted to Khalid on the conquest of Hira. When the bridge was complete, the stage was set for the Battle of Quss Natif, also known as the Battle of the Bridge.

Early in the morning of November 28, 634 [Ramadhan 30, 13 Hijri] the Muslim army began to cross the river by the boat bridge. The Persians stood back as per agreement and made no move for two hours or so while their opponents crossed over to their side, but remained arrayed in battle order in tight formation in such a manner that no outflanking movement would be possible. The strongest element in the Persian army was the group of elephants which stood dispersed in the front rank. Each elephant carried a howdah filled with soldiers armed with javelins and bows, and to each howdah the Persians had tied a palm tree in order to increase the illusion of size. In between the elephants Bahman had deployed his heavy cavalry to form the front rank. The ground which the Persians left for the Muslims to occupy was not very suitable for movement and allowed little room for manoeuvre. The more experienced Muslims looked with misgiving at the Persian battle formation and the situation of the battlefield.

As the crossing progressed, Abu Ubayd, who was among the first to cross, received the tribal contingents on the east bank and placed each one in position for battle. Soon after the last Muslim had crossed, Abu Ubayd was ready for battle. The cavalry was kept in front and the large contingent of the Saqeef, Abu Ubayd's tribe, held the centre where Abu Ubayd himself stood with the army standard.

The Persians made no move. Abu Ubayd at once ordered the attack and the Muslim army, preceded by the cavalry, moved forward towards the Persian front. The Muslims were quite close to the Persians when their forward movement became disorganised. The horses saw the elephants, which, with palm trees apparently growing on their backs, made an unearthly picture. The elephants also had bells tied around their necks, or perhaps their trunks, and their riders were able to make these bells ring, which made the beasts appear even more frightening. And the Persian heavy cavalry, with horse and rider clothed in shining armour, did nothing to reassure the Arab horse. The Arab horse stopped, shied, turned and bolted. The Muslim riders fought to control their mounts and managed to do so before they had gone too far, but the best of the cavalrymen were unable to persuade their horses to advance upon the Persians.

During this confusion the Muslim infantry moved up and engaged in an archery duel with the Persians, in which the latter had the upper hand because of their more powerful bows and heavier arrows. It was an inauspicious beginning for the Muslims. And the situation turned more adverse as Bahman, seeing the state of the Muslim cavalry, ordered the advance, and the Persian army, led by the cavalry and the elephants, moved forward. The noise of the elephant bells now became louder, increasing the din of battle.

This led to a desperate struggle, in which only the courage of the Muslim soldiers and the example of the Muslim officers prevented a collapse. The Persians made masterly use of their bows and drove several wedges into the Muslim front but the penetration was not allowed to go deep. Although crowded and unable to manoeuvre, the Muslims, fighting in groups, beat off the Persian attacks, causing heavy losses, and were able to maintain a fairly orderly formation. But it was obvious that the situation would get still more desperate with time. It was now about midday.

It was at this stage of battle that one of Abu Ubayd's detractors, a man named Maslama bin Aslam, said to him, "O man, you do not have the knowledge that we have. You rejected our advice; and soon all the Muslims will be annihilated with you because of your useless plan."

Abu Ubayd could think of nothing better to say than: "O man, go forth and fight."[48]

There were abler officers than Abu Ubayd in the Muslim army, but there was none braver. He could see that the horses had become ungovernable and it was

---

[48] Masudi: Muruj; vol. 2. P. 316.

a waste of time to try to get them back into battle. Abu Ubayd was not the man to let his horse decide whether or not he should fight. He sprang off his horse and ordered the cavalry to dismount and attack on foot. The Muslim cavalry abandoned its horses, and sword in hand, joined the infantry as Abu Ubayd ordered the attack again.

The Muslims, disencumbered of their horses, rushed at the Persian front line which reeled under the Muslim blows. This now became a battle of foot against horse and foot against elephant. Abu Ubayd, followed by his clan and accompanied by his cavalry commander, Abu Mihjan, led the attack. The Muslim commander shouted to his men to attack the elephants and cut their girths, and the Muslims moved accordingly upon the huge animals. Many were killed and wounded by the javelins and arrows shot by the elephant riders, but several groups reached their quarry and cut the girths, bringing down the riders who were then killed on the ground.

The battle now reached its climax with fierce fighting everywhere. It was still anybody's game, with the odds rather in favour of the Persians whose organisation was still intact.

The largest and more ferocious of the elephants was a white giant which stood in the centre and was doing the most damage. Abu Ubayd, with his standard in one hand and a javelin in the other, advanced upon this elephant, and now began a duel between man and beast. Abu Ubayd approached the elephant and hurled his javelin, which struck and blinded the animal in one eye. Then, with drawn sword, he eluded the flailing trunk and got under the elephant and cut its girth, bringing down the howdah and its occupants. Those of the Persians who could evade the blows of Abu Ubayd's sword dispersed quickly. Abu Ubayd next attacked the elephant from a side and with one powerful blow cut off the elephant's trunk; but this was the gallant Muslim's last blow. The enraged monster knocked Abu Ubayd down with its leg and placed a foot upon its fallen foe. Under the enormous weight of the great white beast, the body of Abu Ubayd crumpled like a plastic toy.

The death of Abu Ubayd marked the turning point in the Battle of the Bridge. His cousin, Abu Mihjan, rushed forward and struck at the leg of the elephant, gashing it badly. He was joined by the fallen commander's brother, Al Hakam, who picked up the standard and assumed command of the army. The two of them drove the elephant back and dragged the mangled remains of Abu Ubayd from the scene of combat. But soon after, AI Hakam also fell and Abu Ubayd's son, Jabr, followed his uncle in command and in death. Then, one after the other, the officers named by Abu Ubayd before battle, all from his own clan, took the standard and one after the other, fought and fell as martyrs. Along the entire front the battle was raging with unrelenting fury, but now as the Muslims came to know that Abu Ubayd and six others in the line of command had been killed in battle, they began to lose heart and to fall back. At this moment Bahman, with superb judgement, sensed the turn of the tide and ordered his front rank to counterattack. Meanwhile the white elephant had died of its wounds.

The Saqeef were the heaviest sufferers on the Muslim side. Their commander, his brother and his son, and four others of his clan-warriors who were among their best, had commanded the army and died in the thickest of the fighting. With them had also fallen many more of the tribe. This turned the mood of some of them into a violent, suicidal one. One especially - Abdullah bin Marsad - decided that none should survive this battle. Under the pressure of the Persian heavy cavalry, which was exhilarated by the scent of victory, the Muslims began to retreat rapidly towards the bridge with the intention of crossing to safety. Seeing this move, Abdullah bin Marsad rushed to the bridge, shouting: "O people, die for what your commanders have died for, or fight till victory."[49] As he got to the bridge he cut the cords which held the nearest boat, and the bridge floated away. The only route of Muslim escape was severed.

The Muslim retreat turned chaotic as they rushed to the site of the bridge, while the exulting Persians attacked with great vigour to finish the army of Islam. All order vanished from the Muslim ranks, and it was clear that few if any would escape. A large number of Muslims, not knowing what else to do, plunged into the river, even those who could not swim. And the Persians pressed closer and increased the violence of their assaults, confident that not one of their foes would escape the slaughter.

But the Persians had not reckoned on Muthana. This grand soldier once again rose to glory in the darkest hour which the Muslims were to know in their campaign against Persia. He took command of the army, under circumstances when few would dare to even attempt to take command, and organised a rear guard for the close defence of the bridge site. Along with his own veterans he fought off the Persians as they struggled to get to the helpless, seething mass on the river bank. With Muthana stood Saleet, Abu Ubayd's deputy, and a man who had been one of Khalid's ablest lieutenants - Asim bin Amr. The Persian

---

[49] Tabari: viol. 2, p. 642.

storm broke on the rock of Muthana's rear guard and the Muslims gained a much needed respite.

Muthana ordered the repair of the bridge and work began at once at the bridge site. He called to the men: "O people, I am with you." Just such an assurance from Muthana could restore order, for the presence of Muthana was a battle winning factor. "Cross calmly and do not panic. Do not drown yourselves. I shall remain at my post until the last of you has reached the other bank."[50]

Under the shield provided by Muthana and his veterans, the bridge was repaired and the defeated army began to cross. At the site stood Abdullah bin Marsad, the man who had cut the bridge. He was still trying to dissuade the soldiers from crossing, and he kept at it until someone caught the misguided fellow and brought him to Muthana. Muthana hit the man and asked, "What made you do this?" "So they should fight!" replied Abdullah simply.[51]

As the crossing proceeded, Muthana held the Persians off and slowly began to fall back on to the bridge. Then his own men started to cross and now the Persian attacks increased in fury as their stalwarts struck to cut down the rear guard. Finally only two men remained on the east bank - Muthana and Saleet. Saleet fell dead from a Persian blow; and Muthana, like the celebrated Marshal Ney in Napoleon's retreat from Moscow, was the last man to cross the river.

Muthana was badly wounded. The worst of his wounds was in his face and mouth, where a Persian spear had struck him. After him the bridge was hastily dismantled by the Muslims, of whom only a third remained.

As the Muslims assembled in their camp at Marauha on the west bank, Muthana's greatest worry was that the Persians would rebuild the bridge and cross the river, but he was saved from this predicament by the uncertain politics of the Persian Empire. Bahman had determined to cross the Euphrates and put paid to the Muslim account when news reached him of an uprising against Rustam. The capital apparently was in ferment. Regarding this as a more serious threat to the empire than the broken Muslim army, he at once ordered a return to Ctesiphon and the Persian army marched away, leaving a detachment to watch the river.

Of the 9,000 Muslims who had taken part in the Battle of the Bridge, 4,000 laid down their lives, of whom a little more than half were drowned. But the brave

---

[50] Ibid.
[51] Ibid.

warriors accounted for 6,000 Persian lives. 2,000 Muslims, all of Abu Ubayd's army, fled, some from the east side of the river and others after crossing the bridge, and returned to Arabia. When Muthana counted his men he found only 3,000 left, almost all of whom were veterans of his own older army, and many of these including himself and his lieutenant, Asim bin Amr, were wounded. The fugitives who returned to Madina tried to hide themselves, afraid to show their faces. They had actually fought with courage but were nevertheless ashamed of having left the battlefield as vanquished men.

Following a sound strategy, Muthana abandoned Hira and marched with his weary army to Ulleis, there to rest and recoup. He also sent a messenger to the Caliph to inform him of the fate of the Muslim army in Iraq; and in due course this messenger returned with the instructions of Umar: "Stay at your post. Lo! help shall soon come.[52]

This was a terrible blow. Never before had the Muslim state in its brief 13 year history suffered such a crushing defeat, and the impact on Madina was very sad indeed. Umar felt it as a personal loss, because the disaster was due to Abu Ubayd's leadership and he himself had appointed the man to command. It took all the great courage of the man to bear the burden of it with fortitude and equanimity. Those of the fugitives who feared the taunts of others and the wrath of the Caliph need not have done so, for in this tragedy Umar showed how big he was and how broad his shoulders were. "O Lord," he said, "every Muslim is in my charge and I am a refuge for all Muslims. May Allah bless Abu Ubayd! Having crossed the river, if only he had secured his position by the side of a hill! I wish he had not crossed and sought his death, but had returned to me!"[53]

One much respected Muslim named Muadh, a reciter of the Quran, was among those who had fled, and he repented it deeply. Whenever he recited the Quran and came to the verse: "And whoever turns his back to them, except when manoeuvring for battle or rejoining a company, he has incurred the wrath of Allah. His habitation shall be hell, a terrible journey's end,"[54] he would weep bitterly. Umar consoled him: "Do not weep, O Muadh. I am your refuge, and you have returned to me.[55]

---

[52] Dinawari: p. 114.
[53] Tabari: vol. 2, p. 640.
[54] Quran: 8-16.
[55] Tabari: vol. 2, p. 643.

Chapter 4: The Battle Buweb

Muthana, the bravest of the brave, bore his troubles in silence. Not a word of complaint escaped his lips, though he had much to complain about.

When he had first gone to Abu Bakr to suggest an invasion of Iraq, he had hoped that he would be given command of the Iran front, but Abu Bakr appointed Khalid as the Commander-in-Chief. Muthana was disappointed but accepted the Caliph's decision without resentment because of Khalid's great stature and his unique military ability. The best of generals would be happy and honoured to serve under Khalid. When Khalid was sent off to Syria and Muthana appointed Commander-in-Chief in Iraq, he got his just elevation and was satisfied.

After the Battle of Babylon, when Muthana went and met Abu Bakr and asked for reinforcements, he naturally expected that he would remain in command, and this was clearly Abu Bakr's intention also. But then a relatively obscure man whose qualifications for high command were doubtful was placed in command of the army in Iraq. Muthana again felt unfairly treated, but like the good soldier and true Muslim that he was, accepted the Caliph's decision loyally and threw himself without reservation into battle under Abu Ubayd, in spite of the obviously faulty plan of the new commander. And in the disaster of the bridge, it was Muthana who took command when all was nearly lost and saved the Muslims from annihilation, at a personal cost of many wounds. And now that others had messed everything up and left him holding the baby, the Caliph was telling him to stay at his post!

If Muthana had belonged to the Qureish or been a Companion of the Prophet, his fate may well have been different. But he was only from the Bani Bakr, a distant tribe. In grim silence he nursed his wounds and watched the moves of Persian forces. Far from being downhearted, he awaited his next victim. And soon fate provided him with one.

As mentioned in the preceding chapter, Bahman had returned in haste after the Battle of the Bridge to deal with the uprising against Rustam. The details of this uprising are not known but it was some sort of protest against Rustam, and some of the generals too were involved in it. One of these was Jaban, who had fought and survived in battle against Khalid and Abu Ubayd. On the return of Bahman with his victorious army, order was soon restored in Ctesiphon and

Rustam was again as firmly entrenched as ever. But Jaban was now on the run. With some followers he made his way towards Ulleis for reasons not known. Muthana came to know of his arrival in the neighbourhood and leaving Asim bin Amr in charge of the camp, set off with a few stalwarts to engage the Persians. The two parties met; and Muthana and his men sprang at the Persians and overpowered them. Muthana put all of them to death, including Jaban. After this little adventure, which acted as a restorative to the old campaigner, Muthana returned to his camp at Ulleis and awaited the next Persian move. The date of this event is not recorded but would be about January, 635 [Zul Qada. 13 Hijri].

This was an auspicious beginning to the year 635. Things began to look up again for Muthana. The reinforcements promised by Umar started to arrive in groups of various sizes, the largest being that of a veteran named Jareer bin Abdullah. Jareer had fought under Khalid in Iraq and marched with him to Syria, but soon after Khalid's arrival in Eastern Syria, he had found it necessary to return to Arabia for certain reasons. After the Battle of the Bridge, Jareer approached Umar with his clan of Bajeela and asked for marching orders.

"Go and join Muthana," said Umar. "But Syria!" said Jareer. "But Iraq!" replied the Caliph.

Like many Arabs, Jareer and his followers were happier at the prospect of fighting in Syria and not as keen to go and fight the Persians. Umar explained that reinforcements were urgently needed in Iraq and that there was no need for more forces in Syria. "The Muslims in Syria are on top of their enemies."[56]

Jareer remained reluctant and finally Umar was able to persuade him to go to Iraq only by offering his clan one-fourth of the state's share of the booty. Thus the clan of Bajeela would get the usual four-fifths of the booty taken by them plus a quarter of the remaining one-fifth which was the share of Madina. With this understanding Jareer set off for Iraq. Before he left, the Caliph warned him: "Do not cross a river or a bridge except after victory."[57]

Several other tribal contingents also marched to Iraq. Some of these joined Muthana at Ulleis while others joined him at Zu Qar where Muthana later moved up from Ulleis. Among the better known tribal chieftains who went to Iraq to fight in the holy war were Jareer bin Abdullah of the Bajeela, Arfaja bin Harsama of the Azd, who had been one of Abu Bakr's corps commanders in

---

[56] Tabari: vol. 2, p. 644.
[57] Ibid: p. 646.

the Campaign of the Apostasy and Adi bin Hatim of the Tayy. The last named had fought under Khalid in the Campaign of the Apostasy and was one of Khalid's prominent generals in his Iraq campaign. He was also one of the two tallest Arabs in history, about whom it was said that when they sat on a horse their feet touched the ground!

Reports began to trickle into Ctesiphon of the arrival of Muslim reinforcements at Ulleis. These reports were followed by intelligence that Muthana had moved up to Zu Qar, a few miles south of Qadisiyya, and had been joined there by more tribal groups coming up from Arabia. [See Map 1.]

This information caused a considerable amount of alarm in the Persian capital. After Khalid no Muslim was feared more by the Persians than Muthana. He seemed indestructible. He had never lost an action and the violence of his raids was as fearsome as their success was total. No place west of the Tigris was safe from his lightning strikes. Moreover, Muthana appeared to be fired not only by the spirit of the holy war but also by an obsessive personal vendetta against the Persians. Something had to be done to prevent the Muslim horse from overrunning the Suwad again. Consequently another Persian army was ordered out of Ctesiphon.

This time a general named Mihran was placed in command of the army which numbered 12,000 soldiers and had three elephants. Mihran was charged with the mission of driving the Muslims out of the region of Hira; and he marched to the Euphrates and camped by the east bank opposite the present Kufa. At about the same time Muthana, advancing from Zu Qar, where the last of the Muslim reinforcements had joined him, arrived on the west bank and camped at Nakheila, which stood roughly in the area where Kufa was later founded. Nakheila was a little away from the river. At this place a last addition was made to Muthana's strength in the form of two groups of Christian Arabs from the tribes of Namr and Taghlib which inhabited Western Iraq. These Christian Arabs were willing to fight along with their fellow Arabs against the Persians, and this brought Muthana's strength up to about 8,000 men. It was now April 635. [Safar, 14 Hijri].

By Nakheila a small river called Buweib took off from the Euphrates where the southern edge of Kufa stands today and flowed southwards, eventually joining the River Ateeq, though its exact junction with the Ateeq is not known.[58] The locality at which this river began was known as Dar-ur-Rizq, and was a low-

---

[58] Yaqut: vol. 1, p. 765.

lying area which became a lake when the Euphrates rose and flooded its banks. This river was to give its name to the battle that followed.

As the two armies settled down in their respective camps. Mihran sent the usual message to the Muslims: "Either you cross over to us or we cross over to you." Muthana was not going to commit the blunder of Abu Ubayd, and replied, "You cross."[59]

Muthana's decision was not only a tactical imperative but also a psychological necessity. The Muslims had taken a terrible beating at the Battle of the Bridge and the wounds of that battle, both physical and emotional, had left deep scars. Should the Muslims suffer another defeat like the last one, it would shatter all hopes of conquest in Iraq and not even Umar would be able to persuade the Arabian Muslims to face once again the much-feared Persian. Moreover, although Muthana could order his men across the river and they would obey, because the state of discipline of this army was very high, the men would keep looking over their shoulders, wondering if Mihran would do to them what Bahman had done. The location of the two camps was only a little upstream of where the Battle of the Bridge was fought, and this itself was an unpleasant reminder of that disaster. Muthana knew that on the outcome of this battle hung the fate of Islam in Iraq, and he was determined to win it.

He turned to a local Arab who stood beside him and asked, "What is the place called where Mihran is camped?" "Basusia," replied the Arab. Muthana then remarked, "Mihran is in a bad way and shall perish, for he is camped at a place which yields nothing."[60] In Arabic, he used a pun on the word "basus", which means a she camel which does not yield to milking.

A bridge was constructed across the Euphrates, and the following morning the Persians crossed to the west bank and stopped at a place called Shumia about half a mile from the river. Here Mihran arrayed his army for battle in three groups, a centre and wings, and placed an elephant in each. The commanders of his wings were Mardanshah and the military commander of the district of Hira; and Mihran placed himself in the centre. He had every intention of emulating the example of Bahman.

The Muslims also moved up from their camp and formed up for battle in front of the Persians. Muthana appointed Adi bin Hatim and Jareer bin Abdullah to command the left and right wings respectively, and these were composed

---

[59] Ibid.
[60] Ibid.

mainly of cavalry. The centre, comprising the infantry, was placed under his brother, Masud - a gallant and much-admired officer, and Muthana formed a small reserve, which was positioned behind the army and was led by another brother, Mu'anna. The army commander himself took up his station in the centre, mounted on his horse "Shamus" - the Refractory One - which was known for its speed and its fine gait. This horse was only mounted by Muthana for battle.

While Muthana was arranging his lines for battle, he saw a Muslim emerge from the front rank and position himself some distance ahead of his comrades. "What is the matter with that man?" Muthana asked. He received the reply. "He is one of those who had run away at the Battle of the Bridge, and is now determined to get killed in battle." Muthana went to him and nudging him gently with the handle of his lance, made him get into line with his comrades.

Mihran awaited the Muslim attack, planning to hold and repulse the Muslims before launching his counter stroke. And Muthana, wishing to seize the initiative at the very start, ordered the attack by his centre and wings, leaving the reserve under his brother Mu'anna out of battle for later employment. The Muslims moved forward, and the two armies met with a clash of steel, each bent on victory or death.

The Persian front remained intact and unshaken. The defenders of the empire, having tasted victory under Bahman, were determined to suffer no more defeats, and fought with courage and discipline to hold their position. For some time the battle raged along the entire front. Then, as the weight of Muslim pressure slackened, the Persians began a forward movement and the Muslims found themselves being pushed back. Clouds of dust blanketed the battlefield and the din of battle sounded like "a roar of thunder."[61]

In spite of their best efforts, the Muslims were unable to stem the tide of Persian advance. Some disorganisation had now set in, as is inevitable in combat, and a few Muslim units even broke contacts and pulled back a short distance. Muthana had his work cut out for him in restoring order and getting his troops to go once again into the attack. He galloped to every part of the front where the Persian pressure appeared to be bearing fruit, and rallied his men with the cry: "To me! To me! I am Muthana!"[62] At times, in a fit of desperation, he would tear at his beard.

---

[61] Dinawari: p. 114.
[62] Ibid.

Then there was a lull in the fighting, though contact remained. The Persians too needed a little rest and reorganisation and Mihran set about re-establishing order in his own formations before dealing the final blow to the Muslims. In this lull the Muslims reformed for the attack. The commanders urged their men to fight even harder, and the men realised that on their actions depended the fate of Islam in this part of the world. Jareer, the commander of the Muslim right, addressed his own tribe: "O people of the Bajeela! Let none advance more speedily against this enemy than you. There is for you in this land, if you conquer it, a greater share than for other Arabs. Fight for one of the two glories."[63] The two glories were victory and paradise.

Once again the Muslims went into the attack, the centre and the wings, and once again the Persians held them. The fighting increased in ferocity. Muthana and his brother, Masud, the commander of the centre, struck to break the Persian centre, and in this fighting Masud fell mortally wounded. Muthana turned to his men and shouted: "O Muslims, this is the way that the best of you die. Raise your standard! May Allah raise you!"[64]

Seeing that the Persians were getting tired, though not more tired than his own men, Muthana now called up his reserve under his brother Mu'anna, and threw it into the centre, and these fresh troops began to play havoc with the Persian front. It was Muthana's intention to break through the centre while his wings held the Persian wings in place.

Mihran was now in a desperate position. His centre was being pushed back towards the bridge. To stop the retrograde movement of his centre, he went forward himself, and at the front he was killed in single combat by a Muslim warrior. According to one account, he was killed by a Christian youth from the Tajhlib, according to another, by Jareer, and according to yet another, by Muthana himself. And Allah knows best!

With the death of their general, the Persian resistance weakened. The Muslim pressure against the centre increased; and at last the Persian centre broke. Muthana wanted the bridge in order to prevent a Persian escape, and made a thrust towards it, but his pace was slowed by stout resistance from groups of Persian warriors who knew the vital importance of the bridge and strove to deny it to the Muslims. The Persian wings too were now in retreat.

---

[63] Ibid: p. 115.
[64] Ibid: p. 114; Tabari: vol. 2, p. 650.

At last Muthana broke through and captured the bridge and stopped all movement over it. Some part of the Persian army had already managed to cross to safety, but the bulk of it was cut off west of the river and here the Muslims inflicted the most fearful, casualties upon their foes. The Persians scattered and fled north and south but were pursued by the Muslim cavalry till nightfall and again the next day. A large number of the fugitives were killed in the pursuit. Those who escaped the slaughter made their way to Ctesiphon to tell a tale of woe which Ctesiphon had heard many times before.

The Battle of Buweb was Muthana's revenge for the disaster of the Bridge. The debt had been cleared. For many years the plain on which this battle was fought was littered with the whitened bones of the Persian fallen, and it was not till two decades later that these bones were covered with sand. This battle also became known as the Battle of Tens, because 100 Muslims killed ten Persians each in combat.

By the evening of the day of battle all the forward supplies of the Persians had fallen into Muslim hands, consisting mainly of sheep and cattle, and Muthana decided to drive the herds to the Muslim camp where the women and children awaited news of the battle. The herds were put in charge of a Christian Arab prince named Abdul Maseeh bin Amr bin Buqeila with instructions to convey them to the camp. As Abdul Maseeh neared the Muslim camp, the women seeing him and seeing some other horsemen with him, feared that this was a Persian raiding party which had got to their camp. The women armed themselves with stones and tent poles and formed a line in front of the children. They were going to fight and die rather than be captured by an unbelieving enemy.

The misunderstanding was soon cleared up, of course, but the Arab prince was amazed at the sight of the Muslim women preparing to fight. He remarked, "Even thus should be the women of this army."[65]

Muthana, who had an unerring and intuitive sense of timing, now threw his army across the Euphrates and the Arab horse again galloped over the fertile plain of the Suwad. Asim was sent to raid Sabat, a few miles west of Ctesiphon, Jareer to the Tigris down to Kaskar, and Muthana himself led a large column to Anbar, then to Bagdad, and then to Tikreet. [See Map 1]. So much booty was gathered by the Muslims that its transportation became a serious problem and Muthana had to order that only gold and silver would be taken in the raids. The

---

[65] Tabari: vol. 2, p. 652.

Suwad once again became the property of Islam; the Persian army once again stood behind the Tigris; and Muthana was once again in his element, master of every inch of land where his horse placed its hoof.

This was not the defeat of one race by another; it was the victory of Islam over an unbelieving empire. The part that the spirit of Islam played in this campaign is evident from the words of Muthana, uttered after the Battle of Buweb: "I have fought Arabs and Persians; fought them in the time of Ignorance and in Islam. By Allah, during the Ignorance a hundred Persians were stronger than a thousand Arabs, but today a hundred Arabs are stronger than a thousand Persians."[66]

The southern part of Iraq was suffering from neglect. After his conquest of Uballa, as Khalid advanced to Hira, the strategic centre of gravity and the focus of attention shifted north-westwards to the Euphrates and the Central Suwad. Uballa was reoccupied by the Persians, who placed a garrison there, and none remained to show the Muslim flag but Qutba bin Qatada with a few hundred followers. Qutba carried out desultory raiding but this theatre was very much in the shadow.

The theatre was, nevertheless, from a long term point of view, of considerable importance. Much of the Persian resources in men and material, needed to sustain the war, came from the province of Fars and passed through the junction of Ahwaz. And all seaborne supplies were landed at Uballa. If these lines of supply could be severed or at least disrupted, the effect on the Persian war machine would be a serious one. Umar decided to do something about it but unfortunately under-estimated the magnitude of the task.

Having despatched Abu Ubayd to the main front in Iraq, he sent Shareeh bin Amr with a few hundred men as a reinforcement to Qutba and instructed him to raid deeper into Persia. Qutba sent Shareeh across the Tigris to carry out the Caliph's orders by raiding Ahwaz. Shareeh advanced upon Ahwaz, but at a place called Daris on the way he was intercepted and killed by a Persian garrison. Qutba resumed his role of observation and pin-pricks. Then took place the Battle of Buweib and the reoccupation of the Central Suwad by Muthana. On getting news of this victory, Qutba wrote to Umar and asked for large scale reinforcements so that he could take a more active part in the war against the Persians. Umar was already contemplating a serious effort in this

---

[66] Ibid: p. 651. The time in Arabia before the coming of Islam is known as the Ignorance.

sector and sent for Utba bin Ghazwan, an Immigrant and one of the early Companions.

"Allah, Most High and Mighty," began the Caliph, "has given Hira and what is around it to your brothers, whose cavalry has subdued the region of Babylon. And He has killed a great one of their nobles." The reference was to the Persian Mihran who had fallen at Buweib.

"I am concerned that their Persian brothers will attempt to help them. I wish to send you to Uballa to prevent people on one side from helping their brothers on the other. Go to the region of Uballa and keep the people of Ahwaz and Fars and Meisan occupied so that they do not help their comrades in the Suwad against your brothers who are there. And keep your forces concentrated at one place.

"Fight them in the hope that Allah will give you victory. March with faith in Allah and fear Allah; be fair in judgement; say your prayers at the appointed times and remember Allah much."[67]

Utba bin Ghazwan set off from Madina with 2,000 men and arrived in the region of Uballa where he took Qutba under command. His arrival took place in June 635 [Rabi-ul-Akhir, 14 Hijri] and he remained here for two months awaiting further reinforcements which Umar was despatching in groups.

There were four Persian districts over which the Muslims would operate and these briefly were as follows: [a] Furat: district on the east bank of the Tigris opposite and below Uballa; [b] Abarqubaz: district on the east bank of the Tigris opposite and below Mazar, in other words, north of Furat; [c] Dast Meisan: district east of Abarqubaz up to Ahwaz; [d] Meisar: district west of the Tigris at Mazar and below.

If these four districts could he occupied by the Muslims, Persian supplies coming from Fars would be seriously affected and would have to use a wide detour from the north. The Muslims were encamped by the side of Basra, the old Basra that is, which is more or less the present Zubeir, twelve miles from modern Basra. But there was no Basra then, for the town had not yet been built. What existed at this place was the ruins of an ancient town; and beside and among these ruins the Muslims had established their camp. Near these ruins was fought the first action in this mini-campaign.

---

[67] Tabari: vol. 3. p. 90; Balazuri: p. 336; Dinawari: p. 116.

The governor of the district of Furat had been receiving reports of the increase in Muslim strength in the bordering desert across from Uballa, and could guess that once Muslim strength had been sufficiently built up their action would be far from passive. This was also obvious from the offensive posture of the Muslims elsewhere in Iraq. He therefore planned to put in a pre-emptive strike and eliminate the Muslim threat on his front. With this aim in view he gathered all his troops, which included the garrison of Uballa, and with 4,000 men marched towards the ruins. He hoped to catch the Muslims unaware in their tents and gave to his men ropes to tie around the necks of the Arabs and bring them in like cattle.

On arrival near the ruins, however, he found an army about as strong as his own awaiting him. In the battle that followed a large number of Persians were killed and the governor was taken captive, while the rest fled to Uballa. The Arab of the desert was a master in exploiting a success and pursuing a defeated foe: and the very next day the Muslims appeared at the gates of Uballa. The Persians, defeated the day before in battle, offered no resistance and Uballa fell to the Muslims for the second time since the beginning of the Muslim invasion of Iraq. This happened in Rajab, 14 Hijri [August or September, 635].

Utba bin Ghazwan lost no time in crossing the Tigris. The district of Furat had little opposition to offer and a few Muslim mounted groups went through it to make sure that no hostile soldiers remained. Then Utba marched into the district of Dast Meisan without, however, going as far as Ahwaz. In this district a small Persian force prepared for battle but it was easily defeated, and having established Muslim authority here, Utba marched westwards into the district of Abarqubaz, which also bowed before the Muslims. The districts east of the Tigris were now in Muslim hands. Utba returned to Uballa and sent a force under one of his officers across the Euphrates. This force captured Mazar and subdued the district of Meisan before rejoining Utba at Uballa. It had hardly returned, however, when news was received that Abarqubaz had revolted. The governor of Abarqubaz was a Persian, named Feelhan, who had accepted Muslim rule as a matter of necessity until he was strong enough to throw off the yoke. Hence he had signed a treaty with Utba acknowledging the Muslims, but now he gathered a small force and prepared for battle. Utba sent Mugheerah bin Shu'ba with the bulk of his small army to Abarqubaz to deal with the revolt. Mugheerah marched to Marghab, where Feelhan awaited him, and at Marghab the Persians were again defeated and their commander killed. Having reimposed Muslim rule over Abarqubaz, Mugheerah returned to Uballa.

Hardly had he got back when Meisan, the district west of the Tigris, also revolted, and pursuing the mission given him by his commander, Mugheerah crossed the Euphrates and crushed this revolt also. This was the last attempt by the Persians to dispute Muslim rule in these districts.

By about Ramadhan, 14 Hijri [October or November, 635], these four districts were in Muslim hands and remained so for some time. This had a restricting effect on the movement of Persian supplies through Ahwaz, but it would be incorrect to say that the route of supply to Ctesiphon was severed. The Muslim strength here was not enough to achieve this end, and they contented themselves with the moderate success which they had gained.

Soon after these actions Utba left Uballa to visit Madina, but died while he was on his way back, and Umar appointed Mugheerah bin Shu'ba as the commander of this front. Mugheerah was a sturdy soldier and a gifted man, whom the reader will come to know better in the chapters that follow.

Chapter 5: Umar and Sa'd

There was much to occupy the mind of Umar as the year 14 Hijri neared its end. His main worry was Iraq.

The trouble with fighting great empires is that one cannot bite off just one province on the frontier and expect to call it a day. The empire fights back to re-establish its boundaries and its glory; and the Persian Empire was certainly too proud and too misty to let the Muslims remain in occupation of the Suwad. The Muslim campaign in Iraq so far had been in the nature of a see-saw. Four times had the Muslims overrun the Central Suwad, and thrice, until Muthana's last victorious entry, had the Persians pushed them out. This gave an element of military and political instability to the Suwad, the people of which began to feel like a wife with two husbands. And now this see-saw action came into play again.

The star of Emperor Yazdjurd had never shone brilliantly but it still had some lustre. Advised by his master strategists, Rustam and Bahman, he set into motion measures which would bring about a titanic contest such as is fought only once in a veneration, or perhaps even in a century. Such demons of war would be unleashed as had never been seen on Persian soil before. More will be said in subsequent chapters about the Persian juggernaut, but suffice it to say that Muthana found it prudent to withdraw his forces from the Suwad. The local inhabitants, of course, again declared their loyalty to the Persian crown. The Muslims even abandoned Hira and withdrew to Zu Qar, a few miles south of Qadisiyya, from where Muthana wrote to the Caliph and conveyed the latest military situation.

The Caliph had already been receiving information about the Persian preparations over the past few weeks, and realised the appalling danger in which the Muslims in Iraq were now placed. They would have to worry not only about Iraq but perhaps also about Arabia. The Caliph at once ordered Muthana to withdraw to the edge of the desert and disperse his army in cases. Consequently Muthana pulled back to the desert region south of the Euphrates and what now forms the north border of Saudi Arabia. This move was carried out in the month of Zul Qada.[68] Muthana took up his station at Sharaf, and the front which he commanded stretched from west of Hira to about opposite

---

[68] As a matter of interest, for those who do not know. the Muslim months are: Muharram, Safar, Rabi-ul-Awwal, Rabi-ul-Akhir, Jamadi-ul-Awwal, Jamadi-ul-Akhir, Rajab, Shaban, Ramadhan, Shawwal, Zul Qada and Zul Haj.

Samawa, with his largest group positioned in the vicinity of Sharaf. In the Uballa sector, which was not under Muthana, the Muslims were encamped in the hills of Ghuzayy, some distance from Uballa. The Suwad and the main cities on the west bank of the Euphrates, including Hira, were in Persian hands.

On the western front against Rome, the campaigns of Abu Ubayda, Khalid and Amr bin Al Aas were making excellent progress. The Romans had been defeated in several bloody battles and at the present moment the main Muslim army under Abu Ubayda was investing Emessa, whose fall was expected any day. Syria had not, however, been completely captured from the Romans and a decisive battle or battles had yet to be fought. The Caliph had no misgivings about Syria, but it was obvious that he could not take away a sizable force from that front to fight against the Persians until the back of the Roman power in Syria was broken.

In Iraq things were heading for a big showdown and it would take months to put into the field the kind of army that was needed in the new situation. One answer was to do nothing about the Persians until the Romans were finally crushed in Syria, and then move a large part of the Muslim army from Syria to Iraq, but the Syrian campaign could get prolonged and there would be a delay in directing Muslim forces to Iraq. This could dampen the Muslim zeal to fight the Persians and could even give the impression that the Caliph was afraid of Persia. Moreover, the remaining manpower in Arabia would get sucked into Syria, denuding the Arabian peninsula of all reserves.

The problem of numbers was partially eased by using the apostates for military service. Some time after assuming the caliphate, Umar had rescinded Abu Bakr's ban on the use of apostates in the holy war, and this action was in fact dictated by necessity. Since the entire Arabian peninsula had apostatised after the death of the Holy Prophet, except for Mecca, Madina and Taif, there were just not enough Muslims in the tribes which had remained loyal, to fight two large scale wars against two mighty empires. Moreover, some of the best Arabian tribes, militarily, had apostatised and since they were now all Muslim again, it was incorrect not to use them in the way of Allah. As a result of Umar's call, the apostates came in their thousands to fight the infidel and all were sent off to Syria, where they were now serving just like other Muslims. Some of the apostate leaders were distinguished officers, whose presence in battle was welcomed by the Muslim generals commanding the corps and armies, and in this history many of them will earn the respect and admiration of the reader. It should be noted, however, that the word "apostate" is used here to classify these people; in actual fact they were ex-apostates, and now Muslims like everybody else.

Umar knew that the days of small armies were over in Iraq, that great and terrible battles lay ahead, and he decided to start preparations straightaway for the war against the Persians. He would launch the Muslims in their initial move for this campaign and hope that the timing of it would fit in with success on the Syrian front, enabling him to switch forces from Syria to Iraq before the main confrontation in battle with the Persians. In early Zul Haj, 14 Hijri, shortly before the annual pilgrimage, a Caliph wrote to all the governors and tribal chieftains: "Leave none who has weapons or a horse or strength or intelligence, but take him and send him to me. Hurry! Oh hurry!"[69]

The response was quite favourable. Some clans living near Mecca and Madina joined the Caliph on his way to Mecca for the pilgrimage, and some soon after. Some clans living nearer the Iraq front moved forward and reported for duty to Muthana. Within a month the first concentration of troops, a small force consisting mainly of the Muslims of Madina and local tribes, had gathered at Madina. Umar established these men in a camp at Sirar, three miles from Madina on the way to Iraq, and also ordered to the camp some of the earliest and most venerated Companions of the Prophet, including Uthman bin Affan, Zubeir bin Al Awwam, Talha bin Ubaydullah and Abdur Rahman bin Auf.

In Muharram, 15 Hijri [latter half of February and first half of March, 636] the first concentration of troops was complete; and Umar moved in person to the camp. He was not sure if he should himself command the army but was prepared to do so, should it be necessary. At Sirar he called the troops for a congregational prayer and addressed them. After explaining the situation in Iraq and the need for pursuing the holy war, he asked the men how they felt about the campaign. With one voice the congregation replied: "Go, and we go with you!"

Umar was still not certain that it was right for the Caliph to go to Iraq with one army while other armies of Islam were engaged on other fronts, all under the strategical guidance and political control of the Caliph, but he gave no definite commitment. "Prepare for war," he said, "and I shall go with you, unless some better counsel comes forth."[70]

---

[69] Tabari: vol. 2, p. 660.
[70] Ibid: vol. 3, p. 2.

Umar decided to call a council of war, to be attended by all the leading Companions. But first he sent for Ali whom he had left in Madina to act as his deputy in case he should march with the army to Iraq. "O Father of Hasan," said Umar to Ali, "what do you say? Should I go or send someone else?" "Go yourself," replied Ali, "for that will have a greater psychological impact upon the enemy."[71]

Then came the council of war, and Talha was of the same view as Ali and the troops, i.e. that Umar should command the army in person. The rest of the councillors, however, were unanimous in opposing this view and felt that it would be incorrect for Umar to go to Iraq with the new army. Abdur Rahman spoke for most of them when he said, "Stay, and send the army; and the will of Allah in respect of your wishes will be apparent in the fortunes of your army. If It is defeated, it will not be your defeat; but if you are killed or defeated, it would be a humiliation and a terrible blow to Muslim prestige."
"Then advise me about the man who should command the army," asked Umar.
"I have found him," replied Abdur Rahman.
"Who is he?"
"A lion with claws: Sa'd bin Malik."[72]
All present agreed to the appointment as commander of the Army of Sa'd bin Malik- better known as Sa'd bin Abi Waqqas.

Later Umar conferred alone with Abdur Rahman. "I know that Sa'd is a brave man" he said, "but I fear that he does not have sufficient knowledge about the strategy of war."

"He is, as you say, in courage," replied Abdur Rahman, making no further comment about Sa'd's military qualifications. He added, however, "He is a Companion of the Messenger of Allah, on whom be the blessings of Allah and peace. He fought at Badr, and will never disobey your orders."[73]

Still later, Umar sought Uthman's opinion about Sa'd bin Abi Waqqas and Umar finally agreed with his appointment. As for the strategy of war, Uthman was of the view that it would be sufficient to tell Sa'd to seek counsel from men of experience and knowledge of war, and not act without their advice.

The following day the Caliph ordered a congregation of the army at Sirar and addressed the gathering:

---

[71] Masudi: Muruj; voi. 2, p. 317.
[72] Tabari: vol. 3, p. 3; Masudi: Muruj; vol. 2. p. 317.
[73] Masudi: Muruj; vol. 2. p. 317.

"Lo! Allah Most High and Mighty has gathered his people to Islam and has joined their hearts and made them brothers one to another. The Muslims are like one body of which all suffers if one part suffers. It is incumbent upon the Muslims to decide their affairs in a council of men of judgement. The troops must follow the one appointed to command by mutual agreement and consent; and the one appointed to command must accept the decision of men of judgement in the strategy of war. O people, I am just one of you, but men of judgement have dissuaded me from going with you. I have decided to remain here and send another in command; and I have consulted all in this matter."[74]

Sa'd was not present at Madina during these proceedings. After the Caliph had addressed the troops, he sent for Sa'd, and as; Sa'd appeared before him, the Caliph said: "I have appointed you commander of the war in Iraq. Remember my words, for you are proceeding on a difficult and fearful mission in which only right can prevail.[75]

Then followed a sermon by the Caliph regarding Allah [swt] and obedience and patience and other virtues.

Sa'd bin Abi Waqqas was a short, stocky man in his early forties, with a large head covered with thick hair. A very strong and vigorous man, he had been an arrow-maker by profession and was one of the best archers of the time. He was the only man to whom the Holy Prophet had said: "I sacrifice my father and mother for you,"[76] and this was at the Battle of Uhud, where he had stood beside the Prophet and with his bow played havoc with the infidels: Once the Holy Prophet had referred to him as his maternal uncle [khal], as a mark of affection, and thereafter Sa'd had become known as the maternal uncle of the Messenger of Allah, although there was no actual blood relationship between the two.

As a Muslim he stood on the highest rung of the ladder and was one of the earliest converts to Islam. He was the 5th or 6th male to accept Islam. Among the Companions of the Prophet there were ten who were held in especial esteem by the people; ten who had been informed by the Holy Prophet in their lifetime of their acceptance by God in paradise, and these ten were commonly known as "Ashra"-The Ten. Sa'd was one of them. And he enjoyed a distinction which none could or ever would challenge: he was the first in Islam

---

[74] Tabari: vol. 3, p. 3
[75] Ibid: pp. 4-5.
[76] This was an Arab way of showing great affection or great reverence.

to draw blood in the way of Allah, and the first in Islam to be wounded in action.

This was the man selected to command the Muslim force assembled in camp at Sirar. He was to be the Commander-in-Chief of the front against the Persian Empire, but it would be some time before he assumed actual physical control of the force. At Sirar he awaited the arrival of more clans, which continued for another few weeks, and during this period he had several conferences with Umar regarding the conduct of the campaign in Iraq.

In Rabi-ul-Awwal, 15 Hijri [April-May, 636], one month after the fall of Emessa in Syria, Sa'd marched from camp with a small army of 4,000 men. Umar addressed the men on their departure and gave Sa'd the parting instruction: "Stop when you get to Zarud and disperse in the region.[77] Urge the people there to join you and take all who have courage and intelligence and strength and weapons."[78]

With these words the Caliph launched the army of Sa'd on its march to Iraq, a march which would culminate in the great battle of Qadisiyya. The army was like a small stream which before long would grow into a mighty river. As Umar saw the army filing out of its camp, he determined to throw into the campaign every man, chief or follower, on whom he could lay his hands. He would leave in Arabia not a chief, not a noble, not a warrior, not a scribe, not a poet, but would hurl him against the Persians.

"By Allah," swore the Caliph "I shall strike the princes of the Persians with the princes of the Arabs."[79]

Sa'd arrived at Zarud and went into camp for a period which he knew would be a long one. He sent couriers to all the tribes in Northern Arabia and himself urged the holy war upon local chieftains. As a result of these efforts, another 7,000 warriors, consisting of tribesmen from the Bani Asad and Bani Tameem, joined his army, and these included Tuleiha the Impostor, a remarkable [ex]apostate chieftain of whom much will be said later. In the meantime the Caliph's efforts to recruit more forces also bore fruit and another 4,000 men were despatched to join the army at Zarud.

---

[77] Zarud was a staging camp 60 miles beyond Feid on the caravan route western Iraq.
[78] Tabari: vol. 3. p. 6.
[79] Ibid: p. 8.

Sa'd waited at Zarud for the build-up of forces, and Muthana waited at Sharaf for Sa'd to come and take over command of the front. Sa'd was expecting Muthana to come to Zarud to make his report while Muthana was expecting Sa'd to come up to Sharaf; since this was a forward movement, there was no point in his going to the rear and then coming up again with the new Commander-in-Chief. This waiting ended when Sa'd had spent about three months at Zarud and, having mustered all the forces that he could find in the region, marched for Sharaf with an army of 15,000 men. But the two principal generals of this theatre were not destined to meet because, before Sa'd's arrival at Sharaf, Muthana died. The wounds suffered by him at the Battle of the Bridge had never really healed.

With the death of Muthana one of the finest generals of the early Muslim period passed from the stage of holy war. A bold, fearless and skilful commander, he was second only to Khalid in military stature and would adorn with lustre the hall of fame of any army in the world. None achieved for Islam in Iraq what Khalid and Muthana achieved, and, but for these two, the story of this war would certainly have read otherwise-less inspiring and less glorious. But like Khalid, Muthana earned the disapprobation of Umar by his sheer success and brilliance. When denying Muthana the command of the Persian theatre, Umar explained his action by saying, as he did with regard to Khalid, that the troops had begun to glorify Muthana and look to him for victory instead of to God.[80]

So Muthana remained an outsider, and because he was an outsider he lived, fought and died in obscurity and his feats never received the acclamation which they deserved. No doubt he was mourned by his tribe-the Bani Bakr, which was acknowledged by all Arabs as the one Arab tribe truly feared by the Persians, but in the rest of the Muslim nation his death evoked no great emotion. Sa'd prayed for his soul and that was all. Unheralded when he appeared, unsung when he fought and conquered, unlamented when he died, Muthana rises as a tragic figure to accuse the historian of unjust neglect.

May Allah be pleased with Muthana bin Harisa!

Sa'd arrived at Sharaf in Jamadi-ul-Akhir, 15 Hijri [July, 636] and again dispersed his forces in the oases of the region. This was to be the last staging arm before the Muslim march to contact the Persians in Iraq. Soon after his arrival he received Muthana's brother Muanna, who had been left in command

---

[80] Ibid: p. 98.

by the departed hero until Sa'd should make other arrangements. With him came Salma bint Khasfa, Muthana's widow, and he delivered to Sa'd the parting words of Muthana:

"The Muslims should not fight the Persians when they are concentrated in their homeland, but should fight them on the boundary between the desert and the sown. Thus if Allah should give the Muslims victory, they will have whatever lies behind the Persians, and if the result is otherwise, they can withdraw into a region whose routes they know best and of which they are masters - until Allah decides that they should return to battle."[81]

Muanna also conveyed his brother's opinion that the battle with the Persians should be fought between Qadisiyya and Uzeib; and he handed over to Sa'd his brother's widow, for she had been bequeathed by her late husband to Sa'd. Apparently this custom was sometimes practised by noble-born Arabs. Sa'd accepted the lady, and after her four months period of widowhood was over, married her. He also took command of Muthana's army and confirmed Muanna as the commander of the Bani Bakr. Muthana had under his command just before his death a force of 12,000 warriors, which included some who had joined him after Umar had sent out his call to arms, and all these men now became part of the army of Sa'd, which swelled to a great force of 27,000 men.

Sa'd wrote to the Caliph, conveyed Muthana's advice and informed him of the location of various contingents deployed along the front from opposite Uballa to opposite Hira. In reply Umar wrote: "When you get this letter, organise the army into tens[82] and let them know their units. Appoint the commanders of the corps and let them see and know their men. Give the contingents Qadisiyya as the meeting point and get Mugheerah bin Shu'ba to join you with his cavalry. And then write to me."[83]

Sa'd acted as ordered and in due course Mugheerah, who was in the Uballa sector, moved to Sharf with 800 men. The army was organised as instructed by the Caliph and the commanders of corps and regiments and tribal contingents were left to get acquainted with their men.

A few days after the first letter, another one arrived from the Caliph:

---

[81] Ibid: p.10.
[82] This was a practice started by the Holy Prophet at Madina.
[83] Tabari: vol. 3, p. 8.

"March with the Muslims from Sharaf towards the Persians. Place your faith in Allah and seek His Help, and know that your are advancing against a people whose numbers are vast, whose equipment is superb, whose strength is great and whose land is difficult. Even its plains consist of rivers and heavily-watered land. When you meet them or any one of them, attack them fiercely, but beware of facing them if they are all together. Let them not trick you, for they are wily plotters and their ways are not your ways.

"When you get to Qadisiyya, remain there and leave not your place. They will find your continued stay intolerable and will come against you with all their strength of horse and foot. And if you stand fast against them, you shall overcome them, and should they ever assemble again in great number they shall do so without hearts.

"And should the result be otherwise, you will have desert behind you and can withdraw into a region which you know and control and of which they are ignorant and afraid. And there you shall stay until Allah decides victory for you and you return to battle."[84]

Sa'd was to spend about two months in Sharaf before marching on to Iraq, and the reader may wonder about this delay. There was actually no delay. According to the strategy adopted by the Muslims, as the reader might have guessed from Umar's last letter and of which more will be said later, it was to be left to the Persians to come and do battle with the Muslims. The arrival of the Muslims on the border of Iraq was to be no more than an invitation to battle. Moreover, it took time to organise the large army which Sa'd now commanded into its proper tactical groups and get every one acquainted with their units. Then there was the situation in Syria. As Sa'd arrived at Sharaf, the Muslims and the Romans were facing each other across the plain of Yarmuk, which was about to explode into the greatest battle of the century. This battle had to be finished before the Caliph could commit another large army against another mighty empire.

The Battle of Yarmuk was fought in Rajab, 15 Hijri [August, 636] and a colossal Roman army of 150,000 men was cut to pieces. Such battles are only fought once in a campaign, and it was obvious, that the Romans would never again face the Muslims in such strength. The Caliph could therefore move some forces from Syria to reinforce Sa'd, and following his instructions, Abu Ubayda sent to Iraq a force of 1700 men under the command of Ash'as bin Qeis, an

---

[84] Ibid: pp. 10-11.

[ex]apostate chief. This was an [ex]apostate group consisting of tribes from the Yemen and Hadramaut and included a prince, Amr bin Madi Karib, and a chief of the Bani Murad, named Qeis bin Hubeira. All these men had fought at Yarmuk. But this force was not to join Sa'd's army till after his arrival at Qadisiyya and about a month before battle, and this would bring the strength of Sa'd's army to about 29,000 men.

Some more weeks passed; then Sa'd received his marching orders front the Caliph: "On [such and such a date] move with your men to between Uzeib-ul-Hijanat and Uzeib-ul-Qawadis, and place your men to east and west."[85] The location of these and many other places will be explained in a later chapter which gives a description of the battlefield.

Sa'd conducted the march to Qadisiyya as a tactical movement. An advance guard was formed and placed under Zuhra bin Al Hawiya of the Bani Tameem, and this force led the advance along the main caravan route and secured Uzeib, where a Persian scout was captured and killed by the Muslims. The main body of the army closed up after Zuhra and the advance guard crossed the Trench of Sabur and occupied Qadisiyya. Again the main body closed up and Zuhra advanced to the bank of the River Ateeq and secured the western end of the bridge. Zuhra also spread out along the Ateeq, occupying Qudeis to the south. Sa'd now moved up and encamped at Qadisiyya, while the advance guard remaind in front as a protective screen. [See Map 3]

---

[85] Ibid: p. 11.

MAP 3: THE APPROACH TO QADISIYYA

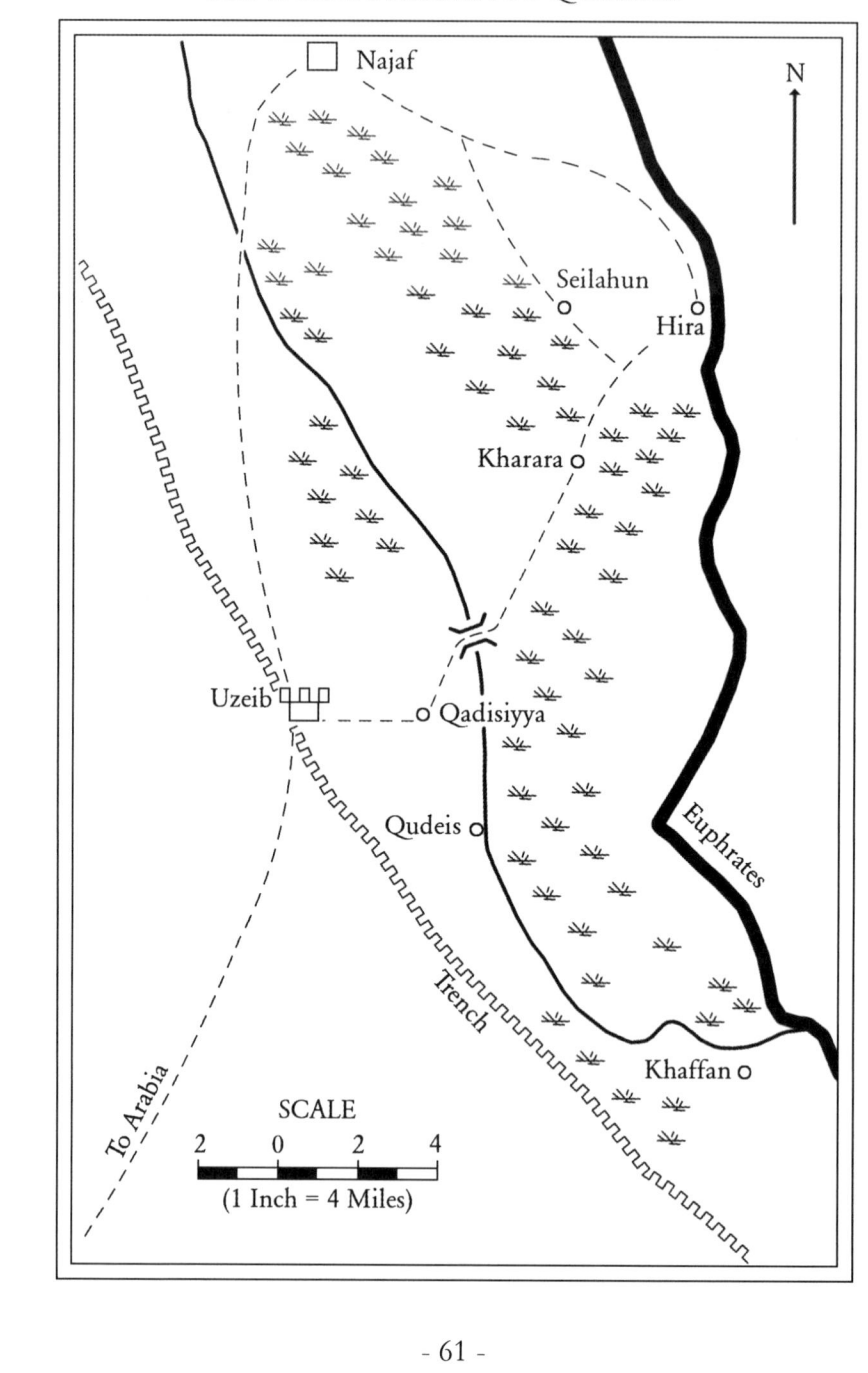

As soon as he had secured the river bank, Zuhra sent a raiding party to the area north of Hira and this party captured a large bridal procession which was taking the daughter of Azazbeh, governor of Hira, to her bridegroom. Several of the guards were killed and the bride, along with 30 noble born maids and 100 slave girls and the entire dowry of the bride, was brought into the Muslim camp. The booty, including the beautiful damsels, was distributed by Sa'd among the members of the raiding party and the Muslims took this as an auspicious and delightful omen.

As soon as the camp was established, Sa'd wrote to the Caliph: "The enemy has sent no one against us and has not appointed, so far as we know, anyone to command the campaign. When we know, we shall inform you and shall seek Allah's help."[86]

A few days later he received the Caliph's letter:
"Strengthen your heart and your army with sermons and right intentions and worthiness; and as for those who forget, remind them. Steadfastness, and again steadfastness! - for help comes from Allah according to one's intentions and His reward according to one's…[efforts]. Caution, and again caution! - for grave is the matter upon which you are embarked. And pray to Allah for His blessings.

"Write to me when you know of the concentration of their army and who commands it, for insufficiency of knowledge regarding their army and its commander prevents me from writing much that I wish to write.

"Describe the place where you are and the land between you and Madain. Describe it so clearly that I can see it with my own eyes and become one of you.

"Fear Allah and in Him rest your hopes."

Sa'd had by now got some information from spies who had been sent into Hira. He sent the required topographical description, and added:

"All those of the people of the Suwad who had entered into covenants with the Muslims have broken them. They fear the Persians and are preparing for war against us. "The commander of their army is Rustam, and he has with him others of his own stature.

---

[86] Ibid: p. 12.

"They seek to weaken us and pounce upon us and we seek to weaken them and attack them. The command of Allah is as good as done and His decision will be according to whatever He wishes for us or against us. We beseech Allah for the best of decisions and the best of judgements."

Umar replied:

"I have received your letter and fully understand it. Remain where you are until Allah fixes your enemy for you. And if Allah should give you victory, cling to them until you fall upon Madain, which, Allah, if He wishes, will destroy."[87]

A few days later another letter arrived from the Caliph:

"My heart tells me that when you meet the enemy you shall defeat him. So dispel all doubt from your mind, and if any of you gives a promise of peace to a Persian, with sign or speech, even if he does not understand it, let him fulfil the promise.

"Beware of jesting. Faithfulness, and again faithfulness. Errors committed in good faith are acceptable but deliberate unfaithfulness leads to destruction. In it will lie your weakness and your enemy's strength, the depression of your courage and the elevation of his.

"I caution you not to bring dishonour to the Muslims nor be a cause of their decline."[88]

This was followed by yet another letter:

"Let not the information which you get about the enemy distress you, but seek Allah's help and in Him place your trust.

"Send to him a man of intelligence and judgement and patience to call him to Islam. As for their wishes, Allah will make them the cause of their decay and defect.

"Write to me every day."[89]

---

[87] Ibid: p. 11-12.
[88] Ibid: p. 12.
[89] Ibid: p. 14.

In this correspondence a month had passed. During this month the Persians made no move from Ctesiphon, and just their local garrisons, which were large enough, remained in the region of Hira and in the area east of the Ateeq and the Euphrates. Meanwhile the supplies brought by Sa'd plus the provisions sent by the Caliph by caravan from Madina, were almost consumed. Sa'd therefore decided to send raiding columns deep into the Suwad, partly to gather supplies to maintain his army and partly to make life miserable for the Persians.

The raids were started in right earnest and the boldest of the Muslim officers were used in this operation. Stalwarts like Muanna and Asim crossed the Euphrates and bypassing Persian garrisons, struck with violence against every town and village that stood in their path. The entire region from Anbar to Kaskar became a hunting ground for the Muslims and vast herds were gathered to feed the army of Islam. Only those animals and those stocks of goods were safe from the raiders which could be kept within fortified towns. The region between the two rivers once again resounded with the cry of "Allah is Great"; and the inhabitants of the Suwad once again turned with piteous appeals to Ctesiphon.

And in obedience of the orders of the Caliph, Sa'd sent a delegation of Muslims to offer Islam to the Emperor Yazdjurd.

Chapter 6: Yazdjurd and Rustam

A large delegation of citizens came to see Rustam. They were openly rebellious and especially resentful of the power struggle that was going on between Rustam and a noble, named Feerzan. While these two wrestled each other in internal politics, the affairs of Persia were going from bad to worse and the Suwad was being ravaged by Muslim raiding columns. This was two years before the arrival of Sa'd at Qadisiyva, in the weeks that followed Muthana's victory over Mihran at Buweib.

The delegates did not mince their words. 'What are you waiting for?" they asked Rustam. "For our destruction? By God, O you people who are in command, this weakness has come upon us only because of you. You have split the people of Persia and diverted their attention from their enemies. Were not the death of you our own destruction, we would kill you this very hour. But if you do nothing, we shall kill you anyway and be ourselves destroyed. Then we shall at least be rid of you."[90]

This rising discontent had the effect of strengthening the hands of the Emperor Yazdjurd. Feerzan somehow disappeared from the political scene and nothing more was heard of him till after the battle of Qadisiyya, while Rustam was cut to size and, metaphorically and literally, put in his place as the head of the Persian military organization - a post for which his talents eminently qualified him.

The Emperor, assisted by his satraps and other nobles, put into motion measures to harness the military resources of the empire for its defence. Contingents of Persians, Turks, Kurds, Armenians and Arabs were called in to join the standard of Persia for a great campaign, and troops marched to Ctesiphon from as far east as Khurasan and as far north as Azarbeijan. A huge cantonment was established at Sabat, three miles west of Ctesiphon, and here the mighty army began to assemble under the command of Rustam, who would himself take the field against the Muslims.

Along with the concentration and preparation of the field army, steps were taken to reorganise the administration of the empire and restore the faith of the people in the government. Smaller forces were moved into the Suwad to clear it of the invaders, and the Muslim outposts, alarmed by the military movements taking place in Persia, vacated their positions and retired west of the Euphrates.

---

[90] Tabari: vol. 2, p. 659.

Muthana moved to Sharaf, in Zul Qada, 13 Hijri, and deployed his small army along the fringe of the desert in south-western Iraq. Even in the Uballa sector the Muslims abandoned their conquests and quickly stepped back into the safety of the friendly desert. With the withdrawal of the Muslims, the inhabitants of the Suwad threw off the burden of allegiance to the Muslim state and reaffirmed their loyalty to the Sasani dynasty; and the Persians took Hira and Najaf and established outposts to watch for further offensive movements by the Muslim army. The domain of Persia was back in Persian hands.

This state of affairs lasted about 18 months till the middle of 15 Hijri. During this period the Persian army was organised, trained and equipped for battle while Yazdjurd awaited the next move of the Muslims. Intelligence about the arrival of the army of Sa'd at Qadisiyya was brought in by Persian agents, but still Ctesiphon waited, wondering when the Muslims would become bold enough to enter the boundaries of Persia again. And then suddenly a dozen rough Arabs turned up in Ctesiphon, claiming to be the envoys of Islam, and demanded to see the Emperor.

Sa'd had selected 12 officers from the army to carry the message of Islam and deliver an ultimatum to the Persian Emperor. They were all noble Arabs, chiefs most of them, but not likely to impress the cultured Persians with their simple desert ways. They rode their horses bareback.[91] Among the 12 envoys were Noman bin Muqarrin, Muanna bin Harisa, Asim bin Amr and Mugheerah bin Zurara, but, in the true spirit of desert egalitarianism, none of them was the leader or chief envoy.

The delegation rode across the Suwad, and since it was on a diplomatic mission, it had no trouble with Persian garrisons and posts on the way. Nearing Sabat, it made a detour of the Persian military camp and entered Ctesiphon. This city, which shared with Constantinople the honour of being the greatest capital of the time, would normally leave any Arabain awe-struck, but these Arabs were Muslims and judged honour and quality by different standards. They came not as humble Arabs seeking the favour of the great king, as their ancestors would have done, but as proud Muslims come to offer Islam and deliver an ultimatum to one whom they regarded as an infidel, and therefore an inferior.

Outside the gate of the palace the Muslims dismounted, tied their horses and demanded of the guard to be taken to the Emperor as envoys of the Muslim power. A large crowd of Persians gathered to stare in amazement at the shaggy,

---

[91] Ibid: vol. 3, p. 16.

neighing horses and the sternfaced men - hard sons of the desert who looked about them with fierce confidence.

Yazdjurd was surprised at the arrival of the Muslims, which was certainly not expected. He hastily, convened a conference of nobles and discussed with them various matters relating to the talks which must now be held with the emissaries of Sa'd. When the conference was over, he sent for the Muslims and prepared to meet them in the great audience chamber of the palace of the Chosroes.

The Muslims, roughly attired but armed with dignity, entered the chamber and sat down in a line in front of the Emperor. Beside Yazdjurd stood the interpreters who would transmit the words of one party to the other, while behind him were arrayed his nobles and courtiers. For some time there was silence as the Muslims looked calmly at the man who in normal times would be too high to be seen by Arabs. Then Yazdjurd broke the silence.

"'What brings you here?" he asked. "What compels you to invade our land and fight us? Is it because we have left you in peace that you have grown so bold?"

Noman bin Muqarrin, who sat in the middle of the Muslim line, said to his comrades, "If you wish I can speak for all of you, unless another wishes to speak." "You speak," replied his comrades. Then, turning to the Emperor, they said, "The words of this man are the words of all of us."

"Lo!" began Noman, addressing the Emperor, "Allah has been beneficent to us. He sent us a Prophet to guide us towards right and enjoin it upon us, and to show us what was evil and forbid it to us, and to make us seek the good of this world and the next. Not a tribe remained but was split in two, one part following him and the other shunning him, though only the good entered his faith.

"So matters remained as long as Allah wished that they should remain; then he was ordered to act against those of the Arabs who opposed him. This he did, and they entered the faith, all of them; and we knew that what he had brought was better than the enmities and hardships in which we had hitherto existed. Then we were ordered to start with those of the nations which lived close to us and to call them to justice.

"Now we call you to our faith - a faith which glorifies all good and condemns all evil. If you refuse, then accept a burden which is lighter than the other burden which you must carry. This is the Jizya; and if you refuse this also, then there shall be war between us.

"If you agree to join our faith, we shall leave with you the Book of God, by the injunctions of which you must live, and we shall leave you to your land. If you pay the Jizya, we shall defend you in return for it; otherwise we shall fight you."

Yazdjurd controlled his temper as he replied, "I do not know of a people on earth more wretched than you, fewer than you in numbers and worse than you in discord. We left you to live beyond our borders and we protected you. The Persians did not invade your land, and had they done so, you would have had no hope of standing up to them.

"If it is hardship that brings you here, we shall send you food according to your needs. We shall honour your leaders, we shall clothe you, and we shall appoint over you a king who will rule benevolently over you."

Now another Muslim. Mugheerah bin Zurara, spoke up: "O king, these men are the chiefs of the Arabs, their leaders, their nobles. The noble treat with dignity the noble; the noble honour the noble; the noble respect the rights of the noble; the noble venerate the noble."

This was a gentle rebuke to the Emperor for not showing more courtesy to the envoys than he had done. It was not intended to, and did not, please the Persian monarch. But Mugheerah continued: "You have described our state without having knowledge of it. As for our distressing condition, there was none in worse condition than us. As for our hunger, there was no hunger like ours. We would eat beetles and scorpions and snakes and regard them as our normal food. Our habitation was the surface of the earth, and we wore whatever we could make of the hair of camels and the wool of sheep.

"It was our way of life to raid each other and to kill each other. Some of us would bury their daughters alive so that they would not have to share their food. Thus did we live in days gone by.

"Then Allah sent us a noble man whose family and whose faith and whose birth were known to us; whose birth was the best of births: whose family was the best of families; whose clan was the best of clans; and who in his own person was the best of us.

"He called us to his faith and none answered him except a Companion he had, who was to be his successor. And he spoke and we spoke, but he spoke true while we spoke false. He rose while we declined and whatever he said came to be. Then Allah cast into our hearts truth and obedience to him, and he became our link with the Lord of the Worlds.

"What he said to us was the word of Allah; the orders he gave us were the orders of Allah. He said to us: 'Your Lord says; "Lo, I am Allah, the One; I have no partners. I was when nothing was, when everything was non-existent except my countenance. I created everything and everything shall return to me. I took you into my mercy and sent you this man to guide you on the path by which you avoid torment after death, and to make you worthy of my home, the home of Islam.'

" We bear witness that he came with the truth from the Truth. And [as] Allah has told us that whoever follows you on this path shall share the good that you possess and bear with you the burdens that you carry. And whoever refuses this, ask him for the Jizya and then defend him against whoever you defend yourselves against. But if he refuses this also, then fight him; and I shall decide between you. And those of you who are killed shall enter my paradise, while those of you who survive shall receive the reward of victory…hence choose as you please: the Jizya, and you shall be subservient to us, or the sword, or accept Islam and save your soul."

Yazdjurd's anger was rising as Mugheerah was making his speech. When Mugheerah stopped, Yazdjurd exploded, "Is this how you address me?"

"I address you because you spoke to me," the Muslim countered. "If someone else had spoken to me I would not have addressed you."

The Emperor was not to be mollified. "But for the fact that envoys are not killed," he shouted, "I would surely have killed you. I have nothing more for you."

He then turned to a court attendant and ordered him to fetch a load of dust. The attendant left the chamber and returned soon after with a basket full of earth. The Emperor commanded, "Place it upon the leader of these people, and drive them forth until they are beyond the gate of Ctesiphon."

He next turned to the Muslim envoys. "Return to your master. Let him know that I am sending Rustam against you and he will destroy you in the trench of

Qadisiyya and teach you a bitter lesson which those who come after you will not forget. I shall then send him to invade your land and visit upon you worse than Sabur had done." The reference was to Sabur of the Shoulders, famous, among other things, for pulling out the shoulders of all Arabs who fell into his hands.

"Which of you is the leader?" asked Yazdjurd. There was silence for a while as the Muslims looked at the load of earth. Then Asim bin Amr spoke, "I am their leader. I shall carry it."

"Is that so?" asked the Emperor of the envoys. "Yes," they replied.[92]

The basket was placed by the Persian attendant on the back of Asim's neck. Followed by the others, he carried his burden out of the palace to where their horses were tied. Here the 12 Muslims mounted their horses and set off at a fast pace for Qadisiyya, their hearts bursting with joy.[93]

Yazdjurd had much to learn. The Arabs regarded the earth of any land as sacred, not the kind of thing to be dished out to anyone who entered the land with hostile intentions. They certainly did not look upon the Emperor's act as humiliating. This was also known to many Persians in Ctesiphon, and soon the capital was buzzing with accounts of the talks and what the Emperor had done in the matter of the earth of Persia.

Rustam heard these reports and was deeply agitated. He went at once to the capital and asked the Emperor how the meeting had gone and how he saw the situation.

"I did not know," said Yazdjurd, "that the Arabs had such people as came to see me, people of intelligence, such eloquence." Then he went on to describe the proceedings of talks between him and the Muslim envoys.

Coming to the end of the account, he said, "They gave me a challenge which I accept, even if it means my death. But I found the wisest of them also the most foolish. When they asked for the Jizya I gave them dust, and he carried it on his own head while he could have given it to another to carry. I know not why."

---

[92] Tabari: vol. 3, pp. 17-19.
[93] This is Tabari, vol. 3, p. 19. According to Balazuri: p. 257, the carrying of the basket was done by Amr bin Madi Karib, the apostate prince, who was also one in this delegation. I favour Tabari's version.

"O Emperor," remarked Rustam, "he was indeed the wisest of them."[94]

Angry and distressed, Rustam returned to the camp. He felt that it was imperative to get the fateful basket back from the enemies of the empire, and at once sent off a group of horsemen to pursue Muslim envoys and snatch the basket away from them before they could cross the River Ateeq. He then turned to one of his officers and said, "If our men catch the envoys, our land is safe. If they fail, then God has given away your land and your children."[95]

The Persian party set off at a brisk pace across the Suwad the road to Qadisiyya, but the heavy Persian charger, ideal for the setpiece battle, was no match for the swift Arabian. The Muslims had crossed the Ateeq bridge to safety long before the Persians arrived to find that they had failed in their mission.

Upon crossing the Ateeq, Asim galloped about the camp with the basketful of Persian earth, shouting to all he passed: "Give the commander tidings of victory. We have won by the will of Allah!"

After a while Asim stopped at his tent where he placed the basket. Then he rode to Sa'd, gave him an account of the talks with the Persian Emperor, and added in conclusion, "We have conquered them. We have subdued their land. Rejoice, for Allah has given us the keys of their kingdom."[96]

Back at Sabat, Rustam heard in grim silence the report of the failure of the Persians to catch the Muslim envoys. He was shattered by the news. "The enemy has taken your land without doubt," he muttered. "This is what the Son of the Hairdresser has done to the country.[97] The enemy has snatched away the keys of the kingdom."[98]

The return of the Muslim delegation with the earth of Persia electrified the army of Islam. No finer omen could have been expected or hoped for. Everyone became eager for battle, confident that God had already granted them victory, had already bestowed upon them the land of Persia. But the

---

[94] Tabari: vol. 3, p. 19.
[95] Ibid.
[96] Ibid; Yaqubi: Tareekh-vol. 2, p. 144.
[97] This is how the detractors of Yazdjurd referred to him. The name will be explained in a later chapter.
[98] Tabari: vol. 3, p. 19; Yaqubi: Tarcekh vol. 2, p. 144.

Persian army had to be drawn out of the security of its cantonments to where the Muslims wished to fight it.

In accordance with the strategy already designed by Umar and Sa'd - and a very fine strategy it was – Sa'd increased the tempo and range of his raids. Fast mounted columns swept the unprotected area right across the Suwad, and penetrated as far as Heet and even Firaz, which marked the border between Persia and Byzantium. The raiders brought in not only cattle, sheep and valuables but even mules and donkeys. A few clashes occurred with Persian troops on these raids but, by and large, the light Muslim cavalry proved too fast and too expert in this sort of warfare to be prevented from doing what it wished to do. This was just as Sa'd wished. He had caught the Persian by the elbow and was twisting that elbow for all he was worth. He was twisting it until the Persian should find the pain unbearable; and the Persian of the Suwad soon cried out in pain.

The raids drove him to madness and to the brink of revolt. Strong delegations of the citizens of the Suwad headed for Ctesiphon and conveyed the same sorry tale and made the same urgent appeal for action, but this time there was a warning in their words, which were as follows: "The Arabs have arrived at Qadisiyya with a posture which is nothing short of war; if they continue doing what they are doing, there will be nothing left for the Emperor; they have devastated the land between the two rivers and only that has survived the raids which could be kept within the safety of forts; if help does not come soon, they [the citizens] would transfer their allegiance to the Muslims."[99]

The Persian feudal lords who owned vast estates in the Suwad also suffered heavily and pressed the Emperor to send Rustam against the Muslims. And Yazdjurd decided that the time had come for action, that no more delay could be brooked. He sent for Rustam.

"I wish to send you for this purpose," he said to Rustam "for the means employed must be worthy of the end and you are the man of Persia today. You can see that the people of Persia have suffered in this situation as they have never suffered since the house of Ardsheer came to power.

"I wish to benefit by your knowledge. Describe to me the Arabs and what they have done since they came to Qadisiyya; and describe to me the Persians and what they have suffered at the hands of the Arabs."

---

[99] Tabari: vol. 3, pp. 20-21

Rustam's reply was brief and to the point. "They are like a wolf who by chance finds the shepherd negligent and does mischief."

Rustam had given an allegorical twist to the conversation, and Yazdjurd too could play that game. "I do not think that such is the case," he observed. "Know from me that the similitude of the Arab and the Persian is thus: An eagle lives on the peak of a mountain; at night a bird steals up to its nest and starts eating the leftover food; when the day dawns the bird watches the eagle apprehensively, preparing to fly if the eagle should strike; if the eagle appears afraid to attack, the bird stays and snatches its food; but if the eagle rises to attack, the bird drops the food and flies away. Thus it is with the Persians and Arabs.

"The worst that can happen to us is that some should seek to save themselves at the expense of others; and if there is disunity in our ranks, no one group can rise against the enemy without being annihilated. Let this guide you in your actions."

To this Rustam replied, "O Emperor, leave the Arabs to me. The Arabs will continue to fear the Persians so long as they have not seriously harmed the Persians. If the empire gains strength through me, it is the will of God.

"We have learned much about the art and stratagems of war; and it is my view that stratagem is more beneficial than certain kinds of victory in battle."

Yazdjurd could guess that Rustam was reluctant to go into a great head-on clash with the Muslims, and asked for more ideas. Rustam went on: "In war patience is better than haste; and today is the day of patience. To fight battle after battle with smaller armies is better than seeking one victory; and this would also be harder on our enemies."[100]

Yazdjurd refused to accept this course of action. His youthful and heroic spirit saw visions of a great historic battle such as had often been fought by his ancestors, and he told Rustam that such a battle would have to be fought. Rustam returned to camp and promptly sent a request to the Emperor to accept his resignation and appoint another in his place. The request was turned down.

---

[100] Ibid.

Over the next few days the pressure mounted on Yazdjurd to do something to save Iraq, and he once again sent instructions to Rustam to march to Qadisiyya and do battle with the Muslims. Again Rustam came to see him and pressed for acceptance of his own strategy.

"O Emperor," said the general. "It is my judgement that leads me to this, and I would not speak of this to you if I did not have to. For the sake of yourself and your family and your empire, let me stay here and send Jalinus with an army to fight them. If he wins, the victory is ours, and if the result is otherwise, I shall send, another to fight them.

"My name is dreaded by the Arabs. I must preserve the image of the undefeated in the minds of the Persians, and the Arabs will remain in awe of me and fear my advance. But if they gain a victory over me, it will embolden them and will mark the end of the days of Persia."

Yazdjurd refused to accept this plan which fell short of his glorious expectation. "If you do not march," he declared, "I shall march in person against them."[101]

The reader might imagine from the foregoing narrative that Rustam was not a brave general; but this would be an over simplification. Judgements in such military situations are far more complex than would be apparent to the untrained mind, and a few words about the strategical situation might help the reader in grasping the implications of the various courses of action open to the Persians.

The Muslims were in an ideal position. Their military aim was to conquer Iraq and they knew that this could only be done by battle. They were determined to fight the battle at Qadisiyya, with their back to the desert and with the Persians across the Euphrates and the Ateeq. And the Muslims were in no hurry. With their base in a safe zone, they were striking with fast columns in the Suwad and taking all the supplies that they needed. This, from their point of view, was an ideal war, a war of which the enemy paid the cost. They were sitting pretty as the guests of the Persians [although uninvited and unwelcome] and were living off the Persians. Their life in camp was no worse than their normal habitation in the desert which they called home. In fact they were enjoying themselves at the expense of their enemy.

---

[101] Ibid: pp. 22-23.

A delay in battle meant no hardship or loss to the Muslims, but the Persians were hurt badly by a continuation of the prevailing situation. The Suwad was losing its wealth and the people were losing their faith in the imperial leadership. This state of affairs just could not be allowed to continue without a possible break up of the empire without battle. The raids could not be stopped except by defeating the Muslim force from which they emanated and by the destruction of their base, and this could only be done by fighting a major battle with the Muslims at Qadisiyya-ground of the Muslim's choice. The situation viewed from any angle favoured the Muslims.

So the Persian Empire cried for battle, and it was justified in doing so. Yet Rustam's strategy of avoiding a major clash was a sound one, and had he been allowed its implementation, it might have led to a better outcome than actually resulted. He was clear-headed enough to know that fighting the Muslims was no easy matter, as had been demonstrated by Khalid and Muthana. Should the Persians seek battle and lose it, the whole empire would fall, and that would be a much worse consequence than the present suffering of one province. On the other hand, by keeping his large army in being with an offensive posture, Rustam could ensure that only raiders would enter Persian territory. Such a strategical plan has often been adopted in history with, in the long run, beneficial results.

But public opinion and political pressure were making it impossible for Rustam to follow his own strategical design and were forcing battle upon him. And here too, in the operational plan which he conceived, he showed himself to be a strategist rather than a mere tactician. He would use several smaller armies, each fresh in its turn to fight the Muslims, and if none of these succeeded in defeating the invaders, he would lead his large army in person to deliver the final blow. This in essence was the same strategy as he had followed against Abu Ubayd, but it was opposed in concept to Yazdjurd's strategy which could be described as a "big bang strategy" - one mighty, decisive, winner-take-all battle.

There was, however, more than stragetical concept which robbed Rustam of his desire for battle. As stated in an earlier chapter, he was an astrologer and his study of the stars revealed to him that the Persians would be defeated in battle by the Muslims. Try as he might, he could find no error in his astrological calculations. Moreover, shortly after the return of the Muslim envoys to Qadisiyya, Rustam had a terrible nightmare in which Caliph Umar came and sealed the weapons of the Persian soldiers. In these superstitious times such a dream could only be interpreted in one way, and Rustam saw in it the destruction of the Persian army and, as a consequence, the death of the empire. But Rustam was a royal son of Persia and prepared to obey the call of the nation and the orders of the Emperor. He despatched an advance guard under Jalinus towards Qadisiyya with the order: "Advance, but do not get involved without my orders." Next he sent Yazdjurd the message: "If God gives us victory, we shall go to their land and engage them in their homes until they submit."[102] Then he set off with the rest of his army for Qadisiyya.

The Persians marched along the main road to Najaf. They made their first long halt at Kusa, a little north of the present Iskandariyya. From here Jalinus advanced, crossed the Euphrates and camped at Najaf, while Rustam went on to Burs, near Babylon. At Burs some Persian soldiers went on a rampage of drinking and rape which led to bitter protests from the populace. Rustam had several offenders beheaded and then marched on until he reached the east bank of the Euphrates at Miltat, north-east of Najaf. The whole army closed up and established a large camp along the east bank from Gharriyeen, opposite the present Kufa, to opposite Khawarnaq, which lay three miles north north-west of Hira.[103]

A few days after his arrival on the east bank, Rustam sent for a delegation of the prominent citizens of Hira. He had not forgiven them for the way they had switched their allegiance to the Muslims whenever the latter occupied Hira and entered the Suwad. When the delegates arrived, he denounced them for what he considered as fickleness and warned them as Christians against having anything to do with the Muslims.

The citizens of Hira did not like this, and felt that the accusation was unfair. They turned to one who stood in their midst, a very old and very distinguished looking man, and asked him to speak for them.

Abdul Maseeh bin Amr bin Buqeila was one of the most illustrious figures in Arab Iraq. He was a prince. Hoary with age, he was known for his wisdom and wit and was held in reverence by the Iraqis, in whose affairs he wielded considerable influence. He had met Anushirwan, the Just, shortly before the latter's death, and warned him that after him his empire would decay. He was the man who had negotiated with Khalid the surrender of Hira and earned Khalid's respect. Abdul Maseeh took a few steps forward and addressed Rustam. "Do not come with your army to us a second time if you cannot defend us and will leave us to defend our land ourselves."

---

[102] Ibid: p.22.
[103] Nothing remains of Khawarnaq except a mound 600 yards west of the Najaf road.

"O enemy of God," Rustam retorted. "You rejoiced over the invasion of our land by the Arabs. You provided them with information and with food."

Then Abdul Maseeh gave it to him, straight from the shoulder: "You say we rejoiced at their coming? And what were we to do? At what did we rejoice? They came and took us to be like slaves. They were not of our faith and called us people of hell.

"You say we acted as spies for them? Well, what made us to do so? Your friends ran away and left the land open to them to plunder as they wished. As for our feeding them, we gave them food so that they would not enslave us and destroy our homes and kill our warriors. After all, you were not there to defend us, and we were helpless to fight them, like those of you who faced them!"

Seeing that his words were having the right effect on Rustam, the old man softened his tone. "By my faith, you are dearer to us than they; and if you will defend us, we will act as spies for you. Lo, we are the hapless ones of the Suwad, slaves to whoever conquers us."

Rustam was silent for a little while. Then he observed quietly, "What the man says is true."[104]

A few more days passed. Then Jalinus advanced to Kharara, beyond Najaf and a few miles short of Qadisiyya, and Rustam crossed the Euphrates with the main body of the army to Najaf. Here again he had the nightmare about Umar sealing the weapons of the Persian soldiers.

Rustam now moved cautiously, for he was within striking range of the main Muslim army. Jalinus with the advance guard marched and occupied Teeznabad, a village between Kharara and the Ateeq. Bahman, commanding a large corps, moved up to Kharara, while Rustam moved with the main body to Seilahun. [See Map 3.] Here the Persians waited a few days, watching the reaction of the Muslims, but there was no major move of Muslim forces from Qadisiyya.

Next Rustam put into effect the last phase of his move, which was a kind of advance to contact. Jalinus moved forward steadily until he reached the River Ateeq and spread his advance guard along the river as far south as opposite

---

[104] Tabari: vol. 3, p. 25.

Qudeis, while at the same time posting a strong guard on the bridge, facing Zuhra and the Muslim advance guard. Bahman advanced and occupied the last camp of Jalinus at Teeznabad and Rustam with the main body moved up to Kharara.

It was a nicely conducted advance, as per textbook, and had taken the Persian army as far as it could go. The next step could only be taken as part of battle, for on the west bank of the Ateeq stood the Muslim army. The Persians now deployed in camp with Jalinus committed along the Ateeq front as a covering force; Bahman commanding a corps behind him, ready to rush into action in aid of Jalinus, should such a move become necessary; and Rustam with the main body of the army standing behind Bahman. [See Map 4.] Rustam had no intention of rushing into battle; he needed time to prepare for it.

The Persian army had a strength of 60,000 men, and these were served by as many followers. It also had 33 war elephants.[105]

---

[105] For an explanation of the strength of the Persian army, see Note 1 Appendix C.

MAP 4: THE PLAIN OF QADISIYYA

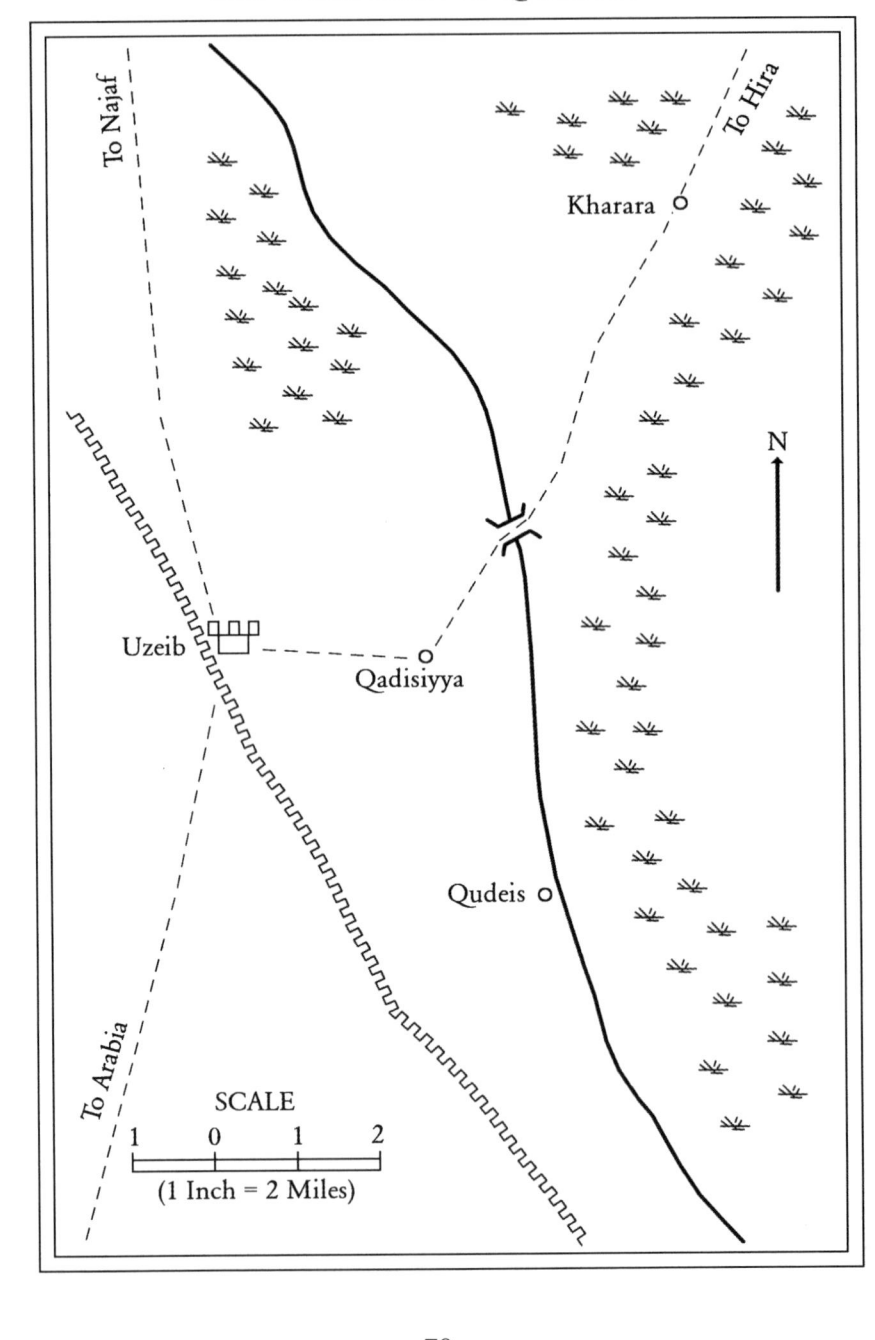

Chapter 7: The Eve of Qadisiyya

From the brief description of the Persian advance in the preceding chapter it might appear that it was an uneventful move. Actually it was not. There were events, in the form of raids and patrol clashes. Rustam had hardly arrived at Najaf when Sa'd sent a large foraging party, which went to Isteemia, a town above Najaf, and collected large flocks of sheep, but Rustam came to know of the raid in time and despatched a cavalry detachment after the raiders. The Persian cavalry succeeded in intercepting the Muslims, who now found themselves in a tight corner, but luckily for them, Asim bin Amr arrived upon the scene and drove the Persians away, whereafter the flocks were brought in safely to the Muslim camp. Asim then went on to raid other places with success, and such was the fear which his name evoked in the Persian mind that on many occasions Persian detachments seeing him coming, just moved out of his path and let him pass.

A few days after the above raid, Rustam started his steady, methodical advance to the battle area, and it was when Jalinus got to Kharara with the advance guard that occurred the incredible one-man raid of the apostate chief who was once known as Tuleiha, the Impostor.

Sa'd was not aware of the arrival of the Persians at Kharara and wished to get information about Persian locations and movements. Consequently he sent two officers, both [ex]apostates, Amr bin Madi karib and Tuleiha bin Khuweilad with instruction to find out all they could and get prisoners for interrogation. Both set off with detachments at dusk, but after crossing the River Ateeq, separated - Amr going left and Tuleiha going right. They had not gone far when Sa'd decided to have another in command of both those officers and sent Qeis bin Hubeira of the Bani Asad with 100 men to follow and take the two officers under command. Qeis caught up with Amr but by now Tuleiha had moved elsewhere. Qeis and Amr marched on to contact the Persians.

When they got near the Persian camp at Kharara, approaching it from the west [See Map 3] Qeis asked Amr what he intended to do. Amr replied that it was his intention to raid the nearest part of the Persian camp. "With just these few men?" Qeis asked in amazement. "Yes," replied Amr.

"You are putting the Muslims to a task for which they do not have the requisite strength," Qeis asserted. "By Allah, I forbid you; and that is that!"

Amr turned upon him in indignation. "And who are you to say so? And that is that!"

"I have been appointed commander over you," Qeis replied calmly. "And even if I were not, I would not permit you to launch your raid; and that is that!"[106] The men who were with Qeis affirmed that he had been appointed commander by S'ad over Amr and Tuleiha.

Amr took it badly. It was a great comedown for him. He was a prince of the Yemen and could claim without dispute to be one of the highest nobles of the Arab race. Madi Karib bin Seif bin Zi Yazn, of the tribe of Mazhij, had defeated the Christian viceroy of Abyssinia in the Yemen with Anushirwan's help, on Anushirwan's behalf, during the last few years of Anushirwan's reign. This had ended Abyssinian rule in the Yemen, and as a reward for his services Anushirawn had made Madi Karib king of the Yemen. But four years later the new king was assassinated by an Ethiopian and Anushirwan appointed a Persian governor to rule the Yemen as a province of the Persian empire. This Amr was a son of that Madi Karib.

The family had followed the Jewish faith, but in 9 Hijri, Amr led a delegation of his tribe to Madina and accepted Islam. In 11 Hijri, upon the death of the Holy Prophet, Amr apostatised, like everyone else, but did not oppose the Muslims in battle. He was eventually taken prisoner and brought before Caliph Abu Bakr who pardoned him, and he became a Muslim again. When Umar raised the ban on the use of apostates in the holy war, Amr with his followers, went to Syria and fought with distinction under Abu Ubayda. He took part in the Battle of Yarmuk, in which he lost an eye.

A skilful warrior and a capable officer, he was noted for his wit and his knowledge of Arab tribes. And although quite old, he was immensely strong and was known as Abu Saur-Father of the Bull. And now he was being put in his place by Qeis bin Hubeira.

The discipline of this army was strict and orders were obeyed without question. But Amr could not help blurting out: "By Allah, O Qeis, the time that you are commander over me is truly, a bad time. I would rather revert from your faith to my original one and fight until death than serve under you a second time. "[107]

---

[106] Tabari: vol. 3, p. 27.
[107] Ibid.

Qeis challenged Amr to say the same before Sa'd, and Amr said he would. On their return to camp both went to S'ad and complained about each other, but Sa'd succeeded in making peace between them and Amr conceded that his plan of raiding a large enemy camp with a handful of men was, militarily, far from sound. Sa'd chided him: "O Amr, I perfer the safety and well being of our men to the destruction of 100 of them in fighting 1000 of the enemy. I thought you knew better than to throw 100 men in action against a large force of Persian cavalry."[108]

Tuleiha, on separating from Amr, moved with his men on a route from the right in the direction of Najaf. There was bright moonlight and movement was easy. But he had hardly gone 4 or 5 miles when he came upon the Persian captain at Kharara, from the lights and noise of which it was evident that a very large force was encamped here. This was Jalinus with the Persian advance guard.

Some of Tuleiha's men, awed by the Persian camp, said, "Return to the Commander. He believed that the enemy was in Najaf when he sent us. We must let him know." Others said, "Let us return so that the enemy does not know that we are here!" Tuleiha insisted that they go on, and when asked what he intended to do, said that he would enter the camp and gather information as per the instructions of the Commander. "I shall risk my life and, if necessary, die," he asserted.

Then his men, who were not apostates, turned against him, and this was easy to do because Tuleiha's past guilt of apostasy put him in a vulnerable position. They did not go near him because he was a dangerous man to tackle in combat, but they gave him a tongue lashing: "No doubt you wish to join them," they sneered. "You are a man with treachery in his heart and Allah will never guide you aright because you killed Ukkasha bin Mihsan. Come back with us!"

"Your hearts are filled with fear," Tuleiha retorted.[109] Thereupon his men left him and returned to the camp where they informed Sa'd of what had happened.

Tuleiha bin Khuweiled was a remarkable man. An able and shrewd chief of the Bani Asad, he was also a poet and a soothsayer and had commanded respect in Arabia during the days of the Ignorance. When the Holy Prophet migrated to Madina, he became one of the most vicious enemies of Islam. He commanded a contingent of the Bani Asad as part of the coalition of infidel tribes which

---

[108] Ibid: p. 28.
[109] Tabari: vol. 3, pp. 2S 29: Dinawari: p. 119.

fought the Muslims at the Battle of the Ditch. Later he sided with the Jews in the Campaign of Kheibar but was worsted by the Muslims. In 9 Hijri he accepted Islam, when all other Arabian tribes did so, but his conversion was a matter of political expediency rather than a genuine change of heart.

Shortly before the Holy Prophet's death in 11 Hijri. Tuleiha renounced his allegiance to the Muslim state and declared himself a prophet. He was an impostor. He went so far as to forbid prostration during prayer and his followers prayed behind him without prostration. Many clans of North-Central Arabia joined him and soon he had become the second most powerful enemy of Islam, the first being Museilima the Liar, also a false prophet.

Tuleiha's reign as chief-of-chiefs and prophet did not last long. He was defeated in battle by Khalid bin Al Waleed at Buzakha, but before that battle he killed, in single combat, a Muslim named Ukkasha bin Mihsan, who was a much loved Companion of the Prophet and a much admired warrior. After his defeat by Khalid he fled to Syria. Later, however, he returned to Arabia and re-entered the faith, but many Muslims held his guilt against him, and their resentment increased when he showed none of the humility which was expected of a penitent, especially one who had killed the noble Ukkasha. But that was now a matter of the past and Tuleiha was a Muslim again, and anxious to redeem himself in the holy war.

Deserted by his men, Tuleiha moved on and got nearer the Persian camp. He tied his horse at a safe distance and strolled into the camp. He carried out a thorough reconnaissance of the camp and shortly before dawn began to pick his way out of the sea of tents. He had not gone far from the centre of this camp when he, came upon a beautiful small white tent, outside which stood a horse such as he had never seen. Tuleiha took the horse but before leaving, cut the ropes of the tent and moved on as the tent collapsed upon its sleeping occupant. Some distance further on he saw another nice tent and another fine horse. He did the same and moved on again. At the edge of the camp he brought down a third tent and took his third horse. And now he was in the open.

When bringing down the first tent, as also the second, Tuleiha did not know that he was disturbing the slumber of not one man but a thousand men!

The Persians had a large number of gladiators chosen for their size, strength and ferocity. Physically powerful and without fear, these men were trained in the arts of combat to such a degree that they could be regarded as the most perfect specimens of the fighting man. They were the champions of the army, heroes of Persia, and took the heaviest toll of enemy lives. They would die in battle rather than accept defeat. Because of their strength and prowess, they were considered the equals of a thousand men and were called as such: Hazar Mard. A Persian general engaged in battle could send such a champion to the part of the front which needed reinforcement, and claim that he had sent a force of a thousand men. And such was the performance of these fearsome fighters that the presence of each one of them in combat was acknowledged as the presence of a thousand men.

One such champion [there may have been others] is known to have faced Khalid bin Al Waleed in a fierce duel.

So Tuleiha brought down the first tent on a hazar mard: Perhaps he chuckled at the idea of a man lying under it, but in the awkward folds of the collapsed tent struggled 'a thousand men.' The `thousand men' were not amused, not about to forgive the perpetrator of the indignity. However, by the time the hazar mard got out, donned his armour and weapons and found another horse, Tuleiha was doing the same to a second Persian, also 'a thousand men,' whose reaction was no more cheerful than that of the first.

Tuleiha, now outside the Persian camp, mounted his own horse and began his return journey, in the pale light of dawn, leading the three captured horses. 'He had not gone far when his three victims caught up with him, followed by a large number of Persian soldiers who came out to see what their champions would do to the intruder. Tuleiha was a brilliant fighter and a fearless man. In fact the only person he feared, and of him he had once lived in mortal dread, was Khalid bin Al Waleed. And now, refusing to flee, he turned to meet his pursuers while the Persians, true to the traditions of Persian chivalry, came at him one at a time, in the order in which their tents had been brought down and their horses taken. This must have been like a tournament of knights except that the contest was in deadly earnest and not a game.

The first hazar mard charged at Tuleiha with his lance and was about to make his thrust when Tuleiha side stepped with his horse and evaded the charge. And as the Persian hurtled past him, Tuleiha swung round in his saddle and plunged his spear in the back of his adversary, breaking the back. In a few moments 'a thousand men' lay dead at the feet of the Muslim's horse. Next the second Persian champion charged and Tuleiha executed exactly the same manoeuvre with exactly the same result. Another 'thousand Persians' perished in combat

The third Persian was somewhat intimidated by the fate of the first two, but, as a proud Persian warrior, had to vindicate his honour. He too charged with a lance and the Persian spectators saw a repetition of the earlier duels, except that Tuleiha did not send his spear home into the receding back of his opponent. Tuleiha had just remembered the instructions of Sa'd to get a prisoner, and decided to take this man alive. He rode after the Persian demanding a surrender, and the Persian, knowing that his life had been spared by his adversary and that the chances of his getting away alive were slim, surrendered to the Muslim. Tuleiha made the Persian ride in front of him and returned to the Muslim camp. Other Persians who had seen his performance in combat wisely stayed out of his path.

An anxious Sa'd had awaited all night the return of Tuleiha or news of him. His return now in this strange manner, leading a fine looking Persian soldier and three magnificent horses, came as a relief but left him perplexed. "Woe to you," he said to Tuleiha. "What have you been doing?"

"I entered their camp," replied Tuleiha, "and saw much during the night. I caught one of the best of them; and here he is."[110]

An interpreter was sent for, who questioned the Persian prisoner, and it was from him that the Muslims learned that the two men killed by Tuleiha were hazar mards; that they were also brothers and the prisoner himself was their cousin. He explained that he had seen war ever since he was a boy and had fought and defeated many champions in his military career, but be had never seen a fighter like Tuleiha. And he gave information regarding the Persian army camped across the Muslim front. At the end of the interrogation the Persian became a Muslim and fought valiantly beside Tuleiha in the battle that was to follow.

After this episode, as the Persian army advanced and camped in its forward position, a number of raiding parties were sent out by the Muslims and more prisoners were taken and more information gathered. Tuleiha and Qeis bin Hubeira played a prominent role in these raids. There were also several skirmishes which had the effect of keeping everybody on his toes.

When the Persians had settled down in their various camps on the east bank of the Ateeq, Rustam carried out a number of reconnaissances. He rode down along the river as far south as opposite Khaffan, where the rightmost Muslim

---

[110] Tabari: vol. 3, p. 29.

unit was camped. He saw every place where a crossing could be made and looked across at every plain on which a battle could be fought. On his way back to his camp he stopped at the main bridge and looked across the river at the Muslim warriors standing on the west bank. Free movement was possible for either army on its own side of the river, and since battle had not yet been joined, one side did not interfere with the movements of the other. Rustam had in mind the possibility of using diplomatic measures to rid Persia of the invaders, without bloodshed, and decided to guage the temper and attitude of the Muslims before initiating formal talks. He sent a messenger across the river to fetch the Muslim commander at the bridge.

The Muslim general here was Zuhra bin Al Hawiyya who had commanded the Muslim advance guard on the march of the army from Arabia and was now in command of the covering troops deployed on the river line. Without hesitation, Zuhra walked over the bridge and came face to face with Rustam, who awaited him with an interpreter.

Rustam was the first to speak. "You are our neighbours," he began, "and many of you lived within our empire. We were good to them as neighbours and saved them from suffering; we bestowed favours upon them and protected them from the people of the wilderness; we allowed their flocks the use of our pastures and gave them provisions from our land. We did not hinder their trade in any commodity of our land, and with us they found their subsistence and a contented living."

"What you say is true," replied Zuhra. "So indeed it was. But we are not as they and our objectives are different to theirs. We have come to you seeking not this world but the next.

"Those of us who came to you in the past submitted to you humbly, seeking what you possessed in your hands. Then Allah Most High sent us a prophet who called us to his Lord, and he answered the call.

"And He said to his Prophet, on whom be the blessings of Allah and peace, 'I have given these people sovereignty over those who have not accepted my religion, and I shall punish those with these. I shall give these the upper hand for so long as they remain faithful to my religion.'"

"And it is the religion of truth. None turns away from it but suffers disgrace. And none clings to it but is exalted."

"And what is this religion?" asked Rustam.

"Its main pillar," said Zuhra. "upon which all else rests, is the declaration that there is none worthy of worship except Allah and Muhammad is the Messenger of Allah; and acceptance of what he has brought from Allah Most High."

"How fine this seems! And what more?"

"Turning the worshippers from the worship of man to the worship of Allah."

"That too is fine; and what more?"

"That all men are children of Adam and Eve, and therefore brothers one to another."

"That too is fine," said Rustam as he continued his questioning

"Now suppose my people and I accept this faith. What would you do? Would you return?"

"Yes, by Allah," Zuhra affirmed. "And we shall never approach your land again except for trade and such things."[111]

Rustam had nothing more to say at this stage and Zuhra returned to the west bank. The Persian general went back to his camp, lost in thought.

For the next three weeks or so there was no major movement of forces on either side of the river. A certain amount of raiding and patrolling went on, but the main activity of the two armies consisted of preparations for battle in a mood of tense expectation. Rustam knew that his army would have to cross the river and had his engineers ready for the task.

On the Muslim side the arrival of the Persians, which they had awaited for months and which fitted exactly with Sa'd's design, was received calmly. But the warriors did not like the close proximity of the Persian camps, which had the effect of restricting the space over which the Muslims could freely move. Some of them approached Sa'd and asked him to attack and push the Persians back, but Sa'd told them to await the decision of those who knew better. The Muslims did not have much to prepare, because a light mobile army like theirs

---

[111] Tabari: vol. 3, pp. 32-33.

was always prepared for battle, but they kept the Persians under surveillance and awaited the next Persian move.

The next Persian move was a diplomatic one. Rustam was fully prepared for a general battle, but before that he would make one final attempt at finding a solution other than military to the present problem. Consequently he sent a messenger to Sa'd asking him to send him an emissary for talks. Sa'd selected seven Muslims, all known for their intelligence and maturity, and was going to send them all together, but at a conference with the seven it was decided that only one man should be sent who would do all the talking necessary. Of the seven, Sa'd chose Rab'i bin Amir as the envoy of Islam to Rustam. Rab'i set off from the Muslim camp, crossed the bridge and made for the headquarters of the Persian Commander-in-Chief.

The Persians were making the mistake, again and again, of regarding these Arabs as Arabs of the Ignorance - a wild, poverty ridden disorganised people, almost barbarian - who would come to Persia seeking plunder or a living, and who were overawed by Persian pomp and splendour. They should have realised by now that these Arabs, upon their conversion to Islam, had become a new breed of men with an entirely different and more exalted set of values. But here again the Persians committed the same error: they prepared to show the Arabs their gold and silver, their emblems of wealth and earthly magnificence. A court was set up for Rustam. The Commander-in-Chief donned his finest uniform, aglitter with precious stones, and sat on a wide gilded throne. Behind and on his flanks stood the nobles of Persia and the high officers of the army, bedecked in all their finery, and surrounding them all were arrayed a large number of local Persian and Arab officials and lower subjects of the empire. Stretching away from the throne lay a splendid carpet, the length of which is said to have been one bowshot, but this is obviously an exaggeration. Over the carpet were strewn the finest cushions which the world of the time could produce. And all this was done to strike awe in the heart of the ambassador of Islam.

The contrast with the ambassador of Islam was stunning. Rab'i bin Amir appeared at the court wearing a coat of shining mail over which was wrapped a coarse woollen cloak, tied at the waist. Around his head was a veil, held by thongs of a camel's girth, but which did not conceal his thick hair which was done in four upstanding plaits, looking like the horns of an antelope.[112] His sword hung at his side in a sheath of coarse cloth; across his chest was strung

---

[112] Tabari: vol. 3, p. 34.

his bow; on his back was slung a shield of cowhide; on the face of which was a brown spot like a loaf; and in his right hand he carried his spear, the handle of which was bound with leather strips. The ambassador of Islam, armed and equipped for battle, arrived at the edge of the great carpet mounted on a short, shaggy horse which looked badly in need of grooming.

The Persians were more awed at the sight of their visitor than they had expected their visitor to be. Seeing him so roughly attired and armed like the commonest soldier, and fearing for their beautiful carpet, they asked him to dismount. Their fears were fully justified, for Rab'i, in utter disregard of the looks of alarm and the pleas of his hosts, rode on to the carpet. When he had covered half the distance to Rustam, he dismounted.

The Persians then asked the visitor to lay aside his arms, to which he replied, "I have not come to you to lay down my weapons at your command. You invited me; and if you do not wish me to come as I wish to come, I shall return."

The Persians looked apprehensively at Rustam, wondering what would happen if the Muslim, armed as he was, should suddenly assault their Commander-in-Chief. But the Persian general said, "Let him come. He is but one man."

Rab'i now advanced towards Rustam, using his spear as a stick, and impervious to the horrified stares of the Persians, with every other step thrust the point of his spear into the carpet or into a cushion. Not one cushion remained in his path but was torn. On getting close to Rustam he drove his spear into the earth through the carpet and sat down on the floor. When asked why he had sat on the floor, Rab'i said, "We do not like to sit in your fashion."

Then began a dialogue between the Persian general and the envoy of Islam.

Rustam:
What message do you bring?

Rab'i:
We have been sent by Allah to take worshippers out of the worship of man into the worship of Allah; to take them from the narrow bondage of the world into freedom; from the tyranny of other faiths into the justice of Islam. We have been sent with His religion to His creation, to call people to Him. Whoever accepts Allah's religion, we accept his acceptance and return, leaving him and his land. As for him who rejects, we fight him until we get to that which is ordained by God.

Rustam:
And what is ordained by God?

Rab'i:
Paradise for those who die fighting the infidel and victory for those who survive.

Rustam:
I have heard what you had to say. Are you agreeable to postponing the decision for some time so that you and we can ponder?

Rab'i:
Yes, how much time do you wish? One day? Two days?

Rustam:
No, we need more time. We need more time because we have to write to the leaders of the nation and to men of judgement.

Rab'i:
It is one of the traditions of the Messenger of Allah that we do not allow an enemy more than three days grace before battle. So we shall keep away from you for three days in which you can reflect upon the matter and select one of, the three: Islam, and we shall leave you and your land; or the Jizya, and we shall defend you unless you do not need our help in defence; or we shall fight you on the fourth day and not before the fourth day, unless you initiate operations. You have my word for this on behalf of my comrades and all those whom you see on your front.

Rustam:
Are you their chief?

Ribi':
No, but the Muslims are like one body, and the lowest is equal to the highest.[113]

Here the conference ended and Rab'i returned to the Muslim camp. Rustam was profoundly impressed by the Muslim ambassador and pondered deeply over his conversation with Rab'i. He saw how futile it was to depend upon the

---
[113] Tabari: vol. 3, pp. 34-35

appearances of the civilization and culture in which he had always believed, in the face of such pure, glowing faith and such simple, earthy realism.

The next day Rustam again sent a request to Sa'd for an emissary, and this time Sa'd picked Hudayfah bin Mihsan, one of the group selected by him the day before. Hudayfah approached Rustam's court in much the same manner as his predecessor had done, and when asked to dismount refused to do so on the grounds that they had invited him and they were the ones who needed the envoy. He rode over the carpet to Rustam's throne, again refused to dismount, and remained seated on his horse throughout the talks with the Persian Commander-in-Chief.

Rustam started by asking why the envoy of the day before had not come, to which Hudayfah replied, "Our commander treats us equally in enjoying favours and bearing hardships. This time it is my turn."[114]

Thereafter Hudayfah offered the Persians the usual three options: Islam, the Jizya and the sword, and without indulging in further discussion, turned his horse and rode away.

Rustam and the Persians were struck by the confidence and easy dignity with which both the Muslim envoys had spoken and their obvious contempt for the pomp and ceremony with which the Persians were trying to impress and browbeat the Muslims, whom they had considered as belonging to a lower order. Rustam felt dissatisfied with the talks which had been held so far; he had not really got into his stride, not really put himself across as he wished. And so on the following day he asked again for an emissary, and this time he received one of the most colourful of the Muslim officers Mugheerah bin Shu'ba.

Mugheerah was received at the bridge by Persian soldiers and escorted to Rustam's court. He had his hair parted twice. North-south and east-west, and made into four plaits.[115] On arrival at the court he crossed the carpet [it is not known whether on foot or on horseback] and on getting near Rustam, surprised everyone by rushing to the throne and sitting down upon it beside the Persian general. For a few brief moments the Persian officers stared at him in stunned silence. Then they sprang at him, pulled him off, the throne and shook him. Mugheerah fought to keep his seat on the throne and in the struggle which followed, protested:

---

[114] Ibid: p. 35.
[115] Ibid: p. 76.

"We had heard of your forbearance, but I do not know of a people more devoid of it than you. We Arabs are all equal and one is not a slave to another. I had thought that you too would treat people as equals, just as we do, but what you have done makes it clear to me that some of you are lords over others.

"You shall not continue to enjoy authority. I have not come to you of my own accord; you invited me; and now I know the weakness of your position. You will surely be overwhelmed, for a state cannot endure which indulges in such behaviour and such thinking."[116]

Rustam ordered his officers to release the envoy who once again sat upon the throne. Then, seeing the look of disdain in the eyes of Rustam's brother, who stood beside him, Mugheerah said, "Do not look so, for by sitting here I do not gain in prestige, nor does your brother lose any."

Order having been restored, Rustam tried to calm his visitor by explaining the behaviour of his officers: "O Arab, on the outskirts of the empire certain things may happen of which the Emperor does not approve but which he had to accept."

He then sought to belittle the Muslims by comparing their weapons with the fine Persian ones. Looking at the short light arrows which protruded from Mugheerah's quiver, he asked, "What do you do with these spindles?"

"We shoot them".

"And why is your sword wrapped in rags?"

"It is clothed in rags but it strikes like steel," replied Mugheerah, drawing his sword and offering it to Rustam for inspection. It was actually an excellent blade. Having made his point, Mugheerah sheathed his sword; and now began the formal talks between him and the Persian.

Rustam:
Since time immemorial we have been established in the land, victorious over our enemies, leaders among nations. In no realm is there greatness such as ours, nobility and power such as ours. We conquered over all men and none conquered over us except for a day or two or a month or two, because of our

---

[116] Ibid: p. 36.

sins. But when God had punished us sufficiently, He turned to us in kindness and restored to us our glory and to our enemy his suffering.

Among the nations there was none as lowly as you. You lived in squalor and wretchedness and we thought of you as nothing. When your land was struck by famine and you suffered from hunger, you came to our borders for succour, and we arranged dates and corn for you and returned you to your land. I know that what brings you here is hardship in your land. I shall give your commander a set of clothes and a mule and 1000 dirhams, and to every man among you two garments and a bag of dates. And you shall go away from us, for I have no desire to kill you or take you into captivity.

Mugheerah: [After praising Allah and invoking His blessings upon the Holy Prophet]: Lo! Allah is the Creator of all things and their Sustainer. And whoever makes anything, it is in fact Allah who makes it. As for what you have said about yourself and your people, of victory over enemies, of power in the land and glory in the world, we are aware of it and do not deny it. Indeed, Allah made you great; and then reduced your power. As for what you have said about the poverty of our condition and the wretchedness of our existence and the discord of our hearts, we know that too and do not dispute it. But Allah was trying us, and we have now become His.

Times change, and ever are people of misfortune turning to ease and ever are people of ease falling into misfortune. Had you been thankful to Allah for what He had given you, the burden of the wrong that you have done would have been lightened, but ingratitude has altered your fine condition.

Lo! Allah Most High sent us a prophet . . . [Here repeated what other envoys had said about the message of Islam and offered the usual three options].

Rustam:
And what will happen if you are killed?

Mugheerah:
Those of us who are killed will enter paradise, and, those of you who are killed will go to hell.

Rustam:
[In great anger]. There can never be peace between us. By the sun as it rises, tomorrow morning I shall slay the whole lot of you![117]

Mugheerah, quoting a Quranic verse: "There is no power to change and no strength except with Allah,"[118] got up and walked away from the throne. Rustam turned to a Persian officer and ordered him to accompany the envoy up to the bridge, and added: "When he has crossed the bridge and got to his comrades, shout to him that I am an astrologer; that I have checked about him and that tomorrow he will lose an eye."

The Persian officer accompanied Mugheerah as he rode to the bridge, and when the Muslim had crossed over to the west bank, conveyed the message as ordered by Rustam. Thereupon Mugheerah replied: "You give me good news. But for my desire to fight infidels like you after this battle also, I would wish to lose the other eye too."[119]

The Persians standing on the east bank laughed, and then became thoughtful as the full import of Mugheerah's words penetrated their minds.

Rustam asked for no more envoys. Sa'd, however, in his initial selection of delegates, had chosen 7 Muslims to represent him and of these 4 remained. So on his own, upon the return of Mugheerah, he sent off these four to reason with Rustam and persuade him to accept Islam or the payment of the Jizya. These four delegates were: Busr bin Abi Ruhm, Arfaja bin Harsama, Qirfa bin Zahir and Maz'ur bin Adi.[120]

Rustam welcomed the delegation in the hope that they had perhaps come round to his terms. He made much the same sort of approach, first belittling the Arabs on account of their past wretchedness and then offering generous rewards if they would return to their desert homes. But this time he also related a few parables:

"We are like the man who had a vineyard and saw a fox in it one day. He said, "What is a fox?" and let it be. But the fox called other foxes to the vineyard and

---

[117] Tabari: vol. 3, pp. 36-39.
[118] Balazuri: p. 257.
[119] Tabari: vol. 3. pp. 37-38.
[120] There are differences among historians regarding the exact composition of this delegation, but the point is not important.

when they had all gathered in it, the owner closed the hole in the wall of the vineyard through which they had entered and then killed all the foxes.

"And you are like the rat who found a jar of grain with a hole in it and went through the hole. His friends called to him to come out but he refused and went on eating the grain until he became sleek and fat. Then he felt a desire to show his friends how beautiful he looked, but found that because of his bulk he could no longer get through the hole. So he complained to his friends of his distress and asked them how to get out. They said, 'You are never going to get out of there until you become as you were when you went in. So starve yourself.' The rat remained inside, starving himself and living in fear, but before he could return to his former thin state, the owner of the jar found him and killed him.

"And you are like the fly that saw a bowl of honey and said to his friends, 'Whoever gets me to that honey shall have 2 dirhams.' The other flies tried to stop him, but he went on to the honey and then into it. As he began to drown in the honey, he cried out, 'Whoever gets me out of this honey shall have 4 dirhams!'

"And you are like the fox who came into a vineyard, thin and starving, and began eating as God wished. The owner of the vineyard saw him and pitying his condition, let him stay. But when the fox had been there for some time and grown big and fat, he turned wicked and started to destroy more grapes than he consumed. This angered the owner, who along with his servants, took a big stick and came after him. The fox dodged them and ran to the hole in the vineyard wall through which he had come, but that hole was big enough for him only when he was thin, and now he was too fat to get through it. So the owner and his servants caught up with him and beat him with sticks until he was dead.

"You came, O Arabs, when you were thin, and now you are fat. See how you get out!"[121]

The Arabs were not amused. They narrated the usual story about Allah and the Holy Prophet and offered the usual terms, emphasizing that what they sought most was the Persians' conversion to Islam.

---

[121] Tabari: vol. 3, pp. 39-40

Rustam was now bored with such statements. He brought matters to a head by saying abruptly: "Will you cross the river to our side or shall we cross to yours?"

"You cross to our side," replied the Muslims.[122]

The envoys returned to the Muslim camp and informed Sa'd of how matters stood. Sa'd at once ordered preparations for occupation of battle positions. Rustam sent a messenger to Sa'd asking to be allowed to use the bridge, but Sa'd returned him with the reply: "No. We have captured it from you and shall not hand it back to you. Take the trouble to make a crossing other than this bridge."[123]

So far the reader has been able to follow with the aid of Maps 3 and 4, the march of the two armies to the area of Qadisiyya. Before we take up the deployment of the two forces and go into the narrative of this historic battle, it would be as well for the reader to get some idea of the terrain over which the battle was fought. What follows in subsequent paragraphs is a topographical description of the plain of Qadisiyya and the area in its vicinity. The reader is advised to refer to Maps 3 and 4 while studying this description.

The plain of Qadisiyya was bounded on the west and east by the Trench of Sabur and the River Ateeq respectively, the space between them being about 4 or 5 miles. The trench had been dug under the orders of the Emperor Sabur as a canal or large ditch and ran from Heet to Kazima on the Bay of Kuweit. It was built as an obstacle against Arab raiders from the desert and was filled with the water of the Euphrates taken at Heet, which eventually flowed into the Bay of Kuweit. Over the generations the trench had suffered from neglect and silted up, but it was repaired in the 6th Century A.D. by Anushirwan, who also built small forts along its length, manned by Persian garrisons which protected the empire from desert raiders. The trench was still there at the time of Qadisiyya, but it was in a state of disrepair.[124] The River Ateeq, which no longer exists, took off from somewhere west of Najaf, from a region of marshes which it drained, and flowed past Khaffan into the Euphrates. It was a sizable river, though not of the magnitude of the Euphrates.

North of the plain of Qadisiyya was a large lake, with two routes going along its sides: one from Qadisiyya to Hira and the other from Qadisiyya around the left

---

[122] Ibid: p. 42.
[123] Ibid.
[124] Yaqut: vol. 2, p. 476.

of the lake. South of Qadisiyya lay a number of lakes stretching up to Walaja, which was a few miles, below Ulleis. The plain was the only stretch of hard ground in the area big enough for a large-scale battle, and to the west, beyond the trench, it merged into the desert.

Astride the trench lay the town of Uzeib. There was a castle here too, at the eastern end of the town and along the eastern edge of the trench. Caliph Umar, to his instructions to Sa'd, had mentioned Uzeiba-Uzeib-ul-Hijanat and Uzeib-ul-Qawadis - and there were two Uzeibs at the time, but we know only of one Uzeib: this one. It marked the very edge of the desert, and the castle was probably one of the larger forts built by Anushirwan.[125]

Information about Qadisiyya itself is confusing. It is known that it was 4 miles east of Uzeib, but historians have also spoken of Qadis and Qudeis, some saying that they were all different names of the same place, others that they were separate places. A detailed study suggests that there were two places, viz Qadisiyya and Qudeis, the first being the more important of the two. The bridge over the Ateeq, on the route to Hira, was known as the bridge of Qadisiyya, and Qudeis was a smaller place on the Euphrates by the lower part of the plain.[126]

Just south of the castle and east of the trench ran a small valley known as Musharraq, and on the eastern edge of this valley stood the village of Ein-ush-Shams. These two - the valley and the village - played no part in the battle except that the Muslim martyrs were buried in this valley.

As soon as the Persian messenger returned with Sa'd's refusal to let the Persians use the bridge, a refusal which the Persians had anticipated, Rustam ordered his engineers to construct a dam over the river Ateeq. Preparations for this work had already been made, stores and material gathered and engineers briefed about the plan of construction. Rustam decided upon a dam in preference to a bridge because it would give him a wider crossing, needed by the vast army with its horses, elephants and baggage would reduce the danger of the bridge being destroyed while the Persians were on the enemy side. The site chosen for the dam was a mile above Qudeis and four miles south of the bridge of Qadisiyya, and would lead to the plain of Qadisiyya on the west bank which Rustam had selected as the battlefield.

---

[125] Tabari: vol. 3, p. 43; Yaqut: vol. 3, p. 626.
[126] Yaqut: vol. 4, p. 7; Tabari: vol. 3, p. 42, 76.

Before nightfall Persian engineers started work on the dam. They must also have constructed some sort of spillway because the level of the water remained constant and no lake formed, but we have no knowledge of the engineering design involved in this construction. The Muslims, acknowledging the need for a Persian crossing to make battle possible, did not interfere with the work of the engineers but withdrew about a mile from the river bank. The dam was constructed of wood, earth and coarse cloth; work continued through the night, and some time after sunrise the dam was complete, affording the Persian army a great road across the river.

The Persian crossing began at once. Troops, horses, elephants and baggage were rushed over the dam and units began to deploy on the west side, according to a plan already given out by Rustam, a short distance beyond the bank of the river. By midday the major groups had occupied their positions for battle, though adjustments were still going on within the groups. As Rustam saw his warriors moving across the river, a great confidence welled up in his breast. "We shall break them into little pieces," he remarked. One of his officers added fervently, "If God wills it;" whereupon Rustam snapped, "Even if He does not!"[127]

The Persian army deployed with five corps holding the front and one corps in reserve, each corps having a depth of 13 ranks one behind the other. [See Map 5.] The commanders of the corps and their locations were as follows:
Centre: Rustam
Left Centre: Beerzan
Right Centre: Jalinus
Left Wing: Mihran
Right Wing: Hormuzan
Reserve: Bahman [Eyebrow]

The Persian army had a strength of 60,000 men, of which about half were deployed in the three parts of the centre. The strength of other groups is not known. In the centre also stood 15,000 Noble-born Persians who formed the hard core of the army, and these in turn included 4,000 Persians from a group which had been settled in Qadisiyya by Chosroes Parwez, but who had to leave their homes on the arrival of Sa'd in the region. All these 15,000 used chains to bind themselves to each other, the chain lengths being for 3, 5, 7 and 10 men.[128] Contrary to general opinion, chains were used in the Persian army not for fear that the men would run away [there was no question of troops running

---

[127] Tabari: vol 3, p. 42.
[128] Ibid: pp. 206; Abu Yusuf: p. 33.

away across the Ateeq] but as a sign of suicidal courage, indicating the mens' willingness to die in battle rather than flee. The chains did have the effect of strengthening morale, but suffered from the grave drawback that in case of a reverse the men could not get away and would fall an easy prey to a victorious pursuer. In any case, Rustam was not contemplating defeat, and by placing his army across the river had already accepted a do or die battle.

There were 33 war elephants in the Persian army, each mounted by several men armed with javelins and bows. These elephants formed the most important and most powerful element of the army, not only for their physical performance as fighting beasts but also for the effect which they had of striking fear in the enemy ranks. Of the elephants, 18 were placed in the centre and 7 and 8 in the two wings; and these beasts were used as squadrons rather than strung out along the entire front of about 5 miles.

In the centre of the elephants stood two huge ones, a white beast and a scabby one, who acted as leaders of their kind and who were expected to set the pace for other elephants. They were also used in time of peace as trainers of war elephants.

Along with the deployment of the army, a human telegraph system to the capital was established. This was a peculiarly Persian communication system and is indicative of the sophistication of the Persian military organization. A line of men, chosen for their powerful voices, was placed at shouting distance all the way from the battlefield to the imperial palace in Ctesiphon. Every event on the battlefield was shouted by A to B, then by B to C and C to D. and so on until the last man conveyed it to the Emperor and his advisers. By this means information regarding the progress of battle could be carried hundreds of miles in a few hours. By establishing the crossing downstream of the Qadisiyya bridge, Rustam had shifted the battlefield southwards by a few miles. At the bridge, however, he left a cavalry detachment to prevent a Muslim tactical crossing during battle. Across from this Persian detachment, Sa'd also left a Muslim mounted group to watch the bridge, as he moved the bulk of his army down to face the Persians.

A large throne like seat was raised near the west bank, shaded by a small canopy, for the Persian Commander-in-Chief. On this sat Rustam, wearing his armour and his weapons. Beside him waved the Dirafash-e-Kavian, the great standard of the Sasanis, which had last been taken into action by Bahman at the Battle of the Bridge. From this seat Rustam had quite a good view of the battlefield which stretched before him, and while looking at the Persian formations taking shape, he suddenly remembered the dream which he had had earlier about Umar sealing the weapons of his warriors. The recollection infuriated him, and he swore "Umar has eaten my heart. May God burn his"[129]

The Muslim preparations for battle began early in the night as soon as the site of the Persian crossing was known. Units and groups, organised on the basis of tribes and clans, side stepped towards the south and in the morning moved into battle positions corresponding to, and about a mile away from the Persian front. The deployment of the army in corps was similar to the Persian one, except that it had a depth of only 3 ranks. In each contingent the first rank was formed by the cavalry; behind it stood a line of men armed with swords and spears or javelins; and, behind it stood a line of archers. The commanders of the corps and their locations were as follows [See Map 5]:

---

[129] Tabari: vol. 3, p. 45.

MAP 5: QADISIYYA - DISPOSITIONS

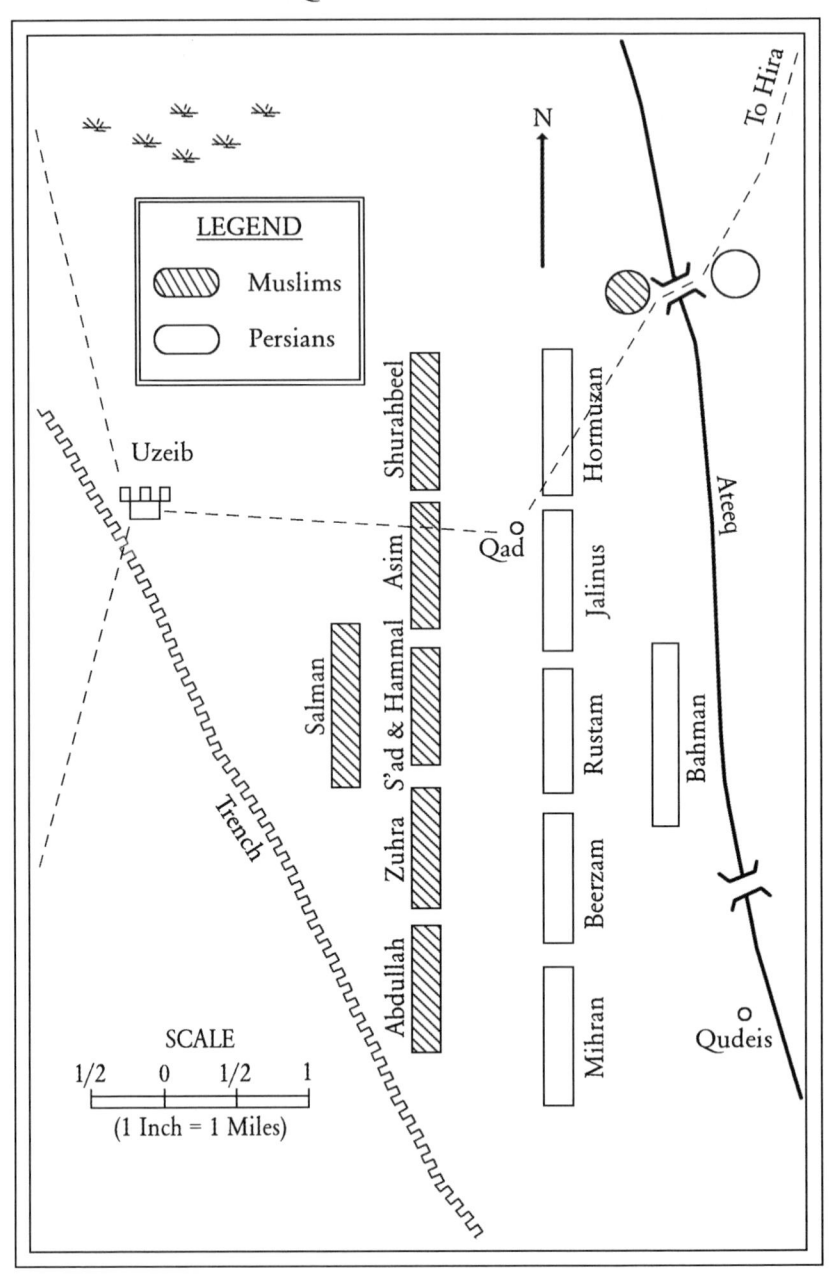

Centre: Sa'd, with Hammal bin Malik as commander of the infantry.
Left Centre: Asim bin Amr.
Right Centre: Zuhra bin Al Hawiyya.
Left Wing: Shurahbeel bin As-Samt
Right Wing: Abdullah bin Al Mu'tim.
Reserve: Salman bin Rabee'a

The Muslim army consisted of 30,000 men in whose ranks were more than 300 Companions, 700 sons of Companions and [the most venerated of all] more than 70 veterans of the Battle of Badr. There were groups of Christian Arabs too in the army, who had joined Sa'd upon his arrival at Qadisiyya, and of these a few had already accepted Islam while the remainder would do so after the battle. And in this army also served some Persian officers and men who had left the Persian empire and, attracted by the new message of Islam, thrown in their lot with the Muslims.

While in the deployment of the army and in making final preparations for battle there was no hitch, the important problem which faced Sa'd was the tactical control of battle. He himself was immobilised by boils on his backside, which prevented him from sitting on a horse. In fact they prevented him from sitting at all. He established his headquarters in the castle of Uzeib and an arrangement was evolved whereby a deputy would be used to convey the orders of Sa'd to the unit commanders and to exercise control where Sa'd was unable to do so. This deputy was Khalid bin Urfuta, who took up his position below the wall of the castle. Sa'd placed himself on the wall nearest the battlefield, from where he could see virtually the entire battlefield; and from here he would throw down written notes to Khalid, with orders, and Khalid would then execute the orders. For any battle action which Sa'd could not see, the deputy would take a decision himself and give orders as necessary. Sa'd had a cot placed on the battlements and lay prostrate upon it with a pillow under his chest, looking upon the plain where the two armies were formed up. He also kept at hand a whole platoon of aides, who would carry his orders direct to the commanders of corps and regiments and would bring him reports about the course of battle. This was an alternative or supplementary arrangement to the command arrangement already described.

When orders for deployment had been issued, Sa'd held a conference of his commanders at which he made a stirring speech about Allah and His blessings, about the need for valour and steadfastness, and ordered his officers to address the men and recite verses from the Quran before and during battle. He also explained his inability to be present with the men in battle because of his condition, and outlined the command arrangements which he had made. All understood and sympathised with him, except a few who uncharitably imputed unworthy motives to his remaining in the castle and commanding the army through a deputy. These officers included Jareer bin Abdullah, who passed rude remarks about the Army Commander to his comrades. When Sa'd came to know of his insubordination he had him thrown into a dungeon and placed in fetters, but Jareer quickly repented and was as quickly pardoned and released.

For the rest of the morning the commanders went about their units reciting Quranic verses and urging the men to fight for Allah. Orators and poets fired the spirit of the men with eulogies on respective Arab tribes and clans. And the Muslim soldiery prepared with grim resolution for a battle which would undoubtedly decide the fate of Islam in Iraq.

Chapter 8: The Day of Disorder

It was a perfect day for battle. The chill of the night was dispelled by the bright sun as it rose in a clear blue sky and painted the plain of Qadisiyya in gentle colours. As it reached its zenith, the rays of the sun were reflected by the rippling waters of the rivers and canals and lakes. It was a glorious day. The sun shone not only upon the peaceful beauty of nature but also upon the magnificent spectacle of two formidable armies, comprising of nearly a hundred thousand men, drawn up for battle on the plain.

The Persian host was the more impressive of the two. Its huge elephants, wearing coats of mail and with their tusks wrapped in silk and velvet, looked like awesome forts; its strong, gaily-caparisoned war horses strained at the bit as well-muscled arms kept them in check; the uniforms and armour of its warriors glittered in the sunlight as their set, strong faces showed their eagerness for battle; its colourful banners fluttered in the gentle breeze, the most splendid being the Dirafsh-e-Kavian, carried by a standard bearer who stood beside Rustam's throne. The most gallant of the imperial soldiers - the flower of Persian manhood - were the 15,000 of the centre who had bound themselves to each other in chains. They had taken an oath by the sacred fire that they would not retreat that they would conquer or die.

The Muslim army was less imposing to look at. Its soldiers had no uniform and just wore the simple coarse cloaks of every day use. Some of them had coats of mail and chain helmets but these did not glitter like the fine armour of their adversaries. Their weapons were less sophisticated. Their largest animals - the camels - were not beasts of battle and their horses were smaller, though also faster and more spirited. But the Muslims made up for what they lacked in numbers and weapons by the strength of their faith in Allah and ark unshakable conviction of victory.

It was a spectacle of a carnival with gallant knights preparing to display their courage and skill. If the sun could think, it would marvel at the beauty and splendour of the scene which stretched in its warm light with the finest manhood of the time arrayed for a titanic contest between a new faith and an old empire. And if the sun could think, it would, three days later, be staggered to find the spectacle of beauty changed into a scene of the most frightful carnage and devastation - It is just as well that the sun could not think!

It was a morning of feverish activity - Thursday, Shawwal 11, 15 Hijri [November 15, 636].[130] The Persians were deploying rapidly with their rear on the bank of the Ateeq and their forward line about a mile to the west. They were prepared for a frontal set-piece battle, and this was inevitable, because by the very nature of his operation, Rustam was confined to the ground which he had occupied and was incapable of any long range manoeuvres. He had established what we would now call a bridge-head across the river, and so long as the Muslims had the power to attack and destroy his crossing site, Rustam had to stay where he was and fight a frontal engagement. Moreover, the marshes on the flanks of the two armies did not permit any wide outflanking manoeuvres. Rustam's cavalry formed the front line in all his corps and behind it stood the infantry. But his strongest element was the elephants which he would use to break the strength of the Muslim cavalry, thus separating the cavalry from the infantry and then attacking with the rest of his army to destroy the Muslim army. This is how he intended to fight each tactical action.

The Muslims on the other hand had more liberty of action, although their freedom of manoeuvre was somewhat restricted by the ground. Their deployment took less time and was simpler. The cavalry formed the front line in each of the corps, with the infantry deployed behind it; and a separate cavalry element formed the reserve under Salman bin Rabee'a. Basically this was to be a battle of guts and stamina rather than brilliant generalship, and would be decided not by fine manoeuvre but by heavy slaughter.

Both the armies were full of spirit, full of confidence, full of a keen anticipation of victory. The Persians exulted in their strength, in their mighty elephants, in the presence on the battlefield of Rustam and the great standard, Dirafsh-e-Kavian, which was for them a symbol of triumph. The Muslim ranks which stretched in front of them were less than awe inspiring. The Muslim mood was more serious, more purposeful, seeing the forthcoming battle as a confrontation between good and evil and a trial of strength between Islam and disbelief. The mood of the Muslims is exemplified by the words of an old woman of the Bani Nakh'a to her four warrior sons.

"You have accepted Islam, so do not betray it" she said to them. "You have left your homes for Islam, and must not regret it. Now you have come here with your old mother and put her in front of the Persians. By Allah, you are the sons of one man and one woman. I was true to your father and I was good to you. Go and be in the fight from start to finish."

---

[130] For an explanation of the date of this battle see Note 2 in Appendix C, but the reader is advised to finish the account of the battle before turning to the appendix.

As the four stalwarts took leave of their mother and departed to take up their positions in the Muslim front line, the appearance of cool courage which she had assumed while facing her sons vanished, and before Allah she became once again a woman and a mother. "O Lord," she prayed, "protect my sons for me."[131]

Arraying the corps and regiments for battle and placing horse and foot in their correct position would take till midday. Before then no serious engagement could be attempted. Sa'd therefore issued instructions that the prayer of the noon be offered at the usual hour, and immediately after that the troops would prepare for battle. There would be four calls for battle, each one consisting of the Takbeer: "Allaho-Akbar." The first two would be warning calls on which the men would don their weapons and armour and prepare for action; the third call would be for individual officers and warriors to go forth and engage in single combat: and this would not only act as a warming up but also eliminate many Persian champions and gain more time for preparation. The fourth call would be for the general attack and at this call the entire army would assault the Persian front as one man. In the attack the cavalry would lead, followed closely by the infantry.

Sa'd had no illusions about being able to seize the initiative and attack the Persians straightaway. In the first place, the Persian army was too large and too strong to be engaged offensively until it had been unbalanced or otherwise weakened. In the second place, the foremost rank of the Persian army included the elephants with which most of the Muslims and their horses were unfamiliar. It was futile to expect the Arabian horse to advance upon the massive beasts, and any attempt to do so while the Persians were in a set, well organised position, would lead to chaos. The Muslim Commander-in-Chief therefore decided to stay on the defensive and await and repulse the Persian attack when it came, and then go on to the offensive when a suitable opportunity offered itself. The fourth call of "Allaho-Akbar" would be for this counter attack.

The prayer of the noon was offered undisturbed. As soon as it was over, Sa'd gave the first call and everyone rushed to his assigned place. This was followed by the second call on which the men prepared their weapons and equipment while the commander carried out last minute checks to see that every man was in position. Then came the third call, the call for champions to engage in single combat.

---

[131] Tabari: vol. 3, p. 53.

The very first Muslim to go forth for combat was Ghalib bin Abdullah of the Bani Asad, which stood in the centre and formed, physically and psychologically, the hard core of the Muslim army. Ghalib rode out into the middle of the no-man's land between the two armies and threw a challenge, which was accepted by the Persian general Hormuz, who had fought and retreated before Muthana at the battle of Babylon. The two champions fought, and the Muslim overpowered and disarmed the Persian, who was then brought to Sa'd and locked up as a prisoner of war.

On the Muslim left the initiative was taken by a Persian officer, who rode forward and called: "Man to man!" His challenge was accepted by Amr bin Madi Karib [Father of the Bull]. The two dismounted and wrestled on foot; and it was not long before Amr threw his adversary and, as the Persian fell, drew his sword and cut off his head. The Muslim then turned and shouted to his men: "When a Persian has dropped his javelin he is useless!"

He had hardly delivered this rather hasty judgement when a Persian horseman advanced, stopped a short distance from Amr and began to shoot at him with his bow. Amr at once closed up, being lucky not to get hit in the meantime, and lifting the Persian off his horse, broke his neck and then cut his throat. Having done so, he gave the further judgement: "When a Persian has lost his bow, he is useless!"

Having triumphed with honour in two duels, the Arab prince returned to his men and as a victory cry, shouted: "I am Abu Saur! Do as I do." To this his comrades, full of admiration, replied, "O Father of the Bull, who can do as you do!"[132]

The next noteworthy encounter was that of the gallant Asim bin Amr who rode out of the Muslim left centre, recited a few extemporaneous verses and threw a general challenge for combat. For some time there was no response from the Persian front, for Asim was a much feared warrior, but after a while a Persian horseman rode forward. When he got near Asim, however, he changed his mind and galloped back to the Persian army. Asim followed him, and as he got near the Persian line, the Persians moved out of his path to let him pass. Asim entered the gap and there, right in front of him, stood a mule loaded with two large saddle-bags and held by an unmilitary-looking and unarmed man. Since no

---

[132] Ibid: p. 48, Balazuri: p. 258.

Persian was coming forth to fight him, Asim took the reins of the mule and led the animal and the muleman back to the Muslim army as a prize.

The mule was led to Sa'd, who found that the muleman was the baker of a Persian prince and that the saddle-bags were full of date-cakes and honey. He sent them to Asim's men as a trophy, and they made a quick snack of the goodies.

Other duels were now in progress and Persian champions too were coming forward to throw their personal challenges. While several of them won their duels, by and large, the honours in this Phase of battle went to the Muslims. Troops of both sides were getting impatient for battle. One Muslim regimental commander lost his patience and ordered his men to advance, but the move was stopped in the nick of time by the deputy commander, Khalid bin Urfuta, who warned the subordinate commander that he would be removed from his command if he took such a rash step again. Another officer, Qeis bin Hubeira of the Bani Asad, rushed to Khalid and said, "O Commander, we have come to these people with a purpose. Launch the attack against them as one attack."[133] But Khalid shook his head; and still Sa'd would not give the signal to attack-the fourth Takbeer. And then suddenly Rustam struck at the Muslims with his elephants and his wings.

Rustam had no intention of letting the initiative slip from his hands to his adversary's. The initial phase of duelling suited him very well because it gave him time to complete his forming up which, with his larger army, naturally took longer. And it is a mark of Persian military efficiency that such a vast array was able to complete its preparations for battle on the west bank by early afternoon. It was Rustam's design to attack and defeat the two wings of the Muslim army and then envelop their centre.

The Persian attack began with heavy showers of arrows. The Persian bows had a longer range and their arrows were heavier, and succeeded in inflicting many casualties on the Muslims and causing a certain amount of confusion in Muslim ranks. The Muslim reaction was an involuntary and spontaneous one: the archers opened up. But while the Muslim bows had sufficient range and their archers were very accurate, their arrows were lighter and less deadly. The Persians laughed at the Muslim arrows and showed their contempt by shouting: "Spindles! Spindles!"[134]

---

[133] Dinawari: p. 122.
[134] Tabari: vol. 3, p. 15; Balazuri: p. 260.

After a little while, when Rustam saw that his archers had gained the upper hand over the Muslim archers, he ordered the attack on the Muslim right, while the rest of the Muslim front was kept engaged by the archers. The 8 elephants in the Persian left led the attack and advanced upon the contingent of the Bajeela, which was under the command of Jareer bin Abdullah. The towering beasts, mounted by javelin throwing warriors, bore down upon the Bajeela and the horses of the Bajeela, frightened by the oncoming menace, broke out of control and fled from their position, leaving the foot soldiers unsupported on the field. The infantry also was thrown into confusion and as the elephants continued their advance, began to fall back, though in fairly good order. Their retrograde movement, however, was a matter of confusion and lack of control rather than fright.

Sa'd could see that the Bajeela were in trouble and something would have to be done to restore the situation on the Muslim right. He did not wish to commit his reserve at this early stage of battle, and seeing no forward move by the Persian centre, decided to rely on units of the forward line to deal with the advance of the Persian left. Consequently he sent orders to Ash'as bin Qeis, who commanded the 700 Kinda in the right centre, and to Hammal bin Malik, who was the commander of the Bani Asad and also of the infantry of the centre, to attack the Persian corps which had occupied the position of the Muslim right and was following up the withdrawal of the Bajeela.

Ash'as at once attacked the flank of the Persian left wing and Hammal, making certain adjustments in the Muslim centre to maintain some sort of a front against the Persians, moved the Bani Asad to face the Persian left wing. The Bani Asad, using javelin and sword, arrested the Persian advance and once it was stopped, the Persians were attacked in front by the Bani Asad and in flank by the Kinda. Both Muslim contingents fought bravely and their chiefs, Ashas' Hammal and Tuleiha, displayed exemplary leadership. At last the Persians were pushed back from the Muslim position. A Persian officer came forward for single combat with Tuleiha and was killed by the ex-impostor.

So far the battle had gone quite well from the Muslim point of view. An initial setback was suffered by the Muslim right, but the situation had been restored and soon the front would be re-established. But Rustam had anticipated such a reaction. His plan was to engage the Muslim right, and either push it back and expose the flank of the Muslim centre or draw Muslim reserves into battle and then attack with his right and throw back the Muslim left. He intended to leave the Muslim centre in its place because his design was of a double envelopment in which the Muslim centre played no part. To execute this design, he launched his reserve under Bahman [Eyebrows] against the Bani Asad to keep what he thought was the Muslim reserve engaged, and ordered his right wing and right centre under Jalinus to advance against the Muslims on their front. The elephants of the Persian right and right centre moved forward, the former to achieve a decisive break-through and the latter to hold and engage the Muslim centre. Thus began the second phase of the Persian attack. [See. Map 6.][135]

Sa'd now found his left under heavy pressure. He was not worried about his right because the Bani Asad, led by redoubtable chiefs, could hold their own against any odds, but on the Muslim left he could see the same sort of situation developing as had happened with the Bajeela, though not as serious. The Muslim horse of the left and centre, severely punished by the Persian archers, became unmanageable and many fell back on the infantry as the elephants, their movement covered by javelins and arrows, bore down upon them. Sa'd did nothing about his left, leaving the problem to the Father of the Bull, but sent word to Asim bin Amr, who commanded the Bani Tameem in the left centre, to do something about the elephants.

Asim led the Bani Tameem forward. He ordered his men to pick off the Persians on the elephants' backs with arrows, to get behind the elephants and then slip in and cut the girths of the howdahs. And this is how the Bani Tameem tackled the elephants-some of the Persian centre and some of the Persian right. There was a great deal of confusion on the battlefield and not one of the elephants engaged by Asim remained with its howdah on its back.

---

[135] On this and subsequent battle maps the names of corps commando have not been shown. because of the scale. For these names the reader should refer to map 5.

MAP 6: QADISIYYA - 1ST DAY

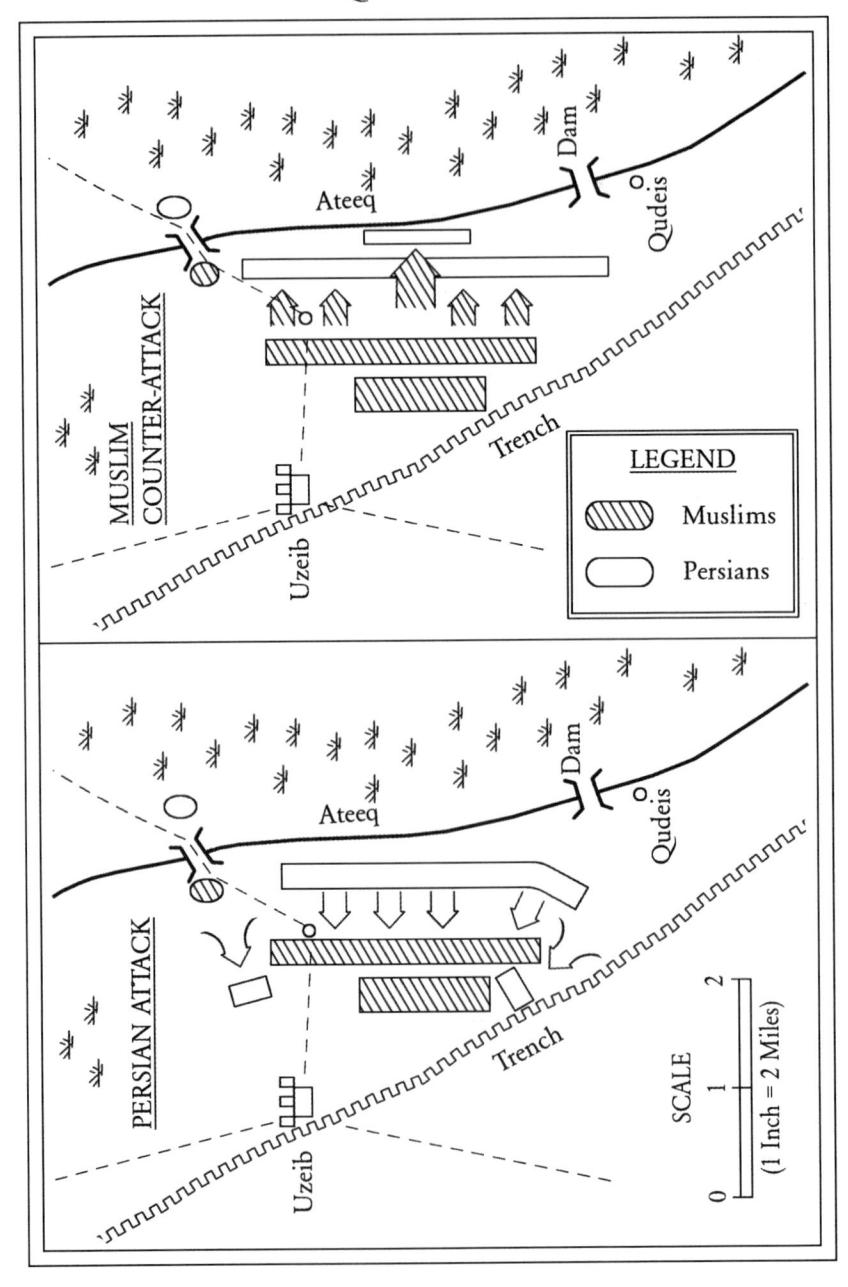

Many Persian elephant-riders were killed as they fell and the rest beat a hasty retreat, leading their elephants to the safety of the Persian position behind the front line. What made the Muslims' task of repulsing the elephants easier was the fact that the beasts came too far ahead by themselves and were not closely supported by the Persian cavalry and infantry.

On the Muslim left Amr bin Madi Karib did much the same to the Persian elephants. Although the commander of the Muslim left wing was Shurahbeel bin As-Samt, most of the tactical actions here were controlled by Amr. He ordered his men to strike at the elephants' trunks, and after some very severe fighting the Persian right was also pushed back to its original position and here too the elephants were withdrawn from combat. And it was while this hard fighting was going on that Sa'd found that his troubles were not confined to the battlefield.

The Muslim Commander-in-Chief lay prostrate on a cot watching and controlling the battle; and beside him stood his newly-acquired wife Salma, widow of Muthana. She too was watching the battle. In her mind Muthana occupied a glorious image, and having seen the wonders that he had performed in many a battle she pictured him as an invincible hero in shining armour mounted on a fiery horse. The contrast with her new husband, with his undignified ailment and his still less dignified position on the cot, was startling. Unaware of military realities, she attributed the pressure on the Muslims and their defensive posture to inadequate leadership, and woman that she was, burst out: "O my Muthana! But there is no Muthana for the cavalry today!"

Sa'd was cut to the quick. The injustice of Salma's words wounded him deeply. He was carrying the extremely heavy burden of military command in a great battle against a fine army, twice as strong as his own and better armed and equipped. And he was in actual physical pain which was acute enough to cause him to groan now and then. And here was this woman! Sa'd realised that the Persians were not the only ones creating problems for him.

With a cry of anger he rose to his feet and slapped the woman. Then he shouted at her: "What could Muthana do about these regiments around which the battle rages?"

Salma was impressed by his violent reaction, but was not yet prepared to give in. "Do you react from a sense of honour or fear?" she asked boldly.

Sa'd now realised that the rules of logic and the military principles that he was trying to apply to the battlefield could not be used against unpredictable women. He controlled his anger and in a voice which was gentler and more reproachful, said, "By Allah, none shall understand my position if you do not. And you can see how it is with me."[136]

Salma turned about and, sulking, walked away.

It was late in the afternoon when the Persian attacks on the Muslim wings were finally repulsed and the Muslim ranks found themselves in about the same position as they had adopted for battle in the morning. The situation was still somewhat confused, as was inevitable, but Sa'd took the immediate decision, and a very sound one it was, to exploit the Persian setback, physically and psychologically, by launching his attack and pressing the Persians back, if possible into the river. Without waiting for the Bani Asad to be re-positioned in the centre, he gave the fourth Takbeer, the call for the general attack.

The Muslim front at once moved forward. The cavalry advanced at a brisk pace along the entire front, followed by the infantry, and on nearing the Persian front the cavalry charged. The Persian front was now weaker than at noon because of the failure of the Persian attack and the severe mauling which they had received from the Muslims, and there were no elephants to strengthen it. But the Persian warrior in his person was no weaker and could fight without elephants. In fact he fought bravely and was able to hold his own at most places.

After the cavalry attack, the javelin-men hurled their javelins and then the swordsmen closed in for a savage contest in which horse and foot were all mixed up and the Muslims were guided only by the laid down direction of the attack and the purpose of breaking through the Persian front or pushing it back. The Muslim soldiers were superior as individual fighting men but the Persians were not wanting in skill and courage and could rely upon their numbers to hold the Muslim attack; and hold it they did. Shortly before sunset, however, as the fighting increased in intensity, the Muslims were able to punch several holes in the Persian front and pressed through the gaps thus created.

One such gap was in the Persian centre, and through this a body of Muslim warriors charged and got very near to Rustam. The Persian Commander-in-Chief now showed himself to be not only a high commander but also a

---

[136] Tabari: vol. 3, p. 51; Balamri: p. 258.

champion, and along with his nobles and other officers, entered the fray with drawn sword. He engaged personally in the fighting, as he was to do several times in this battle, and was able to repulse the Muslims from his headquarters, though at the cost of several wounds on his person.

The Muslim success in this attack was short-lived. The Persians were able to re-establish their front at sunset, by when the fighting could be expected to end for the day; but the two armies were so heavily engaged that the combat continued for some time with each side striving to gain an advantage over the other. It was only at the approach of dusk that the fighting ended; and such was the nature of combat on this day that it became known to the Muslims as "the Day of Disorder."

Both armies returned to their camps, knowing that their ordeal had only just begun. The future held promise of much savage fighting and much sweat and blood. The heaviest odds on the Day of Disorder had been faced by the Bani Asad to whom went the honours of the day. They had lost 500 men.

Chapter 9: The Day of Succour

The night passed. The Bani Asad reoccupied their original position in the Muslim centre. The men rested and fed. Most of the Muslim wounded were evacuated and their wounds dressed, and except for those who were totally incapable of combat, rejoined their comrades for the second day of battle which they hoped would be the last. The Persians had as many followers - slaves and servants - as they had soldiers, and these followers saw to the administrative duties which follow a hard day's fighting. The Muslim followers, however, consisted of the wives and children of the soldiers and these faithful souls did for their men all that was needed. They cooked the food; they dressed the wounded; and, later, they dug the graves and buried the dead.

At sunrise both armies again formed up for battle. Sa'd ordered that the dead be evacuated and buried and a search be carried out for any wounded soldiers who had not yet been found. Some wounded men were found and handed over to the women, and all dead bodies were evacuated from the battlefield and carried on camels to Uzeib, where they were buried on both sides of the Wadi Musharraq-a small valley between Uzeib and Ein-ush-Shams.

This second day of battle would become known as "the Day of Succour." because of the arrival of reinforcements from Syria. It would be a day of chivalry, because of the glorious and exciting duels fought by champions of the two armies. It would be a day on which the Muslims would get very near victory and the Persians would remain on the defensive, because of the heavy casualties which they had suffered the day before and the absence of elephants from the battlefield. Many elephants had been wounded in the first day fighting and all had their equipment, including the howdahs, damaged. This equipment was being repaired and the wounded elephants treated for their wounds.

The two armies watched each other intently till about the middle of the morning; and then the fighting was resumed on the orders of Sa'd and on the same pattern-duels preceding the general engagement.

There were a large number of duels this day. Sometimes a Muslim would advance and throw a challenge and sometimes a Persian. Some duels ended quickly while others were prolonged contests. In some the vanquished withdrew from combat to save his life but in most duels defeat meant death. The corps commanders themselves came out to fight and showed their prowess with arms. Jalinus threw a challenge for single combat which was accepted by Tuleiha. After some fighting, Tuleiha landed his sword on the head of the Persian general and the sword cut the Persian's helmet but stopped just short of the scalp, whereafter Jalinus beat a hasty retreat. And this was just as well for the Persians because he was to play an important part in the conduct of the battle on its last day.

In another duel a Persian officer came forth for single combat. He was killed by his Muslim adversary but before he fell, he was able to inflict a mortal wound on the Muslim, whose name was Ilba bin Jahash. Ilba lay on the ground beside the body of his vanquished foe, with his intestines hanging out of his belly. A little later, with the help of another Muslim, he was able to get them into his body and wrap himself to keep them in. Then he began to crawl towards the Persian front line and was only 15 metres away from the Persians when death overtook him. With his last breath, he recited a couplet:

I look for merit with our Lord.
I was of those who fought the best.[137]

In another duel recorded by chroniclers, A'war bin Qutba fought a Persian noble known as Shahryar of Sijistan; and both killed each other. And so this magnificent and gory drama rolled on, with most of the honours being won by the Muslims, until a little before noon a small cloud of dust was seen rising in the south. At this time, on the western front, the Muslims were besieging Jerusalem. After inflicting a crushing defeat on the Romans at Yarmuk, the Muslims had retaken Damascus and thereafter, on the orders of Caliph Umar, Abu Ubayda had marched to Jerusalem and invested the holy city. The siege was to last more than five months until April 637, but a few weeks before the battle of Qadissiya, while Rustam was on his way to the battlefield, Umar had written to Abu Ubayda to despatch whatever force he could spare from his theatre to strengthen Sa'd against the Persians. In response to the Caliph's orders, Abu Ubayda sent a force of 1,000 men under the command of a nephew of Sa'd named Hashim bin Utba bin Abi Waqqas.[138]

---

[137] Tabari: voi. 3, p. 54.
[138] There is disagreement about the strength of this force. In my book: The Sword of Allah, I had relied on one of Tabari's versions which gave its strength as 5,000. Since then, as a result of more detailed research specific to the campaign in Iraq. I have come to the conclusion that that version is incorrect. Checking with Masudi, Balazuri, Yaqubi, Dinawari, and, of course, Tabari where he quotes other figures. I find alternative strengths of 700 and 1,000. I am now of the opinion that this force was 1,000 strong.

Hashim travelled along the northern Arabian route via Daumat-ul-Jandal [the present Al Jauf]. He sent Qa'qa bin Amr with 700 men ahead of the rest, and Qa'qa, once on his own, was able to secure a whole day's advance over Hashim and the remaining 300. As the first day of Qadisiyya ended, Qa'qa was camped two days' march south of the battlefield on the main Arabian route. And it was in this camp that Qa'qa received information, two days old, that battle was imminent. Taking 100 of his fastest horses and 100 of his bravest men, he set off for Qadisiyya, instructing the remainder to follow on and make the best possible speed.

Arriving near the battlefield, Qa'qa sensed that the Muslims would be under pressure and could do with a morale-boost. He thought of a method which would heighten the psychological effect of his arrival. Dividing his 100 men into tens, he gave instructions that each group of ten would follow the one before it after a short interval so as to arrive on the battlefield separately and thus remind the Muslims, and the Persians, several times that Muslim reinforcements were coming. And in this manner the last stage of the journey was carried out. Qa'qa leading the first group of ten, arrived on the battlefield and came into the Muslim right centre from behind. This was shortly before noon. As he arrived, he gave the cry of "Allaho-Akbar" and this rousing call of Islam was taken up by the Muslims who were thrilled at the arrival of Qa'qa, for who did not know of Qa'qa? - the man who was as good as an army!

Qa'qa was a brother of Asim bin Amr, and two nobler brothers - two more valiant, more dashing, more chivalrous - it would be difficult to find. The two had fought together under Khalid bin Al Waleed in his campaign in Iraq and were his most trusted lieutenants. When Khalid marched to Syria, Qa'qa, went with him and was present at every battle fought in the west where he covered himself with glory. He was one of the two stalwarts who, along with Khalid, had scaled the walls of Damascus which led to the storming of the city and its fall to the Muslims. His worth on the battlefield had been predicted by Caliph Abu Bakr, who once said, before Khalid's invasion of Iraq, "No army can be defeated if its ranks possess the likes of this man."[139] And now Qa'qa had come.

Qa'qa was not the man to waste time when there was good fighting to be done. Disregarding the fatigue of his long ride, he rode forward towards the Persian line and called: "Who will duel?" We do not know why the Persians did not

---

[139] Tabari: vol. 2, p. 554.

come forth to accept the challenge. Perhaps they remembered the Muslim champion from days gone by. Perhaps they recognised him as the brother of Asim. Whatever the reason, there was silence in the Persian front line until at last Bahman came forward to accept combat with the young challenger. 'Eyebrows' was known as a very able general and a gifted fighter, and the fact that he was getting on in years did not deter him from wishing to show the youngsters how great duels are fought.

"Who are you?" asked Qa'qa. "I am Bahman Jazaweih," replied the Persian. Qa'qa at once recalled the Battle of the Bridge of which he had heard accounts in Syria. "Now," he exulted, "I take revenge for Abu Ubayd and Saleet and the people of the bridge!"[140]

Hardly were the words out of his mouth when Qa'qa attacked his adversary. Bahman fought skilfully to defend himself but was no match for the young Muslim champion. Qa'qa killed the Persian general and in doing so inflicted upon the Persian army the greatest single loss that it was possible for it to suffer. This was a kind of death, however, which Bahman himself, a professional soldier, who was once an officer of Anushirawan the Just, would have liked to die.

Again Qa'qa threw a challenge and this time, the commander of the Persian left centre, rode forward, accompanied by another officer. Seeing two Persians emerge from the Persian ranks, one of Qaqa's men rode up to him and the two pairs met in single combat. Qa'qa killed Beerzan and the other Muslim killed the other Persian.

Now Qa'qa returned to the Muslim line. "O Muslims," he called. "Greet them with the sword. Only with the sword do men kill. Do as I do."[141]

The duel with Beerzan was fought at about noon. As the duel ended, Sa'd gave the order for the general attack, hoping to achieve on this day the victory which had eluded the Muslims the day before. The Muslim regiments again swept forward, picking their way over the bodies of fallen foes, and clashed with the Persian mass arrayed in front of them. But the Persians stood like a rock in the path of Muslim attack, and although a large number fell in combat, they repulsed every attack. The most difficult nut which the Muslims had to crack, and they were unable to crack it, was the Persian heavy cavalry which stood forward of the Persian army, intimately supported by the heavily armed

---

[140] Ibid: vol. 3, p. 51.
[141] Ibid: pp. 52-54.

infantry. Fighting increased in intensity and casualties began to mount on both sides, but the Persians could not be shaken. After an hour or two of this the Muslims pulled back to their own position and both sides got a little time to rest.

It was during this break that Qa'qa, with Sa'd's permission, put into effect an extremely ingenious trick. Collecting a number of camels, he got some men to rig up large wooden structures which were covered with cloth and placed firmly on the camels' backs. The faces of the camels were also covered and by the use of props of various kinds, the shape of the camels' heads was distorted to make them look like weird monsters. So camouflaged, these camels were ridden through the Muslim lines and directed at the enemy cavalry which stood nearest to them.

The Persian soldier was tough. He was trained to face any manner of attack, any kind of weapon any race of men and any breed of horse. But he had never been prepared to stand in the path of a huge, towering monster which looked like nothing on earth. He wilted. Many Persians, more intelligent and more steady than others, reasoned that this was a ruse, really camels dressed to look like unearthly creatures. But the Persian war horse could not reason. It knew humans. It knew camels, horses and elephants. But it could not be expected to fight a being which could only be described as "the thing."

There was a short, sharp struggle between horse and rider. Then the Persian horses standing in the path of the oncoming super beasts turned and fled, knocking down Persian infantrymen on way, and nothing but the River Ateeq could arrest their flight.

As the remaining Persians on this part of the front re-established some semblance of order, Qa'qa led the camels along the space between the two armies. After parading his special animals for a short distance, he turned them in the direction of the Persians and no sooner had they got near the Persian front than the Persian horse turned and bolted. In fact the Persian horses were more frightened of the Arab super camels than the Arab horses had been of the Persian elephants. And this went on for some time until most of the Persian cavalry was despatched from the battlefield without a blob, being struck. Had this not been a bloody battlefield with thousands of corpses littering the ground, the scene would have been comical. As it happened, it delighted the Muslims and left the Persians in much confusion and some dismay.

It was now a little before sunset. The time was ripe for another attack. The Persians, abandoned by their cavalry, stunned by the spectacle of the strange beasts, disorganised by the gaps which suddenly appeared in their mist due to the flight of the cavalry, were extremely vulnerable and a determined attack would have every chance of throwing them off balance and robbing them of all cohesion. With clear judgement, Sa'd seized the opportunity and ordered a resumption of the attack.

The Muslim army again went into action. The mounted groups made for gaps left by the departed Persian cavalry and the rest of the army closed up to the Persian line and struck to finish this army once and for all. The progress achieved showed every promise of victory. Some of the Persian units broke under the force of the Muslim attack and made for the river bank, and the exulting attackers drove several wedges into the Persian front. Through the gaps thus created the Muslim horse and foot penetrated deep towards the rear of the Persian army.

Qa'qa had now joined his brother Asim and his tribe of Bani Tameem in the left centre, and the two brothers worked wonders in the hard fighting which was taking place, dazzling everyone, friend and foe, with their skill, strength and dash. On this day Qa'qa made a total of 30 sallies and killed a total of 30 Persians, one in each sally. His last victim was a noble named Buzurjmihr

Along with other Muslim units, the Bani Tameem also struck deep into the Persian mass. Qa'qa led a group of men through the Persian centre towards Rustam's headquarters, and as he approached it, the Persian army showed every sign of collapsing. The Muslim victory was clearly in sight, perhaps only an hour away, and since the sun had just set, there was little time to lose. If they could get Rustam, all resistance would collapse. So Qa'qa made a determined bid for the Persian Commander-in-Chief. [See Map 7.]

Rustam's world was crumbling around him. But he was too great a man and too fine a general to give up the struggle while the least hope remained. Having been in countless battles, he knew that the fortunes of war were fickle and one or two events could turn the tide of battle. There was certainly ample hope. It was getting dark. That helped only a little because there was a good moon, but it was something. If he could keep his army in being over the night, the entire situation would change, for in the morning his elephants would be back in action and then he could turn the tables on the invaders of his land. Rustam drew his sword and personally led a counter attack against the Bani Tameem.

This was a signal for a last desperate effort by the Persians to stave off defeat; and the Persian army rose to heroic heights in fighting off the Muslim groups which had penetrated their front. Soon the sky darkened, but there was no disengagement as the two armies remained locked in fierce combat in the light of a bright, clear moon.

Slowly and steadily the Persians loosened the vice-like grip of the desert army. Slowly and steadily the Muslims were forced out of the Persian position; and having come within an inch of victory, surrendered their gains and fell back to no man's land. Having struggled mightily against a force twice its size, the Muslim army was too exhausted to hold or press its advantage, though not too exhausted to fight on.

The Persians re-established their line of battle as in the morning, but the slogging went on relentless and unmerciful.

One of the bravest of the Muslims was taking no part in this battle. He was lying on the damp floor of a cellar in the castle of Uzeib with his legs in irons. This was Abu Mihjan, of the Saqeef, cousin of Abu Ubayd, martyr of the Bridge.

In the Days of Ignorance, Abu Mihjan had been fond of the bottle and living it up. He was even then a fearless fighter and also a bit of a poet. In early 9 Hijri, when the Holy Prophet besieged Taif, Abu Mihjan's home town, Abu Mihjan fought with distinction against the Muslim army, and with an arrow mortally wounded Abdullah, son of Abu Bakr. Soon after, however, when the Saqeef submitted to the Holy Prophet and accepted Islam, Abu Mihjan too became a Muslim and proved staunch in his new faith, except that he did not totally abjure drink and would now and then give in to the temptation. At the Battle of the Bridge, Abu Ubayd appointed him commander of the cavalry and he showed a great deal of courage in that battle. He was one of those who attacked and drove back the elephant which crushed Abu Ubayd to death.

MAP 7: QADISIYYA - 2ND DAY

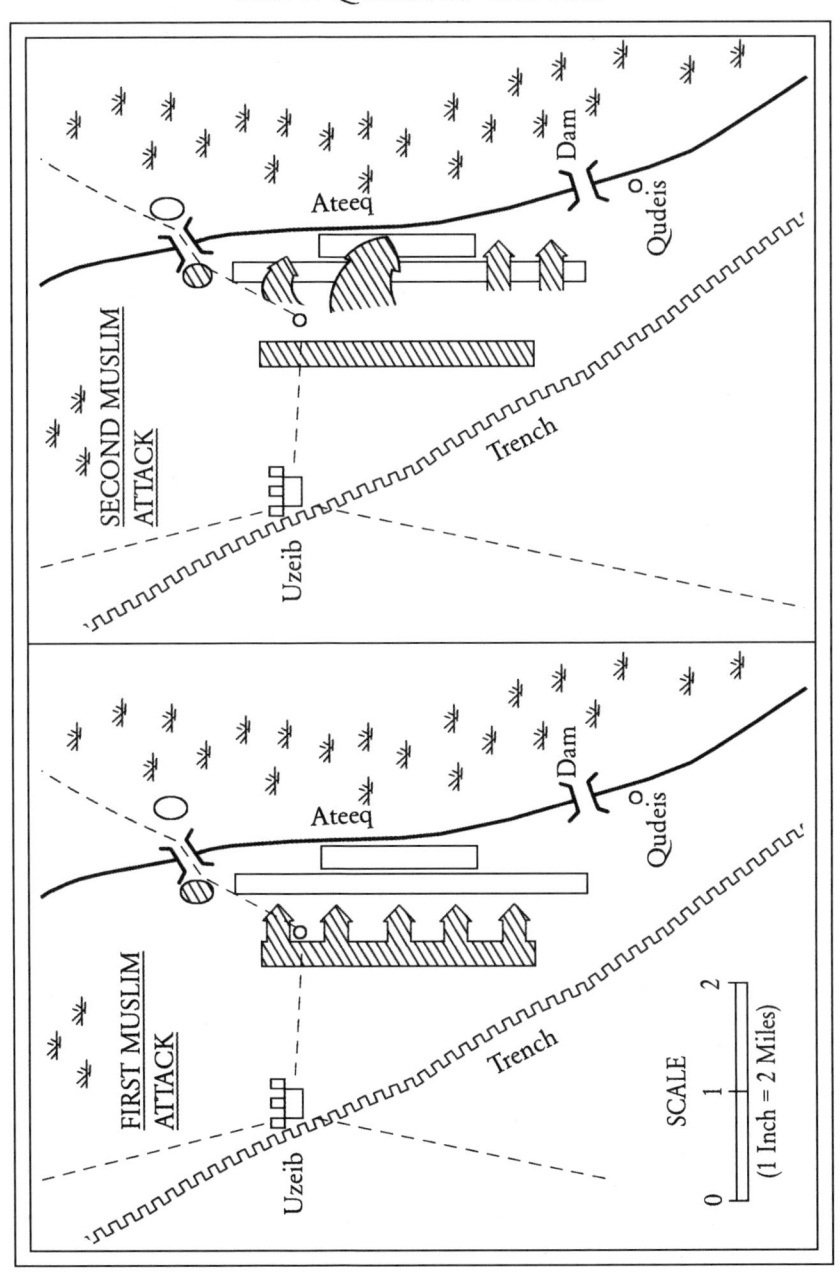

When Abu Ubayd's army disintegrated after the disaster of the bridge, Abu Mihjan stayed on with Muthana at Ulleis for a while and then returned to Madina. At Madina, Umar caught him drinking and exiled him to 'Baze', an island off the coast of the Yemen. We do not know what his sentence was, but shortly before the Battle of Qadisiyya, he was released and came on his own to join the army of Sa'd. In camp however, he drank again and Sa'd on discovering his offence, had him whipped and thrown into a cellar in fetters. And there he lay, hearing sounds of battle. Actually he could walk about the battlements of the castle if he wished to, because his door was not locked. And he yearned to be free and to fight and to satisfy his thirst for glory on the battlefield. He was a born soldier-brave, strong and wild; and he felt very sorry for himself.

The sun had set on the Day of Succour when Abu Mihjan decided to try his luck and plead for his freedom. With the irons restricting his movement, he slowly climbed the stairs to the top of the castle and made his way to where Sa'd lay on his cot. There he sought forgiveness, but Sa'd rebuked him severely and ordered him back to his cellar. Heartbroken at his repulse, he made his way to the floor of the castle and there met Sa'd's wife, Salma. Then it occurred to him that perhaps he could slip out to the battlefield without Sa'd being any the wiser for it.

"O Salma, O daughter of the people of Khasfa," he implored. "Are you inclined to be kind?"

"What is it?" she asked.

"Release me and let me borrow the piebald horse. By Allah I swear that if Allah protects me, I shall return to you and place my feet in the fetters."

"No, I shall not do that."

With his head, Abu Mihjan turned away and slowly dragged his feet towards his cellar. Then, within hearing of Salma, he put his anguish into extemporised verse:

It is sufficient sorrow when you see a cavalier deprived,
Abandoned, and bound in shackles.
When I stand, these irons detain me, trapped,
While others are fighting as if I were deaf to the call.
I was once a man with wealth and kinsmen,
But, have now been left entirely alone.

By Allah, I pledge a pledge which I shall not break:
If I am freed, I shall never visit the tavern again.

This was more than Salma could take. She rushed after him calling: "I seek the pleasure of Allah and accept your promise."

Hastily she released him from his fetters, and while he collected his weapons and prepared for the field, she went out, bridled the piebald and brought it round to the rear gate of the castle which opened on the trench. This magnificent horse belonged to Sa'd and was known by most soldiers in the army. Abu Mihjan came out through the gate and leapt on to the bare back of the piebald.

"Now do as you wish," said Salima,[142] and Abu Mihjan rode away in the bright moonlight.

Abu Mihjan left the castle like a schoolboy coming out school and dashing out to play, like a fierce and hungry tiger leaping out of his cage and seeking his prey. He galloped to the Muslim right, rode through the Muslim ranks and with a cry of "Allaho-Akbar," hurled himself at the Persian front where he killed a man. He galloped back to the rear of the Muslim army and then behind the Muslim ranks, appearing at the Muslim left where again he assaulted the Persian front and killed a man. Then he galloped along the front, between the two armies, thrilled at his freedom, on a horse which was no less thrilled to be in action.

Back and forth he rode between the two armies. Every now and then he would throw a challenge without revealing his name, and his challenge was accepted by many Persian champions, all of whom bit the dust at the end of the Muslim's terrible lance. And as if this were not enough, he even wrestled with some and threw them down. Several times he galloped round behind the Muslim army to reappear unexpectedly between the lines, swooping like an eagle and striking like a lion. Stalwarts like Qa'qa, Asim and Tuleiha had nothing to teach him, for he excelled all. And this went on for several hours while the rest of the warriors, Muslim and Christian, continued to fight as hard as their exhausted strength would permit.

The Muslims marvelled at the wondrous sight of Abu Minjan at war. Some asked, "Who is this warrior, the likes of whom we have never seen?" Others

---

[142] Tabari: vol. 3, p. 56; Masudi: Muruj; vol. 2, p. 323.

said, "He must be one of Hashim's men, came ahead of the rest, or perhaps Hashim himself." The reference was to the commander of the reinforcements from Syria, Hashim bin Utba bin Abi Waqqas, a famed warrior who had lost an eye at Yarmuk. Yet others remarked, "If the Prophet Khizr could take part in battle, this would be Khizr on the piebald. Perhaps Allah has favoured us with him."

Sa'd saw Abu Mihjan from his vantage point on the castle. The bright moonlight provided excellent visibility. Sa'd saw him fight and win, saw him ride about the battlefield and gallop past the foot of the castle behind the Muslim line, but was at a loss to understand what was going on. He muttered: "As for the horse, it is my horse. As for the attack, it is the attack of Abu Mihjan." Then he saw some more of the thrilling spectacle and again felt Perplexed. "By Allah," he said, "were not Abu Mihjan imprisoned, I would have sworn that this was Abu Mihjan and that was my piebald."[143]

This went on till midnight, when the two fronts separated and the fighting ceased. Then the cavalier returned promptly to the castle, led the horse to the stables, took off his weapons and armour and went back to his cell where be put his feet in the fetters.

A glow of pride warmed his heart. Feeling happy and contented, broke into verse:

Have you ever known the Saqeef without honour?
I am the finest of them with the sword;
And the richest of them in full coats of mail;
And the most steadfast of them when men quake in battle,
And I am their champion on every day. If you do not know, ask those who do.
On the night of Qadisiyya they did not know me or of my escape from prison to battlefield.
If now I am imprisoned, it is a test for me;

And if I am freed, I shall make the enemy taste of death.

Salma was listening at the door while Abu Mihjan recited poetry. When he stopped, she entered. "O Abu Mihjan," she asked warrior-poet, "for what reason did this man imprison you?" was still in a huff after the trouble she had had with Sa'd the day before and referred to her husband as "this man!"

---

[143] Tabari: vol. 3, p. 57; Masudi: Muruj; vol. 2, p. 324.

"By Allah," replied Abu Mihjan, "he did not imprison me for anything unlawful that I ate or drank, although I was fond of drink during the Ignorance. I am a poet. Verses slip from my lips to my tongue. He imprisoned me because I recited the verse:

When I am dead bury me by the root of the wine,
So my bones will satisfy their thirst for the juice.
Do not bury me in a desert, for I fear
That when I am dead I may never taste it again.
I shall slake my thirst with clear wine,
For I shall remain its slave even after death.[144]

Salma remained on not-speaking terms with Sa'd till after the battle was over. Then man and wife made peace and she told him the story of Abu Mihjaj. Sa'd at once released his prisoner. He sent for him and said, "By Allah, I shall never whip you again for drinking, after seeing what you have done."

"And I, by Allah," replied Abu Mihjan, "shall never drink again,"[145]

On this day arrived four swords and four horses which Caliph Umar had sent to Qadisiyya with instructions to Sa'd to distribute them among heroes. The swords went to Asim bin Amr of the Bani Tameem and to three warriors of the Bani Asad, including Tuleiha and Hammal bin Malik; the horses went to Qa'qa bin Amr and three stalwarts of the Bani Tameem.

After midnight, as the two armies settled down to rest in their camps after the labours of the day, Sa'd heard the hum of conversation which rose from the Muslim tents. He said to an attendant, "If our men keep talking, do not disturb

---

[144] The reader who is familiar with Persian poetry will notice the similarity between these lines and a quatrain attributed to Omar Khayyam by Edward Fitzgerald. In the original Persian of Omar khayyam, however, I have not found this quatrain, but it is known that Fitzgerald attributed many quatrains to Omar which the latter never wrote. Some of Fitzgerald's quatrains are in fact from Rumi and Hafiz.
[145] Tabari: vol. 3, p. 57; Balazuri: pp. 258 9; Masudi: Muruj; vol. 2, pp. 324-5. According to another version. Sa'd said, "Go I shall not again imprison you for what you say until you do it;" and Abu Mihjan replied, "By Allah, never again shall my tongue praise what is unclean."

me, for then they feel stronger than their enemy. But if they fall silent, awaken me because that would be bad."[146]

Then Sa'd bin Abi Waqqas, like the rest of his men, took a short, well-earned rest.

---

[146] Masudi: Muruj; vol. 2, p. 323.

Chapter 10: The Day of Hardship

There was little sleep during what remained of the night. Exhausted men collapsed in their tents. Persians and Muslims were so emotionally charged that to stay awake and talk of the bloody events of the past two days, seemed the natural thing to do. Many slept; many spent their time of rest in the recitation of prayers. Muslim and Christian, Zoroastrian and Pagan, prayed to God or to whatever they believed in for victory and an honourable end to the horrors of battle, especially such a battle as this. There was no slackening of courage and the mood of the two armies remained determined and hopeful: the Muslims inspired by religious faith and the Persians by imperial pride. The losses suffered were accepted as a fair price for the attainment of the objective. The Muslims had so far lost 2,500 men and the Persians 10,000. There is no record of the wounded, but they were dressed on the Muslim side by the women of the tribes and on the Persian side by trained surgeons.

Others rested, but not Qa'qa. If anyone deserved and needed a break, it was Qa'qa bin Amr, but he had no time to waste in resting. Soon after midnight, when the fighting ceased, he set off on his horse on the Arabian route to receive the remainder of his men whom he had left behind to follow his picked 100. Some distance from the battlefield he met the 600 men, organised them into groups of 100 and instructed them to approach the battlefield soon after sunrise in separate groups, one following the other, so that the Muslims and Persians would be led to believe that large Muslim forces were coming as reinforcements. He also left guides to await the arrival of Hashim and to advise him to make his appearance on the battlefield in a similar manner. Having made these various arrangements, Qa'qa returned to Qadisiyya, arriving there shortly after sunrise.

Rustam was more than relieved at the end of the second day of fighting. He had only just saved the army from annihilation, and having saved it, he had recovered his balance and his army was again in a very strong position. On the third day of battle he would seize the initiative and once more throw his elephants into action. The great war beasts and their equipment had been made fit for combat again. If the elephants achieved a little more success than before, there was no reason why he should not shatter the army of Islam. It was on a confident note that Rustam gave instructions for the morrow; and it was with grim determination that his brave soldiers prepared to execute his instructions.

As night turned to day and the Muslims rose from their morning prayers, everyone moved to battle positions. If the soldiers had too little rest, it was just too bad; there was just no more rest to be had. And as the two front lines re-established themselves, they saw in between a red carpet of corpses, nearly a mile wide, running along the entire length of the front. This was the harvest that the two armies had reaped in two days of bitter fighting, with as yet nothing to show for their labours.

Sa'd ordered the evacuation of the Muslim dead and let it be known that the dead could be buried unwashed and in their blood. The Muslim units pulled out their dead to behind their lines, whence groups specially detailed for the task took over the work of transporting the bodies to the graveyard where the women and children dug the graves and buried the martyrs. One cannot but admire the courage and fortitude of the women and children who, themselves bereaved, dug the graves and buried their own dear departed, - their fathers, their husbands, their sons. There was no time for formalities and condolences and expressions of grief.

The forming up was not complete when the elephants appeared through the Persian position and stopped in front of the army. They were positioned in the central and right corps, with none being left in the Persian left wing. On these animals rested the hopes of the Persians, and to ensure that the Muslims did not get at them, several rings of infantry were thrown around the elephants while their groups of cavalry were positioned a little in advance to protect the infantry. Thus, until the elephants were launched against specific objectives, they would be safe from Muslim attackers. The Persians planned to use their elephants in the attack closely supported by cavalry and infantry, but the elephant riders noticed a certain nervousness in their mounts. The elephants stayed calm and steady when accompanied by men, but if left alone, turned restive and ungovernable.

The arrival of the elephants completely surprised the Muslims and upset their plan of attack. They had believed that they had seen the last of the mighty beasts. Sa'd had intended to once again let his super camels loose against the Persian horse and give the Persians more of the same medicine, but the position of the elephants made this impossible. No camel, however fierce-looking, would advance against an elephant, and that plan would just have to be postponed or entirely shelved. The elephants, surrounded by infantry and preceded by cavalry, were invulnerable and could only be dealt with if they advanced and, in the heat of battle, offered openings. Thus the Muslims were forced to remain on the defensive, and this suited Rustam perfectly.

The Persian attack began at mid morning. Their first action was a storm of arrows let loose against the Muslims, which caused quite a bit of distress in the ranks of the believers. The fire was extremely accurate and to escape the salvoes, several groups of Muslims shifted position, and their ranks were split. The Muslim archers this morning did not prove very effective.

After this had gone on for some time, the leading ranks of the Persian army were set in motion. The elephants moved forward slowly, surrounded by infantry and protected by cavalry on the flanks, and as they got near the first Muslim line, which was composed of cavalry, the attacking infantry moved aside and let the elephants advance upon the Muslims. The effect on the Arab horse was again frightening and many of them broke out of control and panicked. Most riders, however, were able to control their mounts and either pulled back a short distance or moved aside to avoid the elephants. The result was a great deal of confused fighting along the whole front with the elephants charging the Muslim horse and foot, while their own cavalry and infantry were protecting their flanks. The elephants were trained to kill by goring or trampling their victims or picking them up in their trunks and dashing them to the ground; and to this painful fate many Muslims were subjected.

The Persian cavalry and infantry also attacked alongside the elephants and pressed hard against the Muslim army, although their success was not as great as that of the elephants. Fighting against their counterparts, the Muslims were able to inflict considerable damage on the Persian horse and foot, whose losses began to mount sharply, but against the elephants the Muslims found their counter measures ineffective. They could not out manoeuvre the elephants, could not outflank them, could not approach them from the rear, because of the protection which these animals enjoyed from their own soldiers. All that the Muslims could do was to try and pick off the elephant riders with arrows, but in this they had very limited success because of the pressure of Persian soldiers positioned on the flanks of the elephants.

In the face of the elephant advance, the Muslims were slowly pressed back, leaving hundreds of dead and wounded on the battlefield. Several gaps appeared in the Muslim front where warriors had shifted position or withdrawn or been thrown back by the Persians. The confusion increased and Muslim efforts became disjointed, and it was only the heroic labours of their chiefs and the tenacious courage of the rank and file which kept the Muslim army in battle order. The scales were slowly but surely turning in favour of Persia.

Rustam gloated over the success which his troops were gaining. The heavier losses which the Persians suffered were acceptable to him as long as victory was achieved; and victory was clearly in sight. He decided to hasten the process by getting the Muslim Commander-in-Chief, as the Muslims had tried to get him, and ordered a cavalry detachment to attack through a gap which was apparent in the Muslim centre and capture the castle of Uzeib, whereafter it would either kill Sa'd or take him alive. This detachment fought its way through what remained of Muslim resistance in the gap and on arriving at the castle, surrounded it. [See Map 8.]

But the Persians did not get enough time to do any harm to the occupants of the castle. Hardly had they established a ring around the castle when a Muslim cavalry group came to the rescue of their general. Because of their dispersion, the Persians were not in a strong position to fight a proper tactical action and the Muslim cavalry had no difficulty in driving the Persian horse away and back to the Persian position. After this no other Persian unit ventured near the castle of Uzeib.

Sa'd felt relieved as the menace of the Persian cavalry was lifted. But there was no relief from the agonising pressure of the Persian army against the Muslim front, which continued to weaken under the attacks of the Persians, particularly of the elephants. It was only a matter of time; a little more of this and the Muslim front would collapse, and the probable effect of this defeat on the cause of Islam was too horrible to imagine. The main problem was the elephants, especially the two great tuskers mentioned earlier: a scabby one and a white one, which stood in the Persian centre and right centre, respectively, and did the most damage. These animals were bigger and stronger than the rest, more warlike and better trained. They also acted as the leaders of the elephants and on their performance depended the behaviour of others of their kind. Most of the Muslims were terrified of these two, as though they were supernatural. Something would have to be done about the elephants, and if just these two huge monsters could be killed or driven away, the others would become less effective.

MAP 8: QADISIYYA - 3RD DAY

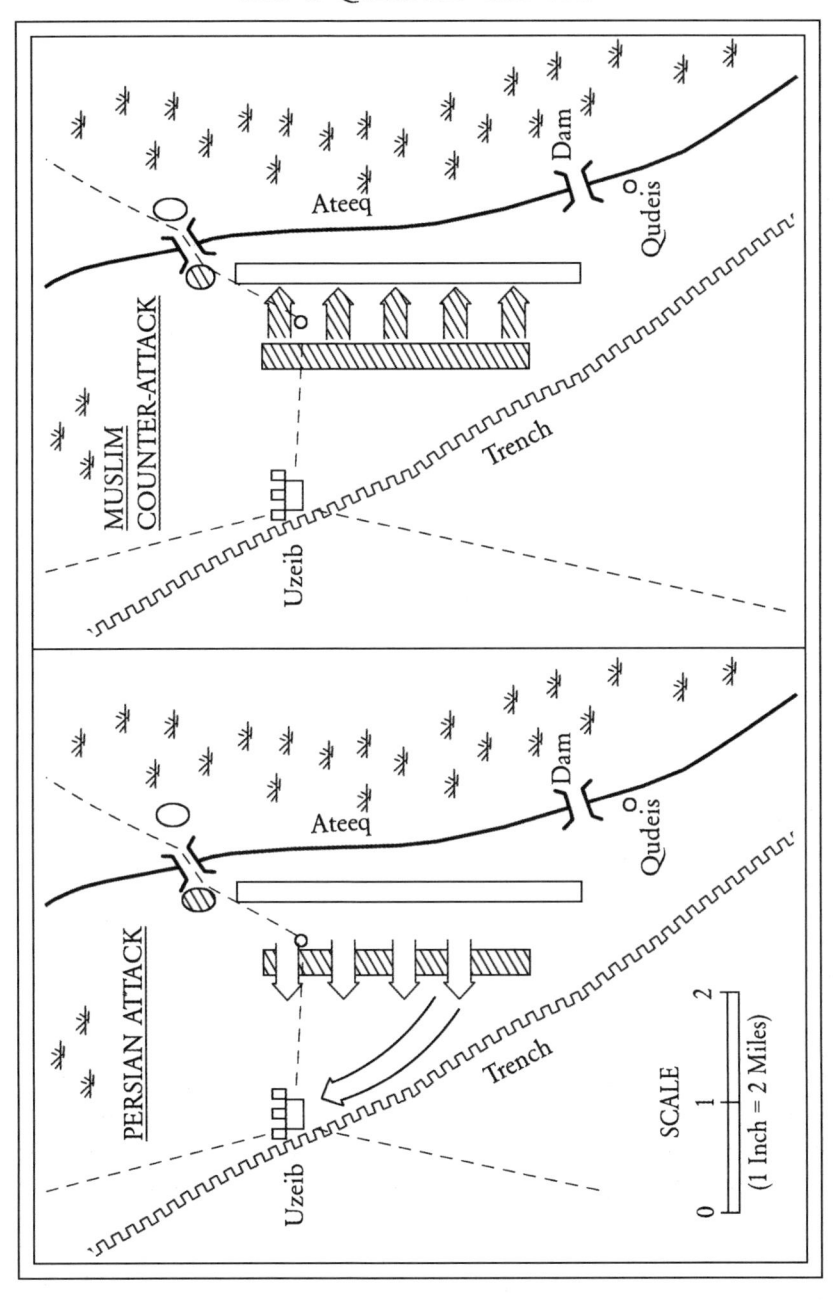

Sa'd sent for some Persian officers who had joined him during the preceding months, had accepted Islam, and were now serving in his army. He asked them what one did about elephants, and they told him that the most vulnerable parts of the elephant were the eyes and the trunk. If the elephant were blinded and his trunk severed, he would be helpless.

Sa'd next sent for two pairs of officers. The first to arrive in his presence were Qa'qa and Asim. "Save us from the white elephant!" said the general. No further instructions or elaboration were necessary, and the brothers walked away. The next to arrive were Hammal bin Malik and Ribbeel bin Amr of the Bani Asad, "Save us from the scabby elephant!"[147] These two also departed to carry out their mission. The four officers knew that on them depended the course of battle, and that there was no time to lose.

It was now midday and the pressure of the Persian attack was at its peak. All of Qa'qa's men from his Syrian contingent had arrived, coming in groups of 100, and a little later, Hashim bin Utba bin Abi Waqqas also joined the Muslim army with the remainder of his men-300, who moved immediately into the Muslim right wing as it was the closest to their route of arrival. The actual strength of reinforcements from Syria did not amount to much-only 1,000 but the psychological effect of their arrival was immense, especially because of the presence in this contingent of stalwarts like Qa'qa and Hashim and an [ex]apostate chief, named Qeis bin Hubeira bin Abd Yaghus of the Yemen.[148]

The first to go into action were Qa'qa and Asim. Taking a strong group of riders and foot soldiers from the Bani Tameem, they moved forward towards the white elephant. Qa'qa gave his plan in a few words before the men went in: they would surround the entire group around the white elephant; they would shout and shoot arrows at the elephant riders; they would close in on the Persian group with the sword from the flanks and rear; they would draw the attention of the Persians away from the front and create as much confusion as possible.

The Bani Tameem charged in with cries of "Allaho-Akbar," struck at the Persians who stood on the flanks of the white elephant and moved through the gaps created by their attack. Soon the Muslims were on the flanks and in the rear of the Persians, and then began their assault from three directions. No Muslims remained in front of this Persian group except for Qa'qa and Asim. In

---

[147] Tabari: vol. 3, p. 62
[148] This chieftain has also been referred to as Qeis bin Makshuh Al Muradi. The Bani Murad was a large and powerful tribe inhabiting the Yemen.

another few minutes all the Persians had concentrated on the flanks and the rear of the elephant to meet the attack of the Bani Tameem, and the front was left completely open. And now the two brothers, armed with long, slim javelin, advanced upon the champion beast which had played such havoc with the Muslim army.

They moved close enough for an accurate javelin throw. They could not move very close as they were on foot and if the elephant were to suddenly charge at them, they would have no hope of getting away. The brothers stopped, raised their javelins and poised for the throw. The elephant riders had their attention riveted to the flank and rear where the Bani Tameem were making a terrible noise, and were paying no attention to the front as there seemed to be no danger from this direction. And then the javelins of Qa'qa and Asim shot through the air as if thrown by a single arm, and pierced the eyes of the great white elephant, getting imbedded in the gigantic head.

With a scream of pain the elephant shook his massive form and all the riders came tumbling down. In a few seconds the brothers were upon them. Qa'qa first dealt with the elephant, delivering a powerful blow with his sword which completely severed the trunk. Then the brothers turned upon the fallen Persians and killed the entire lot of them.

Across the Muslim centre, Hammal and Ribbeel employed the same tactics and achieved the same success: the scabby elephant too was blinded and lost his trunk. And on the Muslim left, Amr bin Madi Karib, Father of the Bull, fought his own battle against the squadron of elephants deployed with the Persian right, which was doing the Muslim left considerable harm. Here too there was a leader elephant which caused the most concern and of which the Muslims seemed most afraid. Amr, although he did not receive any specific instructions from Sa'd, decided that something would have to be done about this elephant, and that he himself was the man to do it.

"I am attacking the elephant and those around it," he said to his men. "If you do not follow me, you will lose the Father of the Bull, but when you find me you will also find a sword in my hand." Having made this pronouncement, which was meant as a challenge to his followers, Amr drew his sword and plunged into the Persian ranks which stood around the elephant. Striking left and right, he was soon lost in the dust and in the Persians.

His men watching him disappear, felt ashamed and left out of combat. "What are you waiting for?" said one to his comrades. "If you lose him, you lose the champion of the Muslims!"[149]

The very next moment they attacked and drove into the Persian ranks which enveloped their chief. After some fierce close quarter fighting they got to him and saw him lying on the ground, wounded, with several dead Persians sprawled around him. One sat astride his chest and was about to deliver the final blow when the Muslims arrived, just in time to drive him away. Amr had not yet reached the elephant but was still conscious and held his sword firmly in his hand. They picked him up and brought his horse which he insisted on mounting again, although he had to be helped to the saddle. A little later the Father of the Bull would be back in action again.

Following this episode, the Muslim left attacked the elephants which by now had lost the protective screen with which they had started the day's operation. The manner and tactics of the Muslim attack in this sector are not known, but they succeeded in blinding and cutting off the trunks of several elephants, which brought the advance of the Persian right to a halt.

The blinding and mutilation of the elephants took the sting out of the Persian attack. The sightless monsters, their world turned to darkness and streams of blood gushing from their faces, screamed as if the devil had taken possession of them, and not knowing what to do nor understanding the reason for their agony, broke into violent movement. They rushed wherever their instincts led or misled them, from one part of the battlefield to another, breaking the ranks of Persians and Muslims, while the combatants momentarily stopped fighting to watch the dramatic suffering of the beasts. Wherever they went, they were pricked with spears to make them move on, and the elephants, maddened by their suffering but unable to retaliate against their tormentors, merely turned away from the source of pain and thumped along as fate guided them. The fearsome beasts, once a source of terror, were now turned into objects of pity- pathetic and helpless.

At last their instincts turned their mutilated heads in the right direction. They faced the Persians and for the last time broke into a run. They bulldozed their way through the Persian ranks, leaving wide trails behind them, and made for the river, followed by the other elephants. Arriving at the bank, unable to see or perhaps still guided by instinct, the leading elephants plunged into the Ateeq

---

[149] Tabari: vol. 3, p. 61.

and the others plunged in after them. How many of them reached the opposite bank is not known, but no elephant remained on the west bank.

Quite a few Persian soldiers, whose number is not known but was probably not large, joined the retreat of the elephants and jumped into the river, swimming to safety on the east bank. The bulk of the Persian army, however, remained on the battlefield and saw with sorrow the flight of its most powerful weapon of war, which also signified the departure of their best hopes. The pillar on which their hopes of victory rested had collapsed.

The effect of a shattering blow differs with the people upon whom it falls. Under its impact the courage of the weak vanishes and leaves them bereft of will and movement; but the courage of the brave hardens and is purified, and they gain the added stimulus of desperation. The Persian soldier took the loss of the elephants with stoic resolve and turned to meet his adversary, determined to fight on and to fight the Muslim army to a draw if not to victory. The Persian army speedily reformed its ranks and once again presented a solid front to the Muslims, who would soon learn that while the elephants were an aid to Persian victory, their absence did not mean a Persian defeat.

Sa'd saw in the flight of the elephants signs which any good general would see-signs of victory. To exploit his advantage, he ordered the attack and the Muslim front, the centre and the wings, moved forward to engage the Persians and push them into the river. The Persians were engaged, but refused to be pushed into the river. The two armies met with a thunderous clash of steel and muscle and brave men lost count of time as they struggled mightily in combat. It was a case of the irresistible force coming up against the immovable object.

Eventually, in the late afternoon, the irresistible force pulled back. Whether this was ordered by Sa'd or was an involuntary breaking of contact is not known. It may have been planned by Sa'd, for his next move was to order the dressed up camels to the front to repeat the stratagem of yesterday. These monstrous looking things moved up and made for a part of the Persian front where a large element of cavalry was positioned, hoping to once again frighten the life out of the Persian war horse. But it was no good. The war horse was either not deceived any longer or was better controlled by desperate men who were not going to be fooled a second time. The Persian horse stood his ground, and the camels returned crestfallen. The stratagem had failed.

But a victory had to be won, and Sa'd again put his warriors into motion, to attack, to pierce the Persian front, to break through the Persians or just wear them down until their resistance collapsed. Tired soldiers again raised their weapons-swords, spears and iron maces and the afternoon wore on, with the Muslims not relenting and the Persians not yielding, on a battlefield of which not one yard of ground remained where either horse or man did not stand or lie dead. The Muslims felt certain of victory but the Persians did not feel certain of defeat, and in the madness of combat the day ended - the hardest day of battle so far, on which both sides suffered equally in relation to their strength and neither could claim success. This day was to become known in history as "the Day of Hardship." The day ended, but not the fighting. Dusk fell, but the violent spasm continued.

Strange are the ways of Allah! One Muslim, named Shabr bin Alqama, a small thin man, went forward in response to the challenge of a large Persian. The Persian at once threw him, sat upon his chest and drew his dagger to cut the Muslim's throat. The reins of the Persian's horse were tied to the Persian's waist, and he was about to strike at the fallen Muslim when for some reason his horse shied and pulled away, dragging the Persian after him. The next instant the little Muslim leapt to his feet, drew his dagger, and fell upon the helpless Persian and killed him. He then stripped the dead soldier of his possessions- armour, weapons, fineries-and took it all to Sa'd, who gave it back to him as rightly his. After the battle he sold the booty for 12,000 dirhams. Strange, indeed, are the ways of Allah!

Chapter 11: The Night of Qadisiyya

There was to be no rest this night. Night came but not darkness, because there was a bright moon. The experience of battle was so harrowing that men were gripped by a kind of insanity, hypnotised by the prospect of destruction from which they could not recoil. So the fighting continued, with Muslim and Persian giving as well as they took and neither, although approaching total exhaustion, showing any weakening of resolve or flagging of spirit.

After a while there was a lull in the fighting, and Sa'd hoped that he would be able to re-establish some sort of control over the situation and get things better organised. He had no intention of allowing the Persians, or for that matter, his own men any peace this night, and was fully determined to slog away until victory was achieved. In sheer stamina the hardy Arab of the desert would outlast the more civilized Persian. Sa'd planned, however, to launch his attack according to a proper design, following a proper programme; but this was not to be. The Muslim contingents went into the assault on their own, without waiting for the orders of their Commander-in-Chief, or even his permission.

This was not so much a lull in the fighting as a lowering of frequency, and it had not lasted long before Qa'qa led the Bani Tameem into a fresh attack. Other contingents followed suit, each leader exhorting his tribe to be foremost in glory, and Sa'd could do nothing but accept philosophically the reports which his officers brought him about the various tribes going into action. Each time he would raise his hands in supplication and invoke God's blessings on the tribe in question.

The madness was upon them again. They were like too mighty bulls, pushing and heaving, with horns locked, neither willing nor able to disentangle them. Very soon the confusion became total, Sa'd and Rustam were both cut off from battle, both helpless spectators of a contest over which neither could exercise the slightest control. The hour of midnight came, and with it a maddened, bleeding world staggered into Sunday. And it was at this time that Sa'd thought he saw a glimmer of victory when an officer conveyed to him a verse which Qa'qa had just uttered:

We have slaughtered a nation and more; In fours and fiver and ones.[150]

---

[150] Tabari: vol. 3, p. 67.

But the hope was illusory, for no change was evident in the situation. And then even the flow of information ceased and both Commanders-in-Chief were left equally in the dark, with the control of battle decentralised to the level of the individual soldier, whom everything now depended.

All night, till the morning, the battle raged. Never again would such a night be lived in the Persian campaign. The shouts and screams of the combatants turned the night into a hell of sound. It was like a fantastic blacksmith's shop with steel striking steel; like a mad choral symphony in which no voice could be distinguished. This night was to become known as "the Night of Snarls."

Through the night the battle raged. In the excitement of combat men who were hungry and thirsty forgot their hunger and thirst; men who were tired forgot their fatigue. They were brave men - these Arabs and Persians - men who knew not fear and were now beyond fear. They knew that there could be life only in victory, that there could be no yielding. They gave no quarter and neither accepted nor received any. They could do nothing but cut and slash and stab and thrust. And so they struggled till daybreak-on the same battle lines as on the previous morning.

At sunrise again the fighting ceased and the belligerents found that for all their efforts and sufferings, neither side had gained or lost a yard of ground. This time it was not a case of the fighting being stopped; it just died down because the warriors were not able to go on. Without plans, without orders, the Muslims gradually disengaged and stepped back out of bow range [about a quarter of a mile], where they stopped, not knowing what to do. The Persian wall seemed impregnable. But they were too dazed, too tired to think. If some hoped that there would be a nice long rest during which their bloody limbs would be washed and dressed, their women would bring a drink of nice cold water and a meal of nice hot food, they were mistaken. With men like Qa'qa around, there could be no rest while there was good fighting to be enjoyed!

"The Night of Snarls" gave way to "the Night of Qadisiyya" It meant day, however, because among the Arabs the 24 hour day was called not day but night, and started at sunset, and the night preceded the day. It was the fourth day of battle and so far as the soldiers knew, might not be the last. The organisation of the two armies had none of the splendour and colour of the first day; their ranks were thinner, their lines dented, and the soldiers did not stand so erect or look so smart. But, as if propelled by fate, they waited for whatever was to happen, and what happened on the Muslim side was Qa'qa.

Qa'qa had not slept a wink for three nights, and if anyone had struggled harder and killed more enemies in this battle, historians have made no mention of him. But now Qa'qa drew his men to him and said, "There is defeat for the enemy after an hour if we start again. So be patient for an hour and then attack once more. Lo, victory springs from steadfastness; so choose steadfastness over grief.[151]

His words were carried to other tribal contingents and the other chiefs, knowing that Qa'qa would steal a march on them if he could, got their men prepared to start attacking again. Amr bin Mali Karib, Qeis bin Abd Yaehuc, Qeis bin Hubeira, Ash'as bin Qeis, Tuleiha, all spoke to their men in similar vein and the spirit of the officers, hardened by a determination to win, transmitted itself to the rank and file. Meanwhile Sa'd and Rustam were able to re-establish a degree of control over their corps, and while Rustam busied himself with putting his corps and regiments in order with a defensive posture, Sa'd began to plan his next attack. His control over the army was not sufficiently strong for him to give detailed orders; all he could do was to lay down directions of attack and this he did as follows: The Kinda and the Bajeela [under Ash'as and Jareer] - the strongest contingents in the Muslim right centre and right wing, respectively - would attack from the right and break through the Persian left flank; on the Muslim left Amr would similarly attack the Persian right flank; the rest of the army would attack frontally; the Muslim wings and centre would meet behind the Persian centre in a converging movement.

Qa'qa was the first to start when, in about the middle of the morning, he led his men against the Persian centre. He was followed by the rest of the Muslim regiments of the centre; and the last to go into action were the Muslim wings, which had to shift their position to engage the Persian flanks. Ash'as bin Qeis, leading 700 men of the Kinda, came up against a Turkish regiment which resisted stubbornly but was at last driven back from its position.

For some time the battle again degenerated into a butchery, and there were signs that it would be fought to a standstill with heavy losses to both sides; but now for the first time in the past 24 hours signs of weakness appeared in the Persian front. Their right under Hormuzan and the left centre were pushed back as a result of the flanking movement; but after withdrawing a short distance they reformed their ranks and stood their ground. And so the situation remained till about noon when Qa'qa pierced the Persian centre, and as the

---

[151] Tabari: vol. 3, p. 68.

Persians scattered before his regiment, made a dash for the Persian headquarters.

Rustam sat upon his throne and waited. He hoped that his army would be able to wear down the Muslims sufficiently for them to suspend their attack; but he also feared that the Muslim pressure was becoming well-nigh unbearable. He had sustained on his person many wounds and displayed an example of professional skill and personal courage which few generals could surpass. And then the sounds of fighting at the Persian centre came closer, and with these sounds came the dust storm.

The storm appeared in the west and blew eastwards. The trampling of tens of thousands of feet had raised a cloud of dust which hung over the battlefield as the belligerents fought in its shadow. Now the storm raised more dust and waves of it were blown in the faces of the Persians. The dust swirled around Persian and Muslim. The storm had assumed serious proportions by the time it reached Rustam, and it picked up the canopy which had been erected over his throne, carried it like a huge bird in the air and dropped it in the Ateeq.

Rustam, no longer under shelter, dismounted from his throne. He was alone. The last of his guards and his personal staff had been thrown into action. There was not an officer to talk to, not a messenger to carry his orders and bring him information, not an attendant to see to the needs of the top general of the empire. The Commander-in-Chief moved a short distance towards the rear, where a mule loaded with two saddle boxes carrying his personal possessions stood in unperturbed silence. Rustam sat on the earth on one side of the mule.

Qa'qa and his men stumbled upon the throne and found it unoccupied. They were at a loss to understand the disappearance of Rustam, but assumed that it would not be possible to find him. One Muslim, however, Hilal bin Ullafa,[152] moved on, looking for nothing in particular, and saw the mule without noticing Rustam. The dust had reduced visibility considerably, and Rustam too was unaware of the approach of any enemy. Hilal got to the mule and struck with his sword at the rope which held the saddle boxes across the top of the mule. The rope was cut and the boxes fell to the ground, one of them on top of Rustam.

It was only now that the Persian general realised his danger, and realised also that the battle of Qadisiyya was, for all purposes, over. He got up at once and

---

[152] Masudi (Muruj: vol 2, p. 325) calls him Hilal bin Alqama.

ran towards the river, while Hilal, hardly believing his luck at finding Rustam, gave chase. Rustam got to the bank and threw himself into the Ateeq, but the Muslim jumped in after him and brought him out on to the dry bank. Then, drawing his sword, he struck several vicious blows at the forehead and face of his victim, mutilating it almost beyond recognition. Next he dragged the corpse along the ground and threw it under the feet of the mule.

Hilal ascended the throne of the dead general and called to those Muslims who were within earshot: "By the Lord of the Kaba, I have killed Rustam. To me! To me!"[153]

Thus died the illustrious Rustam, shorn of dignity, at the hands of a common soldier. He deserved better. The Persian Army remained unaware of the death of Commander-in-Chief, and being unaware of its tragic loss, went on struggling against the attacking army. The storm passed, taking away the dust and clearing the air as if preparing the stage for the final bloody act in this drama. Yet the Persians held on grimly. Their army was actually very near collapse, but this collapse would come not from weakness or wearing down but from the high tension which had been generated by the fierce combat and which would suddenly snap.

It was early in the afternoon when the Muslims put in another determined attack. Qa'qa was already at the Persian headquarters and the Persian wings had been pressed back [See Map 9]. Now the army of Islam attacked as one man and the fighting reached its climax along the semi-circle in which the Persian army had been forced. The mood of the Persian soldier reached its peak as he put up a last heroic resistance. And then the Persian front broke into pieces.

The Persian centre collapsed, and the men fled in panic towards the river. The chained men, 15,000 at the start of battle, stumbled along to escape the pursuing Arabs, but both were so tired that the pursuers could move no faster than the pursued. These soldiers arrived at the bank of the Ateeq. Those who were in line with the dam began to cross the river, but not many had passed when the Muslim centre arrived to pounce upon their backs. The Persians were trapped between the river and the Muslims, and regarding the former as the lesser of the two evils, plunged into the water. The Muslims pricked with their long spears those of the Persians who were near the bank and they died of their wounds. The remainder, weighed down by their armour and chains, were

---

[153] Tabari: vol. 3, p. 69; Yaqubi: Tareekh; vol. 2, p. 145.

drowned in the river. Of the original 15,000 stalwarts who had bravely put on chains, not one survived the battle.

Jalinus, the commander of the Persian right centre, noticed the absence of orders from Rustam, at once assumed command of the Persian army and ordered a general withdrawal towards the dam. Picking a strong group of warriors, he himself made for the dam whence he drove away the Muslims who were there and threw a defensive arc around its western end to keep it safe for use. Towards this perimeter Persian units began to withdraw, and through it they crossed to safety. Troops of several Muslim contingents launched attacks to dislodge Jalinus, but the Persian rear guard held firm and repulsed all attacks. Meanwhile other Persian units were fleeing in other directions.

A large number of Persians, however, were unable or unwilling to retreat. Many had reached a stage of exhaustion where neither the body nor the spirit cared what happened, and the closing stages of this battle saw scenes at once tragic and heroic. More than 30 proud regiments of the imperial army refused to flee and preferred death to life. They were cut down to a man. One regiment actually dug its standard firmly in the ground so that there could be no question of removing it, and the men, having given up the struggle, sat around it, swearing that they would die by their standard. They did. The Muslims, seeing that victory was theirs, now brought up their last reserve of strength and put in a last ferocious attack with sword and dagger.

At length the vanquished who remained on the battlefield gave up even the pretence of resistance. There was nothing left in them, not even a desire to live. Often a Muslim would beckon to a Persian to come to him, and the Persian would come and stand still to be killed. And sometimes a Muslim would stretch his hand, take the Persian's weapon and kill him with his own weapon.

MAP 9: QADISIYYA - 4TH DAY

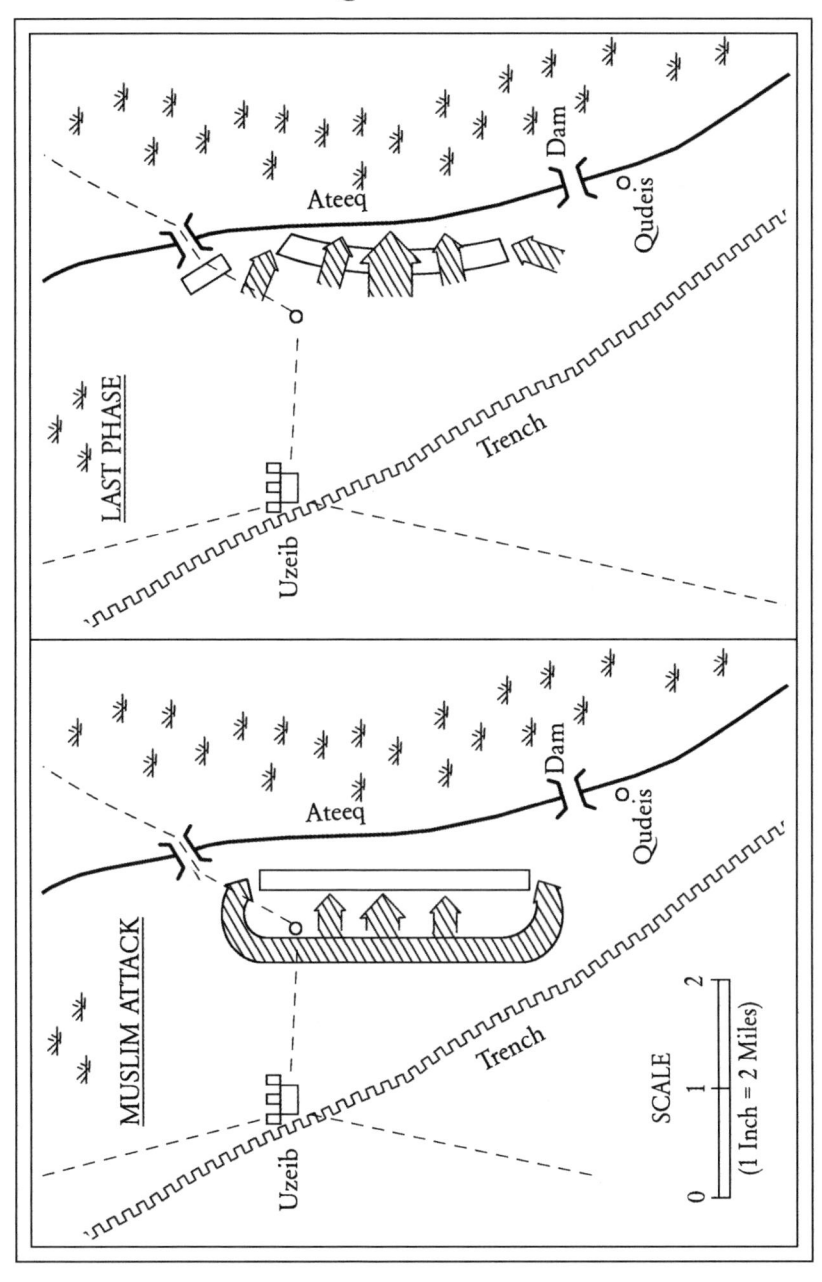

In the savagery of this battle, the quality of mercy was the first casualty.

The human body and the human spirit possess reserves of strength and courage which are seldom taxed to their full capacity. But there are moments when these reserves are exploited; in flight, or in the defence of pride or honour, or in the pursuit of a fleeing foe. Soldiers, exhausted from long days of fighting and believing that they can go on no longer, often go on fighting and are surprised, at their own ability to bear pain and hardship. And now these resources of strength and courage were once again tapped.

Sa'd was a very hard taskmaster and possessed a sternness of character which would later get him into trouble with the Caliph. He was also a good judge of how far men could be driven. He sent immediate orders for Zuhra to move after the withdrawing Persians and pursue them on the road to Najaf. Zuhra, who had commanded the Muslim right centre in battle, picked three hundred of his toughest horsemen and made for the dam. There were not many more left with him in fit condition for a fast-moving operation.

Meanwhile Jalinus had done a commendable job under extremely adverse conditions, getting the remnants of the Persians across the dam to safety. And all this time Hormuzan had stood at the bridge over the main road to Najaf, supervising similar operations. Not too many Persians came to the dam, but those who did, safely got across; and when no Persians remained in sight, Jalinus destroyed the dam and moved upstream along the east bank of the Ateeq. Arriving at the bridge, he took charge of operations from Hormuzan.

Zuhra got to the dam and found it destroyed. There was no trace of any organised Persian force across the river. Intending to give Jalinus no time to reorganise his army for another battle, Zuhra jumped his horse into the river and followed by his three hundred riders, swam across to the east bank. Then he rode along the bank and caught up with Jalinus at the bridge. Here a short action was fought in which Jalinus repulsed the Muslim attack. The bulk of the Persian survivors had already gone up towards Najaf and Jalinus kept with him a body of cavalry, whose strength is not know, to deter and delay pursuit by the Muslims. After a short while Jalinus broke contact and retreated northwards at a fast pace, leaving the bridge intact. Zuhra followed, determined not to let his quarry out of sight.

And so pursuer and pursued moved towards Najaf, both suffering from exhaustion and yet wary of the tricks that the other might play. The Persian horse went past Kharara while the foot soldiers either dispersed or were cut down by Zuhra. About halfway between Kharara and Seilahun, Jalinus turned at bay. There was still plenty of fight left in him and he could think of no better way of discouraging a Muslim pursuit than by killing the commander of the pursuit column. And there was no more chivalrous way of killing the Muslim commander than by doing it himself. Further retreat like a hunted animal was foreign to his gallant nature, and he decided that now was the moment to end the action, once and for all, either in death or in glory. Throwing his cavalry hastily into battle position, Jaliaus rode forward and threw a challenge for single combat with the Muslim commander. From the Muslim front Zuhra emerged.

Two very tired generals fought a duel; and the noble Jalinus met his death at the hands of an equally noble opponent.

As Jalinus fell, the Persians turned and fled, closely followed by the Muslims. The pursuit continued up to Najaf, and all the way large numbers of stragglers were killed by Zuhra's riders. Najaf was reached after sunset and a little later, as night fell, Zuhra turned about and led his column back, marching all night and arriving at Qadisiyya shortly before dawn.

Soon after the departure of Zuhra in pursuit of Jalinus, Sa'd had sent two other columns to pursue scattered parties of Persians. One, under Shurahbeel bin As-Samt, was sent north and the other, under Qa'qa, was sent south. The two columns moved out on horseback. Many stragglers were overtaken in the villages through which these columns passed and all were at once despatched. The columns were back in camp by nightfall.

A strange calm descended upon the battlefield. Where there had been a storm of noise and a hurricane of movement for four action-packed days, there was now silence and stillness. The declining sun looked down upon a scene of desolation and carnage which few battles have produced in history. What had appeared an endless nightmare to the soldiers had at last ended, leaving nightmarish evidence of its passing.

All over the plain the dead lay where they had fallen, alone and in heaps, their sightless eyes staring at the infinity of death. Bodies of Muslims, Zoroastrians, Pagans, lay entangled in a last terrible embrace from which none could separate, no longer Arab and Persian but just broken, twisted, mutilated bodies, lying in grotesque shapes and postures. In death they bore witness that they had been brave men and had laid down their lives for a cause which for them was more important than life; and their broken swords and lances paid eloquent tribute to their valour. The only sound which disturbed the stillness was the groans of the wounded.

Then suddenly other, less warlike sounds were heard on the battlefield - sounds of women and children who rushed up from the Muslim camps. They came with waterskins and rough bandages to slake the thirst and alleviate the pain of the Muslim wounded. They also put an end to the sufferings of the Persian wounded, though in less merciful ways![154]

A total of 6,000 Muslims died in battle and few were those who did not carry wounds on their persons.[155] All the martyrs were buried in the valley of Musharraq, in crude graves hastily prepared for them. The number of Persian casualties is not accurately recorded. We are told that the 15,000 chained men were all killed and on just the last day 10,000 Persians lost their lives,[156] excluding the chained men.[157] Since 10,000 are believed to have died during the first two days of fighting, a fair estimate would place the Persian casualties at not less than 40,000, i.e. two-thirds of the entire army. Many of the top generals had fallen with honour on the battlefield: Rustam, Bahman, Beerzan, Jalinus, as also others less well known. Some able ones survived to fight another day: Hormuzan, Qarin, Khusrau Shanum.

When Sa'd heard that Rustam had been killed by Hilal bin Ullafa, he sent for the man and questioned him about the Persian Commander-in-Chief. Hilal told him that he had left the general's body under the feet of the mule not far from the place where Rustam's throne had stood. On Sa'd's orders Hilal went and brought the body of Rustam, on which were found a hundred wounds from sword and spear.[158] All the possessions of the slain general were awarded to Hilal who sold them for 70,000 dirhams, [Just the cap of Rustam, as a general of the highest rank in the empire, was worth 100,000 dirhams.]

The booty taken at Qadisiyya was vast. Khalid bin Urfuta, Sa'd's deputy commander in battle, was placed in charge of the spoils and everything was properly collected and accounted for. After detaching one-fifth of the spoils for Madina as the share of the state, the remainder was distributed among the

---

[154] Tabari: vol. 3, p. 82.
[155] Tabari: vol. 3, p. 69. There is some doubt about this figure. According to conflicting versions, it could have been 5,000 or 8,500, but the figure which I have given is generally accepted as correct.
[156] Tabari: vol. 3, p. 69.
[157] Masudi: Muruj: vol. 2, p. 328.
[158] Dinawari: p. 122; Balazuri: p. 259.

soldiers. Infantrymen received 7,000 dirhams each and cavalrymen 14,000.[159] The Dirafsh-e-Kavian, the fabulous standard of the Sasanis, made of tiger skin and covered with pearls and sapphires and other gems,[160] was taken by and consequently awarded to Zarrar bin Al Khattab [no relation of Umar], and was sold by him for 30,000 dirhams. Actually its worth, according to one estimate, was 1,200,000,[161] and according to another, 2,200,000.[162] The four sons of the old woman mentioned in an earlier chapter, returned safe and sound to their mother, having earned the admiration of their fellow men in battle, and laid at her feet their share of the spoils, which she happily returned to them, regarding her own sons as her greatest treasure.

The blood had not dried on the plain of Qadisiyya when Sa'd wrote a letter to the Caliph:

Lo, Allah has given us victory over the Persians after a long battle and a terrible earthquake. The Muslims met numbers, such as chroniclers have not heard of, but their numbers proved of no use to them, and Allah gave their possessions to the Muslims. And the Muslims pursued them over rivers and across strongholds and along narrow paths.[163]

He also gave an account of the casualties and mentioned some of the better known of the dead. He then sent for Sa'd bin Umeila of the Bani Fazara, a clan of the tribe of Ghatfan living north of Madina, and instructed him to proceed with all speed to Madina, deliver the letter to the Caliph and tell him all that he knew about the battle. The battle having just ended, others could just fall to the ground where they stood and rest and sleep as long as they wished, but not Sa'd bin Umeila. There was no time for him to rest. He would have to set off straightaway on the desert road to Madina, bearing tidings of victory.

The courier accepted the commander's letter, saddled a fast camel, hastily collected provisions for the journey and took the first step in a journey of a thousand miles.

The journey to Madina would normally take 3 to 4 weeks, depending upon the purpose of the journey and the endurance of the traveller. It is not known how long the courier took to cover the distance, but at last he arrived in sight of the

---

[159] Yaqubi: Tareekh: vol. 2, p. 145.
[160] Masudi: Muruj: vol. 2, p. 328.
[161] Tabari: vol. 3, p. 69.
[162] Masudi: Muruj: vol. 2, p. 328.
[163] Tabari: vol. 3, p. 84.

Muslim capital. Exhausted from his long journey along the sandy road across some of the most desolate desert country in the world, for he had not spared himself, he found the sight of the Prophet's city refreshing. He urged his tired camel on, anxious to complete his mission.

When about 2 miles from Madina, the courier came upon a man sitting by the roadside who stood up at the approach of the camel rider. He was a very tall and broad-shouldered man with a powerful physique and a strong, intelligent face. Yet he wore a long coarse shirt of the cheapest material, patched in several places. There was something contradictory about the man. He was dressed like a beggar but there was nothing beggar-like about him. The rider did not know that this man had for the past several weeks walked every morning to this spot, watched the road to Iraq expectantly and then returned to Madina at noon.

"From where do you come?" asked the tall man.
"From Iraq," replied Sa'd bin Umeila.
The face of the tall man lit up. "O slave of Allah," he said, "tell me all."
"Allah has given the Muslims victory, and the Persians are defeated!"

The tall man was beside himself with joy. "Glory be to Allah!" he exclaimed and repeated the words several times. And since the camel rider had not stopped his mount, being eager to get to Madina and see the Caliph rather than waste time talking to a man who probably had nothing better to do, the tall man fell in beside him and kept pace with the courier at a steady jog.

The rest of the journey passed quickly, with the rider giving an account of the Battle of Qadisiyya and the tall man throwing in questions to keep him going. Sa'd bin Umeila noticed that the man was about 50, and that the hair was thinning on his large head, yet he ran as if a two-mile run was something he would do every day for the fun of it. There was something definitely unusual about the man: the physique of a powerful warrior, the personality of a forceful leader and the clothes of a wretched beggar. The two went on.

They entered Madina. At once a crowd gathered around them. No one knew Sa'd bin Umeila but they all seemed to know the tall man. They hailed him: "Peace be upon you, O Commander of the Faithful!" And again: "Peace be upon you, O Commander of the Faithful!"

At last the courier knew who his companion was. He turned in amazement to the tall man. "Glory be to Allah, and may Allah bless you," he said. "Why did you not tell me that you were Commander of the Faithful?"

"My brother," replied Caliph Umar, "you are not to blame."[164]

---

[164] Tabari: vol. 3, p. 84; Dinawari: p. 124.

Chapter 12: On the Ctesiphon

We go back a few years in history. The Truce of Hudaybiyah was signed in Zul; Qada, 6 Hijri, between the Holy Prophet and the unbelieving Qureish of Mecca, according to which there would be no hostilities between the two parties for 10 years. Having ensured peace with the nearest enemies of Islam, the Prophet turned his attention to neighbouring lands. In Muharram, 7 Hijri, he wrote to the kings of these lands, inviting them to join the new faith, and sent the letters with envoys. Recipients of the Prophet's call included the Roman Emperor, the Negus of Ethipoia and Chosroes Parwez of Persia.

The letter to Parwez was carried by Abdullah bin Hudhafa and read as follows:

> In the name of Allah, the Beneficent, the Merciful. From Muhammad, Messenger of Allah, to Chosroes, the Lord of Persia. Peace be upon whoever follows the Guidance and believes in Allah and His Prophet, and whoever bears witness that there is none worthy of worship except Allah and that I am the Apostle of Allah to all mankind, sent to warn all who live. Accept Islam and be at peace. And if you refuse, then upon you will die the sin of the Zoroastrians.[165]

The emissary of the Prophet delivered the message at Ctesiphon and it was translated to the Emperor by an interpreter. When the interpreter stopped, Parwez took the letter and tore it to pieces. Abdullah returned to Madina and described to the Prophet how his letter had been torn up, whereupon the Prophet remarked: "His empire will also be torn up."[166]

The empire was now being torn up, as predicted by the Prophet 9 years before, and it was the Muslim army of Sa'd bin Abi Waqqas, that was doing the job. It had shattered at Qadisiyya an army which would be the pride of any empire and which would grace any battlefield in the world. Sa'd had won a great and terrible victory, paying a price in Muslim blood such as had never been paid before by the believers in the 15-year history of Islam. He should have expected to relax for a while and enjoy the post-victory glow of pride, along with his dauntless warriors, but much of the feeling of triumph was spoiled by some petty-minded officers in the army. These fellows, many of them simple souls to whom the ideal commander was one who drew his sword and physically and

---

[165] Tabari: vol. 2, p. 295.
[166] Ibid: Ibn Sad: p. 248.

literally led his men in battle, held against Sa'd the fact of his confinement to the cot in the castle of Uzeib.

Jareer bin Abdullah, getting into a poetic mood, said:

I am Jareer and my name is Abu Amr.
Allah helped me in battle,
While Sa'd sat on his cot in the castle.

Jareer was no one to pass nasty remarks about others because his own tribe of Bajeela was the first to break under the Persian elephant attack at the start of battle and had to be helped out by the Bani Asad. Thereafter the performance of the tribe had not been in the same class as that of the Bani Asad, the Bani Tameem, and the Yemenis under the Father of the Bull. So Sa'd paid back in the same coin. He composed some verses of his own and passed them around the army:

What more can the Bajeela hope than that I
Should defer their reward till the Day of Reckoning?
In their courtyard the cavalry moved to advance,
Its glitter the glitter of troops of camels.
Their cavalry clashed with the enemy's horse,
And their horsemen stood under a cloud of blows.
But you would have been like porters persevering in falsehood
Had it not been for the men of Qa'qa bin Amr.
They protected you with spear-thrusts and the blows
Of swords which split the skin.
But for them you would have turned into sheep,
And your regiment would have shrivelled like flies.[167]

This silenced Jareer and the Bajeela, and Sa'd, to leave no doubt in the minds of his men about the real cause of his remaining in the castle during battle, showed his boils to representatives of all regiments. This earned him the goodwill and sympathy of the entire army which was not unmindful of the fact that the record of Sa'd bin Abi Waqqas showed that he was one of the bravest of the Muslims. But another anti-Sa'd verse was going round the army:

We fought until Allah gave us victory,
While Sa'd sat secure at the gate of Qadisiyya

---

[167] Tabari: vol. 3, pp. 79-82.

In conjugal bliss. Many women were widowed
In battle, but not the women of Sa'd.[168]

According to one report, this verse was said while the battle was on and came to Sa'd's attention. Sa'd at once prayed: "O Lord, if what he says be false, save me from his tongue and his hands."[169]

The author of the verse was fighting in the front line when suddenly a Persian arrow struck him in the mouth and pierced his tongue. He survived the wound, but never spoke again while he lived.

In later years, when the conquests of Islam had spread far beyond the borders of Arabia, Caliph Umar wrote to a certain person who was acknowledged as a leading scholar of the time, and asked for a description of the lands under Muslim rule. The scholar replied:

"Know, O Commander of the Faithful, that Allah Most High has divided the earth into regions: the east, the west, the north, the south. The region which is easternmost and cleaves to the place of the rising of the sun, is distasteful because of its burning and the fire and heat, and it burns those who enter it. The region which is westernmost also harms its inhabitants in proportion to the harm which comes to those who go to the eastern extreme. The region which is northernmost harms by its cold and ice, causes calamities to the body and leaves a heritage of sorrow. And whoever goes southernmost is burned by the heat and suffers at the hands of wild creatures. For this reason, all habitation on earth has gathered in a pleasant part which offers moderation, and has chosen as its share the best of regions. I shall now describe, O Commander of the Faithful, the part of the world which is inhabited by mankind."

The scholar described some of the countries which were under Muslim rule. Then he came to Iraq:

"As for Iraq, it is the light-house of the east. It is the navel of the earth and its heart. Into it flow all the rivers; in it meets all brightness and beauty, and in it is every kind of balance. The tempers of its people are purified, their understanding refined, their imagination sharpened. Their cunning becomes powerful, their intelligence strong, their judgement clear.

---

[168] Ibid: p. 79.
[169] Ibid: p. 81.

The heart of the world is Iraq, and it has been so since ancient times. It is the gateway of the east and the path of light. Its people have moderate colouring, pure fancies, superior temperaments, calm dispositions; and they possess all the virtues. Its charms are plentiful: its purity of atmosphere, its fine breezes, its sweet water and the pleasantness of life in it.

Know, O Commander of the Faithful, that Allah Most High divided the earth into parts and made some superior to others; and the best part is Iraq, for it is the prince of lands and has been inhabited by generations of gifted nations."

Umar also asked Kab, the Rabbi, for a similar description. Kab had once been one of the prominent doctors of the Jews but became a Muslim in Umar's time. He said to Umar:

"O Commander of the Faithful, when Allah created things, he joined one with another. Wealth said, "I shall go to Syria;" and Mischief added, "And I with you." Bounty said, "I shall go to Egypt;" and Disgrace added, "And I with you." Poverty said. "I shall go to the Hijaz;" and Contentment added, "And I with you." Distress said, "I shall go to the desert;" and Health added, "And I with you." Intelligence said, "I shall go to Iraq;" and Learning added, "And I with you."[170]

The Muslims had already entered this land of intelligence and learning, but now they would advance deeper into it. Sa'd had an army of about 20,000 men,[171] which he reorganised in five corps, and two weeks after Qadisiyya he started an advance which had as its objective the Persian capital, Ctesiphon, known to the Muslims as Madain. The advance would be carried out in stages with an advance guard marching ahead of the army by a day or two days' march, and stopping at the end of each stage for the rest of the army to close up. The corps of Zuhra bin Al Hawiyya formed the advance guard and was given as its first bound the region of Najaf and what is now Kufa, which would be used as a base for the crossing of the Euphrates and thrusting deeper into the Suwad. Other corps would follow in the order of march: Abdullah bin Mut'am, Shurahbeel bin As-Samt, Hashim bin Utba and Khalid bin Urfuta. The corps were well mounted and well armed, having put into use the thousands of Persian horses and the countless number of Persian weapons captured at Qadisiyya. In fact the entire army was now horse-mounted.

---

[170] Masudi: Muruj: vol. 2, pp. 61-65.
[171] This is an estimate, subtracting 6,000 dead from the original 30,000 with whom he fought Qadisiyya, and allowing for some who would be too badly wounded to indulge in warfare yet.

Zuhra got to the area north of Najaf and occupied it. Other corps moved up and joined him. And then Sa'd gave Zuhra the order to cross the Euphrates and head for Ctesiphon. He was certain that opposition would be met on the way, and was fully prepared to deal with it.

The defeat at Qadisiyya shook the empire of the Chosroes to its foundations. The more thoughtful ones among the Persians must have been reminded of darker moments in their history when their war against the Romans had gone badly and the Romans had knocked at the gates of Ctesiphon. It would be a very long time before the empire recovered from such a defeat, if it recovered at all, and the more clear-headed Persians should have seen the writing on the wall. Perhaps they did, but the military organisation of Persia was not concerned with writings on the wall. It acted with characteristic efficiency and resilience to deal with the Muslim threat to Ctesiphon.

The Battle of Qadisiyya had not yet ended when Yazdjurd sent a body of reinforcements under Nakheer Jan, to augment the strength of Rustam. Nakheer Jan was still east of the Euphrates when he received reports of the disaster of Qadisiyya. He halted his advance and decided to await further orders from the Emperor, meanwhile stopping all Persian survivors who were fleeing northwards and pressing them into his own regiments for further operations.

Yazdjurd and his advisers clearly foresaw the Muslim advance upon Ctesiphon and set about collecting more forces for the defence of the ancient capital. Feerzan, who was once a rival of Rustam and has been mentioned in an earlier chapter, was charged with the mission of preventing or delaying the Muslim advance, and this general at once took over the front from Nakheer Jan. It might not be possible to totally prevent the Muslims from reaching Ctesiphon, but Feerzan selected a series of positions, each on a river or canal, on which a rear guard action could be fought, which would have the effect of delaying the advance of the Muslims and gaining more time for preparing the defences of Ctesiphon, where military engines were being assembled and a great ditch being dug around the western arc of the city.

The first position chosen by Feerzan was at Burs, a few miles south of Babylon on the west side of the Hilla branch of the Euphrates [See Map 10]. Busbuhra, the Persian mayor of Burs, was given a small force to fight on the river line while the bulk of the army, consisting partly of fresh contingents and partly of the remnants of Rustam's army, was positioned at Babylon, east of the river, beside the ruins of the ancient city.

It was at Burs that Zuhra first contacted the Persians and immediately deployed for battle. A short engagement was fought here between the Muslim advance guard and the Persian rearguard in which Zuhra and Busbuhra faced each other in single combat. Zuhra wounded the Persian officer with his spear, but the Persian was able to get away from combat, and soon after this duel the Persian rearguard retreated across the river and rejoined the main body at Babylon. In Babylon, Bushbura died of his wounds.

Following the defeat of the Persians at Burs, the mayor of the district of Burs, an officer named Bastam, approached Zuhra with an offer of peace which was accepted. The Persian administration under Bastam agreed to help the Muslims in every possible way, including constructing bridges for them and providing information about Persian forces. It was from Bastam that Zuhra came to know the details of the Persian strength and position at Babylon and the presence there of the generals: Feerzan, Hormuzan, Mihran and Nakheer Jan.

It was now about the middle of Zul Qada, 15 Hijri [middle of December, 636]. Zuhra wrote to Sa'd, who was still in the area north of Najaf, and gave him all the information which he had received from Bastam regarding the strong Persian position at Babylon. Over the next few days the rest of the Muslim army moved up to join the advance guard.

Then Sa'd pushed Zuhra forward to contact the Persians, and Zuhra's corps, followed by the others in the same order of march as before, advanced to Babylon where the army deployed in front of the Persian army lined up for battle. Some time in the third week of December was fought the second Battle of Babylon [the first being Muthana's against Hormuz].

MAP 10: THE ADVANCE TO CTESIPHON

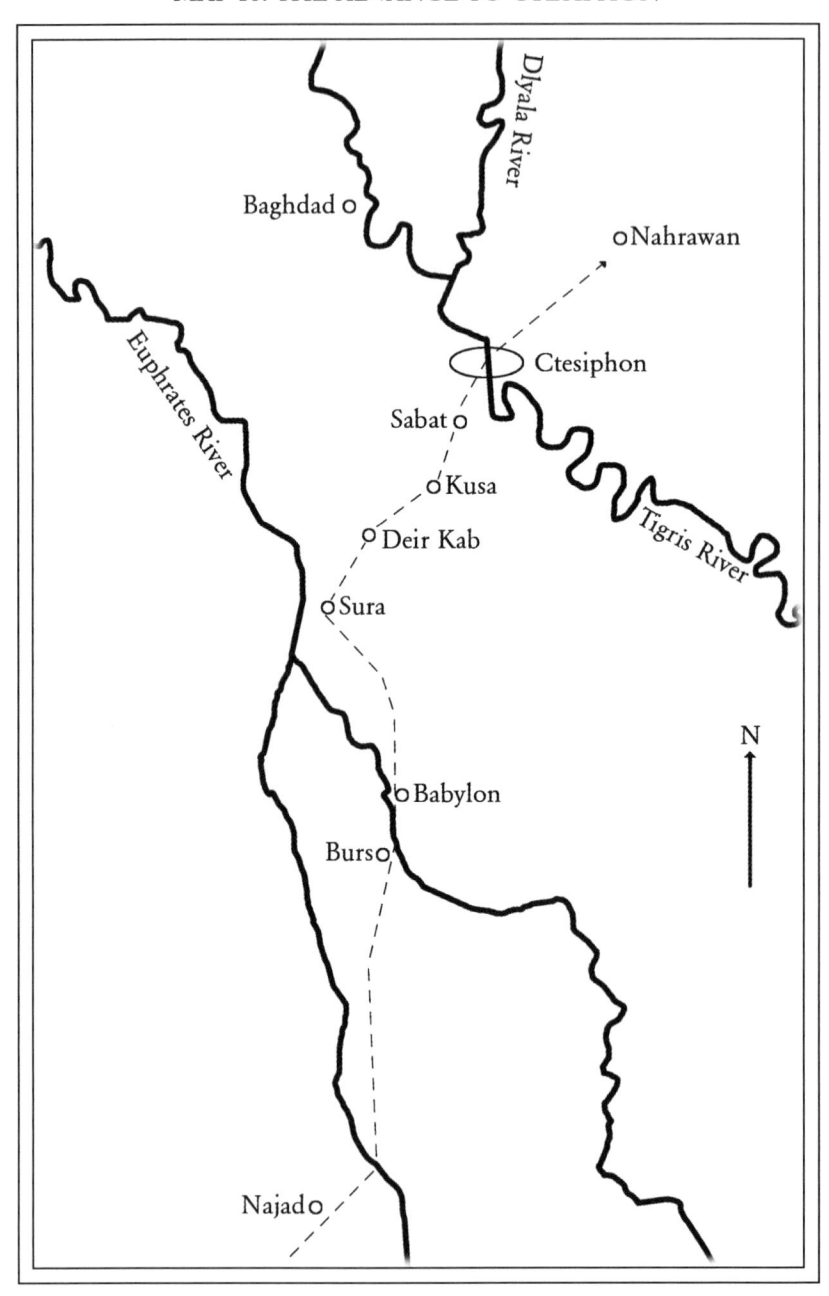

Feerzan had intended to fight a major action here because the river at Babylon was the largest between the Euphrates and the Tigris. He had therefore deployed in considerable strength for a set-piece action and hoped to totally repulse the Muslim attack and discourage any further advance by the invaders. But this was not to be. While the details of the Battle of Babylon are not known, the Persians were again defeated by the Muslims and retreated in good order from the battlefield. Hormuzan, with a large detachment of the army, withdrew south-eastwards to Ahwaz; [it is not known whether this move was on the orders of Feerzan or on his own initiative]; and the remainder of the Persian army withdrew northwards. Feerzan left one detachment at Sura and another at Deir Kab, with instructions to delay the Muslim advance as long as possible, and with the rest of his army took up another position for battle at Kusa.

Zuhra followed the retreating Persians and caught up with the rearguard at Sura, which was a little east of the main branch of the Euphrates, near the Musaiyib of today. The Persian position was on the canal of Sura, but after a short clash their resistance was broken and they were forced to withdraw to Deir Kab, where they joined the other detachment already positioned by Feerzan.

Two days later Zuhra again made contact with the Persians, this time of Deir Kab, on the bank of a canal, and found the Persian position stronger than at Sura. The Persian general Nakheer Jan was in command here, and at the very start of the engagement rode forward and threw a challenge for single combat. From the Muslim side Zuheir bin Suleim rode up in response to the challenge and after an exciting duel, killed the Persian commander. The Persian rearguard continued to resist and fighting became more severe as the Muslim advance guard pressed its attack. Jareer bin Abdullah was able to move round the Persian flank and get to the bridge, which led to some fierce fighting, but soon after this the Persians broke contact and retreated towards Kusa. As the rearguard arrived at this last position before Ctesiphon, Feerzan left a sizable detachment with a general named Shahryar to delay the Muslims, and marched off with what remained of his army to Ctesiphon.

Another few days passed and Zuhra again faced the Persians, with his corps deployed for action against the imperial rearguard, which was arrayed at the forward edge of Kusa, a small town about ten miles short of Ctesiphon. The Persian commander, Shahryar, a huge man – "like a camel"[172]- more arrogant

---

[172] Tabari: vol. 3, p. 115.

than he should have been at this stage of the campaign, threw a challenge: "None but a great and strong knight should come forward so that I may punish him".

It was Zuhra's practice to fight the enemy commanders himself, but he was angered by the insolence of the Persian general. "I was going to fight you myself," he called, "but having heard what you have said, I shall send only a slave to fight you. If you stand up to him, he will kill you for your arrogance, if Allah wills it; and if you run away from him, you will be running away from a slave."[173]

On Zuhra's orders, Nail bin Ju'sham [actually a very good fighter] emerged from the Muslim front line and the two antagonists faced each other mounted on their horses. Shahryar threw away his lance. He was now vulnerable, but for the Muslim to attack him with his lance would be against the rules of chivalry. He too threw his lance away; and the two drew their swords and began to duel. The sword fighting deteriorated into a wrestling match and soon the two champions were locked with each other, still on horse back. Then the two horses pulled apart and both men fell to the ground, Nail below and Shahryar on top. The Persian at once drew his dagger and prepared to strike at Nail's throat, but just then the Muslim, who was holding the Persian's left hand, was able to get the Persian's thumb into his mouth. The Arab of the desert apparently has strong teeth, and this one was able to crush the bone of the Persian's thumb in his mouth. In the few painful moments which followed, in which the Persian was psychologically off balance, Nail threw him off, turned upon him and jumped on to his chest. Now he drew his own dagger and raising the Persian's armour from his belly, struck several times at the exposed flesh until the fallen general had breathed his last.

Following this duel, the Persians withdrew from Kusa, which was then occupied by Zuhra. The rest of the Muslim army marched up again to join the advance guard. During the few days that Sa'd spent at Kusa most of the Muslims visited the place where Prophet Abraham had been imprisoned by the tyrant Nimrod. Sa'd prayed at the site and invoked Allah's blessing upon Prophet Abraham and Prophet Muhammad [on whom be the blessings of Allah and peace].

---

[173] Ibid.

A few days later, in early Zul Haj, 15 Hijri [early January, 637], Zuhra again advanced, on the last leg of his march to Ctesiphon.[174] He arrived at Sabat, the Persian cantonment 4 miles from Ctesiphon, and here he was met by Sheerzad, the mayor of the town, who submitted to the Muslims and offered Sabat as an open city. This Sheerzad had been defeated by Khalid bin Al Waleed at Anbar three years before and had no desire to fight the Muslims again. And now there was no opposition left to the Muslims this side of Ctesiphon.

The military reader will not fail to admire the conduct of this operation by Sa'd and by Feerzan. The Persian general, naturally most sophisticated in matters of war, had carried out a perfect withdrawal, making full use of obstacles and employing several rearguards at the water obstacles to impose delay and wear down the invaders. He had fought a major defensive action at the ideal location-Babylon, where the river obstacle was the largest and would channelise and restrict the Muslim attack. And Sa'd's advance was a fine example of the follow-up of a retreating enemy. He had a strong advance guard to lead his advance, to overcome minor opposition, and in the face of major opposition to form a base and acquire intelligence about the enemy. The main body of the army was held well back, out of contact, protected by the advance guard, and not committed until it was necessary to do so on the army commander's plan. The move of the Muslims was carried out by corps and in bounds to facilitate control and movement.

From Sabat, Zuhra advanced again and approached the western part of Ctesiphon, known as Bahuraseer. His leading elements were very close to the southern edge of the city when large stones, hurled by Persian catapults, began to fall in their midst. The soldiers stopped and quickly pulled back out of range. It was evident that if they wanted Ctesiphon, they would have to fight it.[175]

The origin of Ctesiphon is obscure, veiled by the mist of time. It appears to have first come into existence during the Heroic Age of Persia, when the country was ruled by semi-legendary monarchs whose exploits are glorified in Persian literature. This was during the two millennia before Christ, and before the rise of Cyrus the great, in the Sixth Century B.C.

---

[174] The time of start of this advance from Qadisiyya (late Shawwal) and of its end at Ctesiphon (Muharram) are known. The rough dates given for the various engagements during the advance are the result of my assessment of time and space.

[175] According to Balazuri (p. 263). It was Khalid bin Urfuta who led the Muslim advance from Qadisiyya to Ctesiphon, but I favour Tabari's account in this matter.

The very first reference to the place relates to the time of Zab, son of Budakan, who built the city. Zab appeared in history a little after Moses, and the city was then called "Ateeqa" and lay on east bank.[176] A later monarch, a woman, named Himaya, daughter of Isfandiar and aunt of Darius who was defeated by Alexander, settled near the city.[177] It certainly existed about then because Alexander, on returning from his eastern conquests, visited the place.[178] It is even believed that it was Alexander who built the city [or part of it] and threw a protective wall around it.[179] Alexander was followed by the Seleucids Dynasty, and although the Seleucids had their capital at Antioch, they did make use of Ctesiphon and named the western part of it Seleucia.

Then came the Parthians, and they established a large camp on the eastern side of the Tigris opposite Ctesiphon, which was then apparently mainly on the west side, and, as a result, the city swelled to something much bigger.[180] Later, when the Parthians overthrew the Seleucids and established their own rule over Persia, they turned Ctesiphon into their winter capital. This was some time in the middle of the first century B.C.

The city rose further in importance and grandeur with the fall of Parthia and the rise of the Persian Sasanis. Ardsheer bin Babak, the founder of the Sasani Dynasty, made Ctesiphon his capital and added more to it.[181] Thereafter every big Sasani emperor enlarged it, some building whole new towns beside the old one,[182] until the time of Anushirwan, the Just, when the last new town was added to Ctesiphon. Some of the many towns were Asfabur, Hanbo Shafur and Woh Ardsheer, which the last one was Arabicised by the Muslims to Bahuraseer.[183] Once called Ateeqa, the city was renamed Alexandria, but under the Sasanis it acquired its last historic name of Ctesiphon. The name of Bahuraseer, which was actually one of the cities, was also used by Muslim historians to denote the entire western part of Ctesiphon, on the right bank of the Tigris. And the greatest structure in the capital was the Arch of Chosroes, which rose in majesty to a height of 40 metres.[184]

---

[176] Dinawari: p. 11; Yaqut: vol. 4, p. 446; Yaqubi: Al Buldan: p. 321.
[177] Masudi: Muruj: vol. 1, p. 227.
[178] Dinawari: p. 38.
[179] Yaqut: vol. 4, p. 446.
[180] Gibbon: vol. 1, p. 237.
[181] Dinawari: p. 43.
[182] Yaqut: vol. 4, p. 446.
[183] Ibid: p. 446-7.
[184] Yaqubi: Al Buldan: p. 321.

Anushirwan had, in his glorious campaigns against the Romans in the time of the Emperor Justinian, conquered Antioch. He was so enamoured of the city of Antioch, and apparently of its inhabitants also, that he took them into captivity and transported them to Iraq, at the same time ordering the building of a replica of Antioch at the western edge of the old Ctesiphon. This new city was built on the model of Antioch, and it was so exact a reproduction of the old city that when the captives of Antioch were led into it, everyone went unaided and unguided to his own street and his own house![185] This must be an exaggeration, of course, because so huge a city as Antioch would take years and years to build and would consume more of the imperial revenue than any sensible ruler would expend for a colony of slaves, even to gratify his own vanity, of which Anushirwan had little. It was probably a replica of a part of Antioch which especially appealed to the illustrious Chosroes.

This last addition to Ctesiphon was named Zabr-e-Khusrau, but later came to be known as Rumiyya, and was the last of the 7 cities which comprised the mighty metropolis, of which nothing remains today except the famous Arch. When the Muslims came and found so many cities within a city, they called the place "Madain", i.e. the cities, and so it was ever after called in Muslim history.

---

[185] Dinawari: p. 69.

Chapter 13: The Conquest of Ctesiphon

During the time which elapsed since their defeat at Qadisiyya, the Persians had worked with feverish haste to prepare the imperial capital for battle. After the staggering blow which they had just suffered, it was unlikely that any Persian army would be in a mood to march out for an offensive campaign against the army of Islam; and in any case it was not possible to create another large army to take the field in the time available. The only choice left to the Persians was to fight a defensive action, and with this in view, Ctesiphon was prepared for a siege. While Feerzan was engaged in his delaying action against the advancing Muslims, a large ditch was dug around the perimeter of Bahuraseer, the western part of Ctesiphon, from river bank to river bank. Several military engines-ballistas and catapults-were set up in the capital. These two contraptions were a little different in structure but used for the same purpose, i.e. hurling large stones at the enemy. This was the artillery of the time.

The engines opened up as the Muslim advance guard approached the city. Zuhra quickly pulled his men back and sent parties round to the left to seek entrances into the city, but everywhere his men came up against the ditch, which was manned by Persian posts. Before long the Muslims had established the existence of the ditch along the entire western perimeter of Ctesiphon.

Over the next few days Sa'd, having assumed command of the front, established a large element of his army around the perimeter, keeping suitable reserves in hand. [We know nothing about the dispositions of his corps.] The ditch could not be crossed because of Persian posts covering it; the Persian engines broke up all concentrations which were formed to attempt a crossing; and night attacks, when the engines would not be effective, were just not in fashion. In this manner the situation crystalised into a siege in which the Muslims would starve the defenders into submission.

Sa'd next turned to the subjugation of the neighbouring countryside with the twin objectives of imposing Muslim rule upon the conquered territory and gathering supplies for his army. Raiding parties scoured far and wide and drove in large flocks of sheep and herds of cattle. They also drove in thousands of Persian farmers as captives of war. However, at the intercession of Sheerzad, mayor of Sabat, who had thrown in his lot with the Muslims, Sa'd offered to free the captives on acceptance of Islam or payment of the Jizya. All of them submitted to the payment of the Jizya and were freed, with security of life and property assured, and this action, which in those days would count as an act of mercy, had the effect of winning a tremendous amount of goodwill for the

Muslims. All the property which belonged to the Persian Emperor and the royal family, however, was confiscated.

Begun in Zul Haj, 15 Hijri [January, 637], the siege dragged on for two months, and the Persian garrison and the inhabitants of the city were sorely tried. Supplies from the countryside, on which Bahuraseer depended for its existence, were entirely cut off, and whatever could be ferried across the river from the east was not sufficient to maintain an adequate level of food. As the siege wore on, the Persian population was reduced to eating cats and dogs.[186] During these weeks the garrison attempted a number of sallies across the ditch but all were repulsed.

The Persian superiority in military engines was also neutralised. Sa'd persuaded Sheerzad to build large catapults for him, and Sheerzad soon had 20 of these engines constructed, with which the Muslims began to answer the Persian artillery fire, stone for stone. For the Persians it was bad enough to face an army of fierce desert warriors who in courage and physical toughness had an edge on them; but when these warriors also acquired the sophisticated weapon which had hitherto belonged exclusively to the imperial army and was regarded as its trump card, the situation turned intolerable for them. Moreover, because of the concentration of the Persians in the city, compared with the dispersion of the Muslims in the countryside, the fire of the Muslim catapults was more effective and caused greater suffering.

At last, in Safar, 16 Hijri [March, 637], the Persians decided to make one last attempt to break the Muslim grip. All troops not manning the perimeter were concentrated in one powerful striking force and launched against the Muslims. This led to the hardest fighting of the siege and the corps of Zuhra bore the brunt of the Persian attack, but after some hours of fighting, the attack was blunted. Zuhra was wounded by an arrow, though not seriously, and led a counter attack to drive the Persians back, in which he killed in single combat the commander of the Persian striking force. Upon the death of their commander the Persians withdrew speedily behind the security of the ditch.

This action was followed by a lull in the fighting, and for some hours nothing happened. Then a Persian officer approached the Muslims as an emissary and was confronted by a Muslim who had acquired a good knowledge of the Persian language and was sent by Sa'd to see what the Persian had to say. The Persian message: "The Emperor asks if you would be agreeable to peace on

---

[186] Tabari: vol. 3, p. 119.

condition that whatever we possess on our side of the Tigris up to our hills is ours, and whatever you possess on your side of the Tigris up to your hills is yours. And if your hunger is still not satisfied, God will never satisfy it."

The Muslim had not been empowered to take a decision; he was only to listen to what the Persian offered, but he took it upon himself to reject the Persian offer of peace and did so in an unusual manner. "There can never be peace between us," he replied, "until we get honey out of the lemons of Kusa."[187]

That night the Persian garrison crossed the Tigris and destroyed the bridges behind it. The Persians also took away all the boats and anchored them on the east bank. As the day dawned, the Muslims remained on their guard, watchful as usual and prepared for another sally by the garrison, which actually was no longer there. It was not till some time in the evening that a Persian came out of Bahuraseer and informed the Muslims that the garrison had gone and there were no troops left in the city.

The following night the Muslims entered Bahuraseer, without opposition. Sa'd bin Abi Waqqas disposed the troops at various points in the city where they could rest while awaiting the next move. Half of Ctesiphon was now his.

No sooner had the Persian garrison crossed the Euphrates than Yazdjurd sent off his family and most of the imperial treasure to Hulwan [the present Pul-e-Zohab on the road to Kermanshah], where he planned to establish his court in the event of the fall of Ctesiphon. He was still under the shock of the painful defeat at Qadisiyya and the more recent defeat at Bahuraseer, and was thinking more in terms of security and survival than of victory. But he had not entirely given up hope. He remained in person in the White Palace of Ctesiphon, and appointed the generals Khurrazad [brother of the late Rustam] and Mihran in command of the troops. The generals re-deployed the troops near the east bank of the Tigris and awaited whatever destiny had in store for them.

Across the river stood Sa'd bin Abi Waqqas, looking intently at the swirling waters of the Tigris, half a mile wide. The bridges had been destroyed and all boats removed by the Persians from the west bank for miles upstream and downstream. In front rose the splendid Arch of Chosroes, a wonder of wonders, the ultimate prize of the campaign. He had to get that arch, for the Holy Prophet had predicted that the Muslims would possess the treasure of

---

[187] Ibid: p. 118.

Chosroes. But however was he going to get his desert army across the swollen river?

Sa'd remained uncertain of his next move and impatient of the delay, which he could find no way to end. He was still on the river bank when a Persian came and said: "What are you waiting for? Not another two days will pass before Yazdjurd departs with everything in Ctesiphon."[188] Then another Persian came and offered to show the Muslims a ford where the army could cross the river without boats. Sa'd went with the Persian to see the ford, which was by the village of Sayadeen, just below Ctesiphon, where a dry stem bed [wadi] came down to meet the Tigris at the east bank. Sa'd examined the site of the ford but was put off by the fast current and the deep water, which may have been acceptable to a Persian but was too deep and too fast for Arab. Also, there was a large group of Persian soldiers positioned on the far bank at the site of the fort. Sa'd turned away, his mind torn by doubt.

That night Sa'd got the answer in a dream, and all doubt vanished. In the dream he saw the same waters in frightening motion, the level appearing even higher than in reality, and he saw the Muslim cavalry plunging into the river and swimming across to the east bank.

Early in the morning Sa'd called a conference of his officers and let it be known that the cavalry would swim across the river. Were there any volunteers to lead the assault? Asim bin Amr was the first to answer the call. Sa'd asked for volunteers from the whole army, and the officers dispersed to talk to the men. Before long 700 men were ready to lead the assault across the water.

Plans were made, orders given, horses moved near the bank. Asim would be the first to cross with his 700 men and would be followed by several other regiments. Asim would drive the Persians away from the crossing and establish what we would now call a bridgehead, to secure the bank for the crossing of the remaining regiments. When the crossing was complete, boats from the east bank would be rowed back to the west and used for the transportation of baggage and later of the women and children, but all able-bodied men would cross on horseback, even the Commander-in-Chief.

Asim was soon ready. From his 700 men he picked out 60 who would form the leading wave, and appointed Shurahbeel bin As-Samt, also a volunteer, as his second-in-command. These stalwarts, taking the name of Allah [swt], plunged

---

[188] Ibid: p. 121.

into the Tigris, and the Arab horse, swimming strongly, moved off from the bank. The assault crossing was on-the first such crossing in Muslim history.

Soon after, the remaining men of Asim's regiment entered the river. The Muslims standing on the west bank held their breath and prayed to Allah [swt] for strength and victory; and on the east bank the Persians gazed in astonishment and disbelief at the waves of horse and rider breasting the waters. The Persian commander at the east bank was Khurrazad, who had a score to settle with the Muslims for the death of his brother, Rustam. For some time he stared incredulously at the approaching horsemen doing what would have been deemed impossible. Even this line of defence had collapsed. Then, when Asim was quite close to the east bank, Khurrazad decided that there was a limit to how unkind fate could be.

"O nation of Arabs," he roared at the oncoming attackers, "the river is ours and you have no business to enter it against us."[189] He then got together all the Persian mounted men within sight and ordered them into the river to meet the Muslims in the water, which would surely be to the advantage of the Persians. These soldiers rode in and, covered by the fire of Persian archers, made for the Arabs.

What a scene ensued! Asim and his 60 adventurous souls clashed with the Persians when the Arab horse had only just found its feet on the river bed, but where the current was still strong enough to sweep a horse off its feet and a rider off his horse. The foaming water pressed against the flanks of the horses and the knees of the riders, as brave men, Persian and Arab, fought what should rightly be described as a naval engagement!

Asim was not born to be defeated. He could only live in victory; and Asim lived. He and his men raised their spears and struck at the Persians in close combat in what was undoubtedly one of the most unusual military encounters in history. For some time a mad struggle raged in the swirling waters, and at last Asim prevailed. His men were reckless daredevils, fired by the pure faith of Islam, while the Persians were straight soldiers merely obeying the orders of their commander. Many of them were killed in the water before the survivors turned away, and with cries of: "Devils have come!" and "We are fighting not humans but jinns!" made for the east bank.[190]

---

[189] Dinawari: p. 126.
[190] Tabari: vol. 3, p. 124; Dinawari: p. 126.

By now the remainder of Asim's 700 men had caught up with the leading wave and the entire regiment made for the bank, where Asim threw his dripping riders at the Persians who stood to oppose them. The contest was resumed on the bank with sword and spear and the Persians made one last desperate bid to hold their ground. Sa'd. Watching from the west bank, exclaimed: "By Allah, I wish Qa'qa and Hammal bin Malik and Ribbeel bin Amr were present among them."[191]

He need not have worried. Asim and his 700 men were sufficient for the task. The fighting on the east bank continued for some time and then a Persian, coming from the city, shouted to the soldiers: "Why are you killing yourselves? There is no one left in Ctesiphon."[192] On hearing these words, the Persian unit broke contact and withdrew speedily to the city.

Asim established his regiment deeper inland to protect the crossing of the remainder of the army. He and his men had smashed open the door to the Arch of Ctesiphon.

As soon as Sa'd saw the Persians giving ground to Asim, he knew that the far bank was secure and that the rest of the army could cross the river. He gave orders for the next regiment to cross [this was Qa'qa's regiment] and after that the next and then the next. The regiments followed close upon each others' heels and rode their horses into the Tigris. Their task was relatively easy, for the trail, so to speak, had already been blazed by Asim.

Soon almost the entire army was in the river. It was a mad, confused picture with the river appearing block with bodies of horses and men, except for the waves of foam created by the passage of the regiments. Those still on the west bank could hardly see the water for the bodies. Following the instructions of Sa'd, the men travelled in pairs, one tied to the other loosely with a rope so that if one were in danger of drowning the other could pull him out. After several regiments had gone in, Sa'd also rode into the river, tied to the companion whom he had chosen - Salman the Persian.

Salman the Persian was a native of either Isfahan or Ram Hormuz in Fars. Once a Zoroastrian, he had found the faith unsatisfying and travelled to Syria in quest of the truth. While in Syria he had been taken into slavery, from which some time later he either escaped or was freed. After years of wandering, he arrived at Madina during the early years of the Hijra, became a Muslim and

---

[191] Tabari: vol. 3, p. 121.
[192] Ibid: p. 123.

attached himself to the Holy Prophet. His faith was so pure and he possessed such nobility of character that he became very close to the Prophet and was loved and respected by all. To show the special regard which he had for Salman, the Prophet had said, just before the Battle of the Ditch: "Salman is one of the members of our family."[193]

In fact, in the Battle of the Ditch in 5 Hijri, it was Salman who had suggested the digging of the ditch to keep the infidels out of Madina, a strategem which undoubtedly saved the town. Later, at the Siege of Taif, he had constructed a catapult and a testudo. From this it is reasonable to assume that he was once a soldier of the Persian army, probably a military engineer, and although not one of the *Ten* like Sa'd, he was one of those who, like Abu Dhar and Ammar bin Yasir, had an especially close relationship with the Holy Prophet and were held by the Muslims in deep veneration. And now these two top Companions rode together into the Tigris.

Sa'd recited a Quranic verse: "Sufficient for us is Allah, and what a good Protector He is!" Then he continued, "Allah will help His friends and strengthen His religion and vanquish His foes if there be not in our army evil and sin to overpower the good."

In the mind of Salman even this little doubt did not exist. "Islam is new," he answered Sa'd. "Allah has made the rivers subservient to the Muslims as He has made the land subservient to them. And by Him in whose hands is the life of Salman, they will all come out of the river in troops."[194]

According to Tabari, not a man was lost in the crossing, not an item of baggage. According to other historians, however, one man did drown and only

---

[193] Ibn Hisham: vol. 2, p. 224.
[194] Abū Bakr bin Hafs bin Umar reports that the person travelling with S'ad over the water was Salman Farsi. As there horses swam across, S'ad was saying, "Allah is sufficient for us and He is the best of Defenders. By Allah! Allah will definitely assist His friends, make His Din vanquish all others and defeat His enemies if the wrongs and sins of the army does not exceed their good deeds." Salman then remarked, "By Allah! Although Islam is new, the waters have been made subservient to the Muslims just as the land has been made such. I swear by the Being Who controls the life of Salman that the Muslims shall leave the waters in large droves just as they have entered."
The Muslims then skimmed across the water, as if there where only the banks and no water was visible. In fact, the Muslims were speaking more than if they were walking on land. Just as Salman said, they all emerged safely without anyone drowning and without even losing anything. Tabrani vol.3, p. 121 and Tabari: vol. 3. p. 122.

one, whose name has been given variously as Suleil bin Yazeed[195] and Suleik bin Abdullah.[196] Another rider slipped off his horse and was swept away by the current but luckily, while bobbing up and down in the water, he passed close to Qa'qa who reached out and pulled him up.[197]

In due course of time the entire army got to the east bank, having swum the horses across the great river-an incredible feat. No wonder the Persians thought they were up against devils and jinns! Soon after, on the orders of Sa'd, a large number of boats would be rowed to the west bank and would transport the baggage and the families, but for the time being Sa'd concentrated his attention on locating and disposing of armed Persian opposition, of which at the moment it appeared that none remained.[198]

---

[195] Balazuri: p. 263.

[196] Dinawari: p. 126.

[197] The water was turbulent and while the horses were able to stand up straight, whenever they became tired, a mound would appear for them to rest upon, as if they were on dry land. **There was never an incident more astonishing than this in the history of Madā'in.** It was a day when the water was abundant and it was therefore referred to as 'The Day of Mounds.' Qais bin Abu Hāzim says, "When we entered the Tigris; it was filled to the brim. However (by Allāh's doing), when a horseman stood at the point where the water was at its deepest, it reached only up to his reins." Ibn Jarīr vol.3, p.123.

[198] Habīb bin Suhbān reports that one of the Muslims by the name of Hujr bin Adi said to the others, "What prevents you from crossing over to the enemy? Is it this little droplet? Here he was referring to the Tigris. He then recited the verse: **A person shall die only by the command of Allāh**; (at a time that is) **recorded** (in the Luwhul Mahfūdh), **fixed** (and therefore can neither be postponed nor delayed). [Surah Aale Imrān, verse 14]. He then plunged into the Tigris with his horse and, seeing him, the others followed suit. When the enemy saw them, they exclaimed, **"Madmen!" and ran away.** Tafsīr Ibn Kathīr vol.1 p. 410. Habīb bin Suhbān Abu Mālik narrates that when the Persians saw the Muslims crossing the Tigris the day they conquered Madā'in, they called out in Persian, "Mad devils are coming!" They then said to each other, **"By Allāh! It is not humans that you are fighting against, but Jinn!"** In this way, they were defeated. Abu Nu'aym in Dalāil p.209.

A'mash reports from a companion of his that when they reached the Tigris River, the water level was very high and the Kuffār had already crossed over. One of the Muslims said, "Bismillāh!" and then plunged into the water with his horse. The horse rode over the water. The other Muslims than all said "Bismillāh!" and plunged into the water. Their horse also rode above the water. Seeing them, the Kuffār exclaimed, **"Madmen! Madmen!"** They then all fled. Al-Bayhaqi as quoted in al-Bidāyah wan Nihāyah vol.6 pg.155.

The Persian who had called to his comrades that no one was left in Ctesiphon was more or less right. Yazjurd had left as soon as the crossing began, and after Asim's regiment had landed at the east bank, Khurrazad also pulled back to the city, leaving the Persian unit engaged in the fighting to deal with the situation as best as it could. In Ctesiphon the generals decided that further resistance was futile and marched off with the bulk of the army to Hulwan. One regiment remained in the White Palace adjoining the great Arch, but it is not known whether it was forgotten by the generals or actually ordered to stay. The generals and the army took away part of the imperial treasure left behind by Yazdjurd and as much as they could transport of the valuable possessions of the city. However, what was left behind was far more than what could be saved by the Persians, and the organisation of the evacuation of the treasure was not very effective because part of it was to fall into Muslim stands soon after. On their way to Hulwan, the generals left a detachment at Nahrawan, 30 miles from Ctesiphon, to act as a rearguard and prevent a pursuit of the retreating army.

As soon as Sa'd landed on the bank, he ordered Asim to march on into the heart of the city, and placed Qa'qa's regiment next in the order of march. Asim came up at one place against a few soldiers who offered resistance but the opposition was quickly brushed aside. Deeper into Ctesiphon advanced Asim, and he at last got to the White Palace where a Persian regiment offered opposition. The rest of Ctesiphon was defenceless.

At the White Palace, Salman the Persian acted as a negotiator for the Muslims. He went up to the garrison and said: "I am actually one of you, and I feel for you."[199] In the talks which followed, he offered the usual three choices, and after some deliberation the garrison accepted the imposition of the Jizya and surrendered the palace. Ctesiphon was now in Muslim hands.

Sa'd moved into the White Palace, where he established his headquarters. The great courtyard of the palace was turned into temporary mosque with a pulpit erected for the Imam. [Sa'd himself], and here the Muslim Commander-in-Chief led a mass victory prayer of 8 rakats. In the courtyard stood a large number of statues of horses and men, but these were left in their place. The following day Sa'd kept a fast; and on this day he sent out columns in several directions to deal with Persian stragglers and recover the valuables which were being evacuated by the retreating Persians. The follow-up of the Persians on the main route of retreat was commanded by Zuhra. He got to the Nahrawan

---

[199] Tabari: vol. 3, p. 124.

canal, on the road to Hulwan, just as the last element of the Persian baggage column was crossing the bridge. Here a Persian rearguard was in position to cover the evacuation of the baggage and the retreat of the army, and with the arrival of the Muslims the baggage column hastened its crossing over the bridge, in which process two mules fell into the water. This led to such consternation among the Persians, who worked frantically to recover the mules and their loads, that Zuhra guessed that there was something special about these mules. He at once assaulted the rearguard and pushed it back from the canal, and having captured the mules, followed the Persians and drove them out of Nahrawan before returning to Ctesiphon.

When the boxes on the mules were inspected, they were found to contain the fabulous crown of Persia [which had cracked in the fall of the mule], the court dress and full imperial regalia of the Emperor, several ornaments and the Emperor's armour. On all these objects there was enough gold and precious stones to purchase a kingdom.

Moving in another direction, Qa'qa caught up with a Persian carrying two large leather bags. He killed the man and brought back the bags, which, when opened, revealed 11 swords and 11 suits of armour. These were ornamental as well as functional and were worth a fortune, being the relics of kings and princes. The swords included those of several past emperors of Persia, the Khakan of Turks, the ruler of the Sind and Heraclius of Eastern Rome.

Another Muslim column captured two asses loaded with chests, which carried three very special and precious little animals. There was a horse of gold with a saddle of silver, on which the reins and girth were studded with sapphires and emeralds. There was a horse of silver studded with gems. And there was a camel of silver with a saddle, girth and reins of gold, all studded with jewels. The last mentioned animal also had a rider made of gold and covered with precious stones. Within Ctesiphon the Muslims found a pavilion containing a large number of sealed baskets. When these baskets were opened, out fell utensils of gold and silver. And in the imperial treasury, which also fell into Muslim hands, there was money to the value of 1-1½ billion dirhams.

The history of Islam up to here was a short one - 15 years since the beginning of the Hijra. But in terms of war it was a long history, because into these 15 years the Muslims had packed more battles than other nations had seen in a century. Thus in terms of military action Islam already had a long history, but never before in this history had such rich spoils been taken in war as were taken in Ctesiphon. The Arab of the desert was dazzled. Sa'd excluded a few items from the spoils, of which mention will be made later, took out the value of the one-fifth share of the state, and distributed the rest of the booty among the soldiers. The share of each man came to 12,000 dirhams and all received the same, for all were mounted soldiers. In many cases ornaments and plates of gold and silver were distributed directly among the warriors, who could do as they pleased with their share of the spoils.

Several warriors were too simple to appreciate the value of the good things which they received. One, man who was not happy about the gold dish which he was given and found the silver ones more attractive, went about asking: "Who has a white dish which he will exchange for a yellow one?"[200] Other soldiers found large quantities of camphor, and mistaking it for salt, put it in their bread and cooking pots. When the food tasted bitter, they were nonplussed, and one man rushed around saying: "O people, do not spoil your food. The salt of this land is no good!"[201]

Sa'd also requisitioned the houses belonging to the royal family and the Persian soldiers who had departed the city, and allotted them as quarters to his men, who settled down in them with their families for a brief sojourn.

And now for the first time large scale conversions took place among the Persians. While quite a few of them had already become Muslim during the years preceding the conquest of Ctesiphon and many were even now serving in the Muslim ranks, after this conquest the pace of conversion increased and the citizens came in their thousands to embrace the new faith. This was due partly to the preaching of Salman the Persian, who showed his fellow countrymen the beauty and truth of Islam, and partly to the example of the Muslim soldiery and the justice of the new system of administration established by the conquerors. Ctesiphon was now definitely a Muslim city. There were a number of things which Sa'd did not distribute among his troops, things whose value could not be measured in terms of the money which they would fetch. These things had a special significance because they were the finest trophies of war and symbolised the victory of Islam over the greatest empire of the time. Sa'd therefore despatched these trophies to Madina so that they could be seen by the people back home, who would then have a better appreciation of the achievements of their comrades fighting the holy war far from their native land. The trophies consisted of the swords and armour of the emperors and kings, the Persian Emperor's crown and court dress, and the splendid carpet of Ctesiphon.

---

[200] Tabari: vol. 3, p. 126; Dinawari: p. 127.
[201] Tabari: vol. 3, p. 16.

The carpet from the White Palace was the most gorgeous specimen of craftsmanship of the time, a craftsmanship for which Persia was even then famous. There was nothing like it in the world. It measured 30 metres by 30 metres,[202] and represented a garden such as the faithful might seek in paradise, with glades and trees and flowers. Its base was silk, it was worked with gold, the borders showing fields as in spring when the earth is green with plants. The roads and rivers were of gold. The branches of the trees were also of gold, the leaves of silver, the blossoms and flowers of gold and silver, and the fruits were formed of clusters of gems. Somewhere in the carpet there was a temple, and the entire scene was embellished with figures.[203] It was a thing out of this world.

The astonishment of the people of Madina knew no bounds when they saw the dazzling trophies. They were left spellbound. The more knowledgeable of the Muslims may have heard of such treasures but none had seen them. Caliph Umar, austere, frugal, practical, had no time for such things and promptly had the trophies taken apart and distributed among the faithful at the laid-down scale. But when he came to the carpet, he was stuck for a decision. He sought the advice of the people as to what to do with the carpet, and the people replied that it should be kept by the Caliph.

Umar was averse to keeping such a thing for himself. In any case his house was not big enough to house the carpet, even if all the inner walls were pulled down. He asked Ali for an opinion.

"What they say is right," replied Ali. "But if you accept this today, tomorrow there will be those who claim it, but will not deserve it. Let not your knowledge be wasted and your faith turned to doubt. For you there is nothing of worldly things except your pay and what you wear and what you eat.

"You are right," observed Umar. "You have given sound advice."[204]

The Caliph had the carpet cut up into small pieces and distributed. Ali too got a piece of it and sold it for 20,000 dirhams, and his was by no means the best piece. True to his custom, Ali at once distributed the money among the needy.

---

[202] It was 60 cubits square.
[203] Tabari: vol. 3, p. 130.
[204] Ibid.

Today that carpet would have enjoyed the place of honour in any museum, any palace in the world, but in those early days of Islam it had no value for the Muslims. The Companions of the Prophet sought a different kind of beauty.

Chapter 14: The Battle of Jaluala

Having abandoned Ctesiphon to the Muslims, the Persian army retreated northwards. It was an orderly retreat, secured against interference by the rearguard dropped at Nahrawan, and ended at Jalaula, a hundred miles away. Yazdjurd had established a temporary headquarters at Hulwan [the present Pul-e-Zohab], but the army stopped and faced about at Jalaula. [See Map 1.]

Standing on the east bank of the River Diyala, which flowed down from the hills of Azarbeijan to join the Tigris a few miles above Ctesiphon, Jalaula was a place of strategical importance. It was a kind of bottleneck confining the movement of armies to a narrow gap. West of Jalaula flowed the sizable Diyala River while south-east of the town, starting about 2 miles away, lay a region of hard, broken ground with a distorted surface which rose gradually eastwards into the hills which form the present Iran-Iraq border. Movement was possible over this broken ground but not major military movement. The western edge of this broken ground was 2 to 3 miles from the Diyala, and the space in between was the gap. So long as the Persians held this gap, North Persia was safe from any invader from Central Iraq.

Apart from the necessity of holding Jaluala for reason of Military strategy, there was also the economic advantage of keeping the northern part of the Suwad. As mentioned in an earlier chapter, the Suwad was the most fertile and most fruitful region in the empire and provided more revenue for the imperial treasury than any other region of comparable size. It was the land between the two great rivers of Iraq from Basra to Ctesiphon and stretched further northwards to Mosul and Hulwan. It also included a wide belt of land east of the Lower Tigris, which extended at its southern extremity to Ahwaz. If this entire region were to fall, the most productive part of the empire would be lost to Persia. The Persians determined to keep at least the northern Suwad in their hands, and with this in view, selected Jalaula as the point where they would call a halt to Muslim conquest.

At Jalaula the Persians prepared for a do-or-die battle. Orders for the operation were given by Yazdjurd at Hulwan and large numbers of Persians living in the district of Jalaula came forward to fight for Persia and joined the army of Mihran, who was appointed commander for the defence of Jalaula, with

Khurrazad as his deputy commander and the commander of the cavalry.[205] The two generals at once set about preparing for a great battle against the Muslims. The entire town was converted into a fortress, a deep ditch was dug about 3 miles to the south, enclosing the gap between the river and the broken ground, and various fortifications were constructed behind the ditch. In front of the ditch, wooden caltrops were strewn in large numbers, with certain routes left clear for use by the Persians and known only to the Persians. The caltrop was a small four-pronged contraption which, when thrown on the ground, would automatically land on three points with one pointing up in the air. In size about an inch cross, it was an anti-cavalry obstacle, designed to wound the horses in their hooves and thus put them out of action. The belt of caltrops corresponded to the minefield of today.

The families and the heavy baggage of the army were sent back to Khaniqeen and Qasr Sheereen, and the troops took an oath by the sacred fire that they would die fighting rather than retreat. They prepared the defences of the town with grim determination, and stocked the town with provisions to last a long siege. The preparations were so thorough that any attacker would think twice before tackling such a desperately courageous army in such a formidable position.

Very soon after the defence works were started by the Persians at Jalaula, reports of their activities were brought to Sa'd. The Muslim Commander-in-Chief was as eager to get the northern Suwad as the Persians were to hold it; and for military reasons also it was imperative for the Muslims to capture Jalaula and Khaniqeen [the latter being 15 miles north-east of the former] because the permanent occupation of Ctesiphon could only be assured if the Persians were driven out of the northern plains and the Muslims secured the entrance to the hills of Kirmanshahan. They would then have a more defensible frontier and could prevent the Persians from debouching into the plains from what was the main axis between Ctesiphon and North Persia. The month of Safar, 16 Hijri [March, 637] had not ended when Hashim bin Utba, nephew of Sa'd, set off from Ctesiphon with an army of 12,000 men. With him marched the valiant Qa'qa bin Amr and many Companions of the Holy Prophet.[206]

---

[205] This is from Tabari: vol. 3, p. 138. According to Balazuri (p. 264) and Dinawari (p. 127), Khurrazad was the army commander at Jalaula. They make no mention of Mihran with his army.

[206] Dinawari (p. 127) gives the commander of the army as Amr bin Malik, whom Tabari names as the commander of the force, sent later to Qirqeesia. Tabari does mention him as one of the officers serving under Hashim. Balazuri (p. 624) names Amr bin Utba as the army commander. I accept Tabari's version as it more detailed and probably more

In this march, for the first time in Muslim history, regular Persian troops moved as part of the Muslim army. Some Persian soldiers had already gone over to Sa'd before Qadisiyya and fought against the imperial army in that battle, but after Qadisiyya, and again after Ctesiphon, the numbers of Persian soldiers who accepted Islam swelled to several thousand and included many able officers. These new converts joined the army of Sa'd not as foreign troops but as part of the great brotherhood of Islam. Their existence as separate contingents in the army was a matter of convenience in command and organisation rather than a racial or cultural division with the Arabs.

After some day of marching the army, which now included a separate infantry element, arrived at Jalaula and found itself up against a heavily defended position with fortifications, entrenchments, a deep ditch and as obstacle belt of caltrops. While the gaps left in the caltrop belt were not apparent and known only to the Persians, the gaps left in the ditch could be seen by the Muslims. The entire perimeter was strongly held by Persian troops. Hashim established his camp and deployed his army along the southern arc of the perimeter.[207] [See Map 11.]

This state of affairs, more or less a stalemate, was to last about 8 months, during which neither side could gain an advantage over the other. Persian reinforcements kept coming in driblets from Hulwan, where Yazdjurd was collecting more forces, and he also sent provisions and money. After seeing the first lot of reinforcements arrive at Jalaula, the Muslims got alarmed at the prospect of increase in Persian strength and wished to have an early showdown before the garrison became too large to handle. Consequently Hashim made several attempts to storm the position, during which he was able to get to the ditch but no further; all attacks were repulsed by the Persians. The wooden caltrops did not prove as effective as the Persians had hoped. Although some Arab horses were lamed, most of the caltrops broke under the horses' hooves and could not deter Muslim attempts from getting through the obstacle belt.

---

correct. Tabari is mistaken, however, when he says that Sad wrote to Umar about Persian preparations at Jalaula, and Umar ordered him to send Hashim with an army to Jalaula. This considering that the conquest of Ctesiphon, the Persian retreat and arrival at Jalaula, the receipt of information by Sad regarding Jalaula and the despatch of Hashim, all took place in the same month (Safar, 16 Hijri), is just not possible. Balazuri states that Sad sent the army from Ctesiphon and makes no mention of instructions from Umar.

[207] Since I have not been able to visit Jalaula, my description of this battle is based on maps and the account of the early historians.

When the Persians saw this, they had iron ones manufactured an strewn beyond the ditch, and these caused more damage to the Muslim cavalry.

The Muslims quietened down after this, not knowing how to tackle the situation, and Mihran, thinking that he had taken the wind out of the sails of the Muslim army, began to send detachments out of the position to raid the Muslims. For the next few weeks the Persians maintained an offensive posture and as more reinforcements came in from Hulwan, the strength of their sallies increased. It is reported that Mihran made altogether 80 sallies, but the Muslims held their ground and all sallies were repulsed, with the Persians retiring after each engagement to the safety of their fortifications. Mihran must have enjoyed this phase of the battle, because after Qadisisyya, where he had commanded a corps under Rustam, this was the first time that the Persians were able to wrest the tactical initiative from the Muslims.

The confrontation dragged on. Since no tactical operation was possible across the broken ground and the front of the Persians was too strong to penetrate, Hashim could find no way of breaking the stalemate. When this had gone on for 8 months, he asked Sa'd for reinforcements and the Commander-in-Chief sent 600 infantry and 400 cavalry from Ctesiphon. This force did no more than make up the losses suffered by the Muslims, but their arrival caused more than a little consternation among the Persians. A little later Sa'd sent another 500 cavalry, which arrived over several days and included the redoubtable apostate chiefs: Qeis bin Huberia, Amr bin Madi Karib and Tuleiha. The last of these reinforcements got to the Muslim camp at Jalaula about the end of Shawwal, 16 Hijri [third week of November, 637], and this brought matters to a head.

The Persians were now getting tired of being cooped up in the town, while the Muslims did not show any sign of going away. We have no knowledge of the Persian strength at Jalaula, but it had been augmented considerably by reinforcements sent by the Emperor from Hulwan. The Muslims on the other hand had been recently reinforced and, for all the Persians knew, might receive even larger additions to their strength. The only way to make the Muslims go away was to attack them outside the town and inflict a tactical defeat upon them. With this in view, Mihran began preparations to launch a major attack.

MAP 11: THE BATTLE OF JALAULA - 1

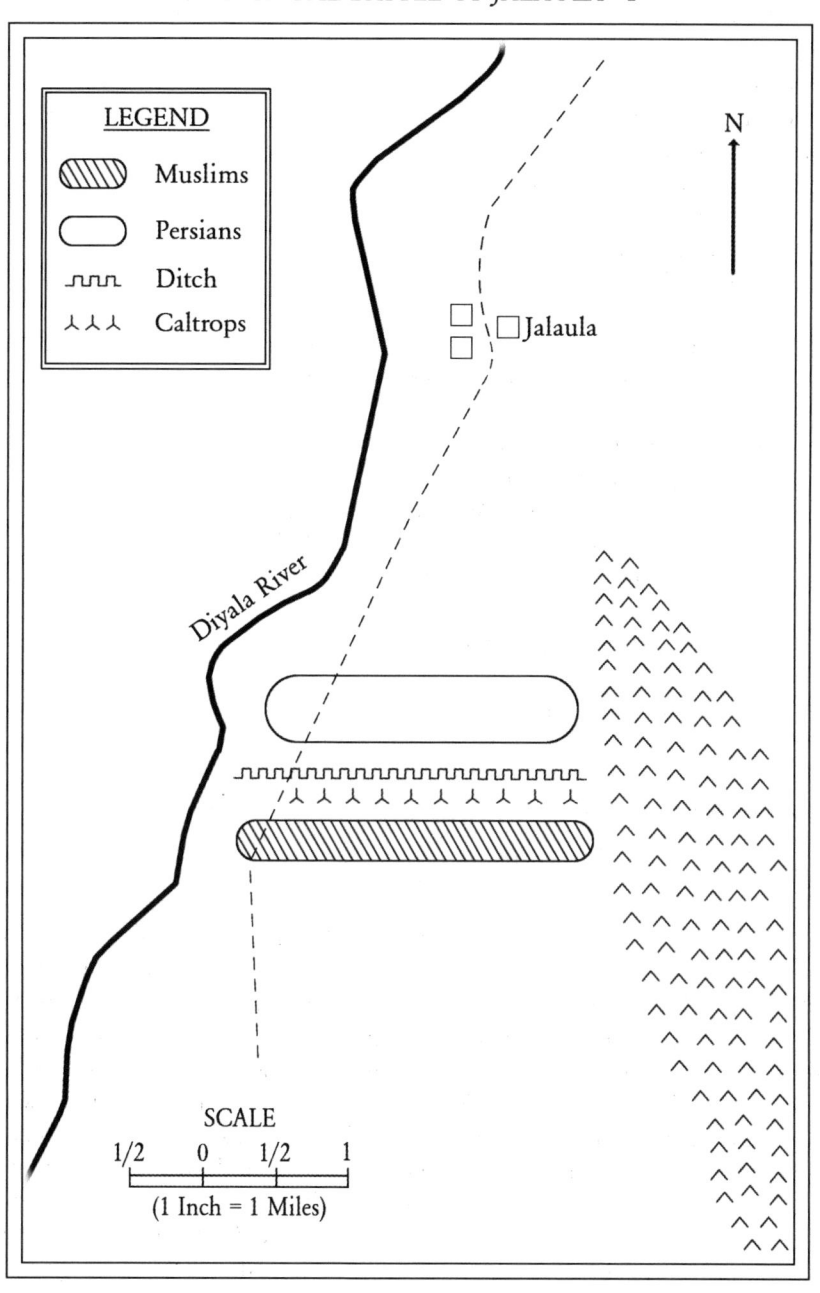

LEGEND
- Muslims
- Persians
- Ditch
- Caltrops

Jalaula

Diyala River

SCALE
1/2 0 1/2 1
(1 Inch = 1 Miles)

- 180 -

These preparations could not be concealed from the Muslims; it was obvious that the Persians were planning offensive action. And while this was the Persian choice, it also suited the Muslims because they were helpless against the fortifications and could wish for nothing better than a great battle in the open. Here the Muslims could fight the ideal battle, with open country behind them in case of a reverse, and ditch behind the Persians, against which the Muslims could drive them in the event of victory, which Allah [swt] would no doubt bestow upon the faithful. The ditch would act as the anvil against which the Muslim hammer would crush the army of Mihran. In fact the Muslims could do another Qadisiyya here, although on a smaller scale.

In keen anticipation of getting his hands on the Persians outside the protection of their defences, Hashim pulled back his army a short distance from the ditch to allow the Persians enough room to debouch and form up for battle, and rearranged his regiments in the camp to correspond to new battle position. The details of the dispositions are not known, but Hashim appointed Tuleiha as commander of the infantry and Amr bin Madi Karib as commander of the cavalry. This was the first time that apostate chiefs had been given important commands in battle in the Persian theatre.

On a crisp winter morning at the beginning of Zul Qada, 16 Hijri [late November, 637], was fought the last and most bloody action of the Battle of Jalaula. The Persian army rushed out of the town, crossed the ditch and the caltrop belt over one main crossing and began to deploy between the caltrops and the Muslims, who were arrayed for battle some distance to the south. Hashim made no move to interfere with the Persian crossing or to disturb the Persians' forming up because he was desirous of getting the whole army out of the fortified zone before the action began.

The action began with a heavy attack by the Persians along the entire front. Fired by hopes of a revenge for Qadisiyya, they struck boldly at the invaders of their land. Initially the Muslims stood their ground, not yielding an inch to the attackers, but after some time a few Muslim units were pushed back a short distance and the danger of a collapse on their front became very real. Hashim himself had to dash around on his horse to various regiments which were showing signs of weakness, and assure them that this was the last battle which they had to fight against the Persians and that there would be none after this. Mihran was undoubtedly having the best of this battle, not knowing that Hashim was deliberately remaining on the defensive and was even prepared to lose ground in order to let the Persians advance farther away from Jalaula.

Hashim had taken a big risk in letting the entire Persian army out of the town; but the greater the risk the greater is the victory which it leads to.

The fighting gradually increased in intensity as the sun rose higher in the sky. Hashim's orders to his men were to hold their ground, and hold it they did, while under the pressure of the superior numbers of the Persian army, the battle became more violent. After some time both sides found that they had expended their arrows and all the javelins and spears and lances were either lost or broken. Thereafter the fighting was carried on with sword and mace with the two bodies locked in a frantic contest, the Persians striving to drive the Muslims back and the Muslims straining every nerve to hold the Persian attack. The Persians had more forces at their disposal and were able to replenish their front line with fresh troops, while the Muslims had practically no reserves, could not be relieved in the line and had to go on struggling without rest. This went on till about noon when one Muslim regiment gave way under the Persia pressure and fell back hastily from its position. The Persians were slow to follow up their advantage, perhaps they were too tired to do so, and Hashim got enough time to shift some troops into the gap created by the retreating regiment.

In no time Qa'qa had got to the beaten regiment. "Has this fighting frightened you?", he asked the men. "Yes," they replied frankly. "We are weary and they are fresh. The weary become helpless." Qa'qa then said, "I am attacking them again, until Allah decides between us."[208]

Qa'qa's words and example had the desired effect and the men moved back into their positions. After this the regiment showed no weakness and fought as bravely as all other Muslim contingents.

Soon after this episode, the Persian attack halted. They were just not able to go on, and both sides disengaged from combat Mihran regarded this as no more than an interval before he resumed his attack, but Hashim had no intention of letting the Persian keep the initiative. In this first phase of battle he had planned to remain on the defensive and wear down the Persians, and after this would come the second phase in which he would counter-attack and drive his adversary back into his own ditch.

After a short rest, Hashim gave orders for the counter-attack, and in the middle of the afternoon the Muslim army went into action along the entire front. The

---

[208] Tabari: vol. 3, pp. 134-5

two forces were again locked in combat. This time the Persians assumed a defensive posture and this combat continued for an hour or two without change or let-up. Then, a little before sunset, came the storm from the south. There was a great wind and "the land went dark."[209] This was more frightening for the sophisticated Persian than for the desert Arab, and Hashim welcomed it as an unexpected blessing. He promptly gave the signal for the manoeuvre which he had already planned with Qa'qa.

The Muslims, attacking with the wind behind them, struck harder against the massed Persian formations but the defenders, though upset by the storm, held on with determination, not giving up an inch of ground. The fighting turned so savage and both sides fought with such fanatical fury that the veterans of Qadisiyya were reminded of the last day of that historic battle. The combat was going on with relentless violence when from behind the Persian ranks, from somewhere near the crossing of the ditch, came a call in Arabic, loud and clear: "O Muslims, here is your commander who has got to the ditch and captured it. Advance to him and let none stand between you and him".[210]

Hearing this call, the Muslims mistakenly believed that Hashim himself had got to the ditch, while the Persians mistakenly believed that the Muslims had somehow got in behind them in large numbers. The moral effect on the two armies can be imagined. The Muslims attacked with even greater zeal and the Persians began to lose cohesion, although they still had plenty of fight left in them.

Hashim had briefed Qa'qa before his counter-attack about the manoeuvre which was to be carried out. Qa'qa would move with his regiment from the left flank, would work his way to the crossing of the ditch and from there would give the call, while Hashim kept the Persian army engaged in front. Qa'qa would then secure the crossing with his regiment and start attacking in the rear of the Persian army at the same time as Hashim pressed from the front, and the Persians would be crushed between the two forces. Just one regiment of Muslims would be enough for this task if it had a man like Qa'qa to lead it, and also because of the tactical advantage of its location in the rear of the Persians and the psychological effect of surprise on the Persian mind. It was a simple plan-brilliantly simple, as some of the finest military plans of history have been.

Qa'qa had moved from the left on receiving Hashim's signal, and leaving his regiment somewhere under cover, had taken a few scouts and an "announcer"

---

[209] Ibid: p. 133.
[210] Ibid.

picked for his powerful voice, and worked his way behind the Persian army. In this move he had been helped by the storm and the fact that the Persian attention was riveted to the front. At last he got to the crossing and ordered the announcer to give the call. Hearing the call, his own regiment rushed forward, attacking the Persian flank and rolling it up, and finally outflanking the Persian army, got to the crossing. From here Qa'qa launched his regiment into the back of the Persian army [See Map 12.]

It is to the eternal credit of Persia that her army held on in spite of being outmanoeuvred and cut off from its base. If the Muslims thought that the Persians would collapse immediately, they were mistaken. The Persians did not collapse, and the battle turned even more vicious with no quarter given or taken. The two armies, one fighting with the courage of desperation and the other fired by the sight of victory, slogged it out on the plain of Jalaula.

Courage and tenacity cannot by themselves save an army from defeat when it is placed in a tactically impossible situation and when its determination is matched by its adversary's. The fighting went on till after sunset and the sky began to darken. Then suddenly Persian resistance broke. The disciplined Persians, so far held together by their officers, turned into a rabble, and order and cohesion vanished except in some regiments. The individuals who had broken away from their units fled in panic from one part of the front and ran into the Muslims' in another part, only to be cut down in the fading light. Many of them tried to flee rearwards and, unable to get to the crossing, made for the ditch, and in the process suffered grievously from the caltrops. Finally, driven on by the main body of Hashim's army, they fell into the ditch where large numbers perished.

Those of the Persian regiments in which some order still prevailed and which were still under the control of their officers, made a determined dash for the crossing which was held strongly by Qa'qa's regiment. Here the last bloody action was fought, and broken bodies fell in heaps as desperate men fought in frenzied combat for the crossing; but Qa'qa and his men held firm. From the south the main body of the Muslim army, attacking as one man, closed up to the ditch, and the battlefield turned into a slaughterhouse. It was quite dark when the last of the Persians ceased to move.

Within the fortified town those of the Persian troops who had been left to guard the place hastily prepared for departure. Knowing the disastrous outcome of the battle outside the town, they could guess that very soon the attackers would enter the town itself since there was no one left to dispute their crossing of the obstacles. And having no hope of either defending the town successfully or saving themselves from certain defeat, they marched out of the town on their way to Hulwan.

These activities were somehow discovered by the Muslims. Hashim was not the man to let his troops rest, no matter how richly they deserved a rest, while there were operational objectives inviting action. He got a few regiments together and launched them into the town where these regiments caught up with some of the retreating elements and put an end to their retreat. By and large, however, the occupation of Jalaula did not lead to serious fighting, and by the morning there were no Persian soldiers left in the town except as prisoners in Muslim hands.

Tabari gives the Persian casualities at Jalaula as 100,000 killed,[211] which is obviously a gross exaggeration, and there is no way of assessing the casualties accurately. The Persian army, in my view was not less than 20,000 strong and may have been even 30,000, and possibly more than half the troops fell in the Battle of Jalaula. By the very nature of his operation, Mihran had gambled for high stakes, and Hashim's strategy of drawing the Persians away from the ditch contributed to the decisive nature of the result and the staggering losses suffered by the Persians. Mihran himself got away. Muslim casualties are not known.

Over the next few days the spoils of war were collected and distributed. Their total value was 30 million dirhams which gave every man a share of 9000. The Battle of Jalaula, similar in conception to Khalid's Battle of Walaja, was fought to a conclusion in the early part of Zul Qada, 16 Hijri [late November, 637]. It was the last major battle in Sa'd's campaign in Iraq and won for the Muslims a large portion of the Suwad. It also broke the power of the imperial army to dispute with the Muslims the occupation of the Suwad or to threaten their hold upon Ctesiphon.

---

[211] Tabari: vol. 3, p. 134.

MAP 12: THE BATTLE OF JALAULA - 2

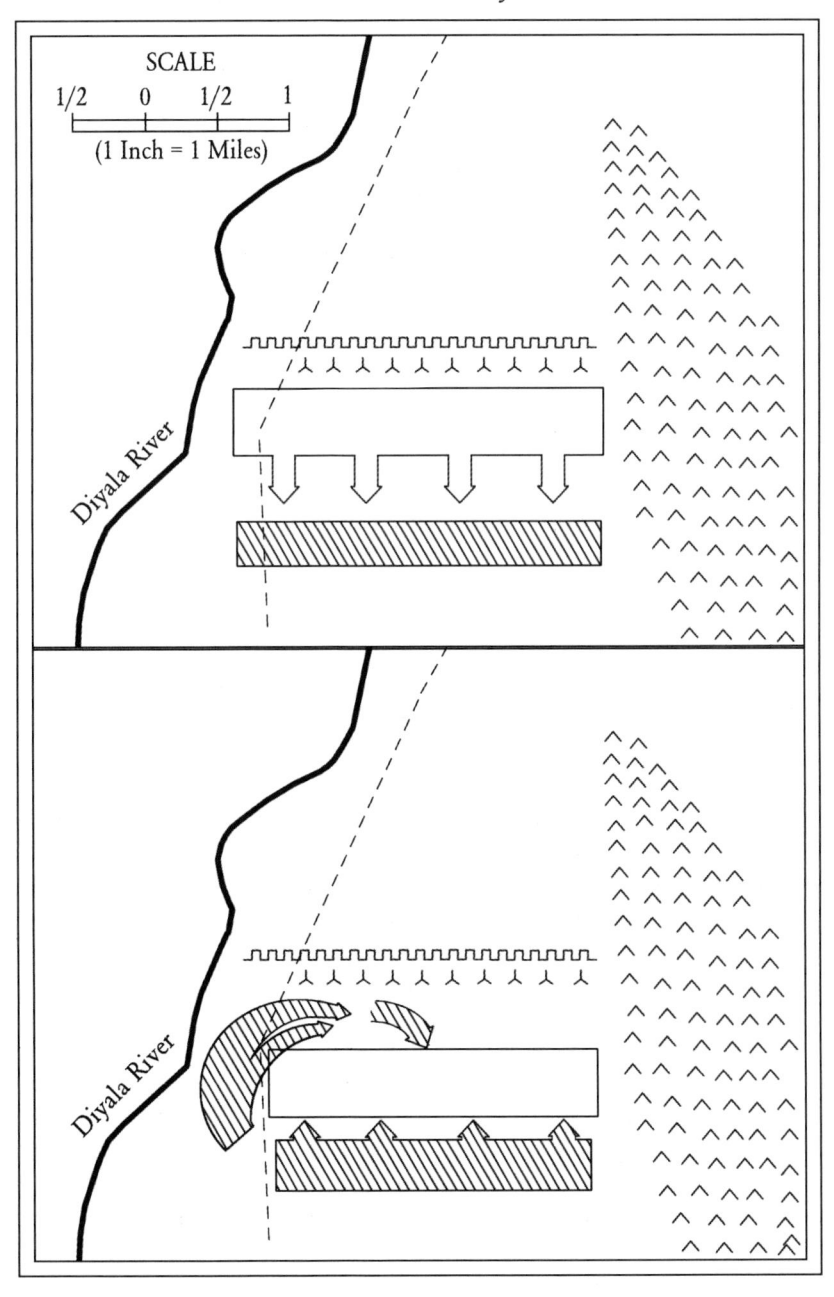

Driven into the foothills of the Kirmanshahan Mountains, which formed part of the Upper Zagros Range, its physical and moral strength shattered at Jalaula, the Persian army could now only hope to hold what remained in its hands and no longer posed a challenge to the army of Sa'd bin Abi Waqqas. But this battle was still on when Sa'd launched an expedition along the Tigris, rightly not waiting for the fall of Jalaula. The Persian governor of Mosul, a man named Intaq, had taken whatever troops were stationed in his region, added a large number of volunteers from Mosul, and moved down the Tigris. On the way he collected large Arab contingents from the tribes of Iyad, Taghlib and Namr and arrived with a sizable army at Takreet, where he had a ditch dug around the eastern arc of the city and prepared for a defensive battle. [See Map 1.]

This happened in early 16 Hijri, about Rabi-ul-Awwal, soon after the confrontation at Jalaula had begun. When intelligence of this move was received at Ctesiphon, Sa'd conveyed it to the Caliph, and in reply, Umar wrote:

"Send Abdullah bin Mu'tam to deal with Intaq. The commander of his advance guard will be Rab'i bin Al Afkal, of his right wing Haris bin Hassaan, of his left wing Furat bin Hayan, of his rearguard Hani bin Qeis, and of his cavalry Arfaja bin Harsama.

If Allah defeats the two armies, the army of Mihran and the army of Intaq, send Qa'qa bin Amr forward so that he is between the Suwad and the hills, on the boundaries of the Suwad, to act as the guard of the Muslims. May Allah preserve the Suwad for you."[212]

In Rabi-ul-Akhir, 16 Hijri [May, 637], Abdullah bin Mu'tam marched from Ctesiphon with a force of 5,000 men. Arriving at Takreet, he invested the city along its eastern arc, and over the next few weeks made 24 attempts to break in but was unsuccessful every time. This state of siege continued for 40 days until late Jamadi-ul-Awwal or early Jamadi-ul-Akhir [June or July] during which Intaq continued to supply his forces by river, and then Abdullah decided to use measures other than military to take the city.

He sent his agents to contact the Arab tribes in the city and promise them safety for themselves if they would join him against the Persians. There was no definite agreement, but the overture had the intended effect of making the Arabs lukewarm in their support of the Persians and anxious to save themselves from the consequences of a defeat in battle. Of the Arab tribes

---

[212] Ibid: pp. 132, 140-1.

present in Takreet, the Taghlib and the Namr had already fought against the Muslims, in the first Muslim invasion of Iraq under Khalid, and had been badly mauled by that great conqueror. And ties of Arab blood also drew them towards the Muslims.

Over the next few days the Persian soldiers noticed that the Arabs would not join them in their sallies and would avoid fighting as much as they could. They suspected the worst, and in this they were right. Consequently they decided not to place any further trust in the Arabs, to abandon their own officers, and to evacuate the city secretly during the night. To put this plan into effect, they began to collect boats on the river front and load their baggage.

Agents of the three tribes came at once to Abdullah with information about Persian intentions, and offered to join him against the Persians in return for a guarantee of their own safety. Abdullah felt that he was now in a stronger bargaining position in relation to the Arabs and made a bolder bid. "If you are sincere in what you assert," he said, "declare that there is none worthy of worship except Allah and that Muhammad is the Messenger of Allah, and accept what he has brought from Allah. And only then must you tell me what you wish to do."[213]

The agents slipped into the city and after discussions with the Arab tribes, returned to inform Abdullah that all had accepted Islam. Abdullah then sent instructions to the Arab chiefs about the part which they had to play in the operation of the coming night: The Muslims would start the attack from the east across the ditch and would announce it with the takbeer; on hearing this, the Arabs would secure the western side of the city, on the river front, and give the same call; after this both sides would move in and sandwich the army of Intaq in between.

Some time early in the night, the Persian soldiers were about to move to the bank to embark in the boats, having withdrawn the guards from the ditch, when sounds of the Muslim advance from the east reached them. The Persians accelerated their move to the bank but before they could get there, calls of Allaho-Akbar were raised from along the river front. Frightened by this unexpected occurrence and believing that somehow the Muslims had been able to land on the west edge of the city and cut their line of retreat, the Persians rushed eastwards, hoping to escape from that side which they hoped would now be clear of hostile troops. Here they ran into Abdullah's army which,

---

[213] Ibid: p.141.

sword in hand, struck at them and drove them back. From the west side the new Muslims advanced and Intaq and his men found themselves under attack from two sides with their escape routes blocked. The Persians were now nothing better than a horde, without officers to guide them and without order to hold them together. It is recorded that not a single man from Mosul escaped death or captivity.[214]

Two days later Abdullah despatched Rab'i bin Al Afkal northwards with a strong detachment of the army and the contingents of the newly converted Arab tribes, with Mosul as his objective. Abdullah sent the Arabs ahead as an advance guard and the Arabs arrived at Mosul and engaged in combat with the defenders. Soon after this Rabi' also got to the town and deployed his force against the defenders, but only a short time had passed when the local warriors surrendered to the Muslims on payment of the Jizya in return for their lives and property.

Following the surrender of Mosul, Abdullah bin Mu'tam also moved up from Takreet to join Rab'i, and remained at Mosul in peaceful occupation until about Muharram, 17 Hijri. Then, on the orders of Sa'd, he left a garrison of Persian Muslim troops under a Persian officer, named Muslim bin Abdullah, and with the rest of his small army marched back to rejoin the main army. The Persian officer left in command at Mosul had fought at Qadisiyya and been taken prisoner by the Muslims, but had accepted Islam, assumed the name of Muslim bin Abdullah, and elected to serve under the banner of Islam.[215]

The tactical confrontation at Jalaula was still on, with a stalemate existing between Hashim and Mihran, when reports were received that hostile Arabs from the Jazeera had gathered at Heet and had prepared the town for action, ditch and all. The Jazeera, which means literally island, was the region between the Euphrates and the Tigris, which falls in what is now north-western Iraq, north-eastern Syria and south-eastern Turkey. Sa'd chose not to do anything about these Arabs because Jalaula needed more forces, and in any case, the Arabs at Heet had a defensive posture and posed no immediate threat to Ctesiphon. Consequently, he used whatever reserves were left in his hands to reinforce Hashim at Jalaula.

Jalaula fell in early Zul Qada, and following the instructions of the Caliph as conveyed by Sa'd, Hashim sent Qa'qa bin Amr to follow the Persians towards

---

[214] Ibid: p. 142.
[215] How this Persian assumed the name of Abdullah for his father is not known, but other Persians did this also.

Hulwan, with a mixed body of Arab and Persian troops. He also left a garrison of 4,000 men under Jareer bin Abdullah at Jalaula to guard against any hostile move from the north, and with the remainder of his army returned to Ctesiphon. We shall take up later the fortunes of Qa'qa, and meanwhile direct our attention to the Euphrates.

As soon as Hashim was back, Sa'd organised an expeditionary force under Amr bin Malik and sent it off to deal with Heet and any other Arab concentrations which he should discover in the Euphrates valley.[216] In late Zul Qada, 16 Hijri [about 3rd week of December, 637], Amr marched from Ctesiphon. Upon arrival at Heet he found the place protected by a ditch covering the southern face of the town. Amr pitched his tents and deployed his force against Heet.

A few days later reports arrived about Arab movements in Qirqeesia, further up the Euphrates [at the junction of the Euphrates and the Khabur] and thinking that he would have a better chance of dealing with them in a surprise action and also win some laurels, Amr left his camp standing, occupied by a detachment under Haris bin Yazeed, and quietly marched off at night with the rest of his army. His arrival at Qirqeesia took the inhabitants completely by surprise and they submitted to Muslim rule and agreed to pay the Jizya.

Amr at once sent a fast courier to Haris, instructing him to inform the defenders of Heet that Qirqeesia had submitted and if they too agreed to the payment of the Jizya, they would be left in peace; if not, Haris was to construct another ditch outside the ditch of the Arabs so that the latter would know that the Muslims meant business and were going to starve them into submission. The Arabs at Heet were glad to accept the offer of Haris; they agreed to the payment of the Jizya and dispersed to their homes. This happened in Zul Haj, 16 Hijri [January, 638].

Upon the peaceful solution of the Heet problem, Haris bin Yazeed returned to Ctesiphon with his detachment, but Amr bin Malik remained at Qirqeesia for another month to watch the Euphrates axis. Then, leaving a Persian Muslim officer, named Ashannaq bin Abdullah, with a body of Persian Muslim troops to garrison Qirqeesia against the Romans and any hostile Arabs, he returned with his remaining force to Sa'd.

Mihran worked fast at Khaniqeen [15 miles beyond Jalaula and near the present Iran-Iraq border] to reorganise the part of his army which had survived with

---

[216] This officer has also been called Umar, and was one of Hashim's generals at Jalaula.

him the defeat of Jalaula. His soldiers were joined by a few more whom Yazdjurd was able to lay his hands on at Hulwan. In this task Mihran was assisted by Feerzan, but he had only a few days to get his army into shape before Qa'qa was upon him. Mihran quickly arrayed his army for battle on the plain outside Khaniqeen.

Qa'qa also deployed for battle, and knowing that the Muslims enjoyed a moral superiority over the Persians as a result of the latter's successive defeats in recent months and wishing to exploit this state of affairs, lost no time in launching his attack. The Persians put up a defence but it did not last long. Mihran was killed in action. We do not know who killed him, but we can hope that he met his death at the hands of Qa'qa, for to be despatched by valiant and noble an adversary was a fate which Mihran, as a veteran general of so many hotly contested battles, richly deserved. With his death, his army lost its feet and was driven off the battlefield. Feerzan, who survived the battle, could do nothing to stem the tide of defeat.

Khaniqeen was taken as a prize of war. A large number of Persian women were treated as part of that prize and distributed among the Muslim soldiery, like many of their sisters taken at Jalaula. Some were kept as slaves but others were married and lived the rest of their lives like normal Muslim wives. This did not please Caliph Umar, but more of that later.

Upon hearing of Mihran's defeat and death at Khaniqeen, Yazdjurd left the defence of Hulawn to a general named Khusrau Shanum, a veteran of Qadisiyya, and journeyed with his entourage to Qum. Qa'qa arrived at Qasr Sheereen and formed up once again to battle the Persians.

Qasr sheereen was one of the marvels of the world. It had been built by Khusrau Parwez, grandfather of Yazdjurd, the one who had torn up the letter of the Holy Prophet. It is said that once while he was feasting in the company of his wife Sheereen and had too much to drink, Parwez turned to Sheereen and told her that she could have anything that her heart desired. She asked that two canals be constructed, lined with stone, in which there would be a perpetual flow of wine; and between these canals a palace be built for her unlike any palace which existed in the empire. And this was done.[217] The construction of such a palace was quite in line with the character of Chosroes Parwez, who, apart from his other luxurious possessions, is said to have had 3,000 women in his harem and possessed 760 elephants, 8,500 horses and 12,000 mules.[218] The

---

[217] Yaqut: vol. 1, p. 113.
[218] Tabari: vol. 1, p. 616.

palace was used by the lady as a winter resort and took its name from her: the Palace of Sheereen.

Around this palace and its construction hangs the marvellous, romance of Sheereen and Farhad, the story of which has warmed the hearts of Muslims for a thousand years. It is probably entirely imaginary, because there is no mention of Farhad anywhere until the poet Nizami wrote the romance. But the story is so moving, as indeed all romantic tragedies are, that the reader will forgive this digression from the bloody assaults of Qa'qa to the mistland romantic fantasy.

When Parwez got down to building the Qasr Sheereen, one of the engineers employed by him for this task was a young fellow named Farhad. As it happened, one day Farhad laid eyes on Sheereen and fell madly in love with her. Apparently she reciprocated his affections, though not perhaps in the same desperate way. However, this created the usual triangle, and since Farhad was too obstinate and strong to be dismissed lightly, it was arranged, at the direction of Parwez, that Farhad should dig a tunnel through a mountain, and if he succeeded in this he could have Sheereen. Farhad agreed, and the mountain chosen was Bisotun [Persian for 'without pillars'], about 20 miles from Kirmanshah.

Farhad got down to work, digging away for all he was worth, using just a pickaxe, and got deeper and deeper into the mountain. He was fortified by his burning love for Sheereen, whose image drew him on and on into the rocky bowels of Bisotun. And the Emperor forgot all about him, not for a moment worried about the possibility of a human being successfully performing the task which he had set Farhad.

Then one day someone informed Parwez that Farhad had just about done it, that he had reached the face of the mountain and was about to break through. Parwez had to act fast if he was to keep his favourite wife to himself. Having lost half his empire to the Romans, he was not about to lose Sheereen to a mere engineer. So he sent for a witch and told her to pass the word to Farhad that Sheereen was dead.

The witch went into the tunnel and found Farhad digging away at the mountain, happy in the thought that victory was near and that Sheereen would soon be in his embrace. Then she told him. When he heard that Sheereen was dead, he raised his pickaxe and plunged it into his breast. He fell down and died; and the Persian couplet runs:

This night the sound of the pickaxe did not come from Bisotun.
Perhaps Farhad has gone into the dreams of Sheereen.

The spirit of Sheereen may have watched the battle which was fought in front of her favourite winter resort. It did not last long. The Persians were again broken by Qa'qa's attack and with Khusrau Shanum in their midst, fled into the hills, while Qa'qa marched on and occupied Hulwan. This action was completed by the very end of the year 16 Hijri. The inhabitants of Hulwan submitted to Muslim rule and agreed to pay the Jizya. Hulwan was then a large city, while today it is a relatively small one called Pul-e-Zohab. The Persians use the name Alvand for Hulwan. This is what the river Hulwan in Iraq is, before flowing into Iraq from Iran, the River Alvand.

When news of the conquest of Hulwan was brought to Sa'd, he wished to continue the advance towards North Persia in the wake of the defeated Persian army, knowing that the sooner this operation was launched the less able the Persians would be to successfully resist the Muslims. He wrote to the Caliph for permission to follow the Persians, but Umar would have none of it. The Muslim army in Iraq was already extended and Umar had an instinctive dislike of water obstacles between himself and his armies. He forbade the operation. "I wish," he wrote to Sa'd, "that between the Suwad and the hills there were a wall which would prevent them from getting to us and prevent us from getting to them. The fertile Suwad is sufficient for us; and I prefer the safety of the Muslims to the spoils of war."[219]

As a result of this ban on further offensive operations, Qa'qa was withdrawn from Hulwan and Jareer bin Abdullah from Jalaula, to rejoin the main body of the army. This happened a few weeks after the capture of Hulwan. Qa'qa left Qubas bin Abdullah, a Persian officer from Khurasan who had fought under him at Jalaula, Khaniqeen and Qasr Sheereen, as commander of a Persian Muslim garrison at Hulwan to guard the frontier of Islam; and himself returned not to Ctesiphon, but to a new cantonment whose construction had only just begun: Kufa.

From Muharram, 17 Hijri onwards [February, 638], all three main approaches into the Muslim-occupied Suwad-along the Tigris Valley, along the Euphrates Valley and down the Kirmanshahan road-were guarded by Persian troops under Persian officers, newly converted to Islam.

---

[219] Tabari: vol. 3, p. 135.

In Iraq the frontiers of the Suwad were being secured by Muslim border posts, and in the capital of the Muslim state a moving drama was being enacted. There in the marketplace, Emperor Yazdjurd's daughter, Shahran, was being sold as a common slave.[220]

Princess Shahran, a girl of tender age, had left Ctesiphon along with her father's household when he abandoned the Persian capital after the fall of its western part. She stayed at Jalaula for a while, but when Yazdjurd moved on towards Hulwan, she was ill and was left behind. She got out of Jalaula apparently just before its fall and moved to some place between that city and Hulwan. And some time after Jalaula, she was travelling with a convoy to Hulwan when Hashim bin Utba fell upon the convoy with a raiding party, killed most of the escort and captured the convoy and its precious passenger. The young princess, the light of her father's eyes, was sent to Madina as part of the spoils of war.

In Madina she was to be sold as a slave to the highest bidder; and there she stood, dressed in her fine clothes, bedecked in her jewellery, with a veil covering her face below the eyes. The Caliph and other important Companions were also present with the crowd. The Caliph said "I see this girl glancing at Hussein bin Ali…and it is obvious that she would prefer him above all men, for none among us is more bright-faced than he."[221]

And while Yazdjurd mourned the loss of his beloved daughter, Shahran was given in marriage to the noble Hussein.[222] While Qa'qa was advancing against opposition on the road to Hulwan, several raids were launched by Sa'd in various parts of the Suwad to bring the region into submission. The deepest of the raids were on the way to Azarbeijan and were led by Hashim bin Utba and Ash'as bin Qeis. The columns had as their objective the area of Daquqa and Khaneejar, on the road to Irbeel, and they succeeded in capturing the area, whose inhabitants submitted to Muslim rule and were left in peace in return for the Jizya.

---

[220] This is the name given by Waqidi. According to Tabari (vol. 3, p. 80) she was called Manjana, but most Persian historians give her name as Shahr Bano.
[221] Waqidi: Futuh-ush-Sham: vol. 2, pp. 139-140
[222] I have given here the account of the Persian Princess being given to Hussain bin Ali as related by the historians. What worries me from the point of view of historical accuracy is the fact that Hussain was born in 4 Hijri and if this episode of the marketplace occurred just after the conquests described (late 16, early 17 Hijri), Hussein would have been a husband at 13. Perhaps the event occurred a few years later, even though the princess was captured just after Jalaula. Or perhaps we are under-estimating Hussein bin Ali!

But while these raids were progressing and Qa'qa was making for Qasr Sheereen, another threat was created by the Persians in the region east of Ctesiphon. A small Persian force under Azeen, son of the Persian general Hormuzan, emerged from the Kirmanshahan Mountains into the plain below. The purpose of this venture is not known. It could only be intended as a diversionary movement to force Sa'd to withdraw Qa'qa and Jareer from the north, but the force was too small to achieve that purpose.

Sa'd sent Zarrar bin Al Khattab [no relation of Umar] with a column to deal with Azeen, and the two forces clashed at Bahandaf.[223] After some fighting, Zarrar captured the Persian commander, whereupon his force broke and fled. Zarrar had Azeen beheaded, and following the retreating Persians, got to Seerwan, the main town in the district of Masabzan, in a valley in the southern slopes of the Kirmanshahan Mountains.[224] He found that the people of the town had fled on hearing of the approach of the Muslims.

Zarrar sent word to the neighbouring villages that the locals could return to their homes in peace and that all they had to do to get protection for themselves and their property was to pay the Jizya. These terms were gladly accepted by the people and they all came back and submitted to the Muslim rule; and as a result of Azeen's rash venture, the district of Masabzan also became part of the new Muslim state. Zarrar remained at Seerwan for a few weeks and then returned to rejoin Sa'd, leaving behind a detachment under Ibn Huzeil to act as a frontier garrison and guard against Persian raids into Muslim territory.

This brings us to the end of Sa'd's campaign against the Persians in 16 Hijri. The only event which remains to be mentioned is that some time after the capture of Ctesiphon, Umar ordered the return to Uballa of the force which had been there before Sa'd's march from Madina and which had joined him on his way to Qadisiyya. Sa'd consequently sent off a force of 800 men under Utba bin Ghazwan and Mugheerah bin Shu'ba; and this force reoccupied Uballa and re-established Muslim government over the local districts.

The year 16 Hijri ended [on January 22, 638] with the entire Suwad except for Ahwaz, in fact all that was best in Iraq, as part of the new empire of Islam.

---

[223] The exact location of this place is not certain. From studies based on Yakut, I place it a little south of Badra, which lies north of Kut-ul-Imara.
[224] Seerwan is now called Sheerwan.

Chapter 15: The Consolidation of Iraq

Soon after the last of the conquests described in the preceding chapter, Sa'd sent a delegation of officers from various tribes to Madina. When the delegates, one of whom was Abdullah bin Mu'tam, conquerer of Takreet and Mosul, came to Umar, the Caliph was taken aback by the pallor of their faces. "By Allah!" he exclaimed, "you do not look as you did when you started from Madina. You look pale. What has changed you?" "The unhealthiness of the land," they replied.

Then came a letter for Umar from a Muslim officer in Ctesiphon, in which he said, "The bellies of the Arabs have gone flabby, their biceps have gone soft, and their colour has faded."[225]

The Caliph was perturbed. The thought of his hardy soldiers losing their toughness because of the enervating effect of the climate and the softening effect of the finer civilisation to which they were exposed in Ctesiphon, worried him, as did the presence of wide rivers between him and the army in Iraq. There was something about large water obstacles which the Caliph did not like. So when another request arrived from Sa'd for permission to follow the retreating Persians, Umar replied firmly, "Stay where you are and do not follow them. Find for the Muslims a place which is open and suitable as a station for war; and let there not be a river between me and the Muslims."[226]

Sa'd, as aggressive as ever in his military intentions towards the Persians, gave more importance to the factor of prosecuting the war against Persia than the mainly psychological advantage of not having a river between the army and the Caliph. He picked on Anbar as a military station, and leaving a sizable detachment in Ctesiphon, marched thither with the bulk of his army in the early part of 17 Hijri. [This could not have been before Muharram].[227] Anbar was an ancient town on the north bank of the Euphrates, 3 miles from the present Falluja, and was well known for its granaries. It was also a trading centre for caravans from Syria and Persia and had been captured by Khalid bin Al Waleed

---

[225] Tabari: vol. 3, p. 145.
[226] Ibid: p. 80; Balazuri: p. 274.
[227] Some historians have placed this move in 15 Hijri but they are not correct. Most of them agree that the move took place in 17 Hijri and are definite about it being after Takreet and Mosul. (Tabari: vol. 3 pp. 129, 145, 147; Balazuri: p. 275; Yaqubi: Tareekh: vol. 2, p. 150.) In fact Tabari places the move in Muharram.

five years earlier by the remarkable expedient of filling the moat which circled the town with the bodies of slaughtered camels to establish a passage across it.

But Sa'd's troops disliked the place. It was hot and full of flies. Having discovered its drawbacks, Sa'd wrote to the Caliph about his problem, and Umar wrote back: "The Arab is like the camel. No place suits him unless it suits the camel and the goat, and has pastures. So find for them a dry plain near the river, and do not place a river between them and me."[228]

On receipt of this instruction, Sa'd crossed the Euphrates and marched to a place known as Kuweifa, not far from the site of the future Kufa, but this did not prove suitable either. It was hot and infested with flies and mosquitoes which bothered the soldiers. Luckily for them, they received as offer of help from Amr bin Abdul Maseeh bin Buqeila, the old Iraqi prince of whom mention has been made in an earlier chapter. He said to Sa'd: "I shall guide you to a land which rises above marshland but is lower than the desert."[229]

The Muslims followed Amr bin Abdul Maseeh and he led them to just the kind of place they were looking for. When the baggage had been unloaded, Sa'd wrote to Umar, "I have moved to Kufa[230] a place between Hira and the Euphrates, where the land is both dry and well-watered and is overgrown with thistles.[231] I divided the army at Madina, left there as a garrison those who liked the place and brought the rest to me."[232]

Thus was Kufa born, in 17 Hijri [638 A.D.] The place was open virgin country which in the past had been known as "Suristan", and here the Muslims got down to building the new city, actually a cantonment. They worked according to a well laid out plan with separate areas earmarked for tribes and clans and the mosque acting as the hub of the city. In fact the first thing to be built was the mosque, and beside it Sa'd had a palatial building put up for himself. This palace of Sa'd, as it came to be called, was designed and constructed by a Persian architect, named Ruzbeh bin Buzurjmihr, a native of Hamadan who had become a Muslim. A large area was also allotted to Persian Muslim soldiers who were now numbered in thousands. These included men who had joined

---

[228] Tabari: vol. 3, p. 81; Balazuri: p. 275.
[229] Tabari: vol. 3, p. 95; Masudi: Muruj: vol. 2, p. 329.
[230] There was no Kufa before this. Kufa means literally a mound of sand, and also an area of sand and pebbles (Balazuri: p. 274). The name chosen by Sa'd was descriptive.
[231] In the Arabic words used by Sad, the reference to thistles may be an idiom indicating vegetation which is both dry and green, i.e., by seasons.
[232] Tabari: vol. 3, p 147.

Sa'd before Qadisiyya, men who had fought against the Muslims at Qadisiyya and had been taken prisoner and then accepted Islam, and many more who had joined the banner of Islam after Qadisiyya. All construction at the new city was of wood, but some time later a big fire destroyed most of the city and it was rebuilt with bricks and earth.

At the same time as Kufa was founded, the foundations were also laid by the Muslims of another great city of the future-Basra.[233] Where Basra was built by the Muslims there had been a city since ancient times, known by the Persian name of Wahshatabad [the city in the wilderness] or Beheshtabad [the city of paradise],[234] which had been used as a frontier garrison by the Persians against the marauding Arab tribes from the desert. But as a result of the raids of Muthana bin Harisa, the Persians in this city had sought refuge in Uballa and Muthana had destroyed the city.[235] The ruins left after Muthana had finished with the place became known to the Muslims as Khureiba, i.e. ruins!

Some time after Ctesiphon, Sa'd had sent to Uballa a force of 800 men under Utba bin Ghazwan and Mugheerah bin Shu'ba the original team which had conquered the districts between Uballa, Ahwaz and Mazar. This detachment returned and reoccupied Uballa, though what opposition, if any, was met is not known. Utba did not find the city of Uballa suitable for permanent habitation, moved his soldiers out into the desert and camped not far from the ruins of Wahshatabad. He then wrote to Umar about the need for a place from which the Muslims could campaign against the Persians and to which they could return after operations; and in reply the Caliph instructed him to concentrate his soldiers at one place, which should be near water and pasture.

Utba set out with his men to look for a suitable place. When they came to a certain area covered with pebbles, the men at once called it Basra. To the Arabs, Basra meant a hard land, full of pebbles and stones, [some say black stones, some say white stones, some say stones with white in them.][236] The place was 15 miles from Uballa. This was to be Basra, and the new city would in its north-eastern part hold the old ruins of Wahshatabad. Utba was happy to

---

[233] Some historians have given the year of Basra as 14 Hijri. This is due to the reason that some of them have mixed up Utba's early battles. In the Uballa region with his reoccupation of Uballa. Like Kufa, Basra also was founded after the conquest of Ctesiphon, Takreet and Mosul.
[234] Tariq al Katib: p. 17.
[235] Ibid.
[236] Tabari: vol. 3, p. 90; Masudi: Muruj: vol. 2, p. 329; Balazuri: p. 336; Dinawari: p. 117; Yaqut: vol. 1, p. 636.

find the place and wrote to the Caliph, "I have found a place which is full of reeds, beside fertile land, and beyond it is a marsh."[237]

All the dwellings in the city were built of wood, and work started at about the same time as at Kufa and followed the same pattern of construction, with a mosque being built first and the houses of the tribes and clans next. Here too there was a fire, though not as bad as the one at Kufa, and after that the city rebuilt with bricks and earth. The following year [18 Hijri], Umar instructed the governor of Basra, Abu Musa, to build a canal for the use of the inhabitants, and Abu Musa had a canal dug for a distance of 11 miles from the Tigris to the city. The canal was constructed by a Muslim, named Maqil bin Yasar, and became known as the canal of Maqil.[238] Later another canal was built to meet the needs of the growing population; and the city founded by Utba bin Ghazwan continued to grow in size and importance for 300 years until the early part of the 10th Century Hijri, when a new Basra [the present one] was built on the right bank of the Tigris and the old one was evacuated by the inhabitants for the new. The old Basra now carries the name of Zubeir.

The Muslims settled down to ruling Iraq as a permanent part of the Muslim empire. There would be no going back from Iraq, nor would anyone take it away from them. They had come to stay, to live, to rule, and to become part of the land. For its military protection against a possible return of the Persians, strong garrisons were maintained at Ctesiphon, Kufa and Basra, while detachments guarded the frontier at Hulwan, Seerwan, Mosul and Qirqeesia. The military commander in Iraq was also the governor of the province with his headquarters at Kufa, from where he saw to the organisation and administration of all Iraq except the region of Basra, which was placed under a separate governor. Sa'd bin Abi Waqqas was assisted by a number of officials appointed by Umar, the more prominent among whom were Ammar bin Yasir, who was given charge of the prayers, and Abdullah bin Masud, who held charge of the treasury and acted as chief judge. For assessment and acquisition of land revenue, Umar appointed Uthman bin Haneef for the region west of the Tigris and Hudayfah bin Al Yaman for the region east of the river. The latter had his post in Ctesiphon.

The people of the Suwad - Persian and Arab - who had entered into treaties with earlier Muslim commanders and then broken the treaties and joined Rustam against the Muslims, were generously treated. They were allowed to return and remain in occupation of their property. But those who had left their

---

[237] Balazuri: p. 341.
[238] Ibid: p. 352.

homes on the defeat of the Persians and even now refused to return to the Suwad, lost their properties, which were confiscated and treated as spoils of war. All property belonging to the Persian royal family was confiscated. Most of the inhabitants of Iraq actually bore no ill-will towards the Muslims. They had joined the army of Persia when the Muslims had been pushed out of the Suwad and they saw this as the only way of survival, but they were now glad to get back home and come under Muslim rule, which they found to be more just and kind than what they had experienced in imperial days.

There were many cases of Muslims marrying Persian women, either Christians who could be lawfully married or those who had got converted to Islam. One of these Muslims was Hudayfah bin Al Yaman, administrator of Ctesiphon. When Umar came to know about this, he wrote: "It has come to my knowledge that you have married a woman of Madain from the people of the book. Divorce her!" Hudayfah knew his law as well as Umar and was not going to let Umar order his matrimonial affairs. "I shall not divorce her," he wrote back, "until you tell me whether it is lawful or unlawful, and what you intend by this." Umar then explained, "It is lawful, but the women of Persia are clinging, and if you go to them they will prevail upon you against your own women." Upon receipt of this letter Hudayfah divorced his Persian wife.[239]

With the occupation of Iraq by the Muslims, one very important question which arose was the possession of landed property by Muslims in the conquered territory. Many of them, those serving in Iraq as well as those living in Madina, felt that since Iraq was theirs, they should be permitted to acquire estates in the province and settle down in permanent ownership. But Umar did not wish the Muslim soldiers to become landed gentry and acquire vested interests which would make them less willing to strike camp and march on to further conquests. He refused to permit the purchase or allotment of land to Muslims, and when he came to know that some officers had already bought land, one of whom was Jareer bin Abdullah, he ordered its return to the former owners.

"Leave the land in the hands of its owners," the Caliph wrote to Sa'd, "and the irrigation and organisation of it in the hands of the old officials, so that the Muslims can get the benefit of revenue. If you take it away and distribute it among the present Muslims, there will be nothing left for those who are to come."[240]

---

[239] Tabari: vol. 3, P. 88.
[240] Balazuri: p. 265.

It was not till the time of Caliph Uthman that the allotment of land to the Muslims was begun, and then there was a rush to acquire property in Iraq. The two main sources of income from Iraq were land revenue and the Jizya. All cultivated land was left in the possession of local owners and a system of taxation was imposed upon farmers and producers. The tax varied with the type of produce and was fairly assessed to the satisfaction of the tax-payer. [The details of the system would not interest the reader].

Then there was the Jizya which, as explained in an earlier chapter, was a tax imposed upon non-Muslim subjects in return for their exemption from military service and a guarantee of safety against external foes. The inhabitants of Iraq in the east and of Syria and Palestine in the west, knowing the rigours that subjection by foreign powers entailed, were happy to secure their lives and property and live in dignity and peace by paying what in most cases amounted to one dinar per head per annum. The tax was paid by all non Muslims- idolaters, Christians, Jews, Zoroastrians. Umar was not sure about the treatment to be meted out to the Zoroastrian and at a conference in Madina, raised the question. Abdur Rahman bin Auf at once replied, "I bear witness that the Messenger of Allah, on whom be the blessings of Allah and peace, said, 'Treat them like the people of the book'."[241]

But there were some exemptions from the Jizya: old people with no income, those of infirm mind, priests and monks of any faith, and those who were not in a position to pay.[242] All non-Muslim Persians who served as soldiers with the Muslim army were also exempt from this tax, but the largest single group exempted was the large Christian Arab tribe of Bani Taghlib, which inhabited north-western Iraq and the southern part of the Jazeera.

A part of the Bani Taghlib had accepted Islam at Takreet, as narrated in the preceding chapter, but the bulk of the tribe was still Christian. They were a fiercely proud people who regarded themselves as above the rest of the Arabs in the region and in spite of their defeats at the hands of the Muslims, felt that they were powerful enough to claim special privileges. A delegation from the tribe travelled to Madina to see Umar and requested that they should not have to pay the Jizya as it would be an affront to their dignity. They were prepared to pay more in any other way but not in the form of Jizya. At first the Caliph refused to accept their request and the delegation threatened that the tribe would migrate to the Roman Empire and join the Romans against the forces of Islam in Syria. Umar told them that they could go where they wished and the

---

[241] Ibid: p. 267.
[242] Abu Yusaf: p. 123.

Muslims would still catch up with them. After some discussion, Umar allowed that while the Muslims would claim and receive Jizya, the Taghlib could call it by any other name. Eventually, on the recommendation of other prominent Muslims, Umar relented and exempted them from the Jizya, but imposed a double rate of Sadqa, a voluntary contribution made by Muslims for the use of the needy. Umar also laid down as one of the terms of agreement that the children of those of the Taghlib who had accepted Islam would not be brought up as Christians. The tribe was happy to accept these terms and returned home.[243]

The revenue flowing into Madina from various taxes turned into a generous flood and created problems for the Caliph, who had to make sure that it was spent wisely and not allowed to be wasted or unfairly distributed.

The coffers of Madina had begun to fill soon after the Muslim armies were launched across the borders of Arabia in the time of Abu Bakr. The victorious armies marched from triumph to triumph and gathered vast spoils after every battle, of which one-fifth was sent to Madina as the share of the state, and to this was added the Jizya paid by those of the conquered peoples who did not accept Islam as their faith. But so simple were the financial needs of the Muslim administration of the time that all the wealth which came in was distributed among the Muslims as a gift of God. Abu Bakr made no distinction between various classes and categories of Muslims and gave equally to all. However, there was no proper financial system or economic structure and the prosperity of the Muslim state depended upon the fortunes of its armies in battle.

The problem became more complex in Umar's time and he was faced, more than his predecessor, by the big question: What to do with all the money which was pouring in? Finally, in late 15 Hijri, after Qadisiyya and Yarmuk, when the treasury was bursting at the seams, Umar decided that something had to be done to deal with all the wealth and a proper system devised for spending the state revenue. He called a conference of the Companions.[244]

Umar first asked for opinions about the general principles of dealing with the wealth which had accumulated in the treasury. Ali said, "Distribute every year whatever money is gathered. Keep nothing back." Uthman gave the opinion: "I see a lot of wealth in the treasury which will enrich people, and if we do not

---

[243] Balazuri: p. 186; Tabari: vol. 3, pp. 145, 158.
[244] The date of this event is disputed. Balazuri and Yaqubi place it in 20 Hijri, but there is incontrovertible evidence to support Tabari's version which I have used here.

keep account of who receives and who does not, I fear it will all be lost."[245] Then a veteran of Syria said that in Syria the Romans had a regular system of pay for their men and had organised military districts in their domains. So far the Companions were in mutual accord and opinions expressed found acceptance by the Caliph. But one man struck a discordant note by saying, "O Commander of the Faithful, you should leave something in the treasury as provision in case of need."

Umar turned upon him in anger: "That is something that Satan has put in your mouth. Allah has saved me from this evil and it will be a trial for those who come after me. I shall provide them with what Allah and his Prophet have commanded. The obedience of Allah and his Prophet is the provision with which we have got so far, as you can see; and if this wealth is the price of the faith of any one of you, then you are doomed."[246]

The man said no more. Actually what he said makes sense and he would have proved a good economist today, but the poor fellow was obviously living before his time!

It was agreed that all the state income should be distributed every year and nothing kept back. The next question was: How to distinguish between various kinds of recipients and how to determine their worthiness? One present reminded the Caliph that Abu Bakr used to treat all Muslims equally in the matter of distribution of money, but this was not acceptable to Umar. "No", he said, "I shall not place those who fought against the Messenger of Allah, on whom be the blessings of Allah and peace, as equal to those who fought by his side."[247] The principle of gradation was also accepted and it was a sound one, because it placed the early Muslims who had suffered for Islam at a higher level than those who accept Islam later when the going was good or when they had no other choice anyway.

Then came the question as to how much a man needed and was entitled to. On this the general opinion was: "His food and the food of his family, neither more nor less; clothes for him and his family for summer and winter; two riding beasts to carry him on the holy war and on the pilgrimage. The rest of the money to be distributed justly among those tried in war, according to their merits, and to meet the needs of the people."[248]

---

[245] Tabari: vol. 3, p. 278; Balazuri: p. 436.
[246] Tabari: vol. 3, p. 110.
[247] Balazuri: p. 437.
[248] Tabari: vol. 3, pp. 110-1.

This too was accepted, and now came the question: What basis should be used for placing some above others? Umar asked with whom he should start, and several Companions, including Abdur Rahman bin Auf, said, "Start with yourself." "No", replied Umar, "the Messenger of Allah is our leader and I shall start with his clan, then those next to him, then those next to them."[249]

This principle having been decided, the Caliph gave three Companions the task of compiling a list of persons in the order of their nearness to the Prophet. These gentlemen produced the list clan-wise, in which the first clan to appear was the Bani Hashim [the Prophet's clan], then Abu Bakr and his clan, then Umar and his clan. This placed Umar higher in nearness to the Prophet than he considered himself, and he rejected it. "I wish you were right", he said. "I shall decide this on the basis of nearness to the Messenger of Allah, on whom be the blessings of Allah and peace; those nearest him, then those next in nearness. And I shall place Umar where Allah has placed him."[250]

The clan of Umar, the Bani Adi, found themselves the losers by this decision and approached Umar to accept the proposal which placed him and his clan higher; but they had not judged their clan leader right. "Fie, O Bani Adi!" the Caliph rebuked them. "You desire that you should eat off my back and my good deeds be lost on your account! By Allah, we have received no merit in this world and we do not hope for God's bounty in return for our actions except through Muhammad, on whom be the blessings of Allah and peace; He is the highest of us and his clan is the highest of the Arabs. So I shall determine this by nearness to the Prophet. By Allah, if non-Arab Muslims bring good deeds and we do not, they will be closer to Muhammad on the Day of Judgement."[251] When later the question of clans was also accepted as one factor, though a less important one, for determining worthiness, the clan of Bani Adi came sixth.

When all was said and done, the main factors which decided merit were entry into the faith and performance in battle, the battles too being taken in chronological sequence. The scales of pay given by historians vary in regard to some details, but by and larger there is agreement on the main categories of recipients and what they were paid. The scale given below is a synthesis of the details given by various sources.

---

[249] Balazuri: p. 440. There are some variations of the opinions given at this conference, as described by the historians, but the sense is the same.
[250] Tabari: vol. 3, p. 278; Balazuri: p. 436; Yaqubi: Tareekh; vol. 2, p. 153.
[251] Tabari: vol. 3, p. 278; Balazuri: p. 436.

The highest were the veterans of Badr, Islam's first battle, who received an annual allowance of 5,000 dirhams, freeman and slave. Next were those who had become Muslims by the time of the treaty of Hudaybiyah: 4,000 dirhams; then those present at the Conquest of Mecca: 3,000; those Meccans who got converted as a result of this conquest received 2,000. The veterans of the Apostasy got 3,000, those who fought in subsequent battles up to Yarmuk and Qadisiyya 2,000, and those fighting after Qadisiyya would receive 1,000. Of the veterans of Qadisiyya, 25 were picked out and given a special additional grant of 500 per annum; and some others were chosen for their excellence in battle and given 2,500 extra, but none could receive a higher pay than the veterans of Badr. Others came in descending order down to 250 dirhams.

What is given above was based on war performance and time of conversion, but there were others whose special claims were acknowledged. The widows of the Holy Prophet received 12,000 each and Abbas, uncle of the Prophet, got 5,000 [or 7,000]. The Prophet's grandsons, Hassan and Hussein, and three Companions who were very close to him, viz Abu Dhar, Ammar bin Yasir and Salman the Persian, received 5,000 each. There was also a scale, varing according to merit, for the women and children of veterans and of the early Muslims, and the lowest in order-the poor who had no claim of any kind-were granted a fixed ration of grain every month. Even Persian officers featured in this bounty. The son of Nakheer Jan and the son of Busbuhra [the generals who were killed in the Muslim advance to Ctesiphon] and other nobles were granted a pay of 1,000 dirhams; and those Persians who accepted Islam and fought under Sa'd bin Abi Waqqas in Iraq received the same pay as laid down for Arab soldiers in that campaign. Only in one case was such a thing laid down as pay of appointment, and this was for the senior generals. The commanders of corps and armies were given an annual pay which varied from 7,000 to 9,000 dirhams, according to the importance and size of their commands.

Everyone entitled to pay would receive it in the month of Muharram every year.[252]

This fixation of the scale of pay was accepted by all as just and fair, but there were exceptions. Some of the noble Qureish who had become Muslims after the conquest of Mecca refused their lower pay because they did not acknowledge anyone as finer than themselves. Umar explained, "I have decided

---

[252] These scales are taken from Tabari: vol. 3, pp. 72, 109-112. Balazuri: pp. 435-442; Abu Yusuf: pp. 43-6.

the scale according to merit by entry into Islam and not by position."[253] They accepted this explanation and their money.

But the most interesting dispute arose in the case of Umar's own son Abdullah, who was given 3,000 and was hurt because a sum of 4,000 was allotted to Usama, son of Zayd, who had been the Prophet's freedman and adopted son. Both young men were of the same age and good soldiers. Abdullah complained to his father, "You have given me 3,000 and Usama 4,000. You have placed him higher than me one who is not better than I. I have fought in more battles than he."

Umar replied, "I have given him more because he was dearer to the Messenger of Allah than you, and his father was dearer to the Messenger of Allah than your father."[254]

---

[253] Tabari: vol. 3, pp. 108-9.
[254] Balazuri: pp. 437-8, 443.

Chapter 16: The Conquest of Ahwaz

The year 17 Hijri, corresponding generally to 638 A.D., was for the most part a year of consolidation. However, while there was quiet on the north-eastern front, where the Persian army had withdrawn after the loss of Hulwan, the Muslims found it necessary to launch two operations, one to the north-west and the other to the south-east. The first was a diversion designed to reduce pressure on the Muslims in Syria, and the second a limited tactical action which was meant to deal with the pinpricks started by the Persian general Hormuzan, but which led in the course of things to the conquest of Ahwaz. We shall take the diversionary operation first.

In August, 636, was fought the bloody battle of Yarmuk, in which Khalid broke the back of a vast Roman army. Following this victory, the Muslims recaptured Damascus and then laid siege to Jerusalem. The holy city surrendered in April, 637, and thereafter Abu Ubayda and Khalid advanced into Northern Syria, taking city after city, until they got to the famous metropolis of Antioch, where the Romans made their last determined stand in Syria. Here too the Romans were trounced, and after quickly clearing up the few cities that remained, Abu Ubayda settled down in military occupation of Syria, with his headquarters at Emessa.

Heraclius, the Byzantine Emperor, had left Syria even before the Battle of Antioch, Knowing that the chances of holding this lovely province against the all-conquering Muslim army were slim. Departing northwards, he had taken one last sorrowing look at Syria and lamented, "Salutations to thee, O Syria, and farewell from one who departs. Never again shall the Roman return to thee except in fear. Oh, what a fine land I leave to the enemy!"[255]

But to keep the Muslims occupied in Syria and dissuade them from following up their conquests, be instigated the Christian Arab tribes of the Jazeera to make an attempt to recover Syria.[256] These tribes, bound to Heraclius by bonds of religion, responded bravely to the call and gathering in their thousands, marched to Emessa in the mid-summer of 638. As soon as Abu Ubayda heard of the preparations being made in the Jazeera against him, he concentrated his army to fight a defensive battle in the fortified city of Emessa, and asked Umar for reinforcements. Umar ordered Sa'd to send Qa'qa bin Amr with 4,000 men

---

[255] Tabari: vol. 3, p. 100; Balazuri: p. 142.
[256] As explained earlier, the Jazeera was the land between the Tigris and the Euphrates in what is now north-western Iraq, north-eastern Syria and south-eastern Turkey.

from Kufa to join Abu Ubayda, and also instructed him to launch a three-pronged invasion of the Jazeera from Iraq under Suheil bin Adi, Abdullah bin Utba and Waleed bin Utba, with Ayaz bin Ghanam as overall commander of the invasion force.

The Christian Arabs of the Jazeera arrived at Emessa to find the Muslims securely fortified. They laid siege to the city, but hardly had the siege begun when messengers came galloping from the Jazeera to inform them that three Muslim columns were approaching their land from Iraq. The Arabs realised the absurdity of their situation: while they were fighting in Syria, pulling Heraclius' chestnuts out of the fire for him, their own land was about to fall to the Muslims coming from another direction. They raised the siege and hastened back to their homes, which was the only sensible thing to do. The Muslims came out of Emessa and redisposed themselves in occupation of Syria.

The three Muslim columns invading the Jazeera stopped when they heard of the return of the Christian Arabs, and soon after were withdrawn to Iraq by order of Umar, who did not wish to get involved in a major campaign beyond Iraq and Syria at this stage. Qa'qa arrived at Emessa with his 4,000 warriors two days after the departure of the Arabs, but a little later was recalled to Iraq. However, Abu Ubayda asked the Caliph to let him have Ayaz bin Ghanam for the Syrian theatre and this general was duly transferred from Iraq to work under Abu Ubayda, and was used by Abu Ubayda for raids into what is now Southern Turkey.

The diversionary move had worked brilliantly and achieved all that it was intended to achieve. The Muslims in Iraq would not hereafter have to worry about the Jazeera or go to the aid of their brothers in Syria. During the following year and the year following that [18 and 19 Hijri], Ayaz bin Ghanam invaded the Jazeera from the Syrian side and conquered all of it as far north as Amid [the present Diar Bakr]; and in 20 Hijri, Ayaz died in the Jazeera.[257]

Hormuzan, veteran of Qadisiyya, had remainrd with the survivors of the Persian army in their retreat to Ctesiphon. After the Persians were again defeated at Babylon by Sa'd during his advance to the Persian capital, Hormuzan and his followers detached themselves from the main body of the

---

[257] Tabari has wrongly given the year of the conquest of the Jazeera as 17 Hijri, although he does quote Ibn Ishaq as saying that it was taken in 19 Hijri. I regard Balazuri (18, 19 20 Hijri) as more accurate in this matter. Tabari probably erred on account of the diversionary operation which he confused with the actual conquest which followed later.

Persian army and travelled to Ahwaz, of which he was governor and prince. Here he set about gathering forces for another trial of strength with the Muslims.

There were seven families in Persia which formed the highest tier of the nobility of the land and stood second in rank only to the royal family. Each of these families had a feudal overlordship over a region of Persia-a kind of duchy or princedom-and one of these families was headed by Hormuzan. His region consisted of Ahwaz [the province now known as Khuzistan] and the district of Mihirjanqazaf which lay in the southern foothills of the upper part of the Zagros Mountains, south-east of Hulwan.[258] The main city of Mihirjanqazaf was Seimara, where Hormuzan had a ducal palace, but the city of Ahwaz was a bigger and more important place and it was here that Hormuzan directed his energies towards continuing the war with the Muslims.

Some time after his arrival at Ahwaz, he began to send raiding parties into the Suwad. The weight of these raids fell mainly on the local Arabs and Persians and Hormuzan failed to consider what would happen to him once the wrath of the Muslims was aroused, but he went on with his raids in the belief that he was hurting the new Muslim state of Iraq. One of these raids was led by his son Azeen, who was captured and killed by Zarrar bin Al Khattab, as described in the last chapter but one. After the death of Azeen, the raids were confined to the southern part of the Suwad, mainly the districts of Meisan and Dast Meisan, which lay astride the Tigris north of Uballa; and for these raids Hormuzan formed two bases a little forward of Ahwaz, one by the River Teeri and the other at Manazir, both of which were districts of Ahwaz.[259]

Meisan and Dast Meisan, the districts afflicted by the Persian raids, fell under the jurisdiction of Utba bin Ghazwan, Governor of Basra. Utba had brought from Ctesiphon only 800 men, and finding this force insufficient to repulse or discourage the raids, he appealed to Sa'd for help. Sa'd sent a force of unknown strength under Noman bin Muqarrin with instructions to place himself opposite the Teeri and await the orders of Utba. Meanwhile Utba was about to recruit more warriors from among the local Arabs who had been converted to Islam, and pushed a force forward from Basra to position itself in front of the

---

[258] There is no such district as Mihirjanqazaf today. The area falls in the present Province of Luristan.
[259] There is no trace of Manazir or the River Teeri, and there is some confusion among local scholars about their location. The version which best fits in with military logic places them in the area of Howeizeh, a village 40 miles west of Ahwan. Of the exact location we cannot be certain.

Persians at Manazir. This force was under the command of a Companion, named Salma bin Al Qein; and this happened in late 17 Hijri, about Shawwal [October/November, 638].

Noman and Salma, having established their camps in front of the two Persian bases, agreed upon a coordinated plan of attack, making full use of speed and surprise, to capture the Persian bases. Consequently, a simultaneous attack was launched and Hormuzan's army positioned at the bases was defeated and driven back. The Persian withdrew his troops to Ahwaz and deployed them in the city along the left bank of the River Karun. The Muslim detachments, the Kufans under Noman and the Basrans under Salma, followed the retreating Persians and secured the right bank of the Karun. The two forces then stood and glared at each other across the river, each safe on its own bank.

Hormuzan was thoroughly shaken by the action at the Teeri and Manazir and feared for Ahwaz. He did not yet have a sufficiently large force to engage in a major battle with the Muslims, but he was a wily general and decided to play for time and postpone a showdown until he was prepared for it. He sent word to the two Muslim generals on the west bank that he wished to make peace. This led to an exchange with Utba and a treaty was signed with Hormuzan whereby his entire princedom of Ahwaz and Mihirjanqazaf would come under Muslim rule and would pay the Jizya and other taxes, though governed by Hormuzan and not occupied by the Muslims. The part of Ahwaz already in Muslim hands, however, was outside the scope of this treaty because it had been taken by the sword, and would remain under direct military rule. Salma took over the administration of the district of Manazir and a Muslim officer named Hurmila was placed at the River Teeri.

In the province of Basra there would be no further military action during what remained of the year 17 Hijri and the year would end peacefully, except for a Muslim named Ula bin Al Hadrami, who pushed the Muslims into an adventure which can best be described as the Fiasco of Fars. Fars was the Persian province lying south-east of Khuzistan, south of Isfahan, and west of Kirman.

Ula, originally an inhabitant of Hadramaut, was quite an important Companion. During the apostasy, Caliph Abu Bakr had appointed him to command an independent corps and charged him with the mission of destroying the apostasy and re-establishing Islam in Bahrain. This task he effectively completed towards the end of 11 Hijri, and thereafter the Arabs in Bahrain remained true to Islam. Peace prevailed in the province with Ula as its governor. When Umar assumed the caliphate, he confirmed Ula at his post, later removed him from the appointment and placed another man as governor, but still later dismissed that other man and reinstated Ula as governor of Bahrain.

There was nothing wrong with Ula bin Al Hadrami, except that he did not like Sa'd bin Abi Waqqas. There had been trouble between the two during the apostasy and Ula thereafter held a grudge against Sa'd. Then as Sa'd became the Commander-in-Chief in Iraq and went on from victory to victory, defeating the great Persian host at Qadisiyya and taking Ctesiphon, Jalaula, Takreet, etc., the fire of Ula's resentment and envy begun to burn more fiercely. His own province of Bahrain was a military backwater; nothing ever happened here and no glory came to the lot of those who had to live in the province. So Ula began to get impatient to do something big in the war against Persia and win fame as a general. He would show Sa'd!

The trouble was that there was no enemy in Bahrain. The nearest enemy was in the Persian province of Fars, across the Persian Gulf from Bahrain, and if he wanted to fight Persians on his own he would have to get to Fars. And this could not be done without disobeying the Caliph, who had given very clear orders that no attempt would be made to cross the Persian Gulf. Umar was a much-feared ruler and dread of what Umar would do to him, if he disobeyed the master, held Ula in check for some time. But at last the desire for fame and envy of Sa'd got the better of him and he made up his mind to cross the gulf and do battle with the Persians, Umar's instructions notwithstanding.

He called the local Arabs to arms and they responded eagerly to the call. Sufficient numbers came forward for Ula to form three large regiments, which were placed under the command of Jarud bin Mualla, Sawwar bin Hamam and Khuleid bin Munzir: with the latter also acting as force commander. This force was transported in sea-going vessels across the gulf by order of Ula. What its exact geographical objective was is not known. The Muslims landed upon the coast of Fars and advanced in the direction of Persepolis, which may have been the objective of the campaign, but had only gone as far as Tawoos when they found their way barred by a sizable Persian force consisting of the inhabitants of Persepolis who had been led out to battle by their high priest. Tawoos, also known as Tawwaj, was in the plain a few miles north of the present Borazjan, just before the hills began.[260] [See Map 13.] As the Muslims stopped to take stock of the situation and prepare for battle, the high priest sent a fast detachment around their flank to get to the coast and destroy the vessels which had brought them across the sea.

---

[260] Dinawari (p. 132) gives the location of Tawoos as 32 farsakh, or 120 miles, from Shiraz.

Khuleid prepared for battle. He made a long speech, embellished with Quranic verses, which fired the spirits of the Muslims, and soon after midday a hard battle began. During the early stages of the battle two Muslim regimental commanders, Sawwar and Jarud, who had thrown themselves fiercely at the Persians, were killed. Their regiments were taken over by their sons, Abdullah bin Sawwar and Munzir bin Jarud, and these young lions, following in their fathers' footsteps, also died a glorious death in combat. Then Khuleid took personal command of the three regiments and conducted the battle very skilfully, with the result that by sunset the Persians had been defeated and driven from the battlefield.

As a battle this was a gallant show and many of the Muslims, including two regimental commanders and their sons, came to a noble end; but as a military campaign it was stupid, pointless, futile. After burying his dead, Khuleid led his men to the coast, only to find his boats burned. He changed his direction and started on the coastal road towards Basra, but when he arrived near Ghub, a small coastal town, he found a Persian force blocking his path-a force too large for his weary soldiers to overcome.[261] Khuleid at once went into camp and prepared for a defensive action. Opposing him was Shahrak, governor of Fars, and Shahrak was determined to wipe out the Muslims, being encouraged, in his resolve by the knowledge that the Muslims were cut off from all aid and from escape. He launched several attacks on the Muslim camp but was beaten off every time. The courage of the Muslims was hardened by desperation, and the Persians could make no dent in the Muslim defence. After a few unsuccessful attempts, Shahrak withheld his attacks and began to wait for Muslim supplies to run out. Meanwhile Khuleid had been able to find a boat of some sort and a messenger to the Caliph to inform him of the plight of the Muslims in Fars.

---

[261] I cannot locate Ghub and no one is Ahawaz or Shiraz has heard of it. In view of the cause of events, it was probably somewhere near the port of Jannaveh.

MAP 13: KHUZISTAN AND FARS

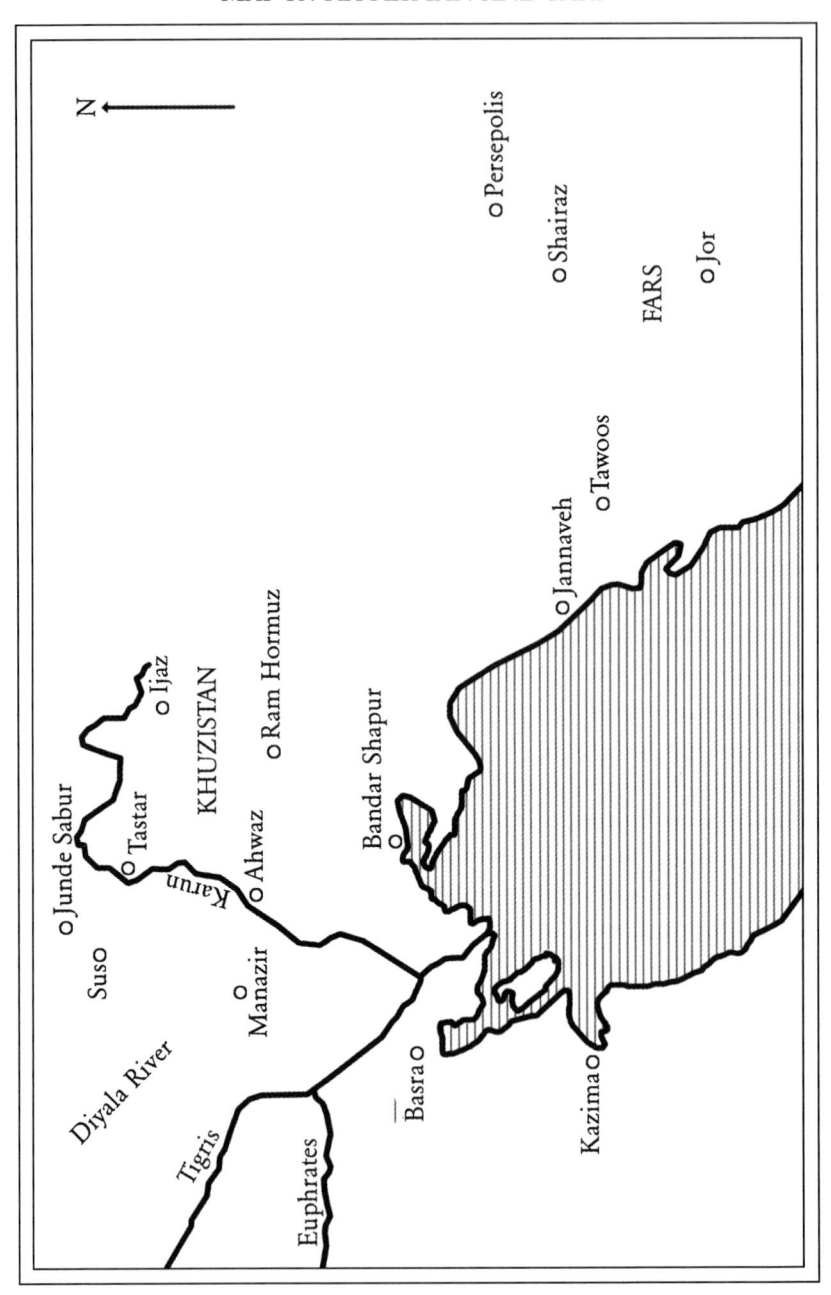

Umar's aversion to water obstacles has already been mentioned. He did not trust water, and resisted all attempts by his generals to go across the sea to farther territories. Three years later, in 20 Hijri, he would give permission for a naval operation against the Romans, and a force was transported in 20 vessels from the North Syrian coast towards some objective in "Rome"-probably the south coast of what is now Turkey. But the entire force, boat and man, which was under an officer, named Alqama bin Mujazziz, came to grief, and Umar wished he had stuck to his earlier resolve against seaborne operations. He swore that this would never happen again.[262]

So now, when he heard of the fate of the Muslims in Fars, the Caliph's anger knew no bounds. He at once wrote to Utba bin Ghazwan and urged him to raise a large force from Basra and despatch it immediately to Fars to extricate the Muslims.

Utba lost no time in carrying out the Caliph's orders and soon had a force ready for action, whose strength is given by Tabari as 12,000 but was probably rather less than that. It contained stalwarts like Asim bin Amr and was placed under Abu Sabra bin Abi Ruhm, and moved by forced marches to Fars, riding mules and leading the horses. As a result of their treaty with Hormuzan, the Muslims felt no danger from the Persian force on their flank as they moved along the coastal route, though this security was due not so much to Hormuzan's intentions as to his inability to interfere with the Muslims.

As Abu Sabra arrived near Ghub, a large Persian reinforcement also appeared from the interior of Fars to join Shahrak. In fact the Muslim relief column was not a day too early. Both Muslim groups, of Abu Sabra and Khuleid, promptly attacked the Persians, who were so surprised and unbalanced by the arrival of the relief column from Basra that they were glad to break contact and get away. The Muslims then marched back to Basra and arrived there after an uneventful journey.

As for Ula bin Al Hadrami, he was forthwith dismissed from his post, and as punishment for his folly and his disobedience of orders, sent to serve under Sa'd bin Abi Waqqas.[263]

---

[262] Yaqubi: Tareekh: vol. 2, p. 156.
[263] The operation described here is Tabari's version. Balazuri, however, gives a rather different story and places the operation in 19 Hijri, while showing it as a successful one. He even says that Umar himself ordered the move across the gulf. Of later historians, Ibn-ul-Aseer supports Tabari while Yaqut supports Balazuri. For Umar to launch such

Soon after the fiasco of Fars, Utba bin Ghazwan left Basra to visit Madina, in about Zul Qada [December-January]. His purpose was the annual pilgrimage to Mecca, but while at Madina he complained to the Caliph about the harsh treatment which he had received from Sa'd while under his command. Umar did not accept the complaint as legitimate, whereupon Utba tendered his resignation, but this too was rejected by the Caliph. Utba had to return to his post at Basra, and as ill luck would have it, fell off his camel on the way and died from the fall. Before leaving Basra he had left Mugheerah bin Shu'ba as his deputy in charge of peace and war. Upon the death of Utba, the Caliph confirmed Mugheerah at his post and the latter took full command of the forces in his theatre and the administration of the districts in his region.

Mention has been made in several preceding chapters of Mugheerah bin Shu'ba. An able general, a brave fighter and a very cunning man, he had become a Muslim in 6 Hijri. He was from the tribe of Saqeef which lived in Taif, had taken part in several battles, including the great battle of Yamama in which Khalid had defeated the redoubtable apostate chief, Museilima the Liar. Mugheerah was the most colourful of the several emissaries who had parleyed with Rustam on the eve of Qadisiyya - so Mugheerah became governor of Basra.

One of the infamous incidents cited in the history books is when he was charged with adultery. This happened soon after he was appointed governor. The lady in question was one, named Umm Jameel and the event in question was seen by four men, the legal minimum number of witnesses required by Quranic law in such offences. The matter was duly reported to the Caliph, who decided to take normal legal action in the matter.

Umar appoints as governor of Basra a man, named Abu Musa, a Companion and general who was destined to make important military conquests, as described later in this book. He was ordered to take over the province and send Mugheerah to Madina for trial, along with the witnesses. Abu Musa travelled from Madina to Basra, took charge of his post, informed Mugheerah of his dismissal and despatched him and the witnesses to Madina.

It appears that Umar himself acted as judge at the trial. Mugheerah pleaded not guilty, taking the stand that the lady was his own wife. The witnesses were called to give evidence. The first 3 made definite statements about the event

---

an operation across the sea is so completely out of character that I prefer Tabari's version and regard Balazuri (or rather his sources) as mistaken.

and identified the woman, but just as the fourth man, one named Ziyad, was called up to make his statement, Umar remarked, "I see the face of a man by whose evidence, I hope, Allah will not disgrace a Companion of Muhammad, on whom be the blessings of Allah and peace,"[264]

Ziyad declared in his statement that while he had seen the event, he had not seen the face of the woman and did not know who she was. Since the minimum of 4 witnesses could not be counted to give evidence against Mugheerah, the accused was acquitted; and because false witnesses in cases of adultery were to be punished with 80 lashes under Quranic law, Umar ordered the three witnesses to be so chastised. And this was done![265]

Mugheerah, happy at his deliverance, became a bit too loud is his expression of indignation at the allegation made against him and had to be warned by Umar,

---

[264] Balazuri: p. 340; Yaqubi: Tareekh: vol. 2, p. 146.

[265] M. Mawdudi writes whilst commenting on Surah an-Nur, 'The facts of the case are that Mugheerah bin Shu'bah, the governor of Basrah, did not have good relations with Abu Bakrah, whose house was opposite to his house across the same street. One day the windows of the two houses were opened by a strong current of wind. When Abu Bakrah got up to his window, he saw through the opposite window across the street Mugheerah in a state of actual sexual intercourse. He asked three of his friends [Nafi bin Kaladah, Ziad and Shibl bin Ma'bad] who were also sitting with him to stand up and witness what Mugheerah was doing. The friends asked him who was the woman. Abu Bakrah said she was Umm Jamil. The next day a complaint to this effect was sent to Umar, who immediately suspended Mugheerah and appointed Abu Musa Ash'ari as Governor of Basrah. Mugheerah along with the witnesses was called to al-Madinah. When they were asked about the case, Abu Bakrah said that they had seen Mugheerah actually committing sexual intercourse with Umm Jamil, but Ziad said that the woman was not clearly visible and that he could not say definitely whether it was Umm Jamil or not. During the cross examination, Mugheerah proved that they could not have seen the woman distinctly from the place where they were standing. He also proved that there was a close resemblance between his wife and Umm Jamil. Besides this, circumstantial evidence also showed that during the Caliphate of Umar, the governor of a province could not have committed this crime in his official residence, especially when his wife was also living with him. Thus the supposition of Abu Bakrah and his companions that Mugheerah was having sexual intercourse with Umm Jamil, instead of his own wife, was nothing but a misplaced suspicion. It was for this reason that Umar not only acquitted the accused but also punished Abu Bakrah, Nafi and Shibl as slanderers. It is obvious that this isolated decision was based on the specific circumstances of the case and not on the principle that the witnesses must be punished when they are not able to prove the charge by their evidence.' *Editor*

"Quiet! May Allah silence your voice! By Allah, if the evidence had been complete, I would have had you stoned."[266]

After this unsavoury episode, Mugheerah bin Shu'ba was detained at Madina by the Caliph for quite some time. He would later have ample opportunity to earn laurels in war and peace, as a general and administrator, but we shall return to him in due course, and meanwhile follow the fortunes of the new governor of Basra - Abu Musa al Ash'ari.

Some time after the affair of Mugheerah bin Shu'ba, and this was in the early part of 18 Hijri [639 A.D.], there was a dispute between Hormuzan and Salma, the commander of the Muslim garrison opposite Ahwaz, regarding the boundary between the land which fell under the treaty and the land taken by the Muslims in war. This boundary could not be clearly defined in the treaty, and Hormuzan sought to take advantage of its vagueness to not honour the terms of the treaty. He refused to cooperate. He had already built up his forces during the few months' respite which he had gained after the treaty, and now hastened to muster more forces, even sending a call to the Kurds who lived in his ancestral district of Mihirjanqazaf to come to his aid.

All this was reported by Salma to Abu Musa, who in turn wrote about it to Umar. The Caliph instructed Abu Musa to take Ahwaz, and Abu Musa marched forth, concentrated his army opposite Ahwaz and faced the Persian army across the River Karun. There was the usual exchange of emissaries: will you cross the river or shall we? Hormuzan invited Abu Musa to cross to his side.

The city for which a battle was about to be fought between the Muslims and the Persians was the capital of the province of Khuzistan, a province which was known to the early Muslims as Ahwaz. The province consisted of a flat, hot plain, very fertile and intersected by many rivers and canals. To the north and east it stretched up to the foothills of the Zagros Mountains, to its west lay Iraq, and in the south its sun-baked shores were washed by the waters of the Persian Gulf. The chief city of the province of Khuzistan [or Ahwaz] had once been named Hormuz Shahr but was known to the Muslims as Suq Ahwaz, i.e., Market of Ahwaz, and we shall, for the sake of simplicity, call it just Ahwaz. The most famous thing about it was that it was a city of misers, and it was said that if you lived in Ahwaz for just one year, you lost your wisdom![267]

---

[266] Tabari: vol. 3, p. 170.
[267] Yaqut: vol. 1, p. 411.

The Muslims crossed the river above the bridge, by the north edge of the city. The Karun is a sizable river and nothing is known of how the Muslims effected its crossing or of the battle that followed, except that it was a hotly contested one in which the Persians were thoroughly defeated. Hormuzan withdrew from the battlefield with the survivors of his army and marched in the direction of Ram Hormuz. This happened in about the second quarter of 18 Hijri, possibly the middle of the year.

Abu Musa took Ahwaz as a prize of war and gathered a considerable amount of booty, of which the usual one-fifth was sent to Madina. He also took many captives who were mainly local farmers, and these too were distributed among the warriors as slaves, but when Umar came to know about this, he wrote to Abu Musa, "You are not able to farm the land, so free the captives in your possession and impose the tax upon them."[268] The prisoners were freed, but the city and the neighbouring countryside were brought under direct Muslim rule.

These measures, however, were taken later. The immediate military action launched by Abu Musa after his victory at Ahwaz was a pursuit column under Juzz bin Muawia, which was ordered to get Hormuzan; and this column caught up with the retreating Persians. Then followed a series of rearguard actions in which Hormuzan skilfully avoided a decisive engagement and extricated his troops from contact every time the Muslims tried to bring on a battle. This mobile action, with retreat and pursuit, continued on the road to Ram Hormuz until the Muslims had occupied Dauraq, chief city of the district of Surraq, some distance from Ram Hormuz. Hormuzan retired east of the river-at Arbuk, where he secured the bridge and turned to face the Muslims once again.[269]

He had, however, no intention of fighting a battle if it could be avoided. He sent an emissary to Juzz and sued for peace. Juzz passed his request on to Abu Musa who in turn passed it on to Umar, and the Caliph gave orders that the offer of peace be accepted and a fresh treaty be signed. This was done. The

---

[268] Balazuri: p. 370.
[269] I have searched in vain for these places in the area between Ahwaz and Ram Hormuz. There is no sign of a town called Surraq, or a river at a place called Arbuk. According to Yaqut (vol. 1, p. 185) Arbuk was famous for its bridge. Some local scholars place Dauraq a good distance south of Ahwaz, but why tactical movements between Ahwaz and Ram Hormuz should take place in such a roundabout way is beyond military understanding. These places are unlocatable.

Muslims, accustomed to keeping their word in their dealings with other peoples, again fell into Hormuzan's trap, believing that he would keep his pledge and unaware that he was merely playing for time until he was strong enough to fight again. However, the district of Surraq also came under direct Muslim rule while the remaining districts of Hormuzan's princedom remained under Muslim suzerainty, though ruled by the Persian prince.

It now appeared that peace would prevail. Noman bin Muqqarrin returned with the Kufans to Kufa; a garrison was established at Dauraq; and the Muslims settled down to ruling their new conquests as part of the province of Basra.

Chapter 17: The Conquest of Tustar

The young Emperor of Persia had left Hulwan when the Muslims took Jalaula. He travelled eastwards to Qum, and news was brought to him of the fall, one after the other, of Khaniqeen and Qasr Sheereen. The Emperor wandered. He went to Kashan and then to Isfahan. Everywhere he urged the people to stand boldly against the menace of the invaders from the desert. He wrote to the governors of his provinces and to the nobles of the land to unite for war, to keep up their resistance and to muster forces not only for the defence of what remained of the empire but also for an offensive campaign to recover the territories lost to the Muslims. His call was answered with varying degrees of enthusiasm, and Persian subjects began to gather, some in large numbers, others in driblets. And this process went on for two years.

He was in constant touch with Hormuzan and encouraged him to continue hurting the Muslim state of Iraq and resisting further expansion by the Muslims. He was faced with a difficult decision about timing: whether to delay all action until a powerful military force had been organised - in which case there was the risk that the people would lose faith in him and accept the Muslim presence as a permanent feature - or to keep the war alive by throwing smaller detachments into action as soon as they were ready for war. Not knowing that Umar had no intention of pressing his advantage and conquering more territory, and fearing that the Muslims would soon be on the war path again, Yazdjurd chose the latter course. Persian reinforcements moved in small numbers into the region of Ahwaz to strengthen Hormuzan, which led to the actions which have already been described. In spite of the treaty signed by Hormuzan, the Persians had no intention of letting the Muslims remain in peaceful occupation of Iraq. Even after the loss of Ahwaz the build-up of imperial forces went on in Khuzistan, concentrating mainly at Tustar and Ram Hormuz, from where a two-pronged counter-offensive could be launched against the Muslims at Ahwaz.

The Emperor also organised, under a one-eyed general, named Siyah, an elite body of champions consisting of 300 knights and including 70 noblemen. Siyah was ordered to gather more fighters as he went on and to operate on the Ahwaz front against the Muslims as suited him best. We do not know whether he was required to join Hormuzan or operate independently, but as it happened, he did not report to Hormuzan and instead moved to Kalbania, some distance north of Sus. We shall come back to Siyah shortly.

Although started in a clandestine manner, the Persian war preparations could not be concealed from the Muslims. By about the middle of 19 Hijri [which began on January 2, 640 A.D.], it was obvious that serious military action was planned by imperial forces. The picture became clearer as pieces of intelligence coming into Basra were put together by Abu Musa and no doubt was left in the Muslim mind that the Persians had broken their pledge [at least Hormuzan had] and had used the peace treaty as a means of gaining time to prepare for war. Abu Musa wrote about this to Umar, and the Caliph determined to settle the problem once and for all by taking Khuzistan and inflicting upon Hormuzan the punishment which he deserved for breaking the treaty a second time.

Umar decided to concentrate forces from Kufa and Basra for dealing with the Persian threat, and sent instructions to Kufa accordingly. But these instructions were not sent to Sa'd bin Abi Waqqas, because Sa'd was no longer there. For the reasons of his removal from command, we must go back to 17 Hijri, when Kufa was founded.

In the new Kufa. Sa'd had a large house built for himself which, according to the simple standards of Arabia, was like a palace, and so it came to be called 'the Palace of Sa'd'. It had a door, and this was apparently a departure from the early Arab custom, for the simple people of Mecca and Madina did not usually have doors in their houses, just a curtain against prying eyes, and there was nothing to prevent one from entering the house. So because of his big house and the large wooden door, Sa'd's men thought that he was living like a lord! Moreover, the Palace of Sa'd was next to the market place whence a great deal of noise arose to disturb Sa'd's peace; and once or twice Sa'd tried to stop this noise. Some people were quick to find fault with him, and it was not difficult to turn people against him because of his stern ways. He was a strict man, a hard driver, and every inch a military commander who would not stand any nonsense from anyone. So the people began to complain, and some saw to it that their complaints were brought to the notice of the Caliph.

The news of Sa'd's living in a palace jarred upon Umar's sense of simple, unspoiled living, as Khalid bin Al Waleed's good living in Syria had done shortly before this. He wrote a letter to Sa'd, gave it to a Companion named Muhammad bin Maslama, and sent him to Kufa with the order: "Burn down his door and then return."[270]

---

[270] Tabari: vol. 3, p. 150.

Muhammad bin Maslama got to Kufa, bought some firewood, took it to the Palace of Sa'd and set fire to the big door. This done, he returned to the house where he had established his quarters. Sa'd was informed that this apparent act of vandalism was the work of the emissary of the Caliph. He sent for the man, but the man refused to come, and the Governor of Kufa had to go himself to the house where Muhammad bin Maslama had put up for his short stay. There the man gave Sa'd the Caliph's letter, which read:

"It has come to my notice that you have built a palace and use it to live as if in a citadel, and it is known as the Palace of Sa'd. And you have constructed a door between yourself and the people. It is not a palace but unsoundness of mind. Come out of it and live in a house next to the treasury, and do not construct a door to prevent people from entering and to deny them their rights. Let them be with you when you sit and when you come out of your house."[271]

Muhammad bin Maslama told Sa'd what was being said against him and Sa'd swore that it was not true. Subsequently Muhammad carried out further investigations and returned to Madina to report to Umar the situation regarding Sa'd and the people. Umar at once accepted Sa'd's denial of the charges and asked his emissary if he had also accepted Sa'd's explanation. Muhammad replied, "If you had wished me to do so, you should have written it for me or instructed me accordingly." Thereupon Umar remarked, "The best in judgement is the man who, even if he does not have definite instructions from his master, acts with resolution."

After this exchange, Muhammad bin Maslama informed Umar that Sa'd was regarded as a just and true man and an efficient administrator, whereupon the Caliph observed; "He is more true than what is said about him and than him who brought me information about him"[272] This happened some time in 18 Hijri, and nothing more came of the complaints against Sa'd.

Sa'd remained at his post for about another year. Then, in 19 Hijri, opposition to him began to mount again and the Kufans, perhaps softened by the good living of Kufa and wishing to take it easy in the belief that the war was over, began to get restive under his firm rule and his no-nonsense approach to military life. Many started complaining and rumours were set afloat. One complaint related to the way that Sa'd conducted the congregational prayers, and people said that it was not the right way, but Sa'd insisted that this was the way that the Holy Prophet himself had conducted the prayers. One of the most

---

[271] Ibid: pp. 150-1.
[272] Ibid: p. 151.

vociferous of his detractors was a man named Abu Sabra. When Sa'd came to know about him, he prayed: "O Lord, if what he says be false, prolong his life and his poverty. Make him blind in mind, and expose him to misery."

The man lived a long life, full of suffering [which included having ten unmarried daughters!], and in later years would lament: "I am in much distress. The curse of Sa'd has got me."[273]

There was something about the curse of Sa'd bin Abi Waqqas, just as there was something about his archery, in which he was unequalled. These gifts had come to him from the Holy Prophet, who had once prayed: "O Lord, answer his prayer and straighten his bow-aim."[274] After that neither the curse of Sa'd nor his arrow ever missed its mark.

The pressure continued to increase, and eventually the Caliph removed Sa'd from command, appointing in his place a Companion, named Ammar bin Yasir, who was known for his nearness to the Holy Prophet and was highly venerated as a Muslim. Sa'd's reaction to his dismissal was the following prayer with regard to the Kufans: "O Lord, let no commander be pleased with them, and let them not be pleased with any commander."[275] This was another of Sa'd's curses and certainly had effect, as students of Muslim history will know.

Ammar remained governor at Kufa for one year and nine months before he too was dismissed by the Caliph on account of the complaint of the Kufans: "He is a weak man. He knows nothing about government." When removing Ammar from his post, Umar exclaimed in exasperation: "Who will plead for me with the people of Kufa? When I appoint a strong man over them they tell lies about him; and when I appoint a mild man they hold him in contempt."[276]

Finally, to replace Ammar bin Yasir, the Caliph chose Mugheerah bin Shu'ba as governor of Kufa, a job for which the man had been angling. He had been detained in Madina by the Caliph ever since the time when he was charged with adultery, and now set out to take command of the region administered from Kufa, at which post he would remain during the rest of Umar's lifetime.
So it was to Ammar bin Yasir, the new Governor of Kufa, that Umar sent instruction, and these were to send Noman bin Muqarrin once again with a detachment to help Abu Musa. He also instructed Abu Musa to organise a

---

[273] Balazuri: pp. 277-8.
[274] Ibn Quteiba: p. 241.
[275] Yaqubi: Tareekh: vol. 2, p. 155; Balazuri: p. 278.
[276] Balazuri: p. 278.

force from his own province and place it under Sahl bin Adi. Abu Musa would then use the army thus created to deal with all the opposition which the Persians offered in Khuzistan. The Basran force organised by Abu Musa included many Companions of high standing, men like Baraa bin Malik, Majza'a bin Saur, Arfaja bin Harsama and Hudayfah bin Mihsan, the last two of whom had been used by Abu Bakr as corps commanders to crush the apostasy in 11 Hijri. The two forces, from Kufa and Basra, would concentrate at Ahwaz whence they would operate against the Persians as decided by Abu Musa.[277]

Abu Musa had several objectives to capture, the biggest being Tustar, but the main enemy was Hormuzan himself and he was at Ram Hormuz. As it happened, Noman, marching with the Kufans across the Suwad, got to Ahwaz before Sahl and the Basrans, who were late in getting started; and Abu Musa sent Noman on to deal with Hormuzan. Sahl arrived at Ahwaz soon after Noman had left and was held back by Abu Musa as a reserve in case the Persians at Tustar advanced against Ahwaz, which was the base from which operations against Ram Hormuz were sustained. It was now about the third quarter of 19 Hijri.

Noman arrived at Arbuk and found the Persians arrayed for battle on the east bank of the river. A short, sharp engagement followed in which the Persians were defeated, and Hormuzan, not wishing to be driven back and away from Tustar, abandoned Ram Hormuz to its fate and with his army marched north-west to Tustar [See Map 13]. Upon arrival here he set about preparations for defence, had the walls of the city repaired, gathered provisions for a long siege, and called upon all local Persians to join battle against the invaders.

Noman marched on and occupied Ram Hormuz, which offered no resistance, and then advanced into Izaj, in the foothills of the Zagros Mountains, which was the easternmost district of Khuzistan.[278] Here too everyone submitted to Muslim rule and to the payment of the Jizya, and Noman returned to Ram Hormuz and sent a report to Abu Musa about the success of his operation.

---

[277] According to Tabari, the entire force was to be put under Abu Sabra bin Abi Ruhm, but other historians make no mention of this man and show Abu Musa as the commander of the force. I find the latter version more correct. Abu Sabra had been appointed Governor of Basra for a short time in 17-18 Hijri, but the battle which was now to be fought took place in 19 Hijri. It could not therefore be correct that Abu Sabra commanded the army.
[278] Izaj is now known as Izeh, a small town which is the tribal centre of the Bakhtiari tribe.

Abu Musa was not like the abler generals who had achieved fame during the war in Iraq before him - Khalid, Muthana, Sa'd - nor did he possess the chivalrous dash or brilliancy of the lower ranking officers like Tuleiha, the brothers Asim and Qa'qa, and the Father of the Bull. Personally a brave man, he was known mainly as a devout Muslim who had accepted Islam just after the Battle of Kheibar in 7 Hijri, and had thereafter served the Holy Prophet well in peace and war. A small, lean man with a thin beard, he had a fine voice for Quranic recitation.[279] He was from the Yemen. As a general he was sensible and steady, with more caution than boldness, and made certain of every move before undertaking it, in order to reduce the element of risk to the minimum. This was, of course, a sensible way of doing things.

When word was brought to him at Ahwaz that Hormuzan had marched to Tustar after his defeat by Noman at Arbuk and was fortifying the city and preparing it for a siege, he chose to make certain of being in the greatest possible strength for the contest before advancing against the Persians. He asked the Caliph for more reinforcements, and the Caliph sent instructions to Ammar bin Yasir to despatch another detachment from Kufa to augment the strength of Abu Musa's army. Ammar despatched a force of 1000 men under Jareer bin Abdullah, but soon after, in response to further instructions from Umar, marched himself with half his army, leaving Abdullah bin Masud as his deputy at Kufa. How much half the army amounted to in terms of men is not known.

While these moves were under way, Abu Musa received another and unexpected addition to his strength, this time from the Persians. Mention has been made earlier in this chapter of a Persian general named Siyah, who with a force of 300 champions had been sent by Yazdjurd to go and fight the Muslims. This force was somewhere north of Tustar, where it just waited and watched, when news was received of the defeat of Hormuzan at Arbuk. Siyah at once decided that it was pointless to oppose the Muslims any longer and the sooner peace was made with them the better. He had a frank discussion with his nobles and they all agreed to end their war with Islam, provided favourable terms were made available to them. In pursuance of this decision, Siyah sent a delegation of ten nobles to Ahwaz to meet the Muslim governor.

The leader of the delegation said to Abu Musa, "We incline to your faith. We are prepared to accept your faith on condition that we fight beside you against Persians but not against Arabs. If any Arabs fight us, you shall have to defend

---

[279] Ibn Quteiba: p. 266.

us. We shall settle down where we wish and among those of you we like; and you shall give us a fixed pay. And for all this the commander over you must give us his assurance."

"No", replied Abu Musa, "you shall have what we have and shall carry the same burden as we do."[280]

To this the delegation did not agree, and Abu Musa had to refer the matter to Umar. The Caliph was more accommodating than his governor and instructed Abu Musa to accept the terms demanded by the Persians. The delegates returned happily to their comrades and the entire body of 300 valiant Persians travelled to Ahwaz under their one-eyed general, accepted Islam and joined the Muslim army. They were to prove to be worth far more than their numbers indicated, for in them Abu Musa found nothing but courage and perseverance in battle after battle. What rate of pay was fixed for them by the governor at this stage is not known.

With the arrival of the forces from Kufa, the Muslim army was ready to tackle Hormuzan. Abu Musa sent orders to Noman to move direct from Ram Hormuz to Tustar, and with the rest of his army advanced from Ahwaz. The entire army concentrated south-east of Tustar and went into camp. Hormuzan was fully prepared for battle. He had been joined by a large number of Persians and had stocked the city for a long siege. The stage was set for the Battle of Tustar, started in late 19 Hijri [640 A.D.]

Tustar was another of the great cities believed to have been built by the illustrious Sasani Emperor Sabur. It was, and still is, known to the Persians as "Shushtar', meaning a very clean place, but it was Arabicised to Tustar, and since all early Muslim history is in Arabic and refers to the place as Tustar, we too shall use that name. It was a walled city, which made it more difficult to attack or raid, and within the city rose a citadel which acted as the inner core of the defence. Its west edge lay on the River Karun and the most unusual feature of the place was a canal lined with stone which brought water into the city from the river and was regarded as a marvel of the time.[281] There were other canals which flowed under the city and which ran mills just below the city after surfacing. [The canals are still there.] And there was a stone dam on one branch of the River Karun which helped in controlling the waters of the river for irrigation. The citadel itself, known as 'Salasil' [the chains], was a remarkable piece of engineering. It stood upon the edge of a cliff which rose sheer from

---

[280] Tabari: vol. 3, p. 186.
[281] Yaqut: vol. 1, p. 848.

the river's edge, and it had a covered stairway dug through the earth like a sloping tunnel to the water's edge. There was also a well, bored down to the water's edge, and a canal, supplying the city with water, ran through the citadel. Its water supply assured, its north-western face resting on the Karun, it was only vulnerable on its south-eastern side; but here the city had the normal protection of a city wall with battlements, etc., and could only be taken by storm. And to further strengthen the defences of the city, Hormuzan had a ditch dug outside the wall along the exposed southern arc [the part not protected by the river] and had it covered by Persian posts located between it and the wall. Tustar was for all purposes unassailable and unconquerable.

The first action which followed the arrival of the Muslims was a set piece engagement outside the city. Hormuzan felt strong enough to fight in the open, and rightly thought that if he defeated the Muslims in a regular battle before they could invest the city, he would not have to be locked up within it. Both sides lined upon the plain south-east of Tustar, and in the fierce battle that followed the Persians were defeated and forced to withdraw behind the safety of the ditch and the wall. Abu Musa then placed several detachments around the city and all avenues of access and escape were blocked.

What followed was a siege which lasted several months, into 20 Hijri. It was an active siege with the Persians making scores of sallies to break the grip of the Muslims, and the Muslims making scores of attacks to cross the ditch and get into the city. There was some very severe fighting and heavy casualties were taken by both sides, but neither could claim success. After some months of this sort of fighting, the Persians made one last desperate sally, which led to the hardest fighting of the siege, but they were again defeated and the Muslims were able to follow at their heels and cross the ditch before the Persians could do anything about it. The Persians got back into the city but lost the obstacle of the ditch, and the Muslims closed up to the wall from all directions, putting the ditch behind them.

Within the city morale sagged, as happens in such situations when food runs short and the spectre of famine raises its ugly head, and when little hope of victory is left against an army which has swept all before it. Hormuzan was determined to fight on for as long as possible, for he knew that he would be given no quarter because of his breach of faith a second time, but many local inhabitants wished for nothing but peace. One such was a Persian named Seena. During the night; shortly after the last abortive sally by the Persians, he slipped out of the city, came to the Muslims and asked to see their commander. When he was brought before Abu Musa, he said that he would show the

Muslims a way into the city which would lead to its quick capture, if they would spare him and his family and give him a fixed pension for the rest of his life. Abu Musa accepted the terms. Then he asked for volunteers who would go and see the way. Many offered themselves for the dangerous task, and of them one named Ashras bin Auf was selected.

Ashras and the Persian set off from the Muslim camp to the west side of the city by the bank of the Karun, where a large sewer discharged water into the river. It was like a tunnel lined with stone. The two entered the sewer and advanced through it, finally emerging at the inner end. Just near this end was the house of Seena, and he took the Muslim inside, dressed him in Persian clothes and then brought him out again. The Persian led the Muslim around the city to show him the entire perimeter of the wall from the inside and the position of the various gates. While they were going round they even passed Hormuzan, and the Persian general actually looked at the two men but could not guess that one of them was an enemy within the fort. At last the Persian led Ashras back into the sewer and out of it and into the Muslim camp. The way in was now known.

The attack was planned for the following night. 40 men were selected as the first group to go in, and another 200 as the group to follow close upon the heels of the first. The second group would join the first as soon as the signal for battle was given, and the remainder of the army, previously positioned by the gate nearest the sewer, would storm the city as soon as the gate was opened by the first group. And this is how the operation was conducted. Complete secrecy was maintained and the Persians had no knowledge of the blow which was about to befall them until 40 brave warriors emerged from the sewer and with cries of "Allaho-Akbar", fell upon the Persian guard at the gate. In no time the soldiers of the guard were killed and the lock and chain that secured the gate broken. Persian units rushed towards the gate but were held off by the second group of 200 men which had emerged from the sewer, and at the same time the main body of the Muslim army began to pour into the city through the open gate.

The last phase of the battle was the bloodiest of all. Hormuzan himself led the struggle and fought ferociously to stem the tide and bottle up the Muslims in the narrow streets in the immediate vicinity of the gate. In the savage contest which followed, large numbers of Persians fell and Muslim casualties also began to mount. Hormuzan himself killed two noble Companions, Baraa bin Malik and Majza'a bin Saur. Many proud Persians, despairing of an honourable survival, killed their wives and children to prevent them from falling into

Muslim hands and living the rest of their lives in slavery. But nothing could stop the Muslim advance. At last the weary Persians gave up and retired to other parts of the city, from where many thousands made a fast exit and fled to Sus. Hormuzan, with a picked group of warriors, withdrew hastily into the citadel where he resolved to sell his life as dearly as possible. The Muslims took the city, surrounded the citadel and began what they believed was the last phase of the siege. In the fighting during the siege, the Persians had lost 1000 killed and 600 captives, and these captives were later executed on the orders of Abu Musa. Muslim casualties are not known but are believed to have been quite heavy.

As the sun rose, the Muslims began to consider ways and means of tackling the Persians in the citadel. Then Hormuzan himself appeared on the wall and called to the Muslims: "What do you wish? You and I are both in a tight situation. In my quiver there are 100 arrows, and you will not get me while a single arrow is left but will lose 100 men, dead or wounded."
"What do you wish?" asked the Muslims.
"I shall surrender". Hormuzan replied, "on condition that Umar himself decides my case as he wishes."[282]

This was agreed to by Abu Musa and Hormuzan gave himself up to the Muslims. The Battle of Tustar was over. A large amount of booty was taken, of which four-fifths was distributed among the soldiers, with the cavalryman setting a share of 3000 dirhams and the foot soldier 1000. This happened in about the second quarter of 20 Hijri.

---

[282] Tabari: vol. 3, p. 182.

Chapter 18: The Rest of Khuzistan

A few days were spent in dealing with post-victory matters at Tustar - the treatment of the wounded, the burial of the dead, the collection and distribution of booty, the establishment of local administration. Then the contingent from Kufa returned to Kufa with Ammar bin Yasir, and Abu Musa set off with his army for Sus, taking the captive Hormuzan with him. The army arrived at Sus to find a sizable Persian force occupying the city, consisting partly of the survivors of Hormuzan's army but mainly of fresh troops from other provinces, augmented by the local inhabitants.

Sus was, and still is, known to the Persians by the name of "Shush". The most famous thing about Sus was the bones of Prophet Daniel which lay in the city. The first resting place of the prophet is believed to have been Babylon, but Nebuchadnezzar, who ruled Babylon in the 7th and 6th Centuries B.C., had permitted the prophet's remains to be transferred to Sus as a water blessing, i.e. the inhabitants prayed by Daniel for water whenever there was a shortage and believed that it was through his intercession that their prayers were answered.[283] Now in the burial city of Daniel, the Persians prepared for a siege under Shahryar, brother of Hormuzan.

The Muslims invested the city and the usual sequence of sally and attack was taken up. Many were killed on both sides and it appeared that the city would be able to continue its resistance for a long time. Then, one day, a Persian Zoroastrian priest appeared on the wall of the city and called to the Muslims: "O Arabs, we know from our ancestors and our wise men that Sus will not be taken except by Dajjal or by a people among whom there is Dajjal. If you have Dajjal among you, you will conquer us; if not, do not bother to besiege us."[284]

Dajjal is the Arabic rendering of what in the English language is known as Anti-Christ, or a quack or impostor. This old belief obviously existed among the Zoroastrians too, but Islam had cleared the minds of the Faithful of all old superstitions [at least early Islam did!] and Abu Musa was not the man to worry about Dajjal. So he continued his attacks but success still eluded him; and once again the Persian priest appeared on the wall to repeat what he had said earlier about Dajjal. After this, a fierce encounter took place near one of the gates

---

[283] Balazuri: p, 371. According to Tabari: vol. 3, p. 188, Daniel died at Sus and his body remained here.
[284] Tabari: vol. 3, p. 187.

which continued till after sunset, but here too there was no decision one way or the other.

Then Abu Musa received a very bright and very daring suggestion from Siyah, the Persian commander of the body of knights which had accepted Islam before the Battle of Tustar. These Persians had fought bravely in the siege of Tustar and were now to play a vital role in the conquest of Sus. Plans were formulated and preparations made to take Sus by guile as well as force.

The night passed uneventfully. As the first light of dawn appeared, the Persian sentries on the wall by the gate saw a Persian officer with his uniform stained with blood, lying on the ground near the gate. There had been fighting close to this spot and the commander of the guard at once ordered that the gate be opened and a few men go out and bring in the wounded Persian who had obviously been outside all night, waiting for help. Poor fellow! A little later the gate was opened and two or three soldiers approached the fallen officer, but they had not yet reached him when the apparently wounded Persian officer leapt to his feet. It was none other than Siyah, who had donned his Persian uniform, stained it with blood, and pretended to be a Persian casualty. In a few moments he had disposed of the Persian soldiers who were coming to pick him up.

The next instant Siyah had rushed to the gate, killing the sentry who stood by it, and got in before the rest of the guards could recover their senses. Here he was immediately joined by another Persian officer, Khusrau by name, who had concealed himself nearby while Siyah was awaiting to be "saved", and now the two stood with their backs to the half open gate, fighting off the soldiers, who strove to get to the gate and close it. The number of Persians increased rapidly as the alarm was raised but none could get past the valiant Muslim Persian champions, who slew every man who came within reach of their bloody swords. The struggle increased in intensity and the Persians attacked with frenzy to knock down the defenders of the gate. At last, as Siyah and Khusrau were about to collapse from exhaustion, the leading company of Abu Musa's army rushed into the breach and took on the Persian soldiers.

The Muslim thrust could not be held. They drove deeper into the city, scattering the Persian defenders, and soon were well established in the nearer sector of Sus. At this stage of battle the Persian commander sued for peace and his surrender was accepted by Abu Musa who wished to spare further bloodshed. Sus was taken, thanks to Siyah. It was now about the middle of 20 Hijri.

Abu Musa made no secret of his admiration for the valour of Siyah and his gallant Persian knights, which seemed to contrast with the impression which he had held earlier of the Persians who fought against the Muslims. "O one-eyed one", he said to Siyah, "you and your comrades are not as we thought you were."[285] Siyah accepted the compliment but complained that he and his fellows were not being paid as well as the best of the Arab warriors, and also pointed out to Abu Musa that they had come to the help of the Muslims when the Muslims needed help most. Abu Musa wrote of this to Umar, and the Caliph ordered higher pay for the Persian knights, six of whom, including Siyah, were awarded 2500 dirhams per annum while 100 of them got 2000 dirhams. What the rest of them were given is not recorded, but perhaps only this number of the original 300 had survived the Battles of Tustar and Sus.

Abu Musa also wrote to the Caliph about the remains of the Prophet Daniel which had not been buried but just lay in a temple, and the Caliph instructed the governor to see that the prophet's remains were properly enshrouded and buried. Abu Musa had the River Shahur diverted, had the prophet buried in its bed, and then let the water run again in its course.[286]

The only place of any military importance which now remained outside Muslim hands in Khuzistan was Junde Sabur, another town built by the great Sabur who appears to have marked the glory of his reign by building cities.[287] [See

---

[285] Ibid: p. 186.

[286] The exact location of the grave of Prophet Daniel is unknown. Under the instructions of Caliph Umar, the Muslims dug thirteen graves and buried the Prophet in one grave and filled the other twelve with dirt so the exact location remains unknown. Dr. Safar Hawali writes in the Day of Wrath, 'In Islamic history there is a well-known event narrated by Ibn Ishaq, Ibn Abi Shayba, al-Bayhaqi, Ibn Abi Dunya and others, from the second-generation Muslims who participated in the conquest of the city of Tustar, including Abul-`Aliya and Mutraf ibn Malik. The particular incident that concerns us here is that the conquering Muslim army discovered the tomb of Daniel. They found his body lying on its bier totally unchanged except for a few hairs on the back of his head. At his head was a scroll which they took and brought to `Umar who called Ka`b al-Ahbar to translate it into Arabic. Abul-Aliya says, "I was the first man to read [the Arabic translation]." The narrator from Abul-Aliya states, "I asked Abul-Aliya, 'what was in it?' He replied, 'All of your history and affairs, the melody of your speech, and what is yet to happen.'" Ibn Kathir: Al-Bidaya wal-Nihaya 1:40-42, al-Bayhaqi: Dala'il al-Nubuwa 1:381, Ibn Abi Shayba: Al-Musannif 7:4, al-Kurmi: Shifa` al-Sudur – edition of Jamal Habib p. 336.

[287] The Iranians call this place Junde Shapur. Sabur is the Arabic form of the name, because of the absence of the letter 'P' in the Arabic language. Nothing ramains of

Map 13.] Junde Sabur was known to contain a strong garrison and while this garrison held, the province of Khuzistan could not be said to belong to the Muslims. So, following the instructions of the Caliph, Abu Musa sent a force under Aswad bin Rabee'a, an early Companion who also had the nickname of Muqtarib, to take Junde Sabur. Abu Musa himself returned to Basra with the rest of his army.

Muqtarib besieged Junde Sabur and several attempts were made to storm the city but without success. Then one day, during a lull in the operation, when all was quiet, the gates of the city opened, the inhabitants of the city emerged unarmed and apparently without fear, cattle were driven out to graze, and shopkeepers began to set up their stalls everywhere. The Muslims stared in amazement at the unwarlike scene, the very peacefulness of which held them back from attacking the Persians.

The Muslims asked what was going on, and the Persians said, "You offered us peace and we have accepted it and agreed to pay the Jizya in return for your protection."
"We did not do so," said the Muslims.
"We do not lie," said the Persians.

Upon enquiry it was found that someone had shot an arrow from the Muslim side into the town, to which was attached a message offering the garrison peace if it would surrender and pay the Jizya. Upon further enquiry it was found that the arrow was shot by a slave named Mukannaf. The Muslims felt that this was going a bit too far and that any negotiation of terms should be done at a higher level of command.

"He is only a slave," said the Muslims.

"We do not know your slaves from your freemen," replied the Persians. "We only know that we received an offer of peace and we accepted it and have stood by it. You can break your word if you wish."

This was rather a severe taunt and no Muslim was prepared to break his word or the word of his brother. So the Muslim commander wrote to the Caliph about the matter while a sort of truce was maintained, subject to the decision of the Caliph. The Caliph's reply, when received, read: "Allah has given

---

Junde Sabur except some ruins beside the village of Shahabad, not far from the present Dezful.

importance to truthfulness. Be true to them; and again, be true to them. And leave them in peace."[288]

Muqtarib accepted the surrender of Junde Sabur on the payment of the Jizya, and after making certain organisational arrangements for the Muslim administration of the district, returned to Basra. Following this action. Abu Musa sent one column eastwards which occupied Zut and Sanbeel, and a second one northwards which occupied Kalbania, between Sus and Seimara. There was no opposition at these places.[289]

All Khuzistan, the plain which stretched to the foothills of the Zagros Mountains, was now in Muslim hands.[290]

On his return from Sus, Abu Musa despatched Hormuzan to Madina with an escort which included two Companions, Uns bin Malik and Ashraf bin Qeis, the former being the brother of one of the two venerable Companions killed by Hormuzan at Sus. This was a strange and less-than-welcome experience for Hormuzan. He, a prince, a lord and son of a lord, he who had spent his life in palaces and in the company of royalty, and was himself one of the minor royalty, was now led into the barren desert of Arabia as a captive with certain death ahead of him. He may also have worried about being in the company of Uns bin Malik, because Arab vindictiveness had always been well known, but nevertheless his fertile brain exercised itself in seeking ways and means of escaping the punishment which lay in wait for him. He was a crafty fellow.

At last the journey ended and they entered Madina. The escort, wishing to dazzle the Caliph by the sight of a Persian prince looking like a Persian prince, dressed Hormuzan in his court regalia, robes of velvet and gold, and placed upon his head his coronet of gold, studded with sapphires. Thus bedecked, Hormuzan was led to Umar's house. Umar was not there. The escort asked some people about the whereabouts of the Caliph and was told that he was in the mosque receiving a delegation from Kufa.

---

[288] Balazuri: p. 375.
[289] Zut and Sanbeel no longer exist: they lay between Ram Hormuz and Arrajan (which is the present Behbahan): Zut 34 miles from Ram Hormuz, Sanbeel 30 miles ahead of Zut; and beyond that, at a distance of 15 miles, stood Arrajan. There is no trace of Kalbania.
[290] For an explanation of the dates of the campaign in Khuzistan, please see note in Appendix C.

They went to the mosque but found it empty. The Kufan delegation had finished its business with the Caliph and departed. They came out, found some boys playing in the street and asked them if they had seen the Caliph. The boys told the group that the Caliph was in the mosque. They went in again and saw a man lying fast asleep in the right side of the mosque, wearing clothes of coarse material and with his cloak folded into an inadequate pillow under his head. In his left hand the sleeping man held a whip.

Hormuzan noticed the reclining figure, and then his gaze travelled around the rest of the mosque. He was looking for the great Caliph who had shaken the empire of Persia to its foundations, but there was no one else there.

"Where is Umar?" he asked his escort.

"This is he." they relied, pointing at the sleeping man.

Hormuzan stared in bewilderment at the poorly dressed man sleeping on the rough matted floor. "Where is his guard?" he asked "And where is his chamberlain?"

"He has no guard, and no chamberlain. He has no secretary; he has no office."

"Then he should be a Prophet." observed the Persian general.

"He is not," said the escort simply.

By now a large crowd had collected in the mosque, attracted by the news of the arrival of the Persian general and eager to see his meeting with Umar. The noise of the crowd awoke the Caliph, who sat up and looked with blinking eyes at the dazzling sight of the splendid attired Persian.

"Hormuzan?" he queried.

"Yes," they affirmed.

For a few moments the Caliph examined the Persian. Then he said, "I seek refuge with Allah from the Fire; and I seek His help. Praise be to Allah who has used Islam to debase this man and his possessions." Then he turned to the crowd gathered in the mosque. "O Muslims, hold fast to this faith and be guided by the teaching of your Prophet. Let not this world lead you astray, for it is full of deceit."

The escort, anxious to get the confrontation going, said to the Caliph, "He is the prince of Ahwaz. Speak with him."

"Not as long as there is anything left on him of his finery," replied Umar. They promptly took off everything that Hormuzan wore except a few garments to cover him. And then began a dialogue between the simple Muslim and the sophisticated Persian with Mugheerah bin Shu'ba acting as translator. Everyone believed that it would not be a long dialogue; that soon Hormuzan would be sentenced to death for treachery and that would be the end of him. They were under-estimating the wily prince.

"O Hormuzan," began Umar, "what do you think now of the dangers of treachery and of punishment by order of Allah?"

"O Umar," replied Hormuzan, "you and we existed in olden days, and God kept us apart. And when God was neither with us nor with you, we overpowered you; but when He was with you, you overpowered us."

"You overpowered us during the Ignorance only because of your vast numbers and our disunity. Anyway, what excuse do you plead for breaking your pledge time after time?"

Umar was just being a good judge, not knowing that he was up against one of the sharpest minds of Persia. Hormuzan suddenly assumed an apprehensive look. "I fear you will kill me before I can tell you" he said.

"You need have no fear on that account." the Caliph reassured him.

Hormuzan then asked for a drink of water and it was brought to him in a crude cup. He looked at the cup disdainfully for a moment. It was the sort of cup which even his slaves would not use in Persia. "I would rather die of thirst than drink from a cup like this," he snapped. The Arabs would not normally let themselves be put on with such airs, but the man was to die and so had to be honoured. They brought water in a more presentable vessel and Hormuzan took it with a trembling hand. It was obvious that he was afraid of being killed at once.

He looked at Umar. "I fear I shall be killed while I am drinking this water."

"You are in no danger until you have drunk the water," Umar assured him.

Hormuzan at once put the cup away. Umar, not realizing his purpose, said to the Muslims, "Give it to him again. Do not, inflict both death and thirst upon him."

"I have no need of it," said Hormuzan calmly. "I only asked for it to save myself by it." He had the Caliph's word that he would not be harmed until he had drunk the water, and now he would not drink it!

This made Umar angry. "I shall kill you!" he threatened.

"But you promised me safety!"

"You lie!" roared the Caliph, seeing how he had been tricked.

And now Uns bin Malik came into the conversation and, incredibly, took the side of the man who had killed his brother. Such was the sense of truth and justice among the Companions of the Holy Prophet.

"What he says is right," he said to the Caliph. "You promised him safety."

"Woe to you, O Uns." Umar turned sharply on the Muslim. "Would I promise safety to the killer of Majza'a and Baraa? You shall find a way or I shall chastise you!"

Uns stood firm. "You said he was in no danger until he had spoken with you. You said he was in no danger until he had drunk the water."

Others also spoke up and took the same stand: the Caliph had given an assurance of safety and the assurance had to be honoured. Umar turned in exasperation to Hormuzan. You have deceived me; and by Allah, a Muslim is not deceived."

Umar was furious at the turn that events had taken. He had no doubt in his mind that Hormuzan would have to face death for breaking his pledge not once but twice, and it would be a just punishment for such an offence, but by his clever handling of the proceedings Hormuzan had talked his way out of what was coming to him. This did not seem right. For a few minutes there was silence, then Umar began the dialogue again.

"From what land are you?" he asked the Persian general.

"From Mihirjanqazaf."
"Tell me what you wish to say."
"Shall I make the speech of the dead or the living?"
"The speech of the living."
"You have promised me safety."
"You deceived me. In war the deceived have the power to retaliate."

There was another pause while the onlookers watched in tense silence to see how the encounter would go. Then Umar turned to Uns bin Malik. "What do you say?" he asked.

"I have left behind a great power and a determined enemy," said Uns to the Caliph. "If you kill him, the Persians will abandon all hope of life and their strength will harden with desperation. On the other hand, if you let him live, the Persians will look forward to life."

"Glory be to God!" Umar burst out impatiently. "He has killed Baraa bin Malik and Majza'a bin Saur!"

"You still have no way to kill him," insisted Uns, brother of Baraa. "You promised him safety."

With a great effort of will Umar controlled himself. What Uns had said about the effect of the killing of Hormuzan on Persian resistance made sense, but more important than that was the principle of the thing. The Caliph had promised the accused safety, and if the accused were now killed, the Caliph would himself be guilty of the offence with which the accused was charged, i.e. the breaking of a pledge. Umar relented and accepted the situation, which he could in any case not change without the naked and unprincipled use of absolute power. He would let Hormuzan live, but on his own terms.

"By Allah," the Caliph turned to Hormuzan, "you shall have no safety unless you accept Islam."

The message was clear to Hormuzan. He could live only as a Muslim, and having had the prospect of death as his close companion for so many weeks, and having stared it in the face during the last few hours, he was thankful for life. He became a Muslim. He also settled down as a citizen of Madina and was awarded an annual pension of 2000 dirhams.[291]

---

[291] Tabari: vol. 3, pp. 183-4; Balazuri: p. 374.

Chapter 19: The Persians March Again

With the fall of Khuzistan in the middle of 20 Hijri [about the middle of 641 A.D.] the Muslims found themselves in possession of all that they wanted in the region of Iraq. What they held was mainly the south-western part of the Persian Empire-plain, level, fertile land-all that lay west of the Zagros range. They also had a bit of the hilly region in the north, the area of Kirmanshah, which they had taken in their drive from Ctesiphon after Jalaula and Hulwan. In this northern region they had pushed forward to some point a little beyond Kirmanshah, on the old historic route to Central Persia, along which great armies had marched for centuries past. The frontier garrison of Islam on this highway, under the Persian Qubaz, watched the movement of the Persians in the region of Hamadan. In short, the Muslims had acquired the most fertile and most productive, if not the most beautiful part of Persia.

The Caliph had got more than he wanted, and he certainly wanted no more. "I wish." he said "there were a mountain of fire between us and the Persians, so that neither could they get to us nor we to them."[292] It was a pious hope, but not one destined to be realised.

While the Muslims were content with their territorial gains and would have been happy to establish an enduring peace with the Persians, the Persians were in no mood to establish an enduring peace with the Muslims. The pride of the imperial Persians was too strong to regard as permanent their territorial losses to a people whom they considered as no better than barbarians. Furthermore they saw the victorious army of Islam poised for further conquest and expansion, which could only be prevented by a permanent peace treaty and such a treaty could not be countenanced by their pride and imperial ambitions. They could not have known that the Muslims sought no further gains. Finally, there was the factor of two giants standing close to each other across an undefined border, each conscious of the might of the other, each suspicious of the other's designs. As has happened time and again in history, such a confrontation could lead only to a titanic clash, and here also it did. The drums of war were heard once again in the domain of Persia.

Preparations for the next campaign by the Persians had already begun while Khuzistan was being wrested from them. After the fall of this province, more urgent calls were sent by Yazdjurd to the provinces which remained under his

---

[292] Tabari: vol. 3, p. 176

rule, from Azarbeijan to Khurasan to the Sind, and the people of the provinces themselves wrote to their Emperor, urging him to lead them to victory. Hardened veterans and young volunteers marched in their thousands to join the imperial standard. They came from Fars, Qumis, Isfahan, Yazd, Rayy, Hamadan, Tabaristan. The imperial foundries worked overtime to forge weapons, supplies were gathered from all quarters, and horses and men trained for combat. Able generals were appointed to command major components of the army and all units, except for a few which watched Muslim forward posts, moved to Nihawand, south of Hamadan, where a vast army would be gathered for an offensive campaign against Islam. Being in a hilly region, Nihawand was less vulnerable to Muslim attack and was also suitable as a base from which an offensive could be launched against any part of Iraq and Khuzistan.

It was some time in the third quarter of 20 Hijri that the first lot of contingents arrived at Nihawand. The concentration of the great army would be complete by the end of this year. The army numbered 60,000 men[293] and was placed under a veteran general named Mardanshah, who was also known as Zul Hajib-"the man with the eye-brows."[294] At Nihawand preparations proceeded apace for the forthcoming offensive which would not, however, be launched until every man available for war had reported for duty. The preparations included psychological measures. The officers of Mardanshah spoke to the men:

Muhammad, who brought religion to the Arabs, never troubled us. Then Abu Bakr became their ruler and he too did not bother us except by taking plunder, and that only in the part of the Suwad which was adjacent to their land. Then after him came Umar, and his rule has become very long. He has taken the Suwad and Ahwaz and ridden roughshod over them; and he will not rest until he has got the entire people and land of Persia. He is coming for you if you do not go for him. He has already destroyed the seat of your empire and plunged into the land of your Emperor. There is nothing to stop him unless you drive his army out of your land and capture their two cities,[295] and then engage them in their own land.[296]

---

[293] The figure is from Balazuri: p. 300. Tabari (vol. 3, pp. 209-10) puts the Persian strength at 130,000 and 150,000. I reject the higher figure for the same reason as explained in the case of Qadisiyya, in Note 1 in Appendix C.
[294] According to Masudi (Muruj: vol. 2, p. 331) the Persian general was know as Zul Jinahein-the man with the wings.
[295] i.e. Basra and Kufa.
[296] Tabari: vol. 3, pp. 209-10.

Hardly had the first few Persian contingents settled down at Nihawand when Qubaz, the commander of the Muslim forward troops on the Kirmanshah road, became aware of the move and also came to know of the expected arrival of more troops. He at once informed the Governor of Kufa, Ammar bin Yasir, who in turn wrote to the Caliph about it. Ammar left no doubt in the mind of the Caliph that the Persian army now concentrating at Nihawand would be a numerous one and that the Persians intended something very big. "If they come to us before we can strike at them" wrote the Governor, "they will multiply in strength and courage."

The messenger who brought the despatch from Kufa was named Qareeb bin Zafar. As Muslims know, every Arab name has a meaning, and this man's name had a meaning which delighted the Caliph - Qareeb, meaning near, son of Zafar, meaning victory. When the Caliph had read the letter, he asked the messenger his name.

"Qareeb," replied the messenger.
"And whose son?"
"Zafar."

Umar saw this as an auspicious omen. "Victory is near;" he exclaimed, "if Allah wills it. And there is no power except with Allah."[297]

As the movement of Persian contingents continued towards Nihawand, fast messengers kept travelling to Madina to keep the Caliph posted about the latest situation, and at last Umar had a clear picture in his mind of what the Persians intended and what was needed to thwart their design. A major military campaign would be necessary against the imperial army at Nihawand. The Caliph called a congregation of the citizens of Madina and addressed them:

"This is the day on which the future depends. I have been occupied with a matter which I wish to present to you. So listen to me and do not give way to dispute, for that will weaken your resolve and take away your courage.

"O nation of Arabs! Lo, Allah has helped you with Islam and created amity among you after discord and given you wealth after hunger and made you victorious over your enemies in every land where you have fought. You have never been defeated and never overpowered. But Lo, Satan has gathered a

---
[297] Ibid.

gathering to extinguish the light of Allah. And here is a letter from Ammar bin Yasir."[298]

He then read out to the citizens of Madina the letter of the Governor of Kufa. He spoke of the threat from the Persians to the Muslims at Basra and Kufa, and declared his intention of going in person and positioning himself between the two cities while the main army in Iraq fought the Persians at Nihawand.

Most of the senior Companions of the Prophet, who sat near the Caliph, did not agree that he should go in person to Iraq. They said that the Muslims had won victories and defeated every enemy they had met in battle, that the best of Arab manhood and the finest Arab champions were already with the army, that the army in Iraq needed permission to fight and the guidance of the Caliph rather than his physical presence. Next followed a discussion of how to put into the field a force large enough to match the expected strength of the Persians. Uthman said: "I think, O Commander of the Faithful, that you should write to our people in Syria to march from their Syria, and write to our people in the Yemen to march from their Yemen, and write to our people at Basra to march from their Basra. Then you yourself should march with the people of these two holy places,[299] to the two cities of Basra and Kufa; and let the host of the unbelievers meet the host of the Muslims. If you do this, you will have a larger army than theirs and the vast numbers of the enemy will appear small."[300]

Strangely enough, most of those present agreed with Uthman's proposal, although Umar himself had doubts about its political and strategical wisdom. He turned to Ali: "What do you say, O Father of Hasan?"

Said Ali: "If you send our people in Syria away from their Syria, the Romans will recapture it. If you send our people in the Yemen away from their Yemen, the Ethiopians will recapture it. And if you march from this land with its people, the land will disintegrate from the sides, so that you will find a more dangerous situation behind you than in front. Let all people stay in their places.

"Write to the people of Basra to divide into three groups. One group should stay and look after the families, one should watch the conquered people so that they do not break their treaty, and one group should go to help their brothers in Kufa.

---

[298] Ibid: Dinawari: p. 134.
[299] i.e. Mecca and Madina.
[300] Tabari: vol. 3, p.211; Dinawari: p. 134.

"As for the strength of the Persians, we have in the past, in the time of the Messenger of Allah and thereafter, fought not with numbers but with the help of Allah."[301]

Umar agreed with Ali and chose to act accordingly. He also decided and announced the name of the general who would command the Muslim army in the campaign which was to follow - Noman bin Muqarrin.

Ubayd bin Aus was one of the early Companions, an Ansar of Madina. His claim to fame rested on his taking part in the Battle of Badr in 2 Hijri, during which he captured four infidels and tied them up. As a result of this he was given the name of Muqarrin, i.e, the Binder, and so he has been known to posterity.[302]

Muqarrin had many sons; and what fine sons they were! Each of them was a good soldier, an able officer and a competent administrator. During the early stages of the Campaign of the Apostasy, Abu Bakr relied heavily on the young brothers, using them as commanders of the main components of his small army for the 2 or 3 tactical actions against the apostates which Abu Bakr led in person. The brothers, and there were several of them, served under Khalid bin Al Waleed in his Iraq campaign and even he employed them after his victory for administration and collection of taxes. The brothers continued to fight in Iraq and were present in practically every campaign, and it is not surprising that Sa'd bin Abi Waqqas also entrusted them with administrative responsibilities when the fighting had ended in his theatre. Noman bin Muqarrin was sent by him to Kaskar, on the east bank of the Tigris [where the city of Wasit was later built] as the Muslim administrator of the district.

Noman bin Muqarrin also acted as the commander of the Kufan reserves, a kind of fire brigade, and would rush down to Basra every time help was needed against the Persians in Khuzistan. He had taken the region up to the west bank of the River Karun at Ahwaz, and later defeated Hormuzan at Arbuk and conquered Ram Hormuz. After the fall of Sus, he had returned to Kufa but immediately after had resumed his governmental post at Kaskar, where he also commanded a small garrison. He was a fine man, a noble Muslim and a true soldier: and like many keen soldiers, preferred battle to administrative duties. He wrote to Umar that Sa'd had appointed him to collect taxes but he would rather have command of any of the Muslim armies engaged in the holy war.

---

[301] Tabari: vol. 3, p.211-1; Dinawari: p. 134-5.
[302] Ibn Hisham: vol. 1, p. 687.

Noman prayed to God for military command, and knew that his wish had been granted when, in about Zul Qada, 20 Hijri [October-November. 641] he received a letter from the Caliph:

In the name of Allah, the Beneficent, the Merciful. From the Slave of Allah, Umar, Commander of the Faithful, to Noman bin Muqqarin.[303] Peace be upon you. I render praise unto Allah, than whom there is no other God.

I have come to know that a vast army of Persians has gathered at Nihawand to fight you. When you get this letter, go by order of Allah and with the help of Allah and the support of Allah, along With those of the Muslims who are with you.

I appoint you commander for the campaign, so march at once until you get to Mah.[304] Lo, I have written to the people of Kufa to join you; and when your army is all together, advance to Nihawand.

In case you fall in battle, the commander of the army will be Hudayfah bin AI Yaman; if he falls, then Jareer bin Abdullah; if he falls, Mugheerah bin Shu'ba; and if he falls. Ash'as bin Qeis.

Do not ill-treat your men or be harsh with them, for then you will come to harm. And do not withhold from them their rights, for then you will be unjust. And do not put them in a position of loss, because every single one of the Muslims is dearer to me than a 100,000 dinars.

Seek the help of Allah and repeat often: 'There is no power to change and no strength except with Allah.'[305]

And again peace be upon you.[306]

At the same time as he wrote to Noman, the Caliph also addressed letters to other commanders who would move with their forces and rendezvous as decided by Noman and operate thereafter under his orders. Hudayfah bin Al

---

[303] The early Caliphs addressed themselves in their letters as Slave of Allah (Abdullah)-a title which they were proud to assume.
[304] Mah means a well-watered area. Here the reference is to the region around Nihawand which later became known as the Mah of Basra; the taxes from here were used to help in running the province of Basra.
[305] A Quranic verse.
[306] Tabari: Vol. 3, pp. 203, 212-3; Balzuri: p. 300, Dinawari: p. 135.

Yemen, administrator of Ctesiphon, would march with the bulk of the forces from Kufa, and Abu Musa with one-third of the Muslim army in Basra. A fresh force would be mustered at Madina, which would include many Companions, including Umar's son Abdullah, and would move under Mugheerah bin Shu'ba. These were the main components which would form the army of Islam against the Persians. But Umar also organised an irregular force from the local Muslim Arabs of the Basra region and the Persians who had joined Abu Musa, and instructed their chiefs to operate as raiders across the hills to disrupt Persian communications from Fars and Isfahan to Nihawand and thus prevent the movement of reinforcements to the Persian army. This would also have the effect of guarding Khuzistan from the north and east, Nothing more is recorded of the actions of the last-mentioned force, and what actual effect its operations had on the main battle which followed is not known.

Noman's mission was clear: he had to fight and defeat the Persian army at Nihawand and eliminate the threat to Muslim Iraq. He had two major axes of approach to Nihawand, one from Kirmanshah and the other from Khuzistan via what is now Khuramabad. He could also go over the hills between these two axes but the lack of communications would restrict his movement and his freedom of manoeuvre. Since the bulk of the Muslim army was at Kufa, Noman chose to take the western axis for operations against the Persians, but he also had to ensure that the Persians did not debouch from the Zagros range into the plain of Khuzistan while the Muslim movement from the west was in progress.

Noman ordered Abu Musa to move to Kufa where the elements from Kufa and Basra would concentrate before marching out for battle. He instructed Mujashe bin Masud to position himself with a detachment between Ghaza-ush-Shajr and Marj-ul Qala in order to prevent the Persians from coming out of the hills and creating a threat behind the Muslims.[307] He ordered Hudayfah bin Al Yaman to march with the Kufans and Basrans along the Kirmanshah road and meet him at Tazar.[308] And Noman himself moved with the few troops who were present with him across the foothills of Masabzan to Tazar. Some distance to the east of Tazar, near Kirmanshah, stood the forward post of Qubaz. [See Map 14.]

---

[307] Marj-ul-Qala is the present Karend, between Kirmanshah and Qasr Sheereen. The location of Ghaza-ush-Shajr is not known, but it must have been somewhere not far from Karend, and to the south of it.
[308] Tazar is the present Khusrauabad, 10 miles south-east of Karend.

These moves, begun in Zul Qada, 20 Hijri, were completed in Zul Haj [November-December 641]. Noman was the first to arrive at Tazar and was joined here by the bulk of the army. When the move was complete, he recalled Mujashe, whose presence as a flank guard was no longer necessary. With the Muslims poised for action at Tazar, the Persians could not leave Nihawand and move southwards because Nihawand and Hamadan would then be exposed. Soon after the bulk of the army had concentrated at Tazar, the large detachment prepared by the Caliph at Madina also joined Noman.

As soon as the troops had settled down at Tazar, Noman sent three officers on the road to Nihawand to carry out a reconnaissance and locate the presence of the Persians. These included Amr bin Madi Karib and Tuleiha the [ex] Impostor. They rode off in the morning. At nightfall one of them stopped and returned to report that all was clear. The other two continued moving during the night till the following morning, when Amr stopped and returned to report that no Persians had been seen. Tuleiha, however, went on and his return was so long delayed that his detractors began to suggest that perhaps he had turned apostate again, as they had suggested at Qadisiyya. But he too returned to inform Noman that he had gone up to Nihawand and found no Persians between Nihawand and Tazar.

The army commander at once set the army in motion with his brother Nueim leading the advance. After some days of marching the Muslims arrived at Isbeezahan, 11 miles short of Nihawand, to find the Persian army assembled for battle in front of them. [Isbeezahan was roughly where the small village of Sa'd Waqqas stands today.] Noman ordered the unloading of the baggage and the pitching of tents.

MAP 14: THE MARCH TO NIHAWAND

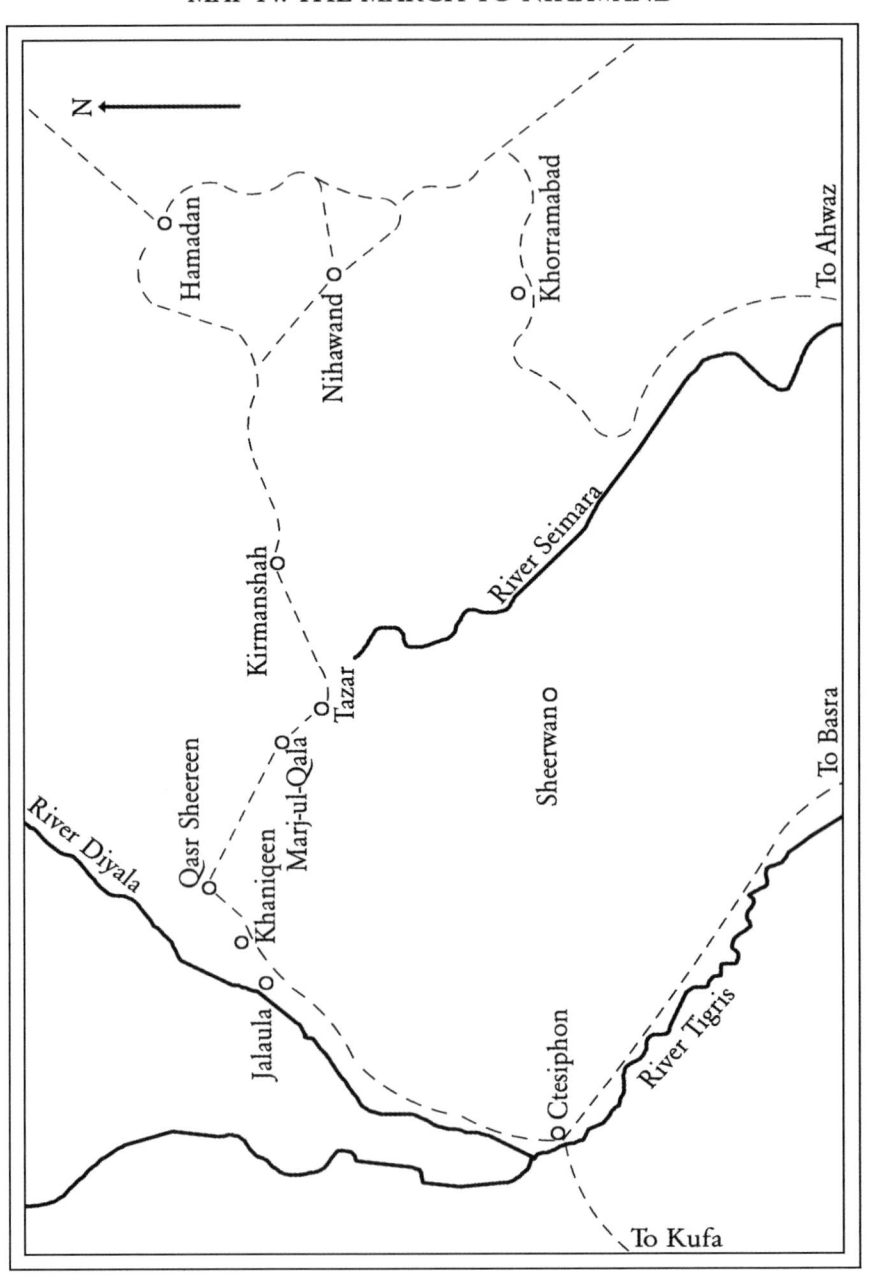

The Persians were in great strength: 60,000 proud warriors, all dedicated to the cause of the empire, all fiercely determined to drive the Muslims out of their land. Yet they were cautious. The psychological effect of the Muslim victories in Iraq lead been such that they regarded the Muslims with something like awe. And Mardanshah, knowing that upon the result of the forthcoming battle hung the fate of the empire, was not averse to negotiations if by that means he could rid Persia of the invaders while avoiding a military trial of strength. He asked for an envoy to be sent by the Muslims for talks. And who should appear from the Muslim side but Mugheerah bin Shu'ba! As Mugheerah arrived at the improvised court established by the Persians, there was an exchange of hot words between him and some Persian nobles who thought that he was not showing sufficient respect to their Commander-in-Chief, but after the unhappy preamble he was offered a seat and a brief dialogue was held. Mardanshah, making the same mistake which his predecessors had made of trying to browbeat the Muslims, said:

"You, O nation of Arabs, are a people farthest of all from good, the most long-suffering in hunger, the most distressed of the wretched, the filthiest of the foul, and the most remote in habitation. The only thing which prevents me from ordering my warriors to kill all of you is my aversion to the pollution which your corpses would cause, for you are unclean. If you go away, we will be rid of you. And if you refuse to go, you will meet your end."

Mugheerah, after praising Allah, replied:

"By Allah, you made no mistake when describing our condition. We were the most remote in habitation, the worst hit by hunger, the most distressed of the wretched and the farthest away from all good, until Allah Almighty sent us His Prophet, on whom be the blessings of Allah and peace. He promised us victory in this world and Paradise in the next.

"By Allah, we have not ceased to receive victory and success from our Lord ever since His Prophet came to us. Now we have come to you; and by Allah, we shall not return to our former wretched condition but will either take what you possess or be killed in your land."

"By God," exclaimed the Persian general," the one-eyed one has spoken honestly."[309]

There was no more to be said, and Mugheerah bin Shu'ba returned to the Muslim camp.

His return was also the point of no return. After this there could only be battle, and the positioning of forces was begun for the battle to be fought the following day. While the forming up for battle was in progress, a messenger came into the Muslim camp from the Persian Commander-in-Chief, and asked if the Muslims would cross or should the Persians cross the small stream bed [wadi] which lay between the two armies and across their front. Noman said that he would cross the obstacle.

The Muslims were in no mood to accept a delay in battle because the season was very cold and this factor suited the Persians more than the Arabs. Noman wished to take the initiative and bring matters to a conclusion as soon as possible. He had an army of 30,000 Muslims, only half the strength of the Persians, but that was good enough. He was reassured by the fact that there were brave generals and splendid champions is his army - Hudayfah bin Al Yaman, Qa'qa bin Amr, Abdullah bin Umar, Jareer bin Abdullah, Mugheerah bin Shu'ba, Noman's brothers Nueim and Suweid, and the dashing [ex] apostate chieftains: Ash'as bin Qeis, Tuleiha the [ex] Impostor and Amr bin Madi Karib [Father of the Bull].

It was Qadisiyya all over again: the same spirit, the same eagerness for battle, the same anticipation of victory, the same sense of destiny.

---

[309] Tabari: vol. 3, p. 206.

Chapter 20: The Battle of Nihawand

It was a cold Wednesday morning in the latter half of December [about the second week of Muharram, 21 Hijri] as the soldiers donned their equipment and prepared for battle.

Their camps lay near the northern edge of the valley of Nihawand, which ran north-west to south-east with a width of about ten miles. At the southern edge of the valley stood a massive range known as Garreen, rising 4-5,000 feet above the valley floor as part of the Zagros Mountains; the northern edge of the valley was not marked by any continuous ridge, but the Persian position was covered on its northern side by a 3,000 feet high ridge called Ardeshan. Down the centre of the valley, more towards the north than the south, stretched another ridge-a low, bare, brown one-which rose about 500 feet and was marked along its southern edge by a prominent stream, or wadi. The battlefield was the northern half of the valley, from Isbeezahan to Nihawand. [See Map 15.]

The Persian front ran generally along the forward slope of the brown ridge and curved up, in front of the Muslim camp, to a prominent spur of the Ardeshan ridge. The Persian right rested on the spur with the ridge itself protecting the Persian flank. The Persian left stood at the eastern end of the brown ridge, a little beyond the village of Zarrameen. [See Map 16.]

To further strengthen their position, the Persians had fortified the villages which lay along the front and improved the wadi as an obstacle. It was a very skilfully arranged position, with their right flank secured by the Ardeshan ridge and their left acting as a refused flank. Any movement by the Muslims towards the Persian left would involve a flank march and expose their base to the Persians. Furthermore, the Persians had the advantage of holding the high ground of the brown ridge which commanded the valley and gave them excellent observation over the approaches to their position. The Muslims would have to not only cross the wadi but also attack uphill, fully exposed to the fire of Persian archers on the forward slope of the brown ridge.

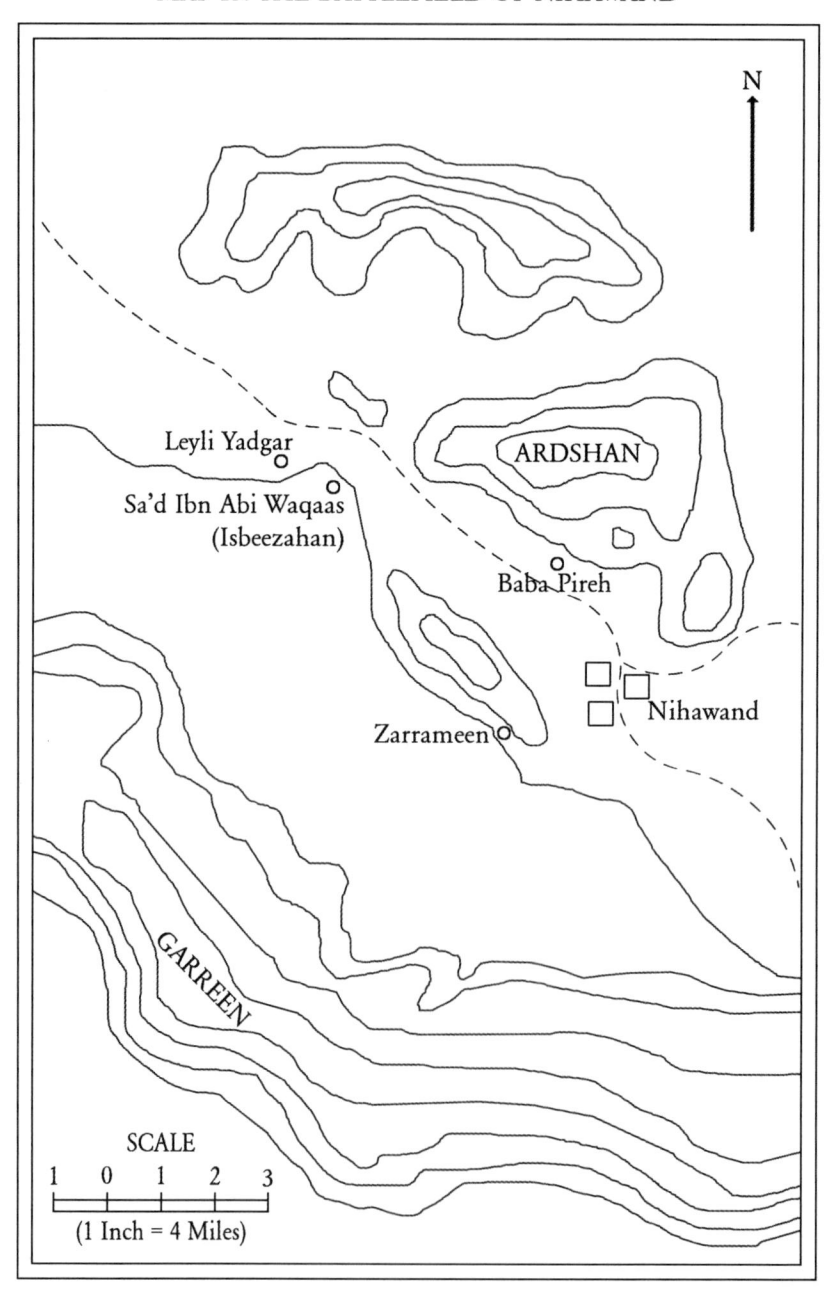

MAP 15: THE BATTLEFIELD OF NIHAWAND

MAP 16: THE BATTLEFIELD OF NIHAWAND - 1

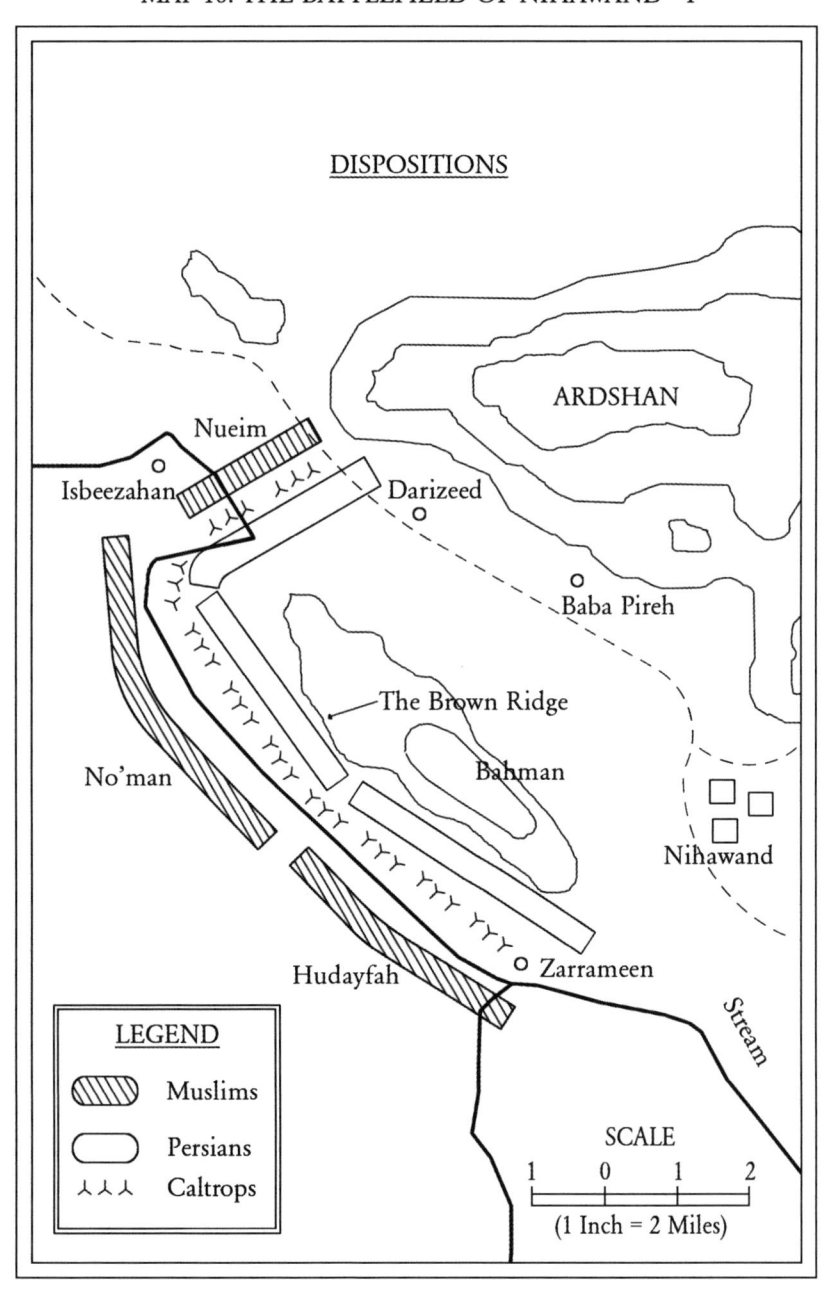

In front of their forward line and behind the wadi, the Persians planted a belt of iron caltrops to lame the attackers' horses - a belt which stretched like a minefield of today from one edge of the front to the other.[310] A few caltrops were also thrown haphazardly in front of the wadi, one of which injured the hoof of a Muslim scout's horse and stuck in it. The scout brought it back to show Noman. Behind the obstacle belt the Persian army stood ready for battle with the infantry bound to each other in chains which were of three lengths, to hold 5, 7 and 10 men together. Equipped with splendid weapons and bound with shining chains, the Persian host looked, in the words of Mugheerah bin Shu'ba, "like a mountain of iron."[311]

There was nothing the Muslims could do about the Persian front. There was no weakness which they could exploit, no tactical error which they could turn to their advantage. It was obvious that no outflanking movement would be possible and it would have to be a frontal clash of arms. Consequently the Muslims did the only thing that was possible; they deployed along the front of the Persian army, on their side of the wadi, from the spur of the Ardeshan ridge to the village of Zarrameen. The Muslim left was commanded by Noman's brother, Nueim, their right by Hudayfah bin Al Yaman, while Qa'qa bin Amr was placed in command of the cavalry. Opposing them, the commanders of the Persian wings were Zardaq and Bahman, and the imperial reserve was commanded by Anushaq.

Both armies remained in their battle positions as the sun ascended slowly to its zenith. Then, just after midday, the Muslims offered the prayer of the noon and Noman had the troops informed that he would give three calls for battle, each consisting of the rousing cry of "Allah-o-Akbar", of which the first two would be preparatory calls and the third one the final call to attack the Persian front. About an hour after the prayers, the Muslim commander gave the calls, and at the third one the Muslim front, horse and foot, heaved into action.

The Muslims got to the wadi and came under withering fire from Persian archers which wounded many of those leading the attack. The attackers got to the far bank of the wadi and plunged into the caltrops. Many horses were lamed

---

[310] As described in an earlier chapter, a catrop was a sharp 4-pronged instrument which, when thrown on the ground, would make a 3-point landing and have one prong facing upwards. About one inch in size, it was designed to lame horses and men-mainly horses. I met a scholar in Nihawand, one named Samee'i, who had actually picked up one of these caltrops in the village of Zarameen, which marked the left edge of the Persian front.
[311] Tabari: vol. 3, p. 206.

but they pressed on, bearing up under fire from the defenders' archers. Then the two bodies of men clashed, brave men drew their swords and raised their maces, and bloody combat was under way. [See Map 17].

This action, begun in mid-afternoon, went on till sunset. Many warriors lay on the battlefield, some motionless, others suffering in pain, but the Muslims could make no headway. On certain parts of the front they achieved some success and pushed the Persians back, but the defenders counter-attacked and re-established their position. At places one, at places the other side was badly hurt, but the battle hung in the balance, and soon after sunset the Muslims, with nothing to show for their efforts except a larger number of enemy dead than their own, broke contact and withdrew to their camp.

The night passed uneventfully. Those of the dead whose bodies could be recovered were buried, the wounded were treated for their wounds. The day's action had proved unproductive. Then dawn approached and the two armies formed up again on the same lines as they had occupied on the previous day. The Persian dispositions did not permit any outflanking movements and Noman decided to try the frontal attack once again. But he did not go into action until the early part of the afternoon, and then gave the order to attack. The Muslim army again swept forward to assault the solid Persian formations.

The second day of battle, Thursday, passed in much the same way. The battle raged furiously for many hours but the Persian army, strengthened by its chains and enjoying the tactical advantage of high ground, remained unshaken, even though large numbers were cut down by the attackers. It was a grim, bloody, relentless struggle, producing a tragic harvest of death but no victory. After sunset the Muslims again disengaged and returned frustrated to their camp.

For the next two days there was no action. Both sides remained on guard, ready for battle, but neither moved to engage the other. Having struck his head twice against the Persian wall with no visible effect on the wall, Noman rightly chose not to pursue the same course a third time. He hoped that the Persians would come forward, outside the protection of their obstacle and the fortifications, but Mardanshah was too wise a general to run such a risk when time was in his favour.

MAP 17: THE BATTLEFIELD OF NIHAWAND - 2

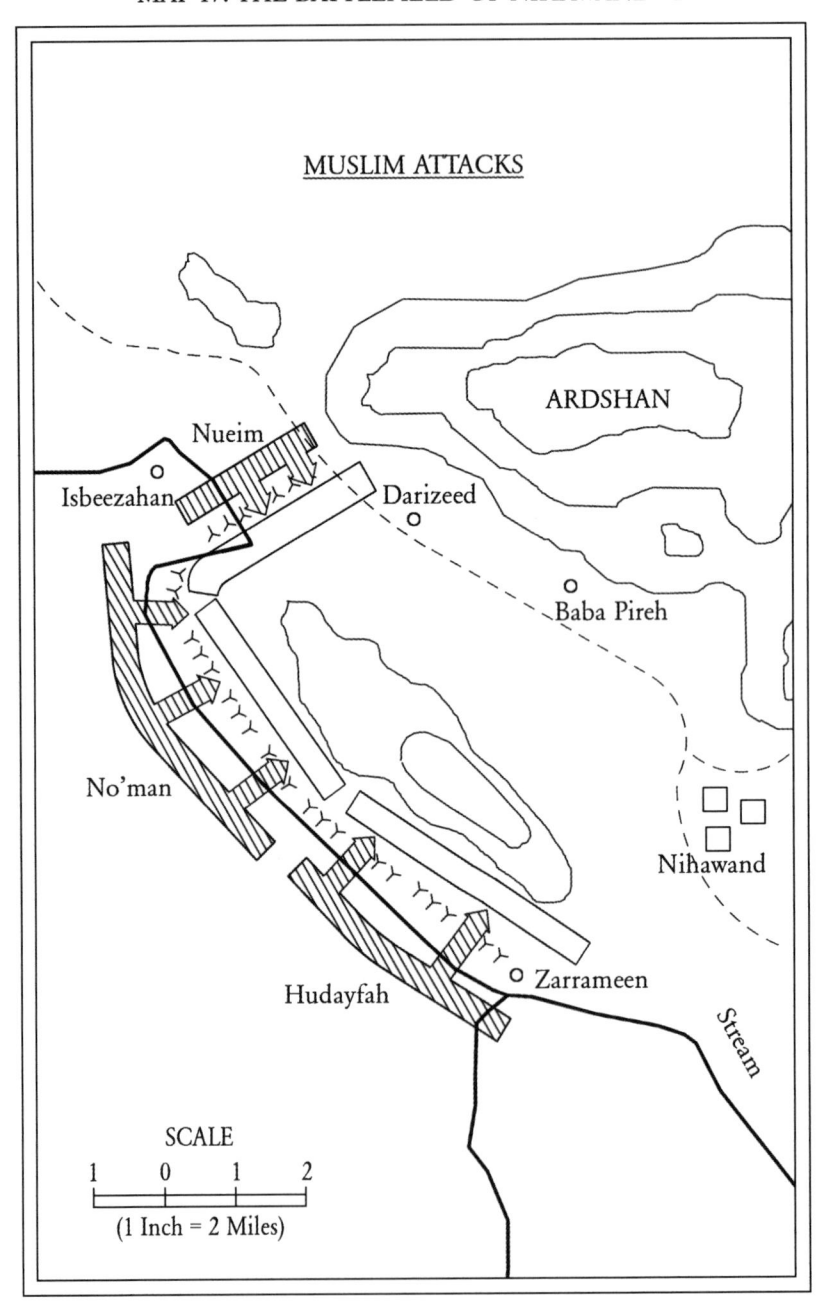

MUSLIM ATTACKS

SCALE
1　0　1　2
(1 Inch = 2 Miles)

After two days the tension left the Persian ranks and they began to raid forward of their position. The Muslims were unable to do much about the raiding parties which withdrew hastily to their own side of the obstacle before the Muslims could take counter-measures against them. In this manner the initiative began to shift to the Persians and the Muslims were left baffled and dismayed. They were brave and eager for battle but just not able to bring on battle, while in the meantime the severe cold caused them much distress and the Persian strength went on increasing with the arrival of reinforcements almost every day. From the point of view of the base of operations also the Persians were better-placed; their supplies and reinforcements could reach them easily from Hamadan, which was quite close: while the Muslims' base for reinforcements, Kufa, was a long way away. Time definitely favoured Persia.

A few days after his last unsuccessful attack, Noman called a council of war. All the generals assembled and many others who were senior in age or were Companions. "You see the infidels and their steadfastness in entrenchments and towns," said Noman. "They only come out when they wish and the Muslims can do nothing against them unless they come out. You can see the difficulties which the Muslims are facing and the initiative which the Persian enjoy. What can we do to get the Persians out to battle and end this delay?"

The oldest man present was Amr bin Subayy, and as the oldest man present he spoke first: "Being under pressure is worse for them than the delay is for you. Let them be. Do not disturb them and fight those of them who come within your reach." This proposal was greeted with a clamour of disapproval. All present were anxious to get the battle behind them as quickly as possible. Another man suggested that the attack against the Persian position be resumed regardless of the consequences, but this too was rejected by the council.

Then Tuleiha came up with a bright idea: "Put the cavalry in a position to outflank them, and show a weak front, making as if to withdraw. Let the Persians hope for victory and advance against us. Then we turn and fight them."

This stratagem was liked by everyone and Amr bin Madi Karib added further to it: "I suggest that we spread the rumour that the Commander of the Faithful is dead. Then you start moving back with everybody. When the enemy hears this he will come after us. Then we turn and fight him."[312]

---

[312] Tabari: vol. 3, p. 215; Dinawari: p.136.

This plan was approved, amplified and put into action.

It was on the following Thursday, when a week had passed since the last Muslim attack, that the Persian heard reports of the death of the Caliph. The news spread like wild fire among the troops and the local inhabitants of the valley. It was the best news they had heard for many years. The joy of the Persians knew no bounds. They were jubilant. How would the Muslims on their front react to the death of their Caliph? Surely, the blow would shatter their morale. They could hardly go on fighting. Now may well be the time to take the offensive and destroy them, before they could withdraw into the plains of the Suwad. The new situation gave a tremendous boost to Persian spirits.

As Friday dawned. Persian scouts reported that the Muslim outposts which had faced them across the wadi were no longer there. This was followed by reports of hectic activity in the Muslim camp where tents were being struck and baggage loaded on the camels. Some men were even seen marching westwards.

Mardanshah read the signs right, as any seasoned and sound general could do. The picture was perfect; every piece of intelligence fitted neatly into it. Now was the time to strike against the invaders of the empire and put paid to their account. And this would be a perfect conclusion to the battle; first fighting defensively to blunt the Muslim attack and wear them down, and then taking the counter-offensive when the Muslims were vulnerable and off balance. According to plans already formulated, several gaps were opened in the caltrop belt on the Persian right, the caltrops being just swept aside, and Persian army began to cross the obstacle in several columns. Its strength was about 50,000 men, but not all of them could take as part in this sally.

The leading elements of each column stopped a short distance beyond the obstacle so that the rest of the column could catch up. It was Mardanshah's intention to form up for battle beyond the obstacle and attack the Muslims with the bulk of his army in one single action, thus achieving maximum superiority of strength at the time and place of engagement. While they were forming up, the Persians saw the Muslims hastily deploying in the valley to face them. This too fitted into the picture. The Muslims were obviously preparing to beat off the unexpected Persian attack so that they would not be caught on the run, and would then continue their retreat unmolested. Well, Mardanshah would show them. But just in case the fighting turned more serious than he anticipated and his men began to look over their shoulders, he had the caltrop belt restored to its full effectiveness, with all gaps filled. It was now an obstacle behind the

Persians. And as a future element of strength to ensure against weakness, the Persian infantry put on its chains.

About two hours before midday, the Persian army, formed in perfect battle order, began to move forward like a monstrous carpet of iron. The Muslims stood still. As the Persians got within bow range of their adversaries, they stopped, and the archers opened up with their bows.

The Muslim plan had gone as designed; the Persians had swallowed the bait. As they had begun to form up on the Muslim side of the obstacle, Noman had quickly thrown his army into battle formation on the same pattern as before but with different commanders of wings - Ash'as bin Qeis on the left and Mugheerah bin Shu'ba on the right. Qa'qa was already in position with a strong cavalry group on the left, obscured from the Persians by the high ground which stretched like a saddle from the western edge of the Ardeshan ridge. Hudayfah and Noman's brothers. Nueim and Suweid, were kept in the centre as reserve officers for use as required.

Noman had a premonition of what fate had in store for him in this battle, and had given orders: "If I am killed, your commander will be Hudayfah bin Al Yaman. If he is killed, Jareer bin Abdullah. If he is killed, Qeis bin Makshuh..." and so he named several officers who would follow in command to a total of 7, the last of whom was Mugheerah bin Shu'ba.[313] This was a change in the order given by Umar who had placed Mugheerah as the fourth in command, and Mugheerah did not take kindly, to his demotion. But he had no option but to accept the orders of the army commander.

When the Persians began to cross the obstacle and get into battle formation. Mugheerah observed these movements closely. He had a very sharp sense of opportunity and his keen eye at once grasped the possibilities which the Persians offered while preparing for battle. He came galloping to Noman from his right wing and asked. "What do you intend to do?"

"When it is past noon," replied Noman, "I shall fight them, for I have seen the Messenger of Allah, on whom be the blessings of Allah and peace, prefer this time."

"If I were in your place, I would hasten to fight them."
"If you hasten to fight them, may Allah not blacken your face!"

---

[313] Tabari: vol. 3, pp. 203, 207.

Mugheerah was irritated by Noman's refusal to exploit the unbalanced state of the Persians. "I never saw such sluggishness in command as today," he said to Noman angrily. "We are letting the enemy form his ranks and not hurrying up against him. By Allah, if I were in command I would attack them at once."

Noman continued to deal gently with Mugheerah: "May Allah show you many days like this one! Let not the waiting irk you. By Allah, nothing prevents me from starting the attack except something which I learned from the Messenger of Allah. When he had to fight, he would not attack during the first part of the day and would not hasten battle until the time had come for the noon prayer and the wind had begun to blow. Only that prevents me from starting combat."

Mugheerah was militarily one hundred per cent right and the timing of the attack as proposed by him was perfect. But this was a matter of judgement and the exercise of reason, while Noman was relying not on reason but on the merit which he hoped to gain by following in the footsteps of the Holy Prophet. The Prophet himself would not have wished such a close and literal emulation of his example, especially where judgement dictated otherwise, but so deep was the impact of his personality upon his Companions that many of them would follow his example blindly, even in matters of form. Noman would do what the Holy Prophet did, and that was that. However, Mugheerah tried once more to taunt him into action: "If I were in command, I would know what to do."

"Steady," replied Noman, without showing any anger, "Allah will not disgrace us, and we hope to attain by waiting what you wish to attain by haste."

He then raised his hands in supplication and prayed: "O Lord, cool my eyes today with a victory which brings honour to Islam and disgrace to the infidels, and then take me to thyself as a martyr." [The phrase: "cooling the eyes." meant making one happy.]

Those present said Ameen, with tears in their eyes.[314]

---

[314] Tabari: vol. 3, pp. 203-8, 216; Masudi: Muruj: vol. 2, p. 332.

MAP 18: THE BATTLEFIELD OF NIHAWAND - 3

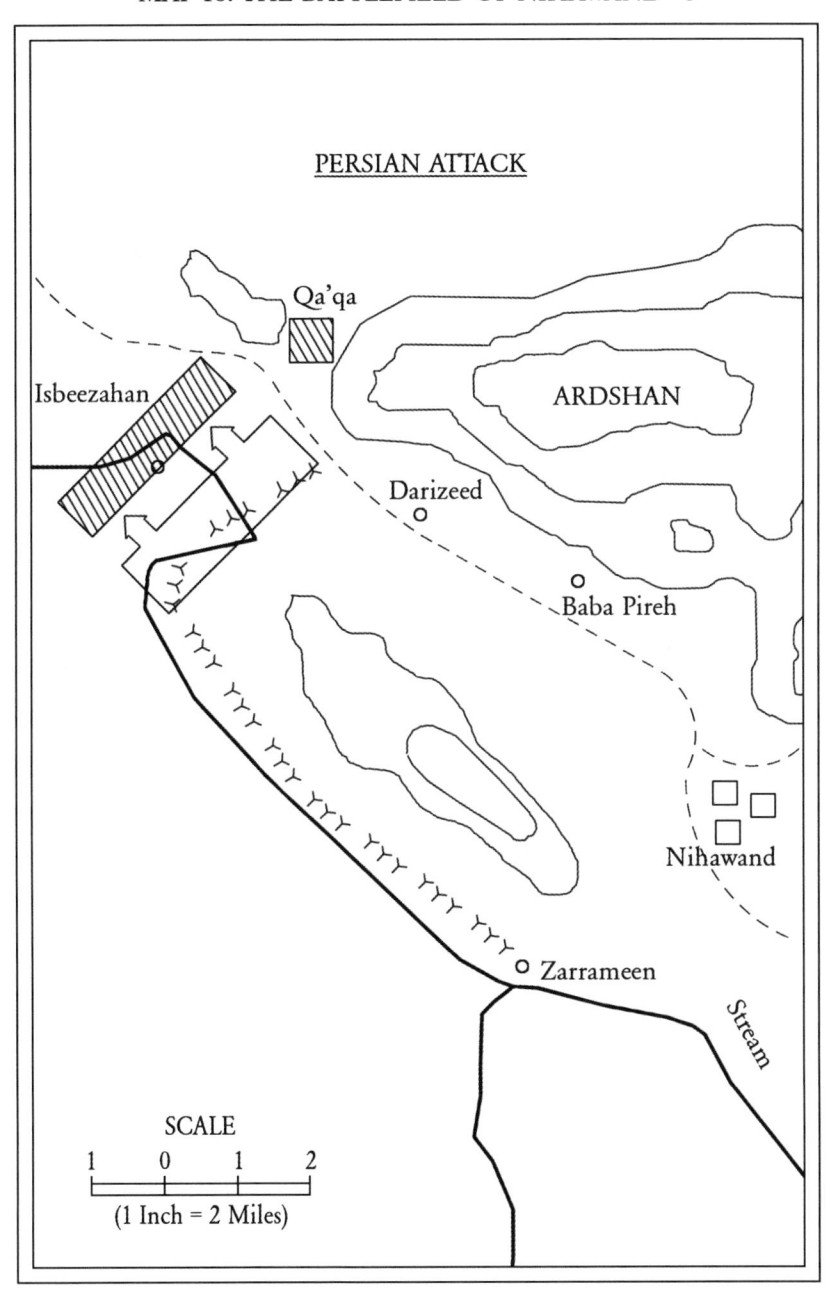

PERSIAN ATTACK

Qa'qa

Isbeezahan

ARDSHAN

Darizeed

Baba Pireh

Nihawand

Zarrameen

Stream

SCALE
1 0 1 2
(1 Inch = 2 Miles)

All this happened while the Persians were forming up on the west side of the caltrop belt. Then the Persians began to advance, and getting within bow range subjected their adversaries to a merciless barrage of arrows. The Muslims stood motionless and used their shields to protect themselves, but in spite of this many were wounded. Their archers were helpless because Persian bows had a longer range while the Persian arrows were bigger and more deadly. The Persian fire was accurate and increased in intensity until most of the Muslim soldiers became impatient to escape the torment of the arrows by closing up with the Persians and engaging them in hand-to-hand combat. Some of them rushed to Noman and complained against their inaction. "Steady! Steady!" replied Noman.

Then the Persians, feeling that enough had been done to soften up Muslim resistance, advanced, and on getting to close quarters, attacked with swords and maces. [See Map 18.] The Muslims fought back but none made a move forward to push the Persians away. The Persian attack was terrible in weight and intensity, and while the Muslims held their own, their inability to move forward imposed a heavy strain upon them. Again some of them rushed to Noman, and again he said, "Steady! Steady!"[315]

So the rest of the morning wore on with the Persians pressing their attack and feeling elated in the mistaken belief that the lack of offensive action on the part of their opponents was due to the shock of their Caliph's death. The Muslims held on with superhuman patience and self-control, but the physical and emotional strain of their remaining on the defensive became more and more intolerable, while their instincts cried out to them to charge back at the Persians. By the time the sun had passed its zenith, their patience had reached its breaking point. Then they heard the call of "Allaho-Akbar" from their Commander-in-Chief. The first was followed by the second call and the Muslims prepared to hurl the Persians back from their position. Then came the heart-warming third call, and with a thundering roar of "Allaho-Akbar", the Muslim army struck back at the Persians and like a powerful bull, locked in a fight to the death with another, pushed forward. At the same time Qa'qa bin Amr broke cover and with his cavalry group galloped for the flank of the Persians between their rear and the obstacle belt, in a manoeuvre similar to the one he had carried out at Jalaula. [See Map 19.]

---

[315] Tabari: vol. 3, p. 216.

MAP 19: THE BATTLEFIELD OF NIHAWAND - 4

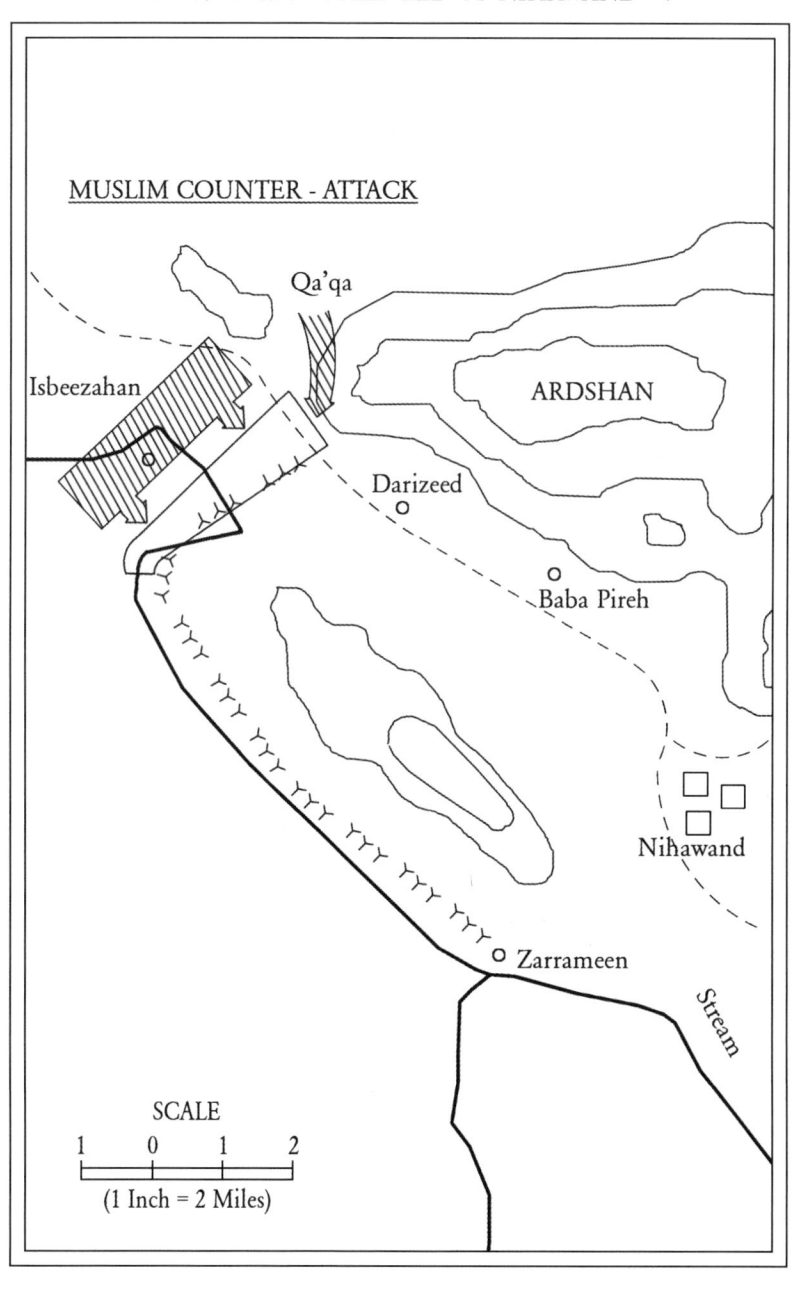

Now came the most bloody and unmerciful phase of the battle. The first Persian reaction was one of amazement at the unexpected nerve of their opponents whom they had presumed to be demoralised, but soon their mood turned to anger as they found a desperate action on their hands. The fighting became more vicious as strong men slashed and stabbed at each other and for a long time nothing could he heard except the sound of iron striking iron. Men fell like flies, dead and wounded, but the Muslims were so worked up that none wished to return to his family except as a victor.[316]

Noman, mounted on his horse and dressed in white, led the attack of the centre, and following his example, others pressed after him, breaking the Persian ranks. The Persians were pushed back in the centre and a little later their wings also fell back a bit, but in perfect shape and with no intention of giving up any more ground than was necessary. In their rear, Qa'qa succeeded in driving a wedge behind the Persian flank but was held before he could get fully behind them. The Persian army fought with desperate courage to stave off defeat and regain the initiative. The time for generalship had passed; it was now up to the soldiers to put every ounce of energy and every bit of courage into the fight and destroy their hated adversaries. And this they did, in an action which recalled to the veterans of Qadisiyya the most bloody part of Qadisiyya.

Some time in the middle of the afternoon, the battle reached its climax. The Muslim wings under Mugheerah bin Shu'ba and Ash'as bin Qeis and the centre under Noman – all three groups led in person by their general – pushed hard against the corresponding Persia formations. Qa'qa struck fiercely against the Persia flank in order to break through and get behind them, but was held by the Persian's who struggled tenaciously to keep their rear clear of the Muslims. Meanwhile the battlefield was soaked with blood, with earth turning into red slush in which often horses and men would slip and fall. At last the first sign of success became apparent and the two locked fronts began to move towards the obstacle. Then suddenly Noman was struck in his side by an arrow. The next instant his horse slipped in the blood-soaked mud and fell; taking its noble rider down with it.

Nueim and Suweid rushed to their stricken brother. He was alive but unconscious, the arrow embedding deep in his side. A few others also gathered around him. They decided to conceal the news from the army until the battle was over. The brothers covered him with his cloak so that no one would know who was laying there, and all agreed not to say a word about the loss of their

---

[316] Ibid: p. 270

commander. Nueim grasped the army standard and took his place in the centre as if he was Noman, and the battle went on with the army unaware of his loss.

The advance of the army of Islam continued slowly and steadily against a stubborn enemy who fought for every inch of ground. Mardanshah was still convinced that Muslim aggressiveness was a passing phase and would end, after which he would strike again and slaughter his foes. At his urging, the Persians fought with the courage of desperation and made the Muslims pay heavily for their limited success. The chains made the Persians more steady, holding them together and discouraging flight. On the flank too they held the attack of Qa'qa, knowing that if he were to achieve his object, all would be lost.

The afternoon wore on, hour after painful hour, the soldiers driven by frenzy to perform superhuman feats of courage and endurance, but by late afternoon the balance had tilted clearly in the favour of the Muslims. Shortly before sunset, the Persian resistance began to weaken and the Muslims, impervious to fatigue and scenting victory, struck with greater violence against the army of chains. Then suddenly the Persian front broke into pieces.

The vanquished soldiers turned and hobbled back in their chains. The Muslims were now faced with an opportunity at which the Arab of the desert excelled- chasing a defeated foe -and with joyous shouts they sprang at the receding backs of the Persian soldiers. For the Persians the terror of the light-armed and fast-moving Muslims coming after them was enough to make them forget that there was another horror awaiting them - the belt of caltrops which they had themselves planted.

The chains which had once given them strength now became fetters which imprisoned them. Where one fell, several were halted and easily cut down. And as the Muslims intensified their assault, the disciplined army of Persia turned into a rabble with no order or organisation and no control by its officers. Many turned and fought bravely to stem the tide, preferring an honourable death to a dishonourable retreat, but the bulk of the army staggered on, driven by a blind desire to get away from it all. The Persian flank guard, however, held its own and in spite of terrible losses did not give ground before Qa'qa. But for the success of this flank guard in holding Qa'qa off, the bruised army of Persia would not have got away from the battlefield. It moved in a chaotic, disorganized manner and arrived at the caltrop belt. It was a body without a head, for Mardanshah was no longer with his army. He lay on the battlefield, covered with blood, redeeming himself in death.

The belt of caltrops could be crossed in daylight with little damage, in a deliberate, planned movement, with soldiers picking their way through it. Thus had the Muslims crossed it over two days a week earlier. But now, for the Persians, such a move was not possible. It was also getting dark. Their fear of the horrid little sharp-pronged contraptions, however, was drowned in their terror of the oncoming victors, and without further thought they plunged into the obstacle belt. Hooves and feet pierced, many fell within the belt, but the rest got across. Some badly lamed, some lucky to escape unhurt, they arrived on the home side of the obstacle and moved on, dragging their feet, impelled by the instinct of survival.

The Muslims came after them. The obstacle gave little trouble because most of the caltrops had been picked up by the hooves of the Persian horses and the feet of the Persian soldiers. In the gathering darkness they went on in relentless pursuit under their new commander, Hudayfah bin Al Yaman. Hudayfah had been informed of Noman's fall soon after the Persians broke, and had taken command of the army and maintained its forward momentum.

A little later, according to Tabari, the Persian horde got to a cleft or ravine which lay near the place where they had camped for battle. This acted as bottleneck, and here occurred what usually occurs at bottlenecks. Everyone made a frantic effort to get ahead to escape the pursuers, and as everyone started pushing everyone else, the fugitives began to fall down the precipice. As the Persians fell, they screamed "Wai khurd," which can be roughly translated as: "O, I am finished!" and as a result of this cry of despair, the ravine became known as Wai Khurd.[317]

Some time during the night, at Wai Khurd, Hudayfah stopped the pursuit.

It was a bright night; but the scene on the battlefield was far from bright. It was a scene from a fevered nightmare. The earth which normally covers the dead was itself covered by dead. There was movement also, where the wounded lay, and men able to give succour gave it to those who needed it. A small group gathered around the body of Noman bin Muqarrin.

Maqil bin Yasar knelt beside the prostrate form. He raised the cloak from the face of Noman and saw that he still breathed, though with difficulty. He gently

---

[317] Tabari: vol. 3, p. 217. I have found no trace of any cleft or ravine in my reconnaissance of the area of this battle, and cannot say where this episode of Wai Khurd could have occurred. Purely as a matter of interest I have narrated the story as related by Tabari.

washed the face of the fallen general. Noman stirred and opened his eyes. "Who is it?" he asked.

"Maqil bin Yasar".

Noman's first thought was for his army. "What have the Muslims done?" he asked.

"Rejoice," replied Maqil, "Allah has given them victory."

"Praise be to Allah." said Noman, as he breathed his last. "Write to Umar."[318]

Noman did not live long enough to be told that thousands of his comrades shared his fate, including the dauntless [ex]apostate chieftains, Tuleiha the Impostor and the Father of the Bull. He had prayed for death in battle as the ideal end of a virtuous life, and Allah had granted his prayer. He drank the cup of martyrdom to the full, and drank it not as a sacrifice or price to be paid for something but as a joy ardently desired and gratefully accepted.

A few soldiers passed that way, wondering why they had not seen their commander lately. "Where is our commander?" they asked.

"Here lies your commander," Maqil told them. "Allah has cooled his eyes and granted him martyrdom."[319]

The following morning Hudayfah advanced with his army to follow the Persians but had not gone far when he found the Persian army arrayed for battle at the small town of Dareezeed, 7 miles from Nihawand.[320] The Persians were an impressive sight and the way they stood in the path of the Muslims gave no hint of a beaten army. They looked fresh and aggressive, under their new commander, Dinar, and every bit a hard fighting army.

Hudayfah decided to give them a hard fight. He deployed his army for the attack but as his front rank came to grips with the Persians, they turned and beat a hasty retreat. This was actually only part of the army which Dinar had used to put up a show of resistance in order to delay the Muslims and gain time

---

[318] Balazuri: pp. 301-2.
[319] Tabari: vol. 3, p. 207.
[320] There is no sign of Dareezeed today. Its location, as given here, is known from Dinawari: p. 136.

for the withdrawal of the bulk of his force and for preparing a more stubborn defence at Nihawand itself.

The Muslim's advanced again and found the Persians at Nihawand, safe behind the walls of the city. They invested the city. Over the next few days the Persians made a few half-hearted sallies but soon lost hope of success. Dinar offered to surrender unconditionally and this was accepted by Hudayfah, after which those of the Persians who were in Nihawand laid down their arms. The Muslims entered the city and took a certain amount of what it had as plunder, because it formed a legitimate prize of war, but soon after, a state of complete peace was established with the Persians agreeing to pay the Jizya and other taxes.

Thus ended the battle of Nihawand, fought over two weeks in Muharram, 21 Hijri [December, 641-January, 642].[321]

But quite a large part of the Persian army was not in Nihawand. This part had maintained its withdrawal towards Hamadan, and as soon as Hudayfah came to know of this, he sent a column in pursuit under Nueim bin Muqarrin and Qa'qa bin Amr. The column moved faster than the Persians, who were in poor condition, and caught up with their rearmost elements a little short of Hamadan. The appearance of the Muslims upon their heels gave wings to the fugitives who moved very fast and got to Hamadan before many could be cut down, but a large mule train carrying baggage fell into the hands of the pursuers. Nueim placed his troops at various strategic places around the city of Hamadan while treating the neighbouring countryside as a prize of war, but hardly had the Muslims settled down in their posts when the Persian commander of Hamadan offered to surrender and pay the Jizya. The Persian general here was Khusrau Shanum, who had fought and survived at Qadisiyya and Qasr Sheereen. His surrender was accepted by Nueim and after the details of payment had been settled, the Muslims returned to Nihawand, leaving Khusrau Shanum as the governor of Hamadan under Muslim authority.

Soon after this, other districts in the region of Hamadan and Nihawand came to know that the inhabitants of the two cities had ended their troubles and won a generous peace from the conquerors by surrendering voluntarily, and they also offered themselves as willing subjects of the new state of Islam. Thus a

---

[321] The year of Nihawand is known-21 Hijri, the month is known-Muharram: the days of the week on which various phases of the battle were fought and the interval between the phases is known: but the exact dates are not known.

large part of the hilly region of the Zagros Mountains came permanently under Muslim rule.

Nihawand was the last of the great battles fought between Islam and Persia. It was on the same gigantic scale as Qadisiyya and marked the turning point in the war against Persia. It was the last time that the Persians put up a fierce and determined resistance, with hopes of reconquest, against the Muslim invasion. It was one of the decisive battles of history, and came to be called by the Muslims: the victory of victories.[322]

It was a splendid achievement by Muslim arms and ranks as one of the finest feats of military history. The Muslim army had faced an army twice its strength, better equipped and armed and fighting on its own ground with the local population behind it, using sophisticated techniques like caltrops and chains. And with all this the bigger army was defeated, not only by the courage and fighting skill of the Muslim soldiers but also the brilliant tactics employed by them-the stratagem proposed by Tuleiha and Amr bin Madi Karib and efficiently put into execution by the Muslim generals. It was a tactical form first used by Khalid at Walaja, then by Hashim bin Utba at Jalaula and now by Noman bin Muqarrin at Nihawand. It had been neatly planned and superbly executed, leading to a beautiful, if bloody end. So superb was the performance of the Muslims at Nihawand that Umar equated them with the veterans of Qadisiyya and granted them an annual pay of 2000 dirhams.

Yet the Persian army was not wanting in courage. Its generals had led the army soundly and commanded it efficiently. Its men had fought gallantly and with the true dedication of good soldiers, laid down their lives in defence of their cause. If the Persian Empire had survived this war, the deeds of its sons at Nihawand would have been recorded in letters of gold. And, had the Persian army been fighting another power, it would probably have won the battle. But it was fighting the new army of Islam, and before this army its soldiers bit the dust.

The Persian casualties were staggering. Of the total strength of 60,000 men which Persia put in the field, more than half failed to survive the battle. Tabari gives the Persian losses as more than 100,000, but this is based on an army strength of 150,000. Since I accept Balazuri's figure of an army strength of 60,000 as more accurate, it is safe to assume that about 40,000 Persians lost their lives in this battle. Of this number, more than half perished in the ravine

---

[322] Tabari: vol. 3, p. 219, Balazuri: p. 302.

of Wai Khurd, and of the remainder more than half fell on the main battlefield while the rest were killed in the follow-up and pursuit. No figures are available to show the Muslim losses, but they are believed to have been considerable.

Quite a large number of Persians were also taken prisoner, which meant that they became slaves, and these included a man named Feroz, who had in earlier years been taken into slavery by the Romans. This was the second such misfortune of his life and he mourned bitterly: "Umar has eaten my heart."[323] To the Arabs this man became known as Abu Lulu - Father of the Pearl - and he was to play an important role as the avenger of the Persians against the Caliph. But we shall come to that later.

The booty taken was immense. It was collected and distributed by Saib bin Al Aqra, an officer appointed for this task by the Caliph. The share of the cavalrymen came to 6,000 and of the infantrymen to 2,000 dirhams, and even those who had stayed behind to guard the Muslim camp were paid their share. In addition, Hudayfah bin Al Yaman made extra payments to those soldiers who had performed heroic deeds in battle.

While the booty was being distributed, the Zoroastrian high priest of Nihawand came to Saib bin Al Aqra and in a conspiratorial tone, whispered: "If you spare me and my family. I shall lead you to the treasure of Nakheer Jan, and that is the treasure of the family of Chosroes. Then it shall be yours and your master's and no one else need share it with you."[324]

The high priest apparently did not know that the Muslims were above corruption and Saib, anxious to get the treasure for Islam, accepted his terms. A man was sent with the high priest, and returned a little later bearing two large boxes filled with pearls and sapphires and other precious stones such as had not been seen in the world. Hudayfah and his advisers agreed that the treasure should not be distributed but sent to the Caliph for use as he wished.

The Nakheer Jan who gave his name to this treasure was the general who commanded a corps under Rustam at Qadisiyya. He survived that battle but later was killed in action during the Muslim advance to Ctesiphon. In past times he had been a great lord and a close companion of the Emperor Parwez, grandfather of Yazdjurd. He had as a wife a girl who was famous in the whole of Persia for her beauty, but for some reason she wanted to belong to the Emperor. When Nakheer Jan came to know of this, he stayed away from her.

---

[323] Tabari: vol. 3, p. 221.
[324] Ibid: pp. 204, 216.

Word of this reached Parwez and one day he said to the lord, "I have heard that you have a spring of sweet water and do not drink from it."

"O Emperor," replied Nakheer Jan, "I have heard that a lion has his eye on that spring and for fear of that lion, I kept away from it."

Parwez was not only flattered but also pleased by the loyalty of his noble subject. He ordered that the girl be brought to his harem, and there he was so struck by her loveliness that he made all the other women of the harem [there were 3,000 of them!] take off their jewels and give them to her. He also had a jewelled coronet made for Nakheer Jan as a mark of special favour.[325]

This treasure remained with the children of the girl and for some reason became known as the treasure of Nakheer Jan. And this treasure came into Muslim hands after the battle of Nihawand.

After the battle, while the siege of Nihawand was in progress, the Muslim martyrs were buried. Many had been buried already during the earlier phases of battle, most of them near the Muslim camp where the village of Sa'd Waqqas stands today; but those who fell on the last, decisive day of battle and during the follow-up of the Persian retreat, were carried forward to a place 4 miles short of Nihawand and buried at the northern edge of the valley. This was the main graveyard, now marked by a shrine known as Baba Pireh. Noman himself was buried a little apart from the others, on a slope just about the valley floor. But there is no graveyard anywhere today and the location of only two important graves is known; the grave of Noman and the grave of Amr bin Madi Karib. The latter is no more than a heap of stones on a bit of high ground beside the village of Leyli Yadgar, 2 miles west of Sa'd Waqqas.

These brave and true men, these distinguished leaders of an invincible army, lie utterly undisturbed. They could have been the humblest soldiers of their land. Over the grave of Noman a simple, small brick structure has been raised-though this must have been made a long time ago-to remind people that he was not a complete nobody. But over the grave of Amr there is nothing, just nothing, and it is only the pointing finger of a local villager which suggests that the now disorderly, scattered heap of stones, unmarked by a slab or a stick or even a dab of white paint, contains the remains of Amr bin Madi Karib, Father of the Bull, knight and prince of the Yemen, the hero of countless duels.

---

[325] Dinawari: pp. 137-8.

These noble Muslims who gave their lives in the way of Allah and who won for Islam the Victory of Victories, are not bothered by devotees and others simple enough to remember and pray. They lie in peace. The grave of Noman is occasionally visited by a few old-fashioned people from Nihawand during the month of Muharram, in the mistaken belief that he was of the family of the Prophet, but in the case of Amr no one makes that mistake. Yet, to a visitor like this writer the graves seem to raise a bitter, wordless protest, with lips that cannot speak, that they deserved better than this. The visitor is poignantly reminded of the Persian couplet:

On the graves of us strangers there is neither a lamp nor a rose.
Neither does the moth burn its wing, nor does the nightingale sing.

The messenger who brought the tidings of victory to Madina was Tareef bin Sahm.[326] Upon his arrival at Madina he went straight to the Caliph.

"What news do you bring" asked Umar.

"Good news, O Commander of the Faithful. Allah has given you a grand victory."

"How has Noman done?"

"Noman is dead."

Upon hearing this the Caliph burst into tears. He cried unabashedly. His weeping got worse, he began to sob, and with his hands over his head bent so low that the messenger, who stood in front of him, could see the middle of his back over his shoulders.[327] After a while he regained his composure and asked about others who had fallen in battle. The messenger named many, and then added, "And there were others whom you do not know."

Umar remarked: "It does not harm them if Umar does not know them, for Allah knows them."[328]

A few days later Saib bin Al Aqra turned up with the treasure of Nakheer Jan. The Caliph ordered him to return to Iraq with the treasure and sell it and use

---

[326] Tabari: vol. 3, p. 219. According to Balazuri (p. 301) he was Abu Usman, but he may have been the same man with two names, as was common among the Arabs.
[327] Tabari: vol. 3, p. 204.
[328] Ibid: pp. 204-5. 208; Balazuri: p. 301.

the proceeds for the pay and sustenance of the Muslims. Saib returned to Kufa and gave the treasure to an Arab of the Bani Makhzum, named Amr bin Harees, in return for two million dirhams. Amr bin Harees, probably the first man in Islam to indulge in big business, resold it at Hira at a hundred percent profit![329]

---

[329] Tabari: vol. 3, p. 208; Balazuri: p. 302.

Chapter 21: The Fall of Persia

We are nearing the end of this history. Although in term of geography more than half the Persian Empire had yet to be conquered, the most interesting campaigns and the most important battles are behind us. The war would go on and Persia would resist the Muslim advance from city to city, from province to province, until the last of the Persians would submit to the inexorable decree of fate. But Nihawand took the wind out of Persia's sails. The fate of Persia was sealed, and if Persia fought on, it was because a great people, faced with national subjugation, prolong their agony through the very pride and stamina which makes them great.

We cannot see in detail the operations fought after Nihawand till the final collapse of Persia, because no details are available. The operations which followed Nihawand are not recorded as minutely as operations up to Nihawand; hence we cannot but be brief in dealing with them. So in this chapter the reader is offered a short summary of the remainder of the war, a bird's eye-view of what for the Muslims was a glorious epic and for the Persian Empire a painful end.

Nihawand was more than a great victory. It was a turning point from which sprang new policies relating to the rule of the conquered territory and further direction of the war. It became clear to the Muslims, as indeed it would have been clear all along, that you cannot walk in and conquer part of a mighty empire and hope that the empire will take its loss philosophically and accept it as permanent. But now the Caliph quite definitely realised this truth and adopted a new direction of political and military policy.

The first of these changes related to Muslims acquiring property in Iraq. Umar had laid an embargo upon this. He had regarded the Muslims in Iraq as a standing army, an instrument of holy war, to be kept free of all local attachments. They were maintained in a state of military alert, to take the field at a moment's notice, which would not be possible if they became land-owners and acquired a vested interest in property.

Ever since his return to Madina from Kufa, Sa'd bin Abi Waqqas had been urging the Caliph to permit the Muslims to settle in the land but Umar had resisted the pressure. After Nihawand, the climate changed and the defects in the Caliph's policy were nicely explained by Ashraf bin Qeis, a veteran of Iraq. "O Commander of the Faithful," said Ashraf, "You have debarred us from settling in the land and made us withhold our hands from what we have conquered. But the Emperor of Persia is alive behind them and they will not cease to contend with us as long as the Emperor is among them. Two kings cannot work together in harmony; one must oust the other. You have seen that we have not taken a city except in countering their moves. It is their Emperor who raises them against us, and this will continue until you permit us to settle in their land and push their Emperor out of Persia and out of the veneration of his people. Then the people of Persia will give up hope of his help and lose their firmness of purpose."[330]

Others present added: "This state of affairs will not change until he is driven out of his realm."[331]

The wisdom of this opinion was undeniable. The Caliph raised the embargo and thereafter the Muslims could purchase land in Iraq and become settlers.

The next problem was Persia itself. The Caliph's policy of being content with what had been acquired and defending the Muslim conquests by taking the field only when the Persians came forward, had not succeeded. During the last five years the Muslims had all along reacted rather than acted. The only way to ensure the safety of the Muslims in Iraq, and of Iraq itself, was to destroy those Persian forces which threatened Iraq, and this could only be done by taking all of Persia so that no armed hostile Persians remained. The Muslims already had Iraq, Khuzistan and most of the district of Kirmanshahan, the last-mentioned being like a bridgehead in the Zagros Mountains. What lay immediately ahead of the Muslim front was: [a] Fars in the south, the province on the Persian Gulf lying south-east of Khuzistan and including the southern reaches of the Zagros; [b] Azarbeijan in the north, a tangled mass of mountains where the Zagros and Elburz ranges meet; and [c] Isfahan in the middle, east of the Zagros. These three formed clear stratagical objectives for further campaigns, and Fars and Isfahan would have to be taken before the Muslims could launch further campaigns on the great Iranian Plateau which stretched beyond, to Afghanistan and Baluchistan.

Umar thought a great deal about his next objective. Then he sent for Hormuzan who, as one of the top generals of Persia, would be just the man to advise the Caliph in such matters. Umar told him the problem, then asked, "How do you think we should start? With Fars or with Azarbeijan or with Isfahan?"

---

[330] Tabari: vol. 3, pp. 184-5.
[331] Ibid: p. 222.

"Fars and Azarbeijan are the two wings and Isfahan is the head," replied Hormuzan, putting an entire strategy into a few words. "If you cut of one wing, the head will stay with the other. But if you cut off the head, the wings will fall. So start with the head."[332]

Umar started with the head.

There was no time to lose. The decision having been made to invade Persia and take all of it, the ideal moment to strike was now, while Persia was still under the shock of Nihawand. That disaster had caused a kind of paralysis in Persia from which it would take a long time to recover, and this time Persia was not to be allowed. A few months after Nihawand, during which preparations were made for the offensive, the Caliph ordered the launching of the first of four campaigns which would shatter what remained of Persian resistance and make Persia a part of the empire of Islam.

The very first operation was directed against Isfahan. Some time in the last quarter of 21 Hijri, Abdullah bin Abdullah bin Utban set off with an army from Iraq and marching via Nihawand, made straight for Isfahan. Some distance short of that city the Muslim advance guard came up against a large Persian detachment and a hard-fought action followed in which the Persians were driven back with heavy loss. The Muslims marched on and arrived at Isfahan to find a Persian army formed up for battle at Jayy, an outer part of Isfahan, to the east of the city.[333] The Muslims attacked at once and the defenders withdrew into the fortified part of the city. The Muslims laid siege to Isfahan.

This siege had gone on for a few weeks when two more Muslim groups joined Abdullah. One was a large corps under Ahnaf bin Qeis, who had been selected by the Caliph for the invasion of Khurasan and was now being positioned at Isfahan, from where he would take off, and the other was a detachment under Abu Musa from Basra. Hardly had these groups arrived when the Persian commander at Isfahan, a general named Fazusfan, offered to decide the issue by single combat with the Muslim commander, the winner taking all.

Abdullah agreed and the two generals met on horseback to fight a duel. The Persian was the first to strike with his sword. The blow did not harm Abdullah

---

[332] Tabari: vol. 3, p. 225; Balazuri: p. 300; Masudi: Muruj: vol. 2, p. 331.
[333] Jayy, still exists as the eastern edge of Isfahan and encompasses some of the villages lying just beyond the edge. This place was later named Shahristan, and even now there is a stone bridge of that name, just below Jayy, dating from Sasani times. Most of the city of Isfahan was then easterly; the western Safavi part was yet to come.

but landed on the front part of his saddle with the result that the saddle broke and slipped off the horse while Abdullah landed on the ground beside the horse. He was up immediately and jumped on to the bare back of his horse, but the Persian, instead of taking advantage of the vulnerability of his opponent, told him that he was much too good a man to be killed and could have Isfahan in peace. Consequently, Abdullah took Isfahan in peace and the Persians laid down their arms.

Upon, the fall of Isfahan, following the instructions of the Caliph, Abu Musa took command of this sector. He marched northwards with a sizable corps and captured Kashan and Qum.

These actions were completed by the end of 21 Hijri and the first part of the campaign successfully concluded. Before its conclusion, Nueim bin Muqarrin, brother of the victor of Nihawand, had been given his warning orders to march with an army of 12,000 men and take Rayy, which, with Isfahan, was strategically the most important city in the central sector and controlled all movement towards the north-eastern part of the empire.[334] On his way he would have to recapture Hamadan, which had revolted and broken the treaty signed just after Nihawand.

In the beginning of 22 Hijri [which began on November 30, 642], his right flank secured by Abu Musa, Nueim marched from Nihawand to Hamadan. This city was again invested by the Muslims but only a few days had passed before Khusrau Shanum, the commander of Hamadan, surrendered to Nueim for a second time. Leaving a small detachment at Hamadan to watch the Persians, Nueim advanced upon Qazween and at Waj Ruz, some distance short of Qazween, came up against a fairly large Persian army under Isfandiar, brother of the late Rustam.[335] A fierce battle followed, which, it is said, was as bloody as Nihawand and in which the Persians were roundly defeated and driven back, some towards Rayy and others towards Azarbeijan.

Nueim sacked Waj Ruz and marched on to Rayy, which he found heavily defended. But the Muslims were able to get inside the fort at night by guile and quickly brought the Persian garrison to its knees. Rayy, too was sacked and a great deal of booty taken, after which the district came under Muslim rule and agreed to the payment of the Jizya.

---

[334] Tehran, of which Rayy is now virtually a part, either did not exist then or was a small unknown village.
[335] I have not been able to locate Waj Ruz.

Nueim established himself firmly at Rayy and sent his brother Suweid to subdue the hilly region to the east, which controlled communications with the north-eastern part of the Persian Empire. One by one, Demawand, Damaghan and Gurgan fell without resistance before Suweid. The administrator of each of these districts agreed to a peaceful surrender and pacts were drawn up, stipulating the payment of the Jizya and other terms. Thus practically the whole of Tabaristan [the region now known as Mazandaran] came under Muslim occupation.

It was still early in 22 Hijri. The first campaign was over. A broad wedge had been driven into the centre of Persia, severing the north from the south, each of which was now on its own. The head had been cut, but the wings would need a little push before they fell. The wing to be eliminated next was the northern one-Azarbeijan. Some time after Nihawand, in 21 Hijri, the Caliph had removed Ammar bin Yasir from the governorship of Kufa. He had been found to be weak in matters of government and not competent enough to run the province with efficiency. In his place Umar appointed Mugheerah bin Shu'ba, who took over the province and at once improved the tone of the administration. As a Muslim he did not compare with Ammar, who was one of the most venerated Companions, but as an administrator Mugheerah was clearly in a higher class.

Mugheerah's task was to prepare the campaign against Azarbeijan. Hudayfah bin Al Yaman was appointed by the Caliph to command this theatre and it was the Caliph's intention to launch him soon after Isfahan was taken and the two wings of Persia had been severed from one another. But there was some delay. Sufficient troops could not be mustered for the operation and Umar found it necessary to use some of the troops from the central sector. Thus Nueim got instructions soon after the re-conquest of Hamadan to send a large detachment to join Hudayfah, but anticipating heavy fighting in his own sector, Nueim delayed implementation of the Caliph's order until he had taken Rayy. Once Rayy had fallen, Nueim despatched the detachment to Hudayfah and soon after that the campaign was launched.

Hudayfa captured Zanjan against opposition and marched on to Ardabeel, which surrendered on terms. From here he continued the offensive and got to Bab, a few miles south of Darband. Bab was an important port on the Caspian Sea, where Anushirwan had built a great wall from the shore of the Caspian into the hills of Azarbeijan to keep the marauding Turks out of his empire. Bab surrendered on terms and the Muslims marched on until they got to Muqan, where they defeated a Turkish army. At about this stage of the campaign,

Hudayfah was removed from command by order of Umar and replaced by Utba bin Farqad.

Utba maintained the momentum of the offensive and after a number of tactical actions, took all of Azarbeijan up to a little south of Darband, and the eastern and northern part of Armenia as far as Tiflis, on the southern slopes of the Caucasus Mountains. During this campaign only at one place did the Muslims suffer a setback and that was at Balanjar, between Bab and Darband, where a Muslims corps was badly beaten by the Turks. Otherwise the Muslim army carried all before it and by the end of 22 Hijri had taken its objectives and brought Azarbeijan and most of Armenia under Muslim rule. How far the Muslims marched into Western Armenia, which was in Roman hands, is not known, but by this campaign Persian power in the north-western wing of the empire was totally eliminated.

The offensive in Azarbeijan was still in its early stages when the Caliph launched the third campaign, deep in the south of Persia. It had become obvious that Azarbeijan would not prove a tough nut to crack and it was not necessary to await its fall. The less time the Persians were allowed to recover in the mainland of Persia, the better it would be for the Muslims. It was military wisdom to press on in the east and penetrate as deep as necessary before the Persians regained their balance and put another large army in the field. Consequently, about the middle of 22 Hijri, Umar decided to strike at the southern wing of Persia. Hormuzan had spoken of Fars as a wing of Persia, but Fars was only the front province bordering Khuzistan. The Muslims would take the entire southern part of the empire, and this would be done with a series of operations by separate corps.

The first one to break into the southern part of the empire was Mujashe bin Masud. He marched with his corps into the district of Ardsheer Khurra, and the first battle fought by him was at Tawoos, [also known as Tawwaj] where the Muslims had fought an action in 17 Hijri during the abortive expedition launched across the Persian Gulf by Ula bin Al Hadrami. Mujashe defeated a Persian force at Tawoos and went on to lay siege to the town of Sabur, 10 miles north-west of Kazerun.[336] In a few weeks the Persians at Sabur had laid down their arms and submitted to Muslim rule.

This was followed by a thrust deeper into Fars by Uthman bin Abil Aas, starting from where Mujashe had left off. Uthman over whelmed a Persian

---

[336] Known to the Persians as Shapur, it was a big city on the bank of the River Shapur. Its ruins are still there, though I did not have time to visit them.

force at Jor [also known then as Ardsheer Khurra],[337] and went on to occupy Shiraz and Persepolis, the historic city, the inhabitants of which had been brutally massacred by Alexander the Great. After Persepolis, Saria bin Zuneim led a column into the district of Darabjurd and captured Fasa and Darabjurd [now known as just Darab].

After this Suheil bin Adi, reinforced by Abdullah bin Abdullah bin Utban who had conquered Isfahan, marched to Kirman. He was faced at the frontier of Kirman by a small Persian army, which he fought and defeated with no difficulty. Following this success, Suheil advanced and occupied Jeeraft, and then turned north to take Beemand and Sheerjan.[338]

The next province to be attacked was Seestan, home of the legendary Rustam of the Shahnama, and here the Muslim commander was Asim bin Amr, our brilliant hero of many campaigns in Iraq. Asim met and scattered a Persian force near the border of Seestan and then marched on to Zaranj [the present Zahidan], to which he laid siege. The siege had not lasted many days, however, when the Persians surrendered to the Muslims.

Only one province remained, Makran - bordering the Sind - and for this Umar formed a strong corps under Hakam bin Amr, which included the column of Suheil bin Adi who had taken Kirman. Hakam marched to Makran and, near the bank of a river, came up against an army led by King Rasil of the Sind, This was the first time that the Muslims had come in hostile contact with India. The position of the river near the bank of which the two armies met is not known, but the presence of an Indian army here suggests that it must have been nearer Sind than Persia. Quite a fierce battle was fought at this place and Allah again bestowed victory upon Muslim arms. The defeated Indians of Raja Rasil withdrew across the river and retreated to the safety of the Sind.

The messenger who brought news of the conquest of Makran to Madina was a bit of a poet. When asked by Umar to describe the country to him, he broke into rhyme:

---

[337] The Jor of old is the Firuzabad of today, which lies to the south of Shiraz.
[338] Jeeraft is the present Sabasevaran; Sheerjan is still there, south-west of Kirman, but I cannot place Beemand.

O Commander of the Faithful,
It is a land
Where the plains are hilly;
Where the water is a trickle;
Where the fruit is inferior;
Where the enemy is brave.
Its good is short;
Its evil is long.
In it many are few,
And a few are helpless,
And what lies beyond it is even worse!

The Caliph looked intently at the man for a few moments, then asked, "Are you a messenger or a poet?"

The man assured the Caliph that he was a messenger and that what he said was true, whereupon Umar swore, "By Allah, no army of mine will fight there as long as I am in charge." And he at once wrote to Hakam bin Amr to go no further.[339]

There was no need to go further, for all of Southern Persia was now in Muslim hands, and it was still early in the year 23 Hijri

After the fall of the Persian south, the only region of Persia which remained unconquered was Khurasan; and since the Muslims had determined to leave nothing of Persia under Persian rule, Umar gave Ahnaf bin Qeis the order to march.

Ahnaf bin Qeis was ready at Isfahan. He had taken part in the siege of Isfahan and then assisted Abu Musa in the conquest of Kashan. He chose to avoid the highway which led from Rayy to Nishapur, because more opposition was likely on this route, and instead struck out across the desert on a less - frequented route which bypassed Nishapur and led to Herat. For an Arab force to cross a desert was no problem, and Ahnaf marched on, took Tabas and Tun-two big towns between Isfahan and Khurasan [these towns are now named Gulshan and Firdaus respectively]-and then went on to Herat, leaving Nishapur behind and on his left. The Persians put up stiff resistance at Herat but were defeated in battle and Herat opened its gates to the army of Islam. This was the easternmost city of Khurasan.

---

[339] Tabari: vol. 3, p. 257.

Leaving a garrison at Herat, Ahnaf detached a column to subjugate Nishapur and Tus, which the column did, and with the rest of the army marched north to Marv. Yazdjurd was at Marv when he heard of the approach of the Muslims and left it hastily for Balkh, and Ahnaf bin Qeis arrived and occupied Marv without opposition. Here he stopped to await the arrival of reinforcements from Iraq.

A few weeks later a contingent arrived from Kufa as reinforcements, and upon its arrival Ahnaf advanced to Balkh, the ancient capital of Bactria, 14 miles west of the present Mazar-e-Shareef. Here Yazdjurd was able to put a small army in the field consisting of warriors from Transoxiana [Mavraunnahr], but it was trounced by the Muslims and forced to withdraw across the River Oxus, leaving Balkh to the Muslims who occupied the city peacefully. After signing the usual pact with the local inhabitants, Ahnaf marched back to Marv and made this place his permanent station. Khurasan now belonged to Islam.

Upon his return to Marv, in the end of 23 Hijri, Ahnaf sent an account of his operations to the Caliph, mentioning in it the fact that he had got to the Oxus. To the dwellers of Arabia the bank of the Oxus, known to them as Jeihun, was a very far-away place, beyond which stretched vast unknown spaces, and to Umar it was another river to worry about. He hastily sent orders to Ahnaf that on no account was he to cross the Oxus![340]

The year 23 Hijri was coming to an end. It had been a glorious year. It had seen the frontiers of Islam established far from its birthplace. In the east, Muslim outposts stood on the borders of India, in Central Afghanistan and on the River Oxus, while in the west the writ of Islam ran in Syria, Palestine and Egypt. Madina was happy. But one man in Madina was not happy; and he walked the streets of the Prophet's city in brooding silence.

This man was Feroz the Persian who had been captured at Nihawand and mourned his misfortune with the bitter complaint: "Umar has eaten my heart!"[341] As a slave he had been bought by Mugheerah bin Shu'ba and now belonged to him. But although Mugheerah was at Kufa, the slave was in Madina, why, we do not know. He was a Christian and a very talented man – an engineer, a carpenter, an engraver and a blacksmith. He worked in Madina and earned money, and as was the custom of the time, had to pay a certain part of

---

[340] The date of this campaign and some other details are disputed. For an explanation of this, see Note 4 in Appendix C.
[341] Tabari: vol. 3, p. 221.

his earnings to his master. The amount in question was very little, two dirhams a day, but it irked him and added fuel to his hatred of the Muslims who were the cause of his being a slave.

In a street of the city this man, whom the Arabs called Abu Lulu - Father of the Pearl - met the Caliph. "O Commander of the Faithful," he said, "help me against Mugheerah bin Shu'ba. He has placed too heavy a tax on me."

"How much is the tax on you?" asked the Caliph.

"Two dirhams a day."

"And what kind of work can you do?"

"I am a carpenter, an engraver and a blacksmith."

"In that case," said Umar, "I do not see the tax as too high, in view of the things you can do. I have heard that you have said that you could construct a windmill."

"I shall make you a windmill," boasted the Persian, "about which people will talk in the east and the west." The windmill which the Persian had in mind was not the kind of windmill which the Caliph wanted.

The following day, Kab the Rabbi came to Umar and said, "O Commander of the Faithful, make your bequests, for you will be dead in three days."

"How do you know that?"

"I have found it in the Book of Allah, the Torah."

"You have found Umar bin Al Khattab in the Torah?" asked the Caliph incredulously.

"O Lord, no. But I have found your description, and your time has come."

The next day Kab, the Rabbi, came to Umar and said, "O Commander of the Faithful, one day has gone and two days are left." The following day he came again. "Two days are gone and a day and a night are left." he said. "They are yours till the morning."[342]

The following morning Umar went to the mosque for the prayer of the dawn. For a few minutes he saw to the dressing of the ranks, then took his place in front to lead the prayer as Imam. At that moment Abu Lulu rushed through the ranks of the Faithful with a dagger. He got to the Caliph and struck him in the belly. Frantic with rage, he struck again and again. After the sixth blow, the huge frame of Umar collapsed on the floor. Near him stood a Muslim, named Kuleib bin Abi Amr, and he came forward to grapple with the assassin, but he too was stabbed and mortally wounded. Then Abu Lulu ran out of the mosque with the dripping dagger in his hand. He was pursued and overpowered.

Three days later, on Zul Haj 26, 23 Hijri [November 2 or 3, 644 A.D.] Umar, son of Al Khattab, Caliph of the Messenger of Allah, Commander of the Faithful, breathed his last.

Upon the death of Umar, his son Ubaydullah, whom Umar had once had whipped for drinking,[343] took the law into his own hands in complete disregard of the processes of justice, went and killed Abu Lulu, Abu Lulu's wife and Abu Lulu's daughter. Next he killed another Persian Christian living in Madina, Jufeina by name, and then went after Hormuzan, the Persian general whose life had been spared by Umar and who had become a Muslim and settled in Madina. Ubaydullah approached Hormuzan quietly from behind, sword in hand, but the Persian glanced back and saw him, and before the fatal blow landed, declared: "There is none worthy of worship except Allah, and Muhammad is the Messenger of Allah." [344]

---

[342] Ibid: pp. 263-4
[343] Ibid: p. 95.
[344] Ibid: p. 303; Yaqubi: Tareekh: vol. 2, pp. 160-1; Ibn Quteiba: p. 187. Some historians note that the reason why Ubaydullah killed Hormuzan was because he had seen him sitting with Abu Lu'lu the day prior to his fathers killing and hence suspected him of some sort of collusion in the murder. Following this, Sa'd ibn Abi Waqqas said that Ubaydullah should himself be killed as the Shariah instructs for he had murdered a fellow Muslim. The new Caliph, Uthman however decided to pay blood money to the family of Hormuzan as compensation as opposed to the retaliatory killing of Ubaydullah. *Editor*

Chapter 22: The Last of the Sasanis

Yazdjurd stands as one of the most ill-fated monarchs of history. Born under an unlucky star, he was destined to live his life in hardship, to have responsibility thrust upon him for which he was never trained, to carry burdens too heavy for the broadest shoulders. He had to spend his youth in obscurity, surviving only by fading out of the public eye, a prince living in humble surroundings, a monarch dragged to the throne because there was no one else, against his own wishes and when the decline of the empire had become so steep that no man born of woman could save it. He saw the light of day when the empire was shaken by misfortune; he was placed upon the throne when the empire had begun to totter; and he was to survive long enough, as a fugitive and a man marked by defeat, to see its final disintegration. Even his birth was unwanted, and for this we go back two generations in history.

Chosroes Parwez sat upon the throne of Persia. This was the emperor who had built the fabulous Palace of Sheereen and created around it an earthly paradise. He lived more lavishly than any emperor before him. He was the one who had 3,000 women in his harem and owned 760 elephants, 8500 horses and 12,000 mules.[345] Parwez had 18 children, the eldest of whom was a boy named Shahryar, born to his favourite wife, Sheereen. As Shahryar grew out of adolescence, some astrologers came to the Emperor and said: "One of your sons will have a son at whose hand this court will be destroyed and this empire lost. And the mark of that boy will be some defect in his body."[346]

Parwez was deeply perturbed by this prediction. He sought to avoid having grandchildren by not permitting his sons any contact with the fair sex. He placed them under a kind of sexual embargo and denied them all access to women.

The prince hardest hit by this ban was the eldest, Shahryar, who was a healthy young fellow and thought that the restriction was most unfair, considering that his father had 3,000 women of his own. He complained to his mother and demanded a woman, threatening to kill himself if his wish were not granted. Sheereen quietly slipped a slavegirl into his chamber, one who used to act as hair-dresser. It is said that she was actually a girl of good birth but Sheereen, in a fit of anger, had sent her to live for some time with barbers, with the result

---

[345] Tabari: vol. 1, p. 616.
[346] Ibid: p. 617.

that she became known as the hair-dresser. However, the young prince had his fun and to Sheereen's horror, the girl became pregnant. Knowing what the astrologers had said and the degree to which the Emperor feared their gloomy forecast, she hid the girl. In due course a baby boy was born and was also concealed by Sheereen. This boy was the Yazdjurd of our history, a man whose detractors would sometimes refer to him as "the son of the hair-dresser."

Five years passed and the child remained undiscovered. Then one day, finding Parwez in a benevolent mood, Sheerern asked him if it would not be nice to have a grandson to play with. The Emperor agreed that it would, and Sheereen promptly produced Yazdjurd. The Emperor was delighted with the boy and kept him in his own chamber and would play happily with him.

Then one day Parwez recalled the prediction of the astrologers. He at once undressed the child and examined him carefully. There was some defect in the boy's hips, and as soon as the Emperor discovered it, he knew that this was the boy the sages had warned him against. He lifted the boy and was about to dash him to the ground when Sheereen snatched him away and clung to him. She would not let him go and begged piteously for the boy's life, which at last Parwez granted, so long as he was sent far away and never appeared before him. The poor, frightened 5-year old child was sent to Seestan.

Parwez got over his fears of what the astrologers had said because the culprit had been found and banished, and now he could have grandchildren. And he did. And 11 years after the banishment of the little prince, Parwez himself was overthrown by his son Sheeruya, who cast his father into a dungeon, where later he was blinded and still later killed. Sheeruya turned against all the male members of the house of Sasan, and in order not to have any rivals, had them killed with the exception of his own son Ardsheer. When this massacre of the princes began, Yazdjurd was moved to Persepolis and his existence was kept a secret from Sheeruya and his assassins.

At Persepolis, Yazdjurd lived in obscurity until 11 Hijri [632 A.D.] when, in the absence of other princes who could be placed on the throne, he was discovered and crowned. He came to the throne utterly unprepared for the responsibilities of kingship and was suddenly called upon to save the empire from falling apart. He was a fine young man of 21, with thick, blue-black hair and beautiful teeth. He wore ear-rings.[347]

---

[347] Masudi: Tanbeeh: p. 93; Tabari: vol. 3, p. 346.

Yazdjurd came to the throne in 11 Hijri, and soon after, Persia was struck by Khalid bin Al Waleed, who raced like a tempest along the Euphrates, flattening every Persian army which stood in his path. The Sword of Allah [as Khalid was called] took the west bank of the Euphrates and raided deep into the Suwad. So roughly did he handle the Persians that by the end of 12 Hijri, they had refused to fight him and had withdrawn into Ctesiphon and to the east side of the Tigris.

Khalid's operations were a model in strategy and tactics - sticking to the fringes of the desert and drawing the Persians away from the well-watered Suwad; rapid movement by forced marches to surprise and outmanoeuvre his enemies; full concentration of effort with his army of 18,000 lightly-armed, fast moving warriors against the Persians and Christian Arabs who usually outnumbered him by 2:1; the violence of his assaults, often from an unexpected direction and at an unexpected time; his own personal victories in single combat over Persian champions-attacking, attacking, attacking. It was a terrible experience for Persia. But Khalid was sent off to Syria by Caliph Abu Bakr, and the Persians breathed easily again.

The campaigns which followed the, departure of Khalid from Iraq have been fully described in this book. Yazdjurd's part in these campaigns was to organise and launch his armies in the field with the advice of top generals like Rustam and Bahman. There was no flaw in his strategy, and Yazdjurd had considerable success in keeping up Persian spirits and strengthening the determination of his people to uphold the empire. The Persians believed in him, rested their hopes in their young sovereign, and there was nothing that he failed to do to justify their trust. If he did not load his armies in person, it was because he was not trained to do so, and under the circumstances it was wiser to let the veteran generals command the armies in battle. It was, after all, their job. Initially the Persians had some success but at the bloody battle of Qadisiyya they were badly defeated and had to fall back upon Ctesiphon.

The trend of military events established at Qadisiyya could not be reversed. One by one, Ctesiphon; Jalaula, Qasr Sheereen, fell to the Muslims and Yazdjurd tasted, one after another, the bitter pills of defeat, retreating before the victorious enemy and, fugitive-like, seeking help at every next stage of his flight. But his resistance continued, and while many Persians in the Suwad abandoned hope, and joined the Muslims, he did not.

After the fall of Qasr Sheereen, he came to Isfahan and then travelled widely in his empire, mustering forces and urging his subjects to stand fast against the peril from the desert. They still believed in him; and he still believed in them. He maintained Hormuzan in Khuzistan with supplies and reinforcements and gave that general all the backing that he needed, but Khuzistan too fell to the Muslims.

Next came Nihawand, and in it the Persians put in everything they had. They hoped that by winning a decisive victory in this one battle they would re-establish the empire, restore its boundaries and rid their land of the invaders. This battle would decide the fate of Persia and the fate of Yazdjurd; and it did. Their fate was sealed. With fading hope, but still unwilling to acknowledge defeat, Yazdjurd came to Isfahan. He had been ruling the empire for ten years - a decade which in crisis and calamity was more than a lifetime. Few monarchs before him had had to carry such a staggering burden and face such a powerful, irresistible, dauntless enemy-an enemy who sought death as ardently as the Persians sought life. We do not know if Yazdjurd's hair turned grey, but it should have done, even if he was now only 31 years old.

A few months later, as the Muslims began their advance to Isfahan, Yazdjurd left the city and travelled to Rayy. His departure did not have a good effect upon the Persians and many of them began to lose hope of ever restoring the empire. Thus, when Abdullah bin Abdullah bin Utban approached Isfahan, Persian resistance was not very stiff and the governor surrendered the city while he could have fought on and prolonged the siege by many months.

The fall of Isfahan, following close upon the heels of Nihawand, had a further depressing effect on Persian morale. The ranks of those who believed in the inevitability of Muslim conquest swelled, and signs of a change of loyalty became apparent. The first man to show this change was the governor of Rayy, whose treatment of the Emperor turned positively disrespectful. This was a cruel blow for Yazdjurd to suffer after all his misfortunes, and he left Rayy with a few trusted followers and went to Persepolis.

Here he stayed for over a year, doing his best to rule efficiently what remained of the empire and to take measures against further attacks by the Muslims, when they came. In this he had some success, for when the Muslims invaded Fars in 23 Hijri, Persian troops put a fairly stiff opposition. But Yazdjurd left Persepolis on the approach of the Muslims and moved to Kirman. The governor of Kirman welcomed him, but when the Muslims continued their advance from Fars, this official also turned cool in his loyalty. One day when Yazdjurd asked for money from the provincial treasury, the governor told him to go. And Yazdjurd went, this time to Seestan. The Muslims followed and took Kirman.

In Seestan it was the same story all over again. The Muslims came nearer, the Persians began to fear for themselves, and Yazdjurd needed money. Nothing could be simpler than to get rid of the unwanted Emperor; and the Emperor, finding little support and seeing clear signs of treachery, took to the road once again. He went to Marv, the north-easternmost part of his empire.

At Marv he stayed in peace for a time. He still had a good deal of the imperial treasure with him. Then Ahnaf bin Qeis, having taken Herat, directed his army towards Marv, and Yazdjurd, feeling like a hunted animal whose pursuers will not relent, prepared to leave for Balkh. He told the citizens of Marv that he would join the Khakan of the Turks or go to China, but they tried to persuade him to stay and make peace with the Muslims, who were more to be trusted than the Turks or Chinese. He refused to stay, whereupon the people took his treasure away and drove him out of their town. Ahnaf bin Qeis arrived soon after to receive the willing submission of the city.

Yazdjurd went on to Balkh and turned once again. He gathered an army from Farghana and as Ahnaf came after him, faced him in battle. But he had no success in the field and was forced to retreat across the Oxus and take refuge in Farghana, where he lived for several years with the Khakan as a king without a kindgom.

After Umar, Uthman became Caliph and in the very first year of his caliphate, 24 Hijri, there was a revolt in Azarbeijan and Armenia, which was put down before it could get out of control. Three years later the Kurds rose in the region of the hills south of Kirmanshah, but they too were quickly brought into line. In 28 Hijri however, the situation became more serious for the Muslims as the Persians made desperate attempts to throw off the Muslim rule in the north-eastern and south-eastern provinces of the empire.

At Persepolis, the Persians rose, defeated the Muslim garrison in action and killed the Muslim commander. Kirman followed suit, and these two provinces for a time again established Persian rule. Yazdjurd appeared in Fars soon after this but could not stay long because Uthman sent another army to suppress the rebellion, which it successfully did; and Yazdjurd withdrew in haste to Kirman.

In 29 Hijri, Khurasan and much of Tabaristan revolted against the Muslims. Details of this uprising are not known and the accounts of the early historians are not only sketchy but also confusing. Anyway, the Caliph had to send another two armies to deal with the revolt, one to the north and the other to the south; and in 30 Hijri the back of the resistance was broken and both regions again brought under Muslim rule. Yazdjurd, who appears to have directed operations from Kirman, found that his fortunes were no better now than they had been during the past 20 years.

Yazdjurd was on the run again. He left Kirman with a body of 4,000 men, including 1,000 noble knights, who had remained Loyal to him and were led by Farrukhzad, brother of the late Rustam, and made for Marv, the citizens of which had driven him out 7 years before. It was now early 31 Hijri [late 651 A.D.[348]], and he was fully determined to raise another army and continue his war against the Arabs, who had not yet retaken Marv.

The governor of Marv was a man named Mahaweih. He was loyal enough to serve and support his master while the going was good, but not loyal enough to stand by him in his hour of need. A perfidious man, he began to prepare the people of the district, even before the arrival of Yazdjurd, to turn against their Emperor, but on his approach made a show of obedience and loyalty. Yazdjurd entered Marv, unaware of the scheming nature of his governor, and wrote letters to the King of Farghana and the Emperor of China, asking for their help against the Arabs. There was also a polite exchange of letters with Neizak Tarkhan, the Khan of the Turks living in the province of Khurasan, who owed allegiance to the Persian Emperor. At this moment Neizak was the most powerful man in Khurasan.

A month passed during which strong suspicions arose in Yazdjurd's mind about Mahaweih's integrity and honesty in administration and his loyalty as a subject. He thought to dismiss the man from his office and asked him to produce an account of all the revenue received by him. Upon this Mahaweih, knowing that he had to act fast if he was to save himself, went into action.

He wrote secretly to Neizak Tarkhan that Yazdjurd was a defeated monarch and a fugitive; that he intended to harm both of them; that they should move against him jointly and overpower him, whereafter they could either kill him or take from him what they wished. Neizak, no more loyal than the governor of Marv, responded to this conspiratorial invitation by writing to Yazdjurd and seeking the hand of his daughter.

---

[348] This is Tabari: vol. 3, p. 342. Masudi (Tanbeeh: p. 90) places this event in 32 Hijri, but Tabari's date is generally accepted as correct.

Yazdjurd may have been a victim of misfortune but he still had his Persian pride and was indignant at the insolence of a subject asking for the daughter of his sovereign. He told his secretary to write to Neizak that he was one of his slaves and how dare he ask for the Emperor's daughter! Upon receiving this rude reply, Neizak gathered an army of Turks [it was not a very large one] and marched against Marv. The news of this event reached Marv soon after and Yazdjurd ordered Mahaweih to call out his troops, which the governor did, having no doubt in his mind that the Turks would win. With this army, which included the Emperor's 4,000 loyal warriors, Yazdjurd advanced to meet his rebellious Turkish subject. The two armies met at Jaleendan, not far from Marv.[349]

Here a battle was fought between Yazdjurd and Neizak Tarkhan with Mahaweih keeping up an appearance of fighting but not actually doing so. Yazdjurd's 4,000 loyal troops gave an excellent account of themselves and pressed hard against the Turks, who were pushed back. It soon became obvious that victory was about to fall into the Emperor's lap, and this was something which Mahaweih could not permit. At a critical moment in battle, the treacherous man took his own soldiers of Marv away from the Emperor and went over to join the Turks.

The defection of this sizable force turned the scales against Yazdjurd. Neizak and Mahaweih attacked fiercely and the loyalists found themselves vastly outnumbered. The battle did not last long. Most of Yazdjurd's men were killed, and the Emperor fled from the battlefield.

He got to Marv, but the fickle inhabitants of this city, seeing his condition and sensing that he was a fugitive, refused to open their gates to him. Yazdjurd was all alone. He dismounted from his horse, which had been wounded in battle, and walked away on foot. He dragged his feet. There was nowhere for him to go.

Yazdjurd was a child of misfortune. He appeared on the stage of history at the wrong time. He not only had to carry the burden of the sins of many predecessors but also had to face the all-conquering thrust of the new faith of Islam, which moved like a vast tidal wave across much of the known civilised world-a tidal wave which saved the world from itself, swept away its evil and purified mankind.

---

[349] Tabari: vol. 3, p. 346. Balazuri (p. 213) gives the location of this battle as Junabiz, near Nishapur. In view of Yazdjurd's movements after, this battle, Tabari has to be correct.

History, like the world, worships the rising sun. Yazdjurd was a setting sun. He has been compared with Darius III, the last of the Achaemenians, with whom the earlier Persian empire collapsed before Alexander, but the comparison is not a fair one. Unlike Yazdjurd, Darius was born and brought up at court and trained to rule; unlike Yazdjurd, he came to power during a period of greatness and strength and had time to consolidate his position before being struck by a great conqueror; unlike Yazdjurd, he had vast armies on call to throw into the field against the invader. In these respects, Yazdjurd had all the disadvantages, but unlike Darius, he fought on for a long time-20 years-and went on fighting to the end. And in the end, all his labours wasted, Yazdjurd also suffered the cruel treachery of his own subjects, who not only abandoned their sovereign in his darkest hour but also came to destroy him. One is reminded of the lines of Hannah More Daniel:

A crown! What is it?
It is to bear the miseries of a people!
To hear their murmurs, feel their discontents,
And sink beneath a load of splendid care;
To have your best success ascribed to fortune,
And fortune's failures all ascribed to you!
It is to sit upon a joyless height;
To every blast of changeless fate exposed.
Too high for hope! Too great for happiness!

Yazdjurd; abandoned by all and having abandoned all hope, walked the earth of Marv in the fading light. Soon it was dark. After wandering about 7 miles, he came upon a miller's house by the River Murghab. He entered the room which faced him as he approached the house. It was unoccupied. He threw himself on the floor and slept the sleep of the utterly exhausted.

The following morning the miller entered the room and stared in astonishment at the strange visitor. He had never before seen such a splendidly-dressed man. He asked the Emperor if he was a man or a jinn. The Emperor affirmed that he was a man and called for food. The miller brought food for his unknown guest. Another day and night passed. Then the miller asked for money with which to buy food, but Yazdjurd had no money. He offered his bewildered host his jewel-encrusted belt, but the miller declined the gift, saying that he would prefer

4 dirhams. Yazdjurd replied that he did not have 4 dirhams. Then, with a bitter laugh, he said: "I used to be told that I would want and not have 4 dirhams."[350]

The next day Yazdjurd asked for a certain kind of bread and the miller went to Marv to get it. There in conversation with some soldiers he mentioned his strange guest and described his appearance, and news of this at once spread in the city. Before long it reached the ears of Mahaweih who had been searching for the fugitive Emperor without success. The governor sent for the miller and from his description of his guest, knew that he had found his prey.

He at once ordered some officers to go with the miller to his house, kill the Emperor and bring his head. The high priest of Marv, who was present, protested strongly against this order and warned the governor that since in Persia religion was inseparable from the crown, such an act would be a sacrilege. Some others also joined the high priest in his objections, but Mahaweih refused to listen to them and insisted that his evil design be carried out. The officers followed the miller and got to the mill.

The 41 year old Yazdjurd pleaded for his life. He offered the assassins what treasures he still possessed-his crown, his belt, his bracelet and his sword - but his pleas had no effect. They moved closer. He then asked them to send him to the Arabs, for they would not kill a fallen monarch.[351] They strangled him with a bowstring.

The body of the dead Emperor was stripped of all its finery. His head was severed from the body and the corpse was thrown into the Murghab. It flowed down the river until it hit a partially submerged log and stuck against it.

A few Persian Christians from Ahwaz were visiting Marv and heard of the fate of Yazdjurd. They and some local Christians, headed by the Bishop of Marv, went to retrieve the Emperor's body. They had a special regard for him because of his grandmother, Sheereen, who was a Christian and always showed kindness to the Christians. They took his body out of the river and buried him with honour in Marv. And over his grave they built a wooden structure to mark the last resting place of the last of the Sasanis.[352]

---

[350] Tabari: vol. 3, p. 346.
[351] Ibid: p. 347.
[352] According to some versions, Yazdjurd was killed by the miller who coveted his jewels, and later the Persians of Marv killed the miller and his family and destroyed his mill. It could be so. Most historians have described both versions and left the reader to take his choice.

The Sasani empire was crushed by the young giant of Islam which arose in Arabia. The empire had lived a full life, marked with glory and power, and in its decline gave way to a new and stronger culture which derived its strength from the divine word of the Quran and the example of Muhammad, the last of Allah's apostles. But while the Sasani empire was destroyed by the sword of Islam, Persia herself was saved by the spirit of Islam and given a new and longer lease of life as a nation and empire. Before we go into this further, however, we must deal with an important misconception about Islam - a misconception arising from conquests such as those described in this volume and actively encouraged by the enemies of Allah - that Islam was spread by the sword.

For centuries the world of Islam has heard this charge; and as proof has been told that Islam spread as its armies marched and conquered. The charge is, of course, untrue and unworthy of intellectual acceptance, but even some Muslims have begun to believe it, being unable to distinguish between the spread of the empire and the spread of the faith - two different things. The Muslim empire was certainly established by the sword, but the Muslim faith was not.

It must be understood that all empires spread by the sword. There is no other way to establish an empire. A would-be conqueror does not walk up to the frontier of the land which he wishes to conquer and politely ask its people to submit so that he can have his empire. Empires are established with military might, assisted at times by guile and treachery. One glance at the blood-soaked history of man will prove this point and the reader will not find a single instance in history of an empire spreading by love and peace. So how could the Muslim empire spread except by the sword?

And yet it is to the everlasting credit of Islam that unlike all other empires of history, its armies marched not to conquer but to convey the message, and this is particularly true of the early conquests of Islam. As illustrated several times in this book, the Muslims first made an offer of their faith to the Persians and Muslim envoys gave a guarantee that if their faith were accepted, they would return to their own land and not come again except for trade. This was not done before nor ever again by any other army creating an empire. It took the early Muslims to set this standard, and to keep their operations free of trickery and deceit.

The next point to bear in mind is the distinction between the spread of the empire and the spread of the faith. According to Ibn Khaldun, a conquered people come to regard their conquerors as a superior nation by the very fact of their success, and tend to adopt the conquerors' ways as their own. The ways of Islam were superior to all ways and this made the new faith even more acceptable to the conquered peoples. Not only were the early Muslims models of the perfect conqueror, but the light of Islam which shone upon the conquered nations made all other religious and cultural lamps appear dim in comparison. Thus the Persians and other peoples conquered by Islam embraced the new faith readily and willingly, and in it they found their salvation.

Nearer our time we have seen European powers conquering vast areas of Asia and Africa. As a result of this colonial expansion, western civilization spread over these continents. Yet we have never heard a European historian say that western civilization was spread by the sword! It would indeed be absurd to say that it was, though not more absurd than to say that Islam was spread by the sword.

Islam offered complete equality and full justice to all conquered peoples and created a degree of equality between conqueror and conquered which never existed before. The much-maligned system of the Jizya, which was a tax paid by non-Muslims only, was actually a concession in that it absolved the non-Muslim from military service. In other words he was permitted to buy himself out of a heavy responsibility at a nominal price. Where the non-Muslim preferred not to pay the tax and serve in the army, he was inevitably petted to do so, and many Christians and Zoroastrian served in the Muslim armies under Muslim commanders and took the same share of the spoils as Muslim soldiers. The generous and humane treatment of the conquered peoples by the Muslims stemmed not only from the teachings of the Quran but also from the example of the Holy Prophet, who would instruct his generals: "Fight in the name of Allah; fight but do not exceed the bounds; and do not be treacherous; and do not mutilate; and do not kill women and children; and do not kill the inhabitants of monasteries."[353]

The sword of Islam knocked Persia down. The spirit of Islam picked Persia up and gave her the shot in the arm which she needed, The old man became a youth again, finding new life in Islam and discovering new horizons. But for Islam, Persia today may have been a small, insignificant country like Greece or Austria or Mongolia, reminding the world of its vanished imperial glory. Empires have their time and when that time is over, they vanish for ever. They

---

[353] Abu Yusuf: pp. 193-5.

can live again in greatness only as a new people with a new culture; and this is how Persia gained a new life. She assimilated Islam, embellished its culture with beauty and made it part of her own heritage.

The Persian intellect, never fully manifested before Islam, found in Islam the right motive power and in Arabic the right vehicle of expression. The combination of the three was stupendous. While Persian poets and mystics continued to use Persian, which itself was strengthened by Arabic, their thinkers, philosophers and scientists broke out in Arabic and gave the world the finest literature of the age. Avicenna, Al Biruni, Al Khwarizmi, Al Ghazali, Ar Razi and a host of others bestrode the world of thought like colossi and laid the foundations of modern science and philosophy. A great deal of what is now known as Muslim literature arose from Muslim Persia.

As a nation and a political entity also the Persians rose again, first as small kingdoms and then as an empire. Islam gave them the strength and resilience to withstand the shock of such cataclysms as the invasions of Changez Khan and Timur [Tamerlane], and to retain their identity as a people. After Timur the empire rose again under the Safawis, who re-established the imperial traditions of Persia. With varying fortunes, after some glorious rises and some pitiful falls, the imperial destiny of Persia finally manifested itself in the Pahlawi Dynasty which appeared after the First World War and which now rules Persia.

Today one sees Persia as a country at once old and young; old because it carries with it the presence of its grand past stretching back to the heroic age of Persia; and young because it vibrates with the spirit and vigour of youth; a nation proud of its past, conscious of its strength and confident of its future as, under its brilliant monarch, it marches on to overtake the world.

The most distinctive quality of Persia today, which her history emphasises and which strikes the visitor with force, is BEAUTY...

...the beauty of her great cities, full of character and style, towering monuments to the glory and grandeur which have marked Iran for 25 centuries of history...
...the beauty of her broad valleys flanked by rugged mountains which are all the more majestic when they are bare of trees, the fertile earth of these valleys, now red, now brown, now light brown, the colours seeming to change as the moving sun paints the landscape in gentle hues...
...the beauty of her way of life, the perfect manners, the warm greetings and affectionate courtesy, the honey-sweet language which sings at it goes and in

which even military words of command remind one of Hafiz, the loving nature of the people...

...the beauty of her arts and crafts, the silverwork and miniatures of Isfahan, the inlays of Shiraz, the pottery of Hamadan, the peerless carpets of so many places, too many to mention, all reflecting the delicate sensibilities of the Iranian people and challenging the world to match them...

...the beauty of her fascinating culture, an amalgam of literature, sculpture, song and dance, spanning 25 centuries, combining the grandeur of the past with the sparkling gaiety of the present, from the proud bas-reliefs of the early Achaemenians to the modern, vibrant singing of the incomparable Gougous......the beauty of her people, the fine, stalwart, soldierly men; the pretty, pink-cheeked, bright-faced children; the lovely women who enhance with modern beauty techniques what is already the finest example of Aryan womanhood, while retaining the saltiness of the oriental and the alluring charm of the Persian peri, the effect of their rich colouring heightened by their dark, deep eyes...

This was the land of beauty which Islam conquered and made its own. May it remain so till the end of time!

The Appendices

APPENDIX A

BIBLIOGRAPHY

1. Ibn Hisham: Seerat-un-Nabavi, Cairo, 1955.

2. Waqidi: Maghazi Rasulillah, Cairo, 1948.
   Futuh-ush-Sham, Cairo, 1954.

3. Ibn Sa'd: Tabaqat-ul-Kubara, Cairo, 1939.

4. Ibn Quteiba: Al Ma'arif, Cairo, 1960.

5. Yaqubi: Tareekh-ul-Yaqubi, Beirut, 1960.
   Al Buldan, Lieden, 1892.

6. Balazuri: Futuh-ul-Buldan, Cairo, 1959.

7. Dinawari: Akhbar-ut-Tiwal, Cairo, 1960.

8. Tabari: Tareekh-ul-Umam wal-Muluk, Cairo, 1939.

9. Masudi: Muruj-uz-Zahah, Cairo, 1958.
   Al Tanbeeh wal Ashraf, Cairo, 1938.

10. Ibn Rusta: A'laq-un-Nafeesa, Lieden, 1892.

11. Abu Yusuf: Kitab-ul-Kharaj, Cairo, 1962.

12. Yaqut: Mu'jam-ul-Buldan, Tehran, 1965.

13. Abul Fida: Taqweem-ul-Buldan, Paris, 1840.

14. Muhammad Tariq Al Katib: Shatt-ul-Arab wa Shatt-ul-Basra wat Tareekh, Basra, 1971.

Ibn Hisham. His abridgement of the last pioneering work, Seerah Rasoolullah, by Muhammad bin Ishaq, is invaluable. Portions of Ibn Ishaq have recently been recovered and published. Muhammad bin Ishaq [who died in 150 or 151AH], is unquestionably the principal authority on the Seerah [Prophetic biography] and Maghazi [battles] literature. Every writing after him has depended on his work, which though lost in its entirety, has been immortalised in the wonderful, extant abridgement of it, by Ibn Hisham. Ibn Ishaq was one of the Tabieen [second generation who saw the Sahabah but not the Prophet [saw] himself] of humble beginnings as a former slave. Ibn Ishaq's work is notable for its excellent, rigorous methodology and its literary style is of the highest standard of elegance and beauty. This is hardly surprising when we recall that Ibn Ishaq was an accomplished scholar not only in Arabic language but also in the science of hadith. For this reason, most of the isnad [chains of narration] that he gives in his Seerah are also to be found in the authentic books of hadith. Ibn Ishaq, like Bukhari and Muslim, travelled very widely in the Muslim world in order to authenticate the isnad of his hadith. It is reported that Ibn Ishaq saw and heard Saeed bin Al-Musayyib, Aban bin Uthman bin Affan, Az-Zuhri, Abu Salamah bin Abdur-Rahman bin Awf and Abdur-Rahman bin Hurmuz Al-Araj. It is also reported that Ibn Ishaq was the teacher of the following outstanding authorities among others:

[a] Yahya bin Saeed Al-Ansari
[b] Sufyan Ath-Thawri
[c] Ibn Jurayh
[d] Shu'bah bin Al-Hajjaj
[e] Sufyan bin Uyainah
[f] Hammad bin Zaid

Al-Waqidi. The second most authoritative book on Seerah is that of Al-Maghazi by Muhammad bin Umar Al-Waqidi Al-Aslami [who lived from 130 to 207AH and is buried in Baghdad]. This book was widely read in various parts of the Muslim world.

Ibn Sa'd. The third authoritative work on Seerah is Ibn Sa'd's *Tabaqat-ul-Kubara* [nine volumes]. Ibn Sa'd was both the student and the scribe/secretary of Al-Waqidi. The quality and scholarly excellence of the *Tabaqat-ul-Kubara* of Ibn Sa'd say a great deal about the academic competence of his teacher and patron.

Al-Yaqubi. [Ahmad bin Jafar bin Wahb, died 292AH]. Al-Yaqubi's work is unique for its examples of the Prophet's [saw] sermons, not to be found elsewhere, especially those containing instruction and admonition.

Al-Baladhuri. [Ahmad bin Yahya bin Jabir, died in 279AH]. The work of this early historian is valuable for the texts it contains of certain important agreements which the Prophet [saw] concluded with some groups and individuals: among others, the texts of his agreements with the Christians of Najran, his agreement with the people of Maqna, his book to Al-Mundhir bin Sawi and to Akaydar Dawmah.

At-Tabari. [Ibn Jareer, died in 310AH] in his monumental world history *Tareekh-ul-Umam wal Muluk*. At-Tabari was not merely a historian, but also an unrivalled authority on the Arabic language and grammar, on hadith and fiqh, and on the tafseer [exegesis] and interpretation of the Quran. Evidence of the excellence of his scholarship, his prodigious and untiring intellectual genius, is provided by his major works which run into many lengthy volumes each.

Al-Masudi. [Abul-Hasan Ali bin Al-Husain bin Ali Al-Masudi, died in 346AH]. A well-known Arab historian, descendent of one of the Companions of the Prophet [saw], Abdullah bin Masood [ra], author of two books on history including long sections on Seerah, both mentioned above.

APPENDIX B

THE HIJRI AND CHRISTIAN YEARS

Hijri Year	Day	Christian Date	Hijri Year	Day	Christian Date
1	Fri	16 July 622	21	Mon	10 Dec 641
2	Sat	5 July 623	22	Tue	30 Nov 642
3	Sun	*24 June 624	23	Wed	19 Nov 643
4	Tue	13 June 625	24	Thu	*7 Nov 644
5	Wed	2 June 626	25	Sat	28 Oct 645
6	Thu	23 May 627	26	Sun	17 Oct 646
7	Fri	*11 May 628	27	Mon	7 Oct 647
8	Sun	1 May 629	28	Tue	*25 Sep 648
9	Mon	20 Apr 630	29	Thu	14 Sep 649
10	Tue	9 Apr 631	30	Fri	4 Sep 650
11	Wed	*29 Mar 632	31	Sat	24 Aug 651
12	Fri	18 Mar 633	32	Sun	*12 Aug 652
13	Sat	7 Mar 634	33	Tue	2 Aug 653
14	Sun	25 Feb 635	34	Wed	22 Jul 654
15	Mon	*14 Feb 636	35	Thu	11 Jul 655
16	Wed	2 Feb 637	36	Fri	*30 Jun 656
17	Thu	23 Jan 638	37	Sun	19 Jun 657
18	Fri	12 Jan 639	38	Mon	9 Jun 658
19	Sat	*2 Jan 640	39	Tue	29 May 659
20	Sat	*21 Dec 640	40	Wed	*17 May 660

* Leap Year.

APPENDIX C

NOTES

Note 1: The Persian Strength at Qadisiyya

Most Muslim historians of later periods have given the Persian strength as 120,000 men, and in my book: *"The Sword of Allah,"* I have mentioned the same figure. As a result of further detailed research, however, I have now concluded that the Persian army at Qadisiyya was 60,000 strong, and I have shown it as such in my account of this battle.

The early Muslim references to Persian strength are given below:-

    a. Tabari: vol 3, p 26:   120,000, including mercenaries.
    b. Tabari: vol 3, p 22:   120,000.
    c. Tabari: vol 3, p 38:   60,000.
    d. Tabari: vol3, p 46:   120,000.
    e. Tabari: vol 3, p 76:   60,000 excluding followers.
    f. Balazuri: p 256:   120,000.
    g. Masudi: Muraj; vol 2, p 320:   60,000.

I have accepted the figure given by Masudi and by Tabari in two of his references. I have done this for the following reasons:-

    a.   It is normal to exaggerate the enemy's strength. Thus when the figures vary, the lower end of the bracket is more likely to be correct.

    b.   An army of 120,000, or really of anything much more than 60,000, could not have completed its crossing of the river and forming up for battle in the time available between sunrise and early afternoon, while crossing the river by one crossing.

    c.   The ground over which this battle was fought did not allow any depth to the Persians, and the entire army, but for Bahman's corps, was in the front line. This front line of about 5 miles could not take more than 60,000 men.

    d.   If the Persians had been four times as strong as the Muslims, Sa'd could not have defeated Rustam. Khalid bin Al Waleed, yes; but Sa'd bin Abi Waqqas, no!

Note 2: The Date of Qadisiyya

On this point there is a great deal of variation, and in explaining the point, since many readers are unfamiliar with the Muslim months, I shall give the months as: 1/14 for Muharram [first month] of 14 Hijri 9/15 for Ramadhan [ninth month] of 15 Hijri, etc. This will help the reader to make his own calculations.

Basically the dates of battle given by the early historians are as follows:-

Tabari: Monday, early 1/14 [pp 44, 49].
Balazuri: Thursday to Saturday, end of 16 Hijri [pp 256, 259].
Ibn Ishaq: Late 15 Hijri [quoted by Tabari: p 75].
Waqidi: 16 Hijri [quoted by Tabari: p. 89].
Masudi: 14, 15 or 16 Hijri [pp 321, 328].
Yaqut: 16 Hijri [vol 4, p 7].

This will give the reader some idea of the confusion, and to compound this confusion, Tabari himself, having placed the battle in 1/14, gives the following timings of events:-

   a. Umar sent out the call to arms in 12/13 [vol 2, p 660].
   b. The first concentration at Sirar, near Madina, took place in 1/14 [vol 3, p 2].
   c. Sa'd stayed at Qadisiyya for 1 month before Rustam began his move from Sabat [vol 3, p 14].
   d. 4 months elapsed from the start of Rustam's march till the battle [vol 3, p 26].

And other historians have added:-

   a. Sa'd stayed at Sa'labiyya [this was near Zarud], on his march to Qadisiyya, for 3 months [Balazuri: p 255].
   b. He moved to Uzeib in 15 Hijri [ibid].
   c. Rustam camped near Hira for 4 months before battle [Dinawari: p 120; Balazuri: p 256].
   d. The talks after Rustam's arrival in his forward camp lasted 1 month [Dinawari: p 120].

The main error of Tabari lies in his chronology of earlier battles. He mistakenly places the Battle of Yarmuk in 13 Hijri [though acknowledging reports of its being fought in 15 Hijri], and having committed this error, he naturally places

Qadisiyya in 1/14. Actually Yarmuk was fought in 7/15, on which there is now almost complete agreement among historians, and so the earliest that Qadisiyya could have been fought is 10/15, to allow for the first lot of reinforcements from Syria, under Asha's bin Qeis, to join Sa'd before battle, and the second lot under Hashim to join him in mid-battle. 9/15 was in any case the month of fasting, and had the battle been fought in this month the historians, who have given a very detailed account of this battle, would surely have mentioned the fast and the breaking of it over four days of fighting.

Then there are the dates of operations after Qadisiyya, as given below:-

a. The march from Qadisiyya began two months after the battle, and the date of the march was 28-11-15 [Tabari: vol 3, p 113].
b. Western Ctesiphon was reached in 12/15 [Tabari: vol 3, p 116].
c. The siege lasted:-
    2 months, to 2/16 [Tabari: vol 3, pp 119, 120, 125, 129].
    1½ months [Yaqubi: vol 2, p 145].
    9 or 18 months [Balazuri: p 262].
    28 months [Dinawari: p 126].
d. Ctesiphon was conquered in 2/16 [Yaqut: vol 4, p 446]; in 16 [Balazuri: p 263].
e. The march for the next battle after Ctesiphon began in 2/16 [Tabari: p 133].

It is generally accepted that Ctesiphon was conquered in 2/16. For the duration of the siege, Tabari's is a low estimate as is obvious from b. above, which places the Muslim arrival, as stated by Tabari, in 12/15. The advance from Qadisiyya, with the deliberate, methodical way it was conducted and the opposition offered by Persian rearguards, would have taken not less than one month. Hence the march from Qadisiyya would rightly have begun in late 10/15.

To arrive at the right date of Qadisiyya, I have worked out a timetable for the march of the two armies and their halts at various places. Sa'd's start from Sirar; his wait at Zarud for reinforcements sent by Umar and his own mustering of warriors from local tribes; his wait at Sharaf where a contingent joined him from Uballa, his arrival at Qadisiyya and the despatch of the envoys to Ctesiphon; the march of Rustam from Sabat and the four months period between then and the battle.

All this places the battle in 10/15. The exact date is a synthesis, and includes the Thursday-Saturday of Balazuri and the bright moonlight. There was a great deal of fighting at night and this could not have been done in the dark, especially the nocturnal daredevilry of Abu Mihjan, which was seen clearly not only by the troops in the front line but also by Sa'd from the castle at the rear edge of the Muslim battle position. Since the Muslim month is a lunar one, the battle could only have been fought around mid-month [full-moon time] and Thursday fell on Shawwal 11, three nights before full-moon, giving us three bright moonlit nights for the battle.

The two-month stay at Qadisiyya after the battle is out; it just does not fit in. This stay was more likely 2 weeks, which is militarily more acceptable and more sound.

Note 3 : The Campaign in Khuzistan

The period of the campaign in Khuzistan was 17-20 Hijri and there were 5 main battles in this campaign, viz. Ahwaz, Ram Hormuz, Tustar, Sus and Jundei Sabur. The accounts of the early historians are conflicting and sometimes self-contradictory, with the result that the dates of the battles have had to be assessed, and in this I acknowledge the possibility of error.

The data available on this are as follows:-
  a. Ahwaz. Tabari, Balazuri and Yaqut place it in 17 Hijri. The Muslim commander according to Tabari was Harqus bin Zubeir, and according to Balazuri and Ibn Quteiba, Abu Musa. [Tabari: vol 3, pp 170, 175; Balazuri: p 370; Yaqut: vol 1, p 412; Ibn Quteiba: p 182.]
  b. Tustar: Tabari places it mainly in 17 Hijri but acknowledges 19 and 20 Hijri as possible years. He names the commander as Abu Sabra with Abu Musa serving under him, but Balazuri and Dinawari name Abu Musa as the commander. [Tabari: vol 3, pp 174, 179, 181; Balazuri: p 373; Dinawari: p 130.]
  c. Ram Hormuz. Tabari places it mainly in 17 Hijri and acknowledges 20 Hijri as possible. He names Noman bin Maqarrin as the commander, serving under Harqus but Balazuri names Abu Musa as the commander. [Tabari: vol 3, pp 179, 180, 189; Balazuri: p 372.]
  d. Sus. Tabari places it mainly in 17 Hijri mentioning the possibility of its being in 20 Hijri; Balazuri in 17 or 19 Hijri. Tabari names both Abu Sabra and Abu Musa, in separate versions, while Balazuri names Abu Musa as the commander. [Tabari: vol 3, pp 179, 182, 186, 189; Balazuri: pp 299, 371.]

e. Jundei Sabur. Tabari places it in 17 Hijri, stating elsewhere that it was taken 2 months before Nihawand, while Yaqut places it in 19 Hijri, [Tabari: vol 3, p 188; Yaqut: vol 2, p 130.]

Now for calculations and deductions. Utba bin Ghazwan, first Governor of Basra, did not leave Sa'd 's army till after the fall of Ctesiphon [2/16] and did not found Basra till after Mosul and Takreet [12/16], So Basra was founded in 17 Hijri. He was commander at Basra during the first clash with Hormuzan in which Manazir and the Teeri were taken and the Muslims occupied the right bank of the Karun.

Utba went to Madina with the intention of performing the pilgrimage [Tabari: vol 3, p 179], and died on his way back. This could only happen in 12/17. Mugheerah bin Shu'ba was then appointed as Governor of Basra and remained so till he was charged with adultery. Abu Musa, who replaced him, went to Basra in Rabi-ul-Awwal [Tabari: vol 3, p 168], i.e. 3 /18.

I accept Balazuri's and Ibn Quteiba's statement regarding Abu Musa being the conqueror of Ahwaz. And this places Ahwaz in the second quarter of 18 Hijri [it could have been a little later]. Incidentally, Tabari also names Abu Musa as Governor of Basra at the end of 17 Hijri, which could not be correct.

We now come to Ram Hormuz. For this, instructions for the move of Noman bin Muqarrin from Kufa were sent by Umar to Ammar bin Yasir, the new Governor of Kufa, after the dismissal of Sa'd. Now Sa'd, according to Tabari [vol 3, p 151] governed at Kufa for 3½ years which takes him to mid-20 Hijri. This could not be correct as it would place Ram Hormuz in mid-or late 20 Hijri, which is too late. We assume that Sa'd governed for 2½ years, and there is evidence that Ammar was governor in 19 Hijri [Balazuri: p 299]. This places Ram Hormuz in the third quarter of 19 Hijri, possibly the fourth quarter.

This action was followed by the siege of Tustar, for which time must be allowed for Abu Musa to convey his request for help to Umar, for Umar to send instructions to Ammar, for Ammar to march to Ahwaz, for the army to march from Ahwaz to Tustar. Hence Tustar began in late 19 Hijri. The siege is known to have lasted several months. So we place its conclusion in the second quarter of 20 Hijri.

Next came Sus, almost immediately after Tustar, and this would be mid-20 Hijri, and soon after, Jundei Sabur fell to the Muslims.

Note 4 : The Fall of Persia

There are some differences of opinion regarding dates and commanders in the campaigns launched after Nihawand, and these are briefly mentioned below:
  a. Isfahan is placed by Tabari in 21 Hijri but by Balazuri in 23 Hijri. Tabari is certainly more correct in this because according to the advice of Hormuzan, upon which Umar acted, Isfahan was the first to be taken.
  b. Hamadan is placed by Tabari in 22 Hijri but by Balazuri in 23 Hijri. Balazuri also names Jareer bin Abdullah as the commander in this battle rather than the Nueim of Tabari. Considering that Hamadan was very close to Nihawand and was taken before Rayy and other objectives deeper in Persia, I regard the earlier date as more likely.
  c. In the case of Azarbeijan, various commanders are mentioned by the historians, including Mugheerah bin Shu'ba. I have taken the ones named by more historians.

In the matter of dates, the major difference relates to Tabaristan and Khurasan, i.e. the central sector conquered after Isfahan. While I have worked on Tabari's version of this-22 Hijri-Balazuri places the former in 29 Hijri and the latter in 30 Hijri, in the time of Caliph Uthman. Balazuri also names different commanders for these campaigns: Saeed bin Al Aas and Abdullah bin Amir respectively. Yaqubi places the conquest of both these regions in 30 Hijri.

Balazuri may be correct, of course, but what is more likely is that the initial thrust of the Muslims led to the conquest of these provinces in 23 Hijri, and they had to reconquer them later when the Persians re-asserted their independence and rose against the Muslims. This went on in many places in the empire in the time of Uthman and Muawia, and the Muslims had to fight again and again to retain their hold over Persia. In fact, Tabari mentions a conquest of these regions in 29 Hijri and a reconquest in 30 Hijri, and I am of the view that the later dates [29 and 30] are of the reconquest while the earliest one is of the first conquest.

Moreover, in the case of Khurasan, I have changed Tabari's 22 Hijri to 23 in my account, for the following reasons:

  a. Khurasan was not included in Umar's initial plan which encompassed only one head [Isfahan] and two wings [Azarbeijan and Fars.] There was no reason for the Caliph to alter this plan, and since Fars and the south-eastern provinces were taken in 23 Hijri, Khurasan, which was a later addition to the plan, could only have been conquered in 23 Hijri, or later.

b. Yazdjurd's flight described in the last chapter of this book shows that Fars and Kirman fell to the Muslims before Khurasan.

APPENDIX D

THE COMPANIONS

Scholars are agreed upon the definition of Companionship by Ibn Hajar Al-Asqalani: *'A Companion is the believer who saw and heard Allah's Messenger at least once and died as a believer'*. Even though some scholars have stipulated that, in order to be ranked as a Companion, a believer should have lived in the company of Allah's Messenger for one or even two years, the majority of the scholars regarded it as enough to have been present in the radiant atmosphere of the Messenger long enough to have derived some benefit from it.

It goes without saying that the Companions are not equal to each other in rank or greatness. Some of them believed in Allah's Messenger at the very outset of his mission, and conversions continued until his saying farewell to the world. The Quran grades them according to precedence in belief and according to conversion before the Conquest of Makkah and after it [Quran 9:100 and 57:10]. The same gradation was also made by Allah's Messenger himself. For example, he reproached Khalid bin Al-Waleed [ra] for offending Abdur-Rahman bin Awf [ra], saying: *"Do not trouble my Companions!"* In the same way, he frowned at Umar [ra], when he annoyed Abu Bakr [ra], and said: *"Will you not leave my Companions alone? Abu Bakr believed in me at a time when all of you denied me."* Abu Bakr knelt down and explained: *'O Messenger of Allah! It was my fault!.'*

As recorded by Tabarani and Ibn Al-Athir, Abdullah bin Masud, who was among the first to embrace Islam in Makkah and sent to Kufa as a teacher by Umar, said:

"Allah looked at the hearts of His true servants and chose Muhammad, upon him be Peace and Blessings, to send to His creatures as a Messenger. Then, He looked at the hearts of people and chose his Companions as the helpers of His religion and the ambassadors of His Prophet, upon him be Peace and Blessings.

The Prophet [saw] said:

"When my Companions are mentioned then withhold." [Sahih At-Tabarani]

"Whoever abuses my Companions, upon them is the curse of Allah, the angels and all the people." [Sahih At-Tabarani]

Twelve Ranks of the Companions

The Companions were divided into twelve ranks by the scholars. This division was made according to the chronological order and some groups are also included in others. It was accepted by the majority of scholars:

1. The four Rightly-Guided Caliphs, namely Abu Bakr, Umar, Uthman and Ali, and the rest of the ten to whom Paradise was promised while alive. They are Zubair bin Al-Awwam, Abu Ubaidah bin Al-Jarrah, Abdur-Rahman bin Awf, Talha bin Ubaidullah, Sa'd bin Abi Waqqas and Saeed bin Zayd, may Allah be pleased with them all.

2. Those who believed prior to Umar's conversion and frequently gathered together secretly in the House of Arqam to listen to Allah's Messenger, upon him be Peace and Blessings.

3. Those who migrated to Abyssinia in the first hijrah [migration] for Allah's Sake.

4. The Helpers [Ansar] who were present at the first ceremony of taking the Oath of Allegiance to Allah's Messsenger at Al-Aqaba.

5. The Helpers [Ansar] who took the Oath of Allegiance to the Messenger at Al-Aqaba, the following year.

6. The first Emigrants [Muhajireen] who joined Allah's Messenger before his arrival in Madinah during the Hijrah [Emigration].

7. The Companions who participated in the Battle of Badr.

8. Those who emigrated to Madinah during the period between the Battle of Badr and the Treaty of Hudaybiyah.

9. The Companions who took the Oath of Allegiance to Allah's Messenger under a tree during the expedition of Hudaybiyah.

10. Those who converted and emigrated to Madinah after the Treaty of Hudaybiyah.

11. Those who became Muslims after the conquest of Makkah.

12. The children who saw Allah's Messenger either during the Conquest of Makka or during the Farewell Pilgrimage, or in any other place and on different occasions.

Excellence of the Companions of the Prophet

Narrated Abu Said Al-Khudri:

"Allah's Apostle said, *"A time will come upon the people, when a group of people will wage a holy war and it will be said, 'Is there amongst you anyone who has accompanied Allah's Apostle?' They will say, 'Yes.' And so victory will be bestowed on them. Then a time will come upon the people when a group of people will wage a holy war, and it will be said, "Is there amongst you anyone who has accompanied the Companions of Allah's Apostle?' They will say, 'Yes.' And so victory will be bestowed on them. Then a time will come upon the people when a group of people will wage a holy war, and it will be said, "Is there amongst you anyone who has been in the company of the Companions of the Companions of Allah's Apostle ?' They will say, 'Yes.' And victory will be bestowed on them."* [Bukhari]

Narrated Abdullah:

The Prophet [saw] said, *"The best of generations is my generation, then those that come after them, then those that come after them."* [Bukhari]

Narrated Abu Said Al-Khudri:

The Prophet [saw] said, *"Do not abuse my companions for if any one of you spent gold equal to Uhud [in Allah's Cause] it would not be equal to a Mud or even a half Mud spent by one of them."* [Bukhari]

The Prophet [saw] said:

"The Jews divided into seventy-one sects and the Christians divided into seventy-two sects. My Ummah will divide into seventy-three different sects, all of which will be in the Fire except one: Those who are on the like of what I and my Companions are on at this time." [Hasan At-Tirmidhi]

Excellence of Abu Bakr [ra]

Narrated Abu Said Al-Khudri:

"The person who has favoured me most of all both with his company and wealth, is Abu Bakr. If I were to take a Khalil [close friend and protector] other than my Lord, I would have taken Abu Bakr as such, but he is my brother and my companion. All the gates of the Mosque should be closed except the gate of Abu Bakr." [Bukhari]

Narrated Ibn Umar:

"We used to compare the people as to who was better during the lifetime of Allah's Apostle. We used to regard Abu Bakr as the best, then Umar, and then Uthman." [Bukhari]

Narrated Jubair bin Mutim:

A woman came to the Prophet who ordered her to return to him again. She said, *"What if I came and did not find you?"* as if she wanted to say, "If I found you dead?" The Prophet said, *"If you should not find me, go to Abu Bakr."* [Bukhari]

Narrated Abu Darda:

"While I was sitting with the Prophet, Abu Bakr came, lifting up one corner of his garment uncovering his knee. The Prophet said, *"Your companion has had a quarrel."* Abu Bakr greeted [the Prophet] and said, "O Allah's Apostle! There was something [i.e. quarrel] between me and the Son of Al-Khattab. I talked to him harshly and then regretted that, and requested him to forgive me, but he refused. This is why I have come to you." The Prophet said thrice, *"O Abu Bakr! May Allah forgive you."* In the meanwhile, 'Umar regretted [his refusal of Abu Bakr's excuse] and went to Abu Bakr's house and asked if Abu Bakr was there. They replied in the negative. So he came to the Prophet and greeted him, but signs of displeasure appeared on the face of the Prophet till Abu Bakr pitied ['Umar], so he knelt and said twice, "O Allah's Apostle! By Allah! I was more unjust to him [than he to me]." The Prophet said, *"Allah sent me [as a Prophet] to you [people] but you said [to me], 'You are telling a lie,' while Abu Bakr said, 'He has said the truth,' and consoled me with himself and his money."* He then said twice, *"Won't you then give up harming my companion?"* After that nobody harmed Abu Bakr." [Bukhari]

Narrated 'Amr bin Al-As:

The Prophet deputed me to read the Army of Dhat-as-Salasil. I came to him and said, *"Who is the most beloved person to you?"* He said, *" 'Aisha."* I asked, *"Among the men?"* He said, *"Her father."* I said, *"Who then?"* He said, *"Then 'Umar bin Al-Khattab."* He then named other men. [Bukhari]

Narrated Abu Huraira:

I heard Allah's Apostle saying, *"Anybody who spends a pair of something in Allah's Cause will be called from all the gates of Paradise, "O Allah's slave! This is good.' He who is amongst those who pray will be called from the gate of the prayer [in Paradise] and he who is from the people of Jihad will be called from the gate of Jihad, and he who is from those' who give in charity [i.e. Zakat] will be called from the gate of charity, and he who is amongst those who observe fast will be called from the gate of fasting, the gate of Raiyan."* Abu Bakr said, *"He who is called from all those gates will need nothing,"* He added, *"Will anyone be called from all those gates, O Allah's Apostle?"* He said, *"Yes, and I hope you will be among those, O Abu Bakr."* [Bukhari]

Narrated Muhammad bin Al-Hanafiya:

I asked my father ['Ali bin Abi Talib], *"Who are the best people after Allah's Apostle ?"* He said, *"Abu Bakr."* I asked, *"Who then?"* He said, *"Then 'Umar."* I was afraid he would say "Uthman, so I said, *"Then you?"* He said, *"I am only an ordinary person."*

Narrated Abu Hurairah:

The Prophet [saw] said: *"Gabriel came and taking me by the hand showed me the gate of Paradise by which my people will enter."* Abu Bakr then said: *"Apostle of Allah! I wish I had been with you so that I might have looked at it."* The Apostle of Allah [saw] then said: *"You, Abu Bakr, will be the first of my people to enter Paradise."* [Abu Dawud]

- 313 -

Excellence of Umar bin Al-Khattab [ra]

Narrated Abu Huraira:

Allah's Apostle said, *"Among the nations before you there used to be people who were inspired [though they were not prophets]. And if there is any of such a person's amongst my followers, it is 'Umar."* [Bukhari]

Narrated Abu Huraira:

The Prophet said, *"Among the nation of Bani Israel who lived before you, there were men who used to be inspired with guidance though they were not prophets, and if there is any of such persons amongst my followers, it is 'Umar."* [Bukhari]

Narrated Ibn Abbas:

When [the dead body of] 'Umar was put on his deathbed, the people gathered around him and invoked [Allah] and prayed for him before the body was taken away, and I was amongst them. Suddenly I felt somebody taking hold of my shoulder and found out that he was 'Ali bin Abi Talib. 'Ali invoked Allah's Mercy for 'Umar and said, *"O 'Umar! You have not left behind you a person whose deeds I like to imitate and meet Allah with more than I like your deeds. By Allah! I always thought that Allah would keep you with your two companions, for very often I used to hear the Prophet saying, 'I, Abu Bakr and 'Umar went [somewhere]; I, Abu Bakr and 'Umar entered [somewhere]; and I, Abu Bakr and 'Umar went out.'"* [Bukhari]

Narrated Jabir bin Abdullah:

The Prophet said, *"I saw myself [in a dream] entering Paradise, and behold! I saw Ar-Rumaisa', Abu Talha's wife. I heard footsteps. I asked, Who is it? Somebody said, 'It is Bilal' Then I saw a palace and a lady sitting in its courtyard. I asked, 'For whom is this palace?' Somebody replied, 'It is for 'Umar.' I intended to enter it and see it, but I thought of your ['Umar's] Ghaira [jealousy regarding women] and gave up the attempt."* 'Umar wept and said, *"Let my parents be sacrificed for you, O Allah's Apostle! How dare I think of my Ghira [self-respect] being offended by you?"* [Bukhari]

Narrated Hamza's father:

Allah's Apostle said, *"While I was sleeping, I saw myself drinking [i.e. milk], and I was so contented that I saw the milk flowing through my nails. Then I gave [the milk] to 'Umar."*

They [i.e. the companions of the Prophet] asked, *"What do you interpret it?"* He said, *"Knowledge."* [Bukhari]

Narrated Sa'd bin Abi Waqqas: Umar bin Al-Khattab asked the permission of Allah's Apostle to see him while some Quraishi women were sitting with him, talking to him and asking him for more expenses, raising their voices above the voice of Allah's Apostle.

When 'Umar asked for the permission to enter, the women quickly put on their veils. Allah's Apostle allowed him to enter and 'Umar came in while Allah's Apostle was smiling, 'Umar said *"O Allah's Apostle! May Allah always keep you smiling."* The Prophet said, *"These women who have been here, roused my wonder, for as soon as they heard your voice, they quickly put on their veils."* 'Umar said, *"O Allah's Apostle! You have more right to be feared by them than I."* Then 'Umar addressed the women saying, *"O enemies of yourselves! You fear me more than you do Allah's Apostle?"* They said, *"Yes, for you are harsher and sterner than Allah's Apostle."* Then Allah's Apostle said, *"O Ibn Al-Khattab! By Him in Whose Hands my life is! Never does Satan find you going on a way, but he takes another way other than yours."* [Bukhari]

Narrated Abdullah: We have been powerful since 'Umar embraced Islam. [Bukhari]

Narrated Aslam:

Ibn 'Umar asked me about some matters concerning 'Umar. He said, *"Since Allah's Apostle died. I have never seen anybody more serious, hard working and generous than 'Umar bin Al-Khattab [till the end of his life]."* [Bukhari]

Narrated Abu Said Al-Khudri:

I heard Allah's Apostle saying, *"While I was sleeping, the people were presented to me [in a dream]. They were wearing shirts, some of which were merely covering their [chests]. and some were a bit longer. 'Umar was presented before me and his shirt was so long that he was dragging it."* They asked, *"How have you interpreted it, O Allah's Apostle?"* He said, *"Religion."* [Bukhari]

Narrated Ibn Umar:

During the lifetime of the Prophet we considered Abu Bakr as peerless and then 'Umar and then 'Uthman [coming next to him in superiority] and then we used not to differentiate between the companions of the Prophet . [Bukhari]

The Ten Promised Paradise

Narrated Saeed bin Zayd:

Abdur-Rahman bin Al-Akhnas said that when he was in the mosque, a man abused Ali [ra]. So Saeed bin Zayd got up and said: *"I bear witness to the Apostle of Allah [saw] that I heard him say: "Ten persons will go to Paradise: "Abu Bakr will go to Paradise, Umar will go to Paradise, Uthman will go to Paradise, Ali will go to Paradise, Talha will go to Paradise: Zubair bin Al-Awwam will go to Paradise, Sa'd bin Abi Waqqas will go to Paradise and Abdur-Rahman bin Awf will go to Paradise. If I wish, I can mention the tenth."* The People asked: *"Who is he?"* so he kept silence. They again asked: *"Who is he?"* He replied: *"He is Saeed ibn Zayd."* He then said: *"The company of one man whose face has been covered with dust by the Apostle of Allah [saw] is better than the actions of one of you for a whole life time even if he is granted the life-span of Noah."* [Abu Dawud]

These Ten Companions are listed below, together with the dates of when they lived and died:

1. Abu Bakr As-Siddiq [51 B.H-13 A.H; 573-634 C.E]

2. Umar bin Al-Khattab Al-Farooq [40 B.H-23 A.H; 584-644 C.E]

3. Uthman bin Affan Ghani Dhun-Nurayn [47 B.H- 35 A.H; 577-656 C.E]

4. Ali bin Abi Talib [23 B.H- 40 A.H; 600-661 C.E]

5. Talha bin Ubaidullah [28 B.H-36 A.H; 596-656 C.E]

6. Zubair bin Al-Awwam [28 B.H-36 A.H; 596-656 C.E]

7. Abdur-Rahman bin Awf [passed away 31 A.H/654 C.E]

8. Sa'd bin Abi Waqqas [23 B.H-55 A.H; 600-675 C.E]

9. Saeed bin Zayd [passed away 51 A.H]

10. Abu Ubaidah Aamir bin Abdullah bin Al-Jarrah.

New and Forthcoming Titles at

Maktabah

www.maktabah.net

Free Online Library

www.maktabah.net

'We aim to create the World's Largest Online Free Islamic Library - In addition to this we are a leading UK independent publisher with a rapidly expanding reputation for excellence across a wide range of subject areas. Our authors are renown experts in their fields, making our publications contribute to lively debate on exciting contemporary as well as historical issues'

All these and **many more** are available to read, listen and watch for free:

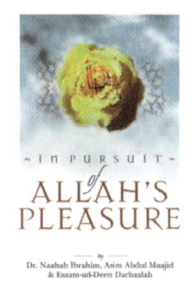

| In Pursuit of Allah's Pleasure | Fortress of the Muslim (Dua Book) | Life and Times of Khattab [video] | The Prophet's Revolution [video] |

| Autobiography of Malcolm X | Islām the Misunderstood Religion | Milestones | 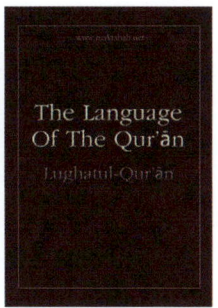 The Language Of The Qur'ān |

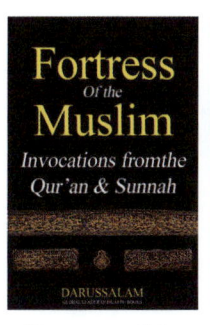

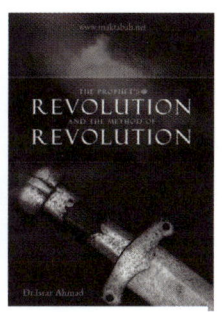

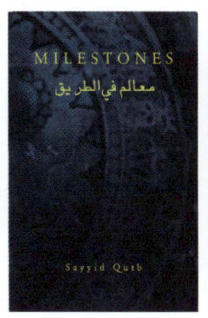

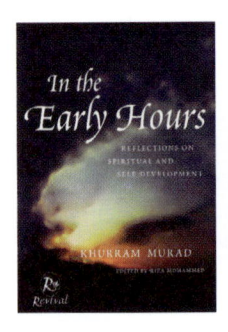

In the Early Hours – Reflections on Spirituality	Fiqh us Sunnah Rulings on Worship	MALCOLM X - PRINCE OF ISLAM [video]	21st Century Crusaders [video]
HAMAS: Behind the Mask [video]	Defence of the Muslim Lands	Signs of ar-Rahmaan in Jihad of Afghan	My Imprisonment
Two Witnesses of Sayyid Qutbs Hanging	Introduction To The Study of the Qur'an	The Obligations Muslims Owe To The Qur'an	Way to The Quran

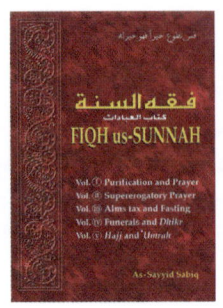

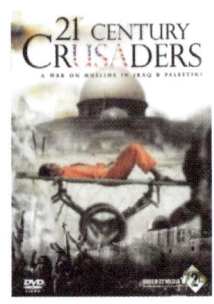

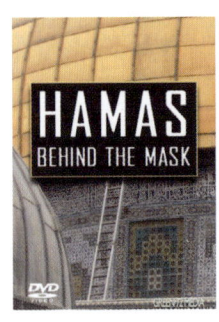

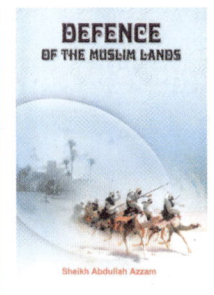

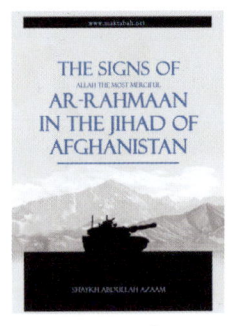

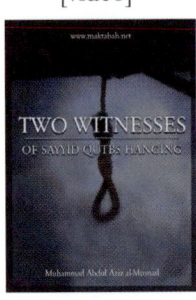

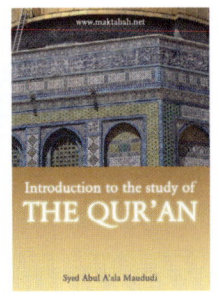

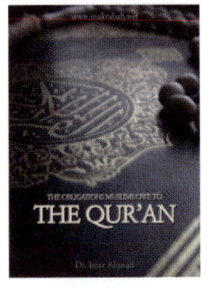

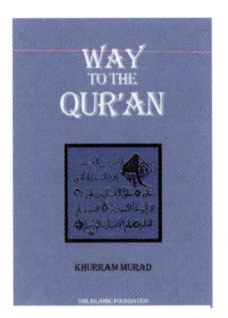

FORTHCOMING TITLES
[insha-Allah]

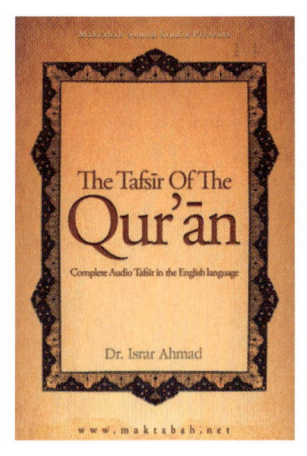

Complete Audio Tafsir of the Qur'an
Dr. Israr Ahmad

Complete Works - Abdullah Azzam
Shaykh Abdullah Azzam

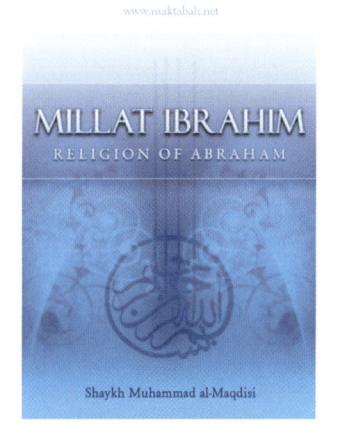

Millat Ibrahim
Muhammad al-Maqdisi

Islamic Military History Series by A.I. Akram

- Khalid ibn al-Waleed: Sword of Allah [printed]
- Muslim Conquest of Persia [printed]
- Conquest of Egypt and North Africa
- The Muslim Conquest of Spain
- Falcon of Quraysh
- Rise of Cordoba

THE QUR'AN PROJECT

www.quranproject.org

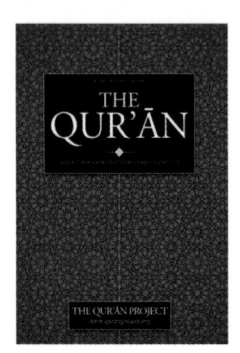

With the help of Allah [swt], we are in the process of printing a free and simple translation [Saheeh International] of the Qur'ān which includes additional chapters produced specifically for non-Muslims.

 Appendices:
- Short Biography of the Prophet Muhammad
- Introduction to the Study of the Qur'ān
- The Unique Qur'ānic Generation
- Preservation and Literary Challenge of the Qur'ān
- Scientific Miracles of the Qur'ān;
  - The Qur'ān on the Origin of the Universe
  - The Qur'ān on the 'Big Bang Theory'
  - The Qur'ān on the Expanding Universe
  - The Qur'ān on the Orbital Movement of the Sun and the Moon
  - The Qur'ān on Duality in Creation
  - The Qur'ān on the Origin of Life in Water
  - The Qur'ān on Seas and Rivers
  - Miracle of Iron
  - The Qur'ān on Mountains
  - The Qur'ān on Human Embryonic Development
  - Scientists Acceptance of the Miracles of the Qur'ān
- Old and New Testament Prophecy of Muhammad
- Women in Islām
- How do I become a Muslim?
- Quick Guide to Ablution and Prayer
- Frequently Asked Questions about Islām - Short Answers -

I want to Support
The Qur'ān Project

Our Aim - To produce a free and simple translation of the Qur'ān which includes additional chapters beneficial for seekers of truth in as many countries as possible.

You can help by donating with the cost of printing further copies –

How can I donate?

- Logon to www.quranproject.org

- Pay direct in to the bank account

    Bank: Islamic Bank of Britain
    Acc name: The Quran Project
    Sort code: 30-00-83
    Acc number: 01200001